Transcendental Phenomenological Psychology

Introduction to Husserl's

Psychology of Human Consciousness

Revised Edition

Order this book online at www.trafford.com
or email orders@trafford.com

Dedicated to the genius of Edmund Husserl

Co-published by Three Rivers Consultancy
and Trafford Publishing

Note for librarians: A cataloguing record for the
original edition of this book is available from Library and Archives Canada at
www.collectionscanada.ca/amicus/index-e.html

Printed in the United States of America.

ISBN: 978-1-4269-6834-1 (sc)
ISBN: 978-1-4269-7214-0 (e)

Trafford rev. 06/21/2011

www.trafford.com

North America & international
toll-free: 1 888 232 4444 (USA & Canada)
phone: 250 383 6864 ♦ fax: 812 355 4082

Contents

Preface to the Revised Edition   *v*

Preface to the First Edition   *vi*

1.
Beginning Considerations

"Why is there no transcendental phenomenological psychology already?"   1

An Organization of Differences   8

The Real and the Irreal   14

Phenomenological Psychology in the Transcendental Register   22

The Phenomenological-Psychological Attitude   25

Pre-theoretical Groundwork   30

Husserl's Psychology with a Soul   35

The Phenomenological Field of Actionality   39

Transcendental Idealism and Phenomenological Psychology   41

Other Theoretical Approaches   43

A Psychology of Consciousness Versus a Philosophy of Existence   51

2.
Uncovering Husserl

The Student Years   56

Husserl's Nascent Phenomenology   60

A Critique of Cognitions   75

The Göttingen Years and a Question of Praxis   81

The Early Freiburg Years and a Question of the Transcendental   89

Our Natural Attitude and the Life-World   95

Eidetic Affairness   102

The Later Freiburg Years and a Question of Renewal   104

Husserl's Last Years   117

3.
Phenomenological Epistemology and Ontology

Eidetic Structures of Sense and Meaning   120

Husserl's "Basic Questions of Epistemology"   123

Embodiment   128

The Transcendental Experience of Intelligibility   132

The Horizon of Ontology   143

A Phenomenological Psychology of Ontic Experience   145

The *Eidos* of *Theme*   154

The Pure Psychology of Transcendental Consciousness   163

"The Dangerous First-Person Singular"   170

4.
The Theoretical Ground of
Transcendental Phenomenological Psychology

A Transcendental Logic of Objects and Acts 173
Genetic Phenomenological Psychology 175
The Transcendental Reorientation: An Affairness of Empathy 184
The Psychological *Epoché* 194
The Practical Performance of Psychosubjectivity 201
An Applied Geometry of "Knowing the Real" 205
The Eidetic Reduction in Pure Psychology 211
The Transcendental Reduction in the Field of Actionality 218
The Psychological Reduction 225
Cognitive Development in the Transcendental Register 232

5.
Applied Transcendental Phenomenological Psychology

An Overview 234
The Psychological Experience of Rational Thought 240
The Affective Unity of Conscious Awareness 244
The Intentional Function of Intersubjectivity 250
The Phenomenological "Person" 253
Generative Phenomenology and Psychology 261
Enworlded Consciousness 266
Final Reflections 273

Bibliography 278

Index 286

List of Figures

Figure 4.1. Under the Ψ *Epoché* 206
Figure 4.2. The Eidetic Reduction 212
Figure 4.3. The Transcendental Reduction 219
Figure 4.4. The Ψ Reduction 226

Preface to the Revised Edition

Since its publication in 2007, *Transcendental Phenomenological Psychology* has been sold on every continent (except Antarctica), and is in the collections of research libraries in North America, Europe, and Asia. Even so, its presentation to the academic community rightly provoked many comments, corrections, suggestions, and criticisms. Such input, while mostly welcome, provided the impetus to publish a revised edition. In keeping with Husserl's revolutionary methodology in the human sciences, I have focused in this edition on breaking away from much of the tedious discourse that threatens to become institutionalized in Continental Philosophy. In doing so, I am reminded of my gaining a more inclusive grasp of social relations when first thinking in gender-neutral terms. A similar experience might be gained by philosophers when reading Husserl's work from a distinctive psychological attitude.

In this light, greater prominence has been given to making Husserl's terminology and insights into our life-span methods of psychic life more accessible to both philosophers and psychologists. For instance, the principle of *psychognosia* that is explicit as praxis in the work of Brentano the psychologist provides a "leading clue" for interpretations of phenomenological psychology in the work of Husserl the philosopher; and in this way, the radical meaning of "the psychological" is emphasized in the Continental tradition of consciousness studies. Contemporary practitioners of so-called talk therapy of the existential, psycholinguistic, or cognitive behavioral variety will recognize the need for such grounding that spells out the normal course of mental life.

The saddest part here is that I must again remind readers that *Transcendental Phenomenological Psychology* is unique in the human sciences. One should not, then, expect to have been previously taught its principles and perspective. I have been told that this situation necessarily impacts the careers of some philosophers and psychologists. Quite frankly, that is not a scholarly concern and it is not a concern here. On the other hand, I have been told as well that the first edition was "too hard for psychologists." If an eidetic psychology is to be understood as an alternative or adjunct to empirical psychology, then it certainly cannot be "easier" to learn or to teach. Still, I have attempted in this revised edition to reformulate paragraphs and subchapters in order to make the reading flow more smoothly. One difficulty remains, however—namely, that Husserl's work is programmatic. This condition promotes run-on sentences and complex phrasings, which I have attempted to limit through a liberal use of the em-dash.

A constant theme of both editions is repeated here for emphasis: Transcendental phenomenological psychology is informed by phenomenological philosophy, but it is not that philosophy itself. When Husserl speaks of "psychology," he refers to the meaning of psychology as a philosophical concept and its domain of study, not to the psychic life *of* that concept. (*see* Fink 1995, §3) Husserl probably went further than others in naming this experience as "pure psychology," but it was not his aim as a philosopher to expand upon its implications for his own work. Instead, discovering and exposing these implications is a goal of transcendental phenomenological psychology.

Preface to the First Edition

The work presented here grew out of my research in phenomenological psychology at Duquesne University and the Saybrook Graduate School and Research Center. It is not an accident that Saybrook's original direction in humanistic psychology to understand the dynamics of a psychologist's own experience is carried over into this book. Colleagues nevertheless recommended that I warn new readers that transcendental phenomenological psychology is controversial, since its rationale calls into question the very meaning of "the psychological" in traditional research and practices. They did not mean to imply, however, that "controversy" is necessarily a pejorative term for humanistic psychology. Some things are perhaps meant to be controversial in everyday judgments and valuations, and should probably remain within that category of expression even in our most sophisticated arguments and debates.

Still, for many in the academic ranks, even for phenomenologists, controversies in this area point toward a lack of rigor in phenomenological psychology as it has been presented so far in classrooms and publications. Sometimes it is forgotten that phenomenological psychology is above all a philosophical psychology of non-physiological consciousness, and is therefore intimately concerned with issues of epistemology and ontology—in phenomenological studies, respectively, what we know and what we mean on the basis of experience. Edmund Husserl's phenomenological epistemology has been used in psychology all too frequently in theory construction without grasping its conceptual basis in fundamental ontology. Husserl's terminology is regularly appropriated in psychological discourse outside the context of its sense and meanings in his cognitive theories of consciousness. Taken together, these practices result in the appearances of key Husserlian concepts and technical language as mere jargon. Sometimes, too, theories given by less rigorous phenomenological philosophers are followed by psychologists for no other reason, it seems, than that they are easier to understand and to teach.

The need for rigor in correct procedures cannot be overestimated when trying to grasp Husserl's phenomenological philosophy in both its original expression and succeeding extentions. Neither should a proper foundation in his concepts be ignored or glossed over when using applied phenomenology as a theory of inquiry in any of the human sciences. The lack of rigor in phenomenological studies and in the development of phenomenological praxis as a revolutionary movement in the philosophy of science has been a problem at least since the turn of the last century. Indeed, Husserl's personal assistant during the movement's most productive years, Edith Stein, felt the need to conduct a so-called philosophical kindergarten for even Husserl's most sophisticated students. (*see* Stein 1993, 17) Furthermore, Husserl mentions in several of his lectures that those not already deeply steeped in his phenomenological methodology are but beginners, and therefore need to be led slowly through advanced phenomenological theories and practices.

I am introducing here an advanced phenomenological theory of inquiry for study of the psychological experience of human consciousness. This experience has its origins in Husserl's (1973a, 392) work as expressions of human "psychic life"—meaning, the intentional activity of the psyche or mind when one is consciously and affectively aware of something. For psychology at least, this book ought not to be controversial. A phenomenological explanation of consciousness has long been sought in regions of cognitive science, psychiatry, and artificial intelligence. I want to stress, however, that Husserl's theories of consciousness have never been seen previously within a systematic presentation for the discipline. Husserl provides little by way of explicit instructions for transcendental phenomenological psychology, except to say that it must "parallel" transcendental phenomenological philosophy, and must proceed step-wise like any applied phenomenology. A parallel, step-wise, introduction is what I am aiming for, where readers are not presumed to be more than beginners with the psychological portion of Husserl's phenomenological studies and its rigorous methodology.

Husserl's methodology guides interpretations of universal psychic life as our intentional methods of cognitive mental life—specifically, as our a-historical methods for transcending primitive elements during consciousness-formation. The psychological thus shows itself with ontic clarity in Husserl's phenomenological philosophy as an epistemology of the free will of the psyche when one is knowingly conscious of something. It follows that I cannot, as one early reader of my work suggested, leave out discussions of Husserl's methodology within a presentation of transcendental phenomenological psychology. Articulating precise human-scientific practices is the continuing work of Husserl's applied phenomenology, both during his lifetime and according to his directions for further studies. This same spirit of passing along high standards of praxis for the ongoing development of his methodology is a reason why many of Husserl's publications are subtitled as an "introduction," and why this same tradition is repeated in the subtitle of this book.

When studying Husserl's approach to phenomenological studies, one cannot lose sight of his aim to notice exemplary cases or events of intentional comportment in order for one to be consciousness of something, and then to apply the essences of those matters to an immediate problem that might vary in similarity or kind. Husserl's practice of noticing and applying things within interactions of the general and the specific (which is itself an experience of transcendence), is not so different from our typical and familiar methods of thinking—except in its intention to be explicit in following strict phenomenological procedures. The phenomenon of human consciousness is ordinarily valued and judged intuitively in our daily lives, not according to a rigorous phenomenological perspective of course, but rather according to the criterion of our attitude for seeing the so-called true nature of things.

We gain a natural attitude toward the sense and meaning of actually real things as the consequence of one's life-span intellectual development within a world of human co-existence. The human world as seen from the natural attitude is indeed Husserl's transcendental phenomenological field of inquiry. What, then, is the criterion of Husserl's transcendental phenomenological attitude and rigorous means for thinking "psychologically" about this _____ Is __ __ ___, ____ ___ _____ ____ __ ___ _____ condition that Husserl relied upon for the development of his phenomenological philosophy were Plato, Aristotle, René Descartes, Immanuel Kant, Friedrich Hegel, David Hume, and Wilhelm Dilthey. Later phenomenologists constructed their own theories based largely on Husserl's phenomenological modifications of the natural attitudes of these philosophers toward what it means to be human. In actual practice, Husserl clarified the essence of the epistemological, ontological, and metaphysical presuppositions of philosophical thinking on the question of human sentient *being*.

During his career-long development of a system of phenomenological observations and interpretations of these essences, Husserl appropriated from the implicit cognitive methods of philosophical thinking on human consciousness certain premises for what came to be in his lifetime a revolutionary attitude and methodology in the human sciences. Five of the most important premises of Husserl's transcendental phenomenological philosophy are grouped and paraphrased as follows:

1. There are things that humans perceive to be objects in space and time.
2. Humans are typically capable of being conscious of said objects in rational thought.
3. In order to be known phenomenally, objects in consciousness are composed from pre-existing essential elements by means of our judgments and valuations in cognitive mental life.
4. Humans use, retain in memory, and speak of these prior compositions during both everyday experiences and theoretical reflections.
5. Upon reflection, humans could have self-knowledge of one's now-transcended elemental compositions and cognitive action.

Husserl added a sixth premise that was appropriated from his teacher, psychologist Franz Brentano:

6. Conditions of transcendence are intentionally used by humans in order to constitute a unity of conscious awareness for an object of actual reality.

Observing these premises in exemplary cases of human thought and speech provides the criterion for investigations of an object of the mind and its correlated cognitive action when one is consciously aware of something. It perhaps come as a revelation to many that in the 1920s Husserl advanced Brentano's "psychognostic investigations" by calling this criterion, *Psychognosia*, the pure method of phenomenological observation and description. (*see* Rollinger 2004, 255) Here, the root "gnosia" signifies knowledge gained by the psyche or mind, such as with "diagnosis" or "prognosis." In the sense adopted by both Brentano and Husserl, *Psychognosia* is not to be confused with contemporary references to parapsychological phenomena. Instead, the concept in its application for phenomenological studies refers to the non-empirical method of thinking that we all use intuitively in ordinary experience and in theoretical reflections.

Husserl's student, Aron Gurwitsch (1966, 65), noticed that *Psychognosia* as practiced by Husserl resembles principles of *Gestalt* psychology. Perhaps, but there is nevertheless a significant difference between the two. *Gestalt* psychology reduces human experience to a field that is analogous with modern physics—meaning, the psychological in human affairs is delimited by objective "laws of nature." On the other hand, *Psychognosia* represents the pre-existing intuitive (and therefore purely subjective) method of universal mental life that enables *Gestalt* psychologists to make such reductions, and to make subsequent associations between parts and wholes of the objective physical plane. Experience with modern physics is a necessity for *Gestalt* psychology, while only experience with the human condition is necessary for *Psychognosia*.

There are two important points of reference that come from familiarity with Husserl's practice of non-empirical thinking. Each seems to be necessary for a proper grasp of transcendental phenomenological psychology. First, Husserl's phenomenological concepts are meant to "mirror" in their application what us humans intentionally experience when we are consciously aware of something—not to advance a mystical tradition or to go beyond the limits of worldly intelligibility. This issue could be described as the mimetic *doing* of Husserl's methodology as praxis, versus the diegetic *telling* of Husserl's philosophy in theoretical discourse. Second, Husserl's phenomenological praxis provides the theoretical groundwork for doing any kind of human science; but it does not generate theories other than for intentional objects and the meaningful human subject, along with the cognitive mental life and psychological processes of the subject's being conscious of those objects.

These last two matters make up parallel areas of a field of conscious awareness. Here, problems of objects and acts are separated and studied according to their respective contents of subjective experience—even as both areas yield to *Psychognosia* for observations, descriptions, and clarifying explanations. When phenomenologists follow these practices closely, they are applying principles of *Psychognosia*; and when used as a method for judgments and valuations, its application coincides with an experience of the "pure psychology" that exists in the depths of thought for everyone. Clearly then, "*Psychognosia*" does not refer merely to Brentano's practice for descriptions and observations. (*see* Husserl 2006, p. 422) Transcendental phenomenological psychology is theoretically grounded in a pure psychology of intentional acts on objects of the mind, where its theory of inquiry traces out what Husserl calls a "phenomenology of phenomenology" for clarifications of key concepts. Indeed, Husserl (1970, §58) considers psychology to be the "decisive field" for further advancements in phenomenological studies.

Based on the premise that one's consciousness of something represents a unity of configuration for an object of the mind, where the "oneness" of conscious awareness is an identifying quality of ordinary thought, Husserl makes the sublime observation that deep reflections on the enduring objects that we tend to think about could lead to an altered state of consciousness for human-scientific practices. From this altered state that is directed toward see-

man concern could be clarified according to their necessary essences or ideas, rather than described solely by the appearances of concrete phenomena of presupposed natural causality—that is to say, according to a criterion for the nature of things in traditional science and philosophy. Making use of this altered state of consciousness on purpose, in order to see a different but necessary reality in human affairs, is called appropriating "the phenomenological attitude." Husserl means for the phenomenological attitude to represent the "working attitude" of human intentionality that pre-exists all constructions of actual reality. This orientation is conceptually opposed to our natural attitude for seeing only the sheer appearances of things in their finished productions or outcomes when given as fully composed unities of thought.

The phenomenological attitude relies significantly more on our intuitive capacity for pictorial reasoning, rather than on our subsequently learned patterns of verbal reasoning or the syllogisms of formal logic in research methodologies. This is the same ability in pure psychology that one would use in order to interpret a graph, recognize a familiar face in a crowd, or to see perspective and scale in the flat plane of a photograph. Along with other reasoning strategies, pictorial reasoning is used within a distribution of cognitive abilities that one might intentionally bring to bear upon a matter of interest. (*see* Giere 1996) Pictorial reasoning is ordinarily applied synchronically in the particular case of an object in conscious awareness; and at the same time, diachronically in the general case of similar objects that one has previously encountered. In Husserl's pictorial reasoning, descriptions of essential parts of an object do not contradict any pre-existing topological features of the whole. With pictorial reasoning applied as rigorous praxis, Husserl would have phenomenologists "turn" in one's imagination the multidimensional qualitative space of a fully composed unity of consciousness in order to see its intentional configuration of essences and relationships of essences here and now.

Husserl never completed his work on a comprehensive science of essences. Neither did he spell out a transcendental phenomenological psychology within this new science. He did, however, continue to call for such a psychology in his later years, saying that its theory of inquiry could be developed through clarifications of the phenomenological method proper. There is a distinction in Husserl's philosophy between his notion of "the phenomenological method" and phenomenological methodology. (*see* Golub 1976, 458) For each of us, even for Husserl, the phenomenological method is the intentional way one's consciousness-of-something comes to presence in thought and speech—more specifically, it is the means by which we are consciously aware of something. (Cairns 1940, 13) Husserl (1970, §9.l) mentions vaguely that according to this universal method of consciousness-formation, our reasoning moves in a "zig-zag pattern" within "a sort of circle" that aims toward unity. In perhaps its most profound impact on the philosophy of science, Husserl's (1983, §65) methodology uncovers and then replicates this method as *praxis*. Failure to notice this distinction in his descriptions and observations of both pre- and post-phenomenological phenomena could lead to a fundamental misunderstanding of Husserl's tradition of inquiry. (*see* Cairns 1976, 52)

The phenomenological method proper is articulated throughout Husserl's work as the universal *way* of non-physiological consciousness that is peculiar to human intentionality—in particular, the intentionality exhibited during both our contingent experiences of conscious awareness and our a-historical performances of consciousness-formation. Clarifications of these two modes of comportment provide what Husserl calls the "leading clues" (*Leitfäden*) for concepts of transcendental phenomenological psychology. Gathering these clues in an organization that accurately represents Husserl's perspective toward the psychic life of human consciousness is the ambitious task that I set for myself in this book. I am approaching transcendental phenomenological psychology as a unique form of theoretical psychology, where decriptions and explanations of psychological phenomena refer back to a philosophical origin of key concepts and logical constructions. (*see* Royce 1987, 1118-19) When following Husserl's lead, substantive theory in the human sciences is never removed from metatheoretical considerations of both the meaning and the achievement of such theory. In light of this principle, transcendental phenomenological psychology is abstracted from Husserl's overall philosophy of what it means to be human in thought and speech.

Before going any further it might be appropriate to remind philosophers of Husserl's "principle of all principles" to take things just as they are intentionally given for matters of sense and meaning. Phenomenological psychology is informed by phenomenological philosophy, but it is not therefore that philosophy itself. Even scholars who seem to have a remarkable grasp of Husserl's philosophy have never seen what is to follow in this book; since for the first time in Husserl's tradition, I am introducing a practice of applied transcendental phenomenology that is intended for the discipline of psychology. I will also present evidence for the notion that Husserl grasped principles of *Psychognosia* in his early studies, extended them as scientific praxis, clarified those principles as a method of consciousness-formation in pure psychology, and then made rigorous use of that method in his later studies when applying his theories of consciousness to issues of philosophical interest.

In the (at least theoretical) unity of the human sciences, it seems no longer relevant that the roots of the discipline of psychology are found in applications of philosophical concepts and practices. But even so, it is the same non-physiological consciousness that provides a metatheoretical venue for both philosophers and psychologists when making phenomenological interpretation of their respective data. In its character as philosophical psychology, phenomenological psychology assumes as a primitive notion for its theoretical constructions that there is but one kind of human mind—namely, our experience of sentient *being*. Setting aside any previously learned misconceptions and prejudices, philosophers could read this book as a review of the argumentation that is meant to advance transcendental phenomenology for human science in general, remembering that passing through psychology is one way to understand philosophy. At the same time, psychologists could introduce themselves to a non-empirical theory of inquiry that raises the bar for serious study of the psychological, just as many of Freud's psychoanalytic theories or Piaget's developmental theories raised the bar for empirical inquiry.

No doubt, it might be more satisfiable for both reader and writer if I were to avoid a transparency of Husserl's methodology and its typical rhetoric during discussions of his key concepts. According to Husserl's explicit instructions, however, phenomenological inquiry in all its forms must be made transparent if it is to be properly appropriated in any human-scientific discipline. And so, I will attempt to create a dialogue of transparency between philosophers and psychologists for phenomenological terms and practices, with Husserl's expressions providing a mediating function for interpretations of transcendental phenomenological psychology. In Natanson's (1988, 183-4) typology of presentational styles for Husserl's tradition of inquiry, this book is distinctly "other" in that it touches at the same time upon what seems to be most familiar and entirely "strange" to everyone.

I am presenting for the first time an explicit *eidetic* psychology in Husserl's tradition of inquiry. This characterization is derived from the Greek term, *eidos*, which refers to the essential form of an idea in conscious awareness. Husserl's science of essences is a science of *ideas*, where *Psychognosia* is the intuitive method of eidetic *seeing* that humans use regularly and consistently during day-to-day experiences and in theoretical reflections. When we apply *Psychognosia* as scientific praxis, we "picture" ideas in our reasoning strategies. Consequently, I follow Husserl (Fink 1995, §3) in recognizing the special character and perspective of phenomenological psychology—namely, that unlike physical things, psychic life is an eidetic affair that cannot be directly observed. The ideas of psychic life can only be represented symbolically in rigorous practices, hence the need for traditional psychologists to operationalize psychological experience by its empirical manifestations.

In other eidetic sciences such as formal logic and mathematics, ideas of essential matters and their relationships are pictured and then represented contingently by symbolic notation. This practice, however, does not exist a-historically as a fundamental method of reasoning. The use of traditional notation—whether logical, mathematical, or statistical—cannot therefore be directly "mirrored" in Husserl's methodology as either a theoretical ground or as a way of proceeding. Instead, I follow Husserl in allowing the deep structure of the subject's own grammar and syntax to represent a symbolic logic of essential ideas in the world that is commonly talked about. Expressions of the concept of *structure* in Husserl's work refer to the interrelation of parts within the eidetic arrangement of a potential whole.

Any prolonged analysis of word-meaning will therefore tend to mask the unitary structure of eidetic sense and intended meaning in Husserl's presentations and mine. Clearly, the meaning, origin, and use of words could be regressed without gaining access to the idea that is referenced by the unity of their expression. Husserl suggests that the eidetic science of geometry best represents a pre-theoretical comprehension of not only the intentional presentations of others, but also his own presentation of key concepts and their practical applications. I bear this in mind throughout this study, and later make use of an illustrative applied geometry in representations of the phenomenological method of reasoning in transcendental phenomenological psychology. Still, this book is not meant to be solely a novel approach for research psychology. It also embraces the hope that human science will find a new common ground and impetus within a revitalized interest in transcendental phenomenology. I believe that this is what Husserl would have intended.

In Husserl's work, the phenomenon of conscious awareness is ordinarily situated in the universal life-world of all potential realities for living as "natural" in human co-existence. This "multifarious" but singular state of affairs is the same "world" of human thinking, feeling, and acting that we commonly talk about as meaningful during our day-to-day activities. It is also the space of human experience that is represented as actually real in our most complex scientific and philosophical constructions. For each of us individually, and for all of us together, the life-world is the intuitive ground of normal praxis—meaning, it typically orients what we intentionally *do* during the normal course of events, including our phenomenological method of reasoning about parts and wholes during performances of consciousness-formation.

When oriented in reasoning solely toward life-world experiences, we have already adopted the natural attitude. Practices of Husserl's transcendental phenomenological studies are intended to grasp the meaning of the human world such as it is during life-world experiences according to one's own constructed truth and reality—but only from the phenomenological attitude for seeing universal concepts as they are intentionally brought to presence in individual thought and speech. Husserl also wants to understand the character of our subjective experiences that are given by the plurality of expressions about the human world from the natural attitude—but only where such expressions allow the same world to remain a unity of meaning during both an instance of individual consciousness and events of communal interactions.

How, then, are we to understand Husserl's philosophy and its parallel psychology, if phenomenological epistemology, ontology, and metaphysics do not belong solely in the substrate of reality for the human world as seen from the natural attitude? More generally, how are we to understand Husserl's expressions that he gives for grasping the human condition precisely as he sees it? The easy answer is to say, "Read the plurality of Husserl's words such that they allow a unity of meaning." This begs what is meant by "Husserl's words." When Husserl set out to present some further development of his phenomenological studies, his habit was to begin by writing down a description of his focused reflective meditations in particularly difficult shorthand. An assistant would then translate that shorthand into German, and the text would subsequently be edited for coherence. In foreign language translations, still more distance from Husserl's original meditations results.

As with any eidetic science, though, there is a valid means for comprehending the deep structure of Husserl's expressions—a practice for any phenomenologist in any native tongue, just as mathematics is not restricted by one's use of ordinary language. German phenomenologist Klaus Held (1998) addressed a group of translators on their project to translate the major works of Husserl and Heidegger into Russian. Held suggested that in order to avoid cross-cultural differences in word-meaning, a "homeworld" (*Heimwelt*) of phenomenological insights and intuitions could guide translations from the original text. He meant that translations could be done from the phenomenological homeworld, one could see a transcendental logic of deep structure in ordinary speech and natural language. This deep structure guides a phenomenologist's insights into the "positing of a relational unity" for what is expressed in any native tongue, but which could be understood in any given language. From the phenomenological attitude, we attempt to comprehend the pre-linguistic *ideas* being communicated by an intentional structure of grammar and syntax.

My mentioning of Held's phenomenological theory of translation is meant to indicate the reason why I read English translations of Husserl's texts from the phenomenological attitude. It would be nonsense, of course, to say that I learned this way of thinking while reading Husserl *from* the phenomenological attitude. This is not the case. I appropriated the phenomenological attitude originally from Martin Heidegger's (1962) *Being and Time*. Later on, the rigorous praxis and possible applications of a phenomenlogical theory of inquiry became clearer with a close study of Heidegger's (1982) *Basic Problems of Phenomenology*. Still later, the direction of my research toward noticing the leading clues for transcendental phenomenological psychology was strongly influenced by Eugen Fink's (1995) *Sixth Cartesian Meditation*. Fink also helped to clarify the difference between a so-called mundane phenomenological philosophy versus philosophy done from the phenomenological attitude—a significant difference that seems exceedingly difficult to grasp by most contemporary phenomenologists. One undeniable aim of this book is to demonstrate how Husserl's tradition of inquiry could be done and expressed from the phenomenological attitude in all the human sciences.

Heidegger's praxis in his existential studies would be out of place in these early remarks, however, except perhaps to reference my own practices for grasping the sense of Husserl's method of phenomenological philosophy as an experience of psychic life. Despite whether Heidegger meant to parody Husserl's "phenomenology," or was indeed being genuine in his prose, one could get the gist of how I initially approached my research into Husserl's work from the following understanding of the "formal meaning" of phenomenology given by Heidegger (1962) in the second part of his introduction to *Being and Time*:

> Thus "phenomenology" means...to let that which shows itself be seen from itself in the very way it shows itself from itself. This is the formal meaning of that branch of research which calls itself "phenomenology." But here we are expressing nothing else than [Husserl's] maxim...'To the things themselves'.... What is it that phenomenology is to 'let us see'? ...Manifestly, it is something that proximally and for the most part does *not* show itself at all: it is something that lies *hidden*...but at the same time it is something that belongs to what shows itself, and it belongs to it so essentially as to constitute its meaning and its ground. (Int. II ¶7)

It might be argued that adopting the phenomenological attitude in order to understand Husserl's theory of consciousness-formation, not only as philosophical discourse but also as Husserl's own psychological experience of phenomenological reasoning, follows Heidegger's technique of hermeneutic interpretations of the "authentic" meaning of symbolic speech and language. To a certain extent this charge would be correct. Husserl's method of reflection for phenomenological interpretations—the eidetic method of *Psychognosia* that I use in this study—is intended to let the deep structures of sense and meaning in referential expressions provide the conditions for interpretations of an original idea in conscious awareness. In this sense, *Psychognosia* is the intuitive ground in pure psychology for making hermeneutic interpretations.

In any event, Heidegger (1962, 1) makes it clear that his interpretations in *Being and Time* allow him to "work out the question" of the philosophical meaning of human *Being*, not to observe and explain either the psychological in human affairs or the phenomenon of human consciousness. It should nevertheless be understood in advance that I do indeed make phenomenological interpretations in order to understand the essence of Husserl's concepts as they pertain to the phenomenological method of consciousness-formation. Furthermore, with my intention to grasp Husserl's overall theory of consciousness as a venue for psychological studies, I follow his eidetic descriptions and clarifications, not Heidegger's existentialism. As to how this is possible from the phenomenological attitude, I recommend Gadamer's (1989, xxx) reflections on variations of hermeneutic interpretations; where in all cases, we are rigorously aware of our "engagement" with expressions of understanding—an engagement with both one's own understanding, and the understanding given by others. In its essence as intentional experience, this practice of interpretation makes use of the method of eidetic *seeing*.

In the following passage relating to his own studies, Welton (2000) gives perhaps the best flavor of my interpretive approach toward Husserl's discourse as it pertains to the phenomenon of human consciousness:

> We must engage in a form of what the later Husserl himself began to think of as "depth history." For it requires us to dismantle, layer by layer, the various levels of Husserl's account, using the one controlling image he was so fond of, that of stratification, as the working picture of how his own thought was put together. Often the strata are fused or mixed together, as is true of most geological layers that undergo periodic upheaval or are exposed to the surface and the elements. But sometimes we can uncover stretches when they are clearly separated and can see the differences. Yet all of this is further complicated by the fact that this was a process of sedimentation in reverse, not one that built "up" from earlier to later but one that built "down" from later to earlier. Accordingly, our reconstruction, to be appropriate, must engage in a form not of *Aufbauen* [building up], as though Husserl's own philosophical development moved from an unchanged foundation to a secure edifice resting on it, but of *Aubbauen* [reduction], of progressively uncovering the underlying strata on which that foundation itself rests, of searching for the ground of the foundation, if you will. (p. 9)

By following this direction for introducing transcendental phenomenological psychology as a necessary "ground of the foundation" for Husserl's phenomenological theory of consciousness-formation, I have made primary use of the most recent English translations of Husserl's major texts. Not only do the most recent translations have the advantage of hindsight into the development of his use and meaning of key concepts, perhaps even more so than an original German text, but they also have the advantage of including the important changes that Husserl made in successive editions. And, too, the most recent translations tend to make use of more idiomatic English. Lauer (1965, 7) points out that often for the sake of accuracy, however, translators will opt to reproduce Husserl's unique grammar and syntax, which "even German readers recognize…as not only difficult but quite un-German." In the opinion of a scholar with considerable experience reading works of Continental Philosophy in both German and English, as difficult as he is to read, Heidegger is a "cake-walk" compared to Husserl.

Husserl's texts are indeed notoriously difficult to read and to understand. Sometimes they are difficult not only because of his choice of words, but also for the way that his words are structured from the phenomenological attitude in paragraphs (not just sentences) in order to present a unity of sense for the meanings being conveyed. In this certain sense, readers of Husserl's text must become translators themselves of his original reflective meditations on both the oneness of human consciousness and on its "hidden" intuitive ground. In citations of the translated works of what one might recognize as classic Continental philosophers (such as Kant, Husserl, and Heidegger), it might have been noticed that I reference the section (§) or the paragraph (¶) of an original German text where it appears. I do this so that those who do not have the most recent translations, or who prefer to read the original German, could follow along with my quotations. Matas (2002) suggests that this is a traditional practice in Continental Philosophy, where sections and paragraphs display thinking "as it has unfolded" into a whole thought.

When I meet with translations of Husserl's German text in the secondary literature, I tend to accept the author's interpretations unless I have reason to believe that Husserl's meaning has been altered to further the arguments of the translating author. In the latter event, I make every attempt to consult the passage in question against the original German. My interpolations in quotations of Husserl's text are meant to put his speech into more idiomatic expressions and to contextualize his comments in as short a space as possible. To a certain extent as well, some of my interpolations represent interpretations of the leading clues for transcendental phenomenological psychology. The accuracy of my interpolations and interpretations could certainly be challenged in the spirit of phenomenological collaboration. In this same spirit, transcendental phenomenological psychology is presented for further study into that portion of Husserl's philosophy which could be evaluated and described psychologically as the cognitive mental life of a human among humans. This is Husserl's primary thesis for a phenomenological psychology of non-physiological consciousness.

1.
Beginning Considerations

"Why is there no transcendental phenomenological psychology already?"

The term "phenomenology" was coined in European alchemical and theological literature during the middle of the 17th century in order to signify the illusionary nature of human perception. The term subsequently entered the philosophical lexicon in the early 18th century as inquiry into the divine system of relations for the appearance of things. In 1764, Swiss-German mathematician Johann Heinrich Lambert was the first to use "phenomenology" in the title of a scientific publication that addressed our capacity for thinking as rational organisms. With this orientation the following year, he provided proof of the irrationality of the number Pi. For Lambert (Moran 2000, 6), a phenomenological study was meant to penetrate the mere appearance of things in order to arrive at knowledge of true being, much as the study of optics leads to discovery of the true features of an object of perception. Lambert's aim was to develop a science that could distinguish between truth and error in claims to knowledge of both the material and the spiritual.

Lambert's contemporary, Immanuel Kant, took up the development of a phenomenology of reason by distinguishing between the appearances of things (called, "phenomena") and the true being of things (called, "noumena"). Here, we gain knowledge of phenomena by the function of objective natural processes, while we come to know the true being of things by the function of our subjective mental processes. In Kant's 1786 *Metaphysical Foundations of Natural Science*, only phenomena could be studied according to principles of empirical observation and experimentation, even as noumena yield only to philosophical examinations. For Kant, phenomenological inquiry is a study of the manner by which noumenal qualities are transcended within the so-called immanent, all-pervasive, "internal" structures of phenomenal reality. An immanent structure of durable qualities is thus a necessary condition for the production of knowledge. In the sense given by Lambert and Kant, our self-knowledge of things is therefore already "transcendental."

The first great work devoted to a growing phenomenological tradition was Frederich Hegel's 1807 *Phenomenology of Spirit*, where he took Kant's descriptions of subjective experience to task for failing to develop a philosophy of mind wherein objective knowledge is produced. For Hegel, if one is to grasp the spiritual (i.e., mental) character of human experience, and of consciousness itself, then we must penetrate the evolution of our collective knowledge of a phenomenon as its true being becomes objectified within a genealogical sequence of moral, ethical, and political renditions. In effect, Hegel clarified our transcendence of the noumenal in historical accounts of a universal human spirit that is engaged in communal life. Moran (2000, 7) records that Hegel had little impact on the phenomenological movement until after the 1920s, when Edmund Husserl formalized and promoted his own approach as a transcendental phenomenology. Especially in Europe during the 1930s and after, Hegel was seen "as the true progenitor" of phenomenological inquiry. Today, phenomenology is perhaps most readily understood in the natural and human sciences as a descriptive study of something objective; and in the vernacular, "phenomenon" is synonymous with "fact." It has nevertheless remained constant from Lambert on that the sheer appearance of something we call a phenomenon is supported in consciousness by a deeper lying structure of sense and meaning that is ordinarily intuitable by humans, both individually and collectively.

Indeed, most of us have an intuitive grasp of what a phenomenon is. If pressed, we might define a phenomenon as something that could be perceived as a matter of fact, such as the wind or the way that chlorophyll is produced. In this sense, wind is a phenomenal characteristic of the weather and chlorophyll production is a phenomenal characteristic of green plants. Sometimes we think of a phenomenon as something extreme or outstanding in the normal course of events. A remarkable fact or achievement is then typically judged to be something phenomenal in ordinary experience. It could be seen with these examples that something perceived as a phenomenon, together with its phenomenal characteristics, refer to an entity that is already known through experience—only now, that same pre-existing entity is being described *as a matter of fact* to one's self and to others as a particular instance or modality of its possible perceptions. The weather is certainly more than the wind, a green plant is more than a chlorophyll-producer, and something said to be phenomenal is more than ordinary in one's ordinary experiences.

Mostly, though, we take for granted an associative linkage in thoughts between phenomena and their phenomenal characteristics. The fact that there is something called "the wind," as we might come to believe, means *of course* that there is something factual called "the weather." Even so, in this construction both the wind and the weather refer to something far more vague than descriptive matters of empirical fact—namely, one's self-knowledge of nature itself as a multi-modal entity in ordinary experience. Constructing a relationship of facts in order to grasp intellectually something that show itself within a plurality of manifestations is one of our earliest and most persistent cognitive skills; for indeed, it leads to the development of our practices of inductive reasoning. Once our self-knowledge of nature itself is accomplished to some satisfaction, this too becomes a matter of factual reality during our judgments and valuations of a particular phenomenon that has a "natural" appearance. One could experience this linkage in thoughts when we respond by saying "naturally," when we *mean* "of course." Describing phenomena to one's self and to others by their particular phenomenal characteristics then takes on the power of an implied natural causality between our perceptions of things and a matter that could be perceived by "everyone."

Although typically restricted in the spectrum of autism, this ordinary skill of reasoning consists of juxtaposing objects of "intellectual realism" and "visual realism" according to one's "inner model" of the plane of reality. (*see* Piaget 1976, 249) This simply means that whatever we have come to expect as real during earlier experience, we are then habitually inclined to perceive *as* real whenever a similar appearance is presented. The psychological phenomenon of an optical illusion, for example, reveals our use of this particular skill when we make judgments regarding the appearance of shapes and their spatial relationships. During its further development, we normally apply this skill of reasoning to areas that do not refer directly to the empirical qualities of nature itself. Nevertheless, we tend intuitively to use the same inductive reasoning that was assimilated during early cognitive development, where we presume a natural cause of occurrence between one's perceptions and whatever is immediately perceived.

One form of contemporary phenomenological inquiry is the study of psychological phenomena that implicitly presupposes an associative linkage of natural causality for the positing of facts. It is not uncommon in this practice for grouped descriptions of phenomenal characteristics to be referred to as a phenomenology *of* some theoretical construction. Here, the researcher builds up a relationship of inferences between a phenomenon and its perceived phenomenal characteristics that satisfies the criterion of natural induction. In this fashion of "doing phenomenology," a researcher's own judgments and valuations imply a natural cause for the validity of any subsequent conclusion of facts. Malmquist (1994) provides the following example of this kind of so-called naturalized phenomenology:

> The phenomenological experience of the depressive-prone child presents an intriguing picture. In some ways they appear as caricatures of the adult intellectual who intensely worries about the state of mankind. With children, the worry is about their own worthwhileness.... Clinicians sense a cautious seeking for attachments in the course of therapy and in reports of their daily life. In contrast to a schizoid child who prefers his withdrawal, the depressed child hungers for a relationship but he is doubtful about its sustainingness.... Sensitive observers sense mild depressive affect when a parent, pet, or friend is absent for more than a short period.... (pp. 194-5)

Although it might not be immediately apparent, the meaningful subject of inquiry in the above example is the narrator. To be precise, it is the clinical observer who presents through this protocol the sense and meaning of an associative linkage between the phenomenon of the depressive-prone child and its perceived phenomenal characteristics. In strictest terms, all that could be validated about the observer's conclusion of facts is the observer's own sensibilities. Still, there is some reason to believe that other clinical observers will share those sensibilities when the same presupposition of natural cause is assumed between one's perceptions and a conclusion of facts. The above example is a description of experience where the readers do not directly or immediately participate. Rather, a reader's participation consists of imagining, or "picturing," the same experience that is presented by the writer—a performance we sometimes called "empathy." When setting down this protocol, the writer presupposes that both the observer and the reader are, as it were, looking in the same direction along the plane of factual reality. A mutual understanding between the narrator and the depressive-prone child might then include the fulfilled since during the normal course of cognitive development, each of us learns to transcend a (noumenal) plane of potentials in one's imagination in order to construct a logical plane of (phenomenal) reality for what is perceived.

In Husserl's approach to transcendental phenomenology, the subject of inquiry is the one who presents the sense and meaning of this transcendence in thoughts—not the third-person scientist or philosopher as in Lambert's, Kant's, or Hegel's phenomenology. In the above example, the clinical observer is the meaningful human subject presented for Husserl's kind of rigorous phenomenological study. Here, the child is the object, not the subject, of clinical inquiry in the writer's descriptions; and here too, the child may or may not live in the same world of phenomenal reality as the observer, where the absence of something could equal depression. This means that the observed child may or may not be referring by its conduct to the same non-empirical matter as that posited by the observer. All that could be verified from the above description is what the observer infers to be the conduct of something named "the depressive-prone child" within a pre-existing system of facts that refers to the phenomenal qualities of what is called in theoretical discourse, "depression." A cognitive process of natural induction for inferences shows itself in the observer's protocol, while no such process of judgments and valuations shows itself directly in the child's described conduct. Throughout his transcendental phenomenological philosophy, Husserl characterizes the perspective on phenomenal reality that presupposes a course of natural induction as "the natural attitude."

Directed in reasoning by our natural attitude, conclusions follow logically from presuppositions of natural cause between perceived phenomenal characteristics and a phenomenon of interest. Facts of reality are then validated by one's experiences within a world of previously constructed factual matters. In this seemingly circular process of reasoning, our natural attitude and skills of induction usually serve us well for comprehending such vague non-empirical things as personal relationships, social dynamics, mathematical functions, morality, and so on. From the natural attitude, we tend to see totalizing associations in causal matters and conclusions within an exhaustive so-called transcendental circle of judgments and valuations. It is therefore not surprising that the natural attitude is carried over into our sciences and philosophies. This does not mean, however, that matters of fact and the world that appears to be made up of phenomena and their phenomenal characteristics do not exist in some form of reality. This only means that in addition to the transcendental objects that are intentionally constructed to be actually real in one's thought and speech, there also exists along the plane of reality certain multi-modal pre-existing things that do not exist concretely and empirically in one's conscious awareness—such as the idea of reality itself.

When the meaningful subject brings its judgments and valuations to bear on an object in space and time, empirical and non-empirical realities typically stand in a relationship of "interlaced" dependence within a circle of transcendence. Husserl's applied transcendental phenomenology aims at gaining *entrée* into this field of consciousness-formation, and then at imaginatively reversing the reasoning process of transcendence. It is perhaps tempting to compare the practices of Husserl's approach toward phenomenological studies with contemporary practices of reverse engineering. Unlike Hegel's historical phenomenology, however, it is not guaranteed in Husserl's theory of inquiry that the subject will succeed in closing the transcendental circle so that an idea comes to fruition as a factual matter of objective knowledge. Neither is it guaranteed, as it seems the case with Lambert and Kant, that errors in judgments and valuations will not be made by the reasoning subject in transcendental phenomenology. In Husserl's methodology, the original idea that is described as a phenomenon by its phenomenal characteristics makes its presence in conscious awareness as something we already intend to know and express as a matter of fact to one's self and to others.

Inquiry into the cognitive action and psychological processes intentionally used within a circle of transcendence—in order for one to be thus conscious of something—is the meaning of transcendental phenomenological psychology that is presented in this introductory study. Years ago, a Husserl-scholar on the cutting edge of the most advanced areas of phenomenological philosophy asked me, "Why is there no transcendental phenomenological psychology already?" I was puzzled myself. I could only say that maybe Husserl's methodology is simply too hard for most. In answering the question, I was thinking of Husserl's approach toward phenomenological psychology as presenting one more methodology for a research psychologist, on par intellectually perhaps with the most sophisticated practices of statistical and experimental inference. I have since discovered that Husserl's distinctive high level of rigor in theoretical inquiry is indeed rarely ever attempted in the human sciences. To the best of my knowledge there is no such thing today as a purely Husserlian psychological research practice; and certainly, no phenomenological psychology captures the original excitement of Husserl's revolutionary attitude as grasped by his contemporaries.

Still, Heidegger (1982, §5) grants that it has been necessary throughout the years to keep Husserl's clarifications of human consciousness in mind as the center around which non-empirical interpretations might revolve. And Foucault (1999, 159) points out that in "the years that preceded the Second World War, and even more so after," clarifications of the subject of human-scientific study "was of course due to the impact of Husserl." Husserl's philosophical studies of human consciousness, however, or of the meaningful human subject, do not necessarily reveal either a firm methodology or a specific application for the discipline of psychology. With rare exceptions in his phenomenological reflections, Husserl keeps a particular philosophical problem in focus without necessarily addressing any of its issues directly for the practice of phenomenological psychology. Perhaps another reason why a Husserlian transcendental phenomenological psychology has not yet been developed is that his transcendental phenomenological philosophy has not been systematized specifically for the discipline of psychology.

There is a conceptual difference that Husserl maintains between philosophical and psychological interests in his theory of inquiry. These differences tend to become blurred in actual practice, however, since each deals primarily with the provides of transcendental consciousness. It is important to remember that in Husserl's kind of transcendental phenomenology, the multi-modal non-empirical things that exist alongside concrete reality are present in consciousness as one's pre-existing ideas about something. For the most part, the practice of Husserl's phenomenological philosophy focuses on the idea of consciousness itself as an object of inquiry—but only as the so-called *indeterminateness* of this idea is intentionally transcended in order to become the self-evident phenomenon of conscious awareness that is recognized as actually real in ordinary experience and theoretical reflections. On the other hand, transcendental phenomenological psychology focuses on the cognitive action that is intentionally brought to bear upon those objects of inquiry *in order* for them to be realized in conscious awareness—including the phenomenon of human consciousness as the intentional object in theoretical reflections. In both cases, all data are presented by the meaningful human subject. In Husserl's terminology, the essence of this subject is referred to as "the pure Ego, *I*,"our universal way of being subjectively human.

It is easily seen that Husserl's terminology is a major cause of difficulty for anyone who intends to acquire and express an adequate understanding of his philosophy. It is certainly no less hard for appropriation in the discipline of psychology. Any new terminology might be difficult to read and to grasp at the beginning of study; and certainly, a difficult terminology requires considerable determined thought on its theoretical foundations and possible applications before one could say that it is well understood. Once Husserl's terminology is appropriated in his style of expression that refers to an intentional parts/whole unity (similar perhaps to the composition of terms for an equation), it must then be remembered in this context in order to make sense of its applications for a particular matter of interest. Considering all this, Husserl's practices are probably no harder to learn than those of any other eidetic science of mathematics, geometry, or formal logic. But instead of making principal use of symbolic notation as in those other sciences, Husserl uses his terms in complex imaginative variations of grammar and syntax in order to signify the idea of something that endures within multiple and simultaneous layers of intelligibility—that is to say, in eidetic strata of unambiguous *sense*, where each is capable of being known with clearness.

The focus of Husserl's reflections is usually first upon a matter of interest given from the natural attitude. Focus here is on the epistemology of a phenomenon in conscious awareness, presented as what is known or said to be known by the meaningful human subject. Sometimes epistemology is presented as one's simple belief or opinion. Epistemology is an *a priori* element of human consciousness in Husserl's work—meaning, it refers to some previous experience. The epistemology of a phenomenon is usually given to reflections from the signifying expressions of another, although at times Husserl seems to engage in introspection. Husserl nevertheless always introduces a phenomenon from the perspective of the natural attitude in ordinary language, but it is described from his phenomenological attitude for seeing real objects in thought and speech along with the intentional cognitive action of the meaningful human subject. This initial focus on epistemology in Husserl's theory of inquiry allows him to begin phenomenological meditations on something that has already gained presence in one's consciousness as actually real.

When focus is on pre-linguistic ("tacit") regions of consciousness, such as our objects and acts of perception and valuation, Husserl uses a descriptive terminology that is intended to evoke the sense and meaning of experiences that each of us could enjoy before we commonly speak of such things. Most of Husserl's distinctive and difficult terminology is meant to evoke one's pre-linguistic feelings of grasping the sense and meaning of an idea in order to be able to speak of it to one's self and to others. For example, in the natural attitude we commonly speak of "perceptual experience." In pre-linguistic stages of a structure of consciousness, however, Husserl refers to "apperceptive experience"—meaning that something is perceived such that it is *known* as being perceived. At each subsequent level of deeper pre-linguistic experience, sense and meaning for what shows itself by its sheer appearances in the natural attitude seem to spread out in Husserl's regressive "reverse" phenomenology. Unities that were presented from the natural attitude are separated within eidetic relationships of parts-to-parts and parts-to-whole in Husserl's reflections on the deep structure of conscious awareness. At lower levels of our pre-linguistic experience with this universal eidetic structure, Husserl makes use of an even more imaginative terminology in order to evoke the vague partial sense and meaning of more primitive regions of human consciousness. In the deeper pre-conceptual regions of regressive reflections (i.e., before an idea is fully represented in pre-linguistic thought), Husserl speaks of non-empirical entities such as *ways, things, stuff,* and *affairs.* At the deepest region possible in his regressive inquiry, Husserl speaks of *a priori* experience with existential things, such as *life, world, I, Other, me, mine,* and *theirs.*

When oriented in reasoning by our natural attitude toward the everyday world and one's place within it, each of us transcends these primitive elements of what it means to be human. Transcendence of these portions of the plane of reality is observed and explained in Husserl's transcendental phenomenology as what he calls a fundamental "clarification" of a matter of interest. A clarification of the phenomenon of the depressive-prone child, for example, would include the goals that are intended to be achieved by the rational and non-rational cognitive action that arise from deeper regions of self-consciousness. In this case, where such action *necessarily* leads to the child's unified phenomenal characteristics that could be described psychologically as "depressive-prone." In Husserl's tradition, a phenomenological clarification of something reduces the course of reasoning presented by the subject to its essence of universal sense and meaning. That essence is a pre-existing idea that is intentionally modified and played out by individuals and groups amid a mutually constructed surrounding of factual reality and objective truth. In its generic sense, this idea is called "the phenomenological *eidos*"—from the Platonic *eide* and its cognate *idea*, meaning a suprasensible reality. Husserl claims throughout his work that the reduced essence of an object of the mind—seen within each potential region of consciousness—is the generalization of how a phenomenological *eidos* shows itself as actually real in ordinary experience, not only within one's own conscious awareness, but also as objec-

7

An Organization of Differences

An introduction to transcendental phenomenological psychology could begin by recognizing broad conceptual differences between purely philosophical and purely psychological interests throughout Husserl's theory of inquiry. In still greater detail, one could see a distinction between a strictly descriptive phenomenological psychology and the course of an explanatory psychology of cognitive action. Generally speaking (Van de Pitte 1981, 39), the difference between phenomenological philosophy and phenomenological psychology is the difference between focus on respectively the objects or the acts when reflecting on human consciousness as a unified experience of subjective origins. Objects have been clarified in Husserl's "theory of elements" from nearly the inception of his studies, while cognitive action in psychological processes only appears explicitly in his more mature transcendental "theory of method." One might say that this division in focus between objects and acts in Husserl's theory of consciousness represents the reduction of a phenomenon to its necessary parts. The formulation of *any* valid scientific theory traditionally requires a system of reductions. (*see* Hempel 1965, 111)

One way to understand what Husserl means by "reduction" is to imagine that something could be separated into its constituent parts that that are necessary to make up a whole thing, perhaps much like an apple could be separated into its stem, skin, seeds, and so on. There comes a point when further separations reveal whatever is *not* necessary for that thing to be a whole, such as the apple's weight or its market price. There comes a point, as well, when further separations are not possible if anything is to exist in its original character as the subject's expression of a whole thing, such as the separation of an apple's parts into chemical compounds. Unlike taste and texture, things like chemical compounds are indiscernible in our subjective experiences of an apple, although the intention to see such things as phenomena themselves is also subjective in origin. Still, it is self-evident that seeing an apple as a whole thing made up of parts is not the same experience as one's intention to see its weight, price, or chemical compound. Something said to be "self-evident" is intuitively valid for subsequent judgments and valuations. An expression of self-evidence is the genesis of Husserl's (1973a, §4) regressive inquiry into the most "primitive operations" of a structure of consciousness.

As separations are made within the unity of configuration for a self-evident object in awareness, discernible parts of the whole are put into so-called brackets ([…]). Phenomenological brackets are used imaginatively and intuitively in order to "index" a sensible relationship of a part to its whole. When no further divisions are deemed possible, Husserl returns to a previously indexed region of the whole to be clarified in reductive focus. In its clarified form of sense and meaning, that region is, so to say, "parenthesized" ((…)) as a unity within the totality of all that is discernible, indiscernible, known, and unknown for that same region to be part of a whole. Something clarified is *necessarily* what it is in reflections, and cannot logically or experientially be anything else. In this sense of phenomenological reduction, objects and acts are bracketed and parenthesized collectively in Husserl's methodology as respectively his theory of elements and his theory of method.

The difference between a descriptive phenomenology of human consciousness, such as with Gurwitsch (1964, 157-97), and an explanatory transcendental phenomenology is perhaps more difficult to grasp. It rests on the distinction between respectively a "static" regressive praxis for evaluations of pre-existing reduced parts, versus a dynamic "genetic" praxis for seeing how something has indeed become a whole, given the previous existence of those same parts. The word "static" is meant to imply that all necessary parts of a whole are already in place at the beginning of inquiry. The term "*genetic*" refers here to the generation of elemental parts through phases or stages in a specific order, rather than to biological inheritability and variation in organisms. Regressive phenomenology is a propadeutic of genetic phenomenology—meaning, it is necessary in the beginning as a stage of the way for a complete and systematic investigation. Descriptive phenomenological psychology is a propadeutic of transcendental phenomenological psychology. In all of this, transcendental phenomenological psychology represents an "act psychology" (i.e., a psychology of cognitive action) amid a genetic phenomenology of intentional experience when one is consciously aware of something.

Husserl (1981, 51) emphasized that phenomenological inquiry in *any* human science "can take root only in radical reflexion upon the meaning and possibility of its own scheme.... [Its practice] must create original concepts, adequately adjusted to this ground, and so generally utilize for its advance an absolutely transparent method." Husserl's point seems to be that his theory of inquiry must be read in part as a method of reasoning about pre-conceptual thought itself within the various phenomenological fields, even before concepts are formed and essential theories about the human condition are constructed. For the discipline of psychology, Husserl's theory of inquiry should therefore be understood as intending to provide a systematic grounding of a phenomenological psychologist's own pre-conceptual experience with psychological phenomena before any observations or analyses begin. The efficacy of Husserl's metatheoretical praxis can be properly debated and extended in applications only when it is understood to be a method of reflection and interpretation within a complex philosophy of human consciousness.

Although Husserl never intended to produce solely a practice of rigorous personal groundwork with his theory of inquiry, there is nevertheless a distinctive phenomenological attitude toward scientific praxis—just as there is a mathematical or a biological attitude toward acceptable ways of proceeding. Husserl's phenomenological attitude is precisely a "working attitude" to see and comprehend how we humans enjoy the capacity to think about the things that matter most to us, and to think in ways that indicate both our individualism and communalism. What matters most from this perspective is the question of what it means to be human in thought, speech, and intentional action. To be sure, it is not always necessary or desirable to apply Husserl's praxis calling for extreme rigor when thinking about the human condition; since as Heidegger (1982, §4) claims, Husserl intended to provide a fundamental ontology of the possibility of cognizing consciousness of human Being as itself a phenomenon for human-scientific study. Heidegger is perhaps correct in his assessment of Husserl's *aim* at fundamental ontology with his phenomenological methodology, but he turns away from Husserl's intentions *for* a fundamental ontology in the full extension of his work.

In the practical experience of Husserl's theory of inquiry, fundamental ontology is the systematic organization and communication of what is invariantly within the human capacity to live in—and be conscious of—a world of things that is already *mine, theirs,* and (for the most part) *ours.* Husserl's fundamental ontology is generally intended to exhaust all potential expressions of the subjective meaning of something that is *being* what it *is* in conscious awareness, including the phenomenon of consciousness itself when we think about it. Husserl's clarifications of the contents of awareness refer to an *a priori* invariance in fundamental ontology for the sense and meaning of what *is* the human condition when we are *being* human. Such clarifications are meant to provide the criteria for all our contingently "truthful" theoretical statements in the human sciences. Yet when Husserl's reflective abstractions of this universal state of affairs are understood solely as theories of existence, or as providing the so-called ontological proof for a conclusion of facts, then his phenomenological clarifications can only be experienced pre-conceptually and understood finally as epistemology—rather than as the ontic support for any epistemological construct whatsoever in the human sciences.

Even so, there is indeed an intuitive phenomenological epistemology running throughout Husserl's work. Specifically, Husserl constructs an ongoing theory of knowledge that provides both the access to, and a confirmation of, his clarified fundamental ontology. In the midst of this theoretical "knowledge-complex" of *being* and *doing,* Husserl's epistemology is descriptive of what is said to be known or understood by the meaningful human subject about a particular phenomenon in conscious awareness. One way to read Husserl's epistemology is as what we might today call a "common sense" theory of evidence. (*see* Smith 1995, 398f) Here, expressions of self-knowledge given by a single subject point toward deeper lying meanings that are believed to be fundamentally valid for all of us. An implied or explicit epistemology in Husserl's work provides *entrée* into ontological conceptualizations of the meaning of what is known to be actually real. Husserl insisted that his phenomenological praxis was meant to be the method of ontology—that is to say, it was intended to be the way of thinking rationally that pre-exists during our expressions of the meaning or existence of things.

In all cases of its articulation, Husserl's (1982, §148) methodology to arrive at a fundamental ontology of *anything* is to be carried out according to irrefutable principles of investigation for both *a priori* and contingent spheres of knowledge. This means, respectively, (a) knowledge accepted from previous experience versus (b) knowledge dependent upon the fulfillment of some experience according to the free will of a human agent. Both spheres of knowledge are given in Husserl's work as "analogies and parallels" of an "extended" concept of formal ontology—meaning, an ordered collection of super-types, types, and sub-types of experience. Husserl's distinction between *a priori* and contingent spheres of knowledge—understood in practice as two essential ways of knowing things—indicates a significant difference for theory construction between his phenomenological praxis of deep reflection and empirical practices of experimental or statistical manipulations. Yet when approaching mental life either phenomenologically or empirically, practitioners concern themselves with the same field of inquiry. The human mind in Husserl's work *is* the human mind for everyone, and no differences in fashion or attitude will change that particular invariant.

Phenomenological praxis for psychological studies in Husserl's tradition is intended to make obvious our experiences in the cognitive mental life of conscious awareness. These experiences include taking positions in judgments and evaluation not only during one's day-to-day activities, but also during our practices of scientific concept formation and theory construction. These latter activities would of course entail the mental life of doing both empirical and phenomenological psychology. Still, Husserl's intention to provide a more complete ground of pre-theoretical experience for psychologists has perhaps gone unnoticed or has been forgotten through the years because of phenomenological psychologists "being 'in love with philosophy.'" (Moustakas 1994, 25) At the same time, Husserl (1970, 207) mentions that there will perhaps always be some philosophers who see an interrelation of philosophy and psychology as a "betrayal" of their "true undertaking," and will therefore avoid dealing with the psychological in any rigorous sense.

Perhaps, too, a failure to grasp Husserl's metatheoretical approach toward all the human sciences precludes seeing any need to develop a phenomenological psychology to its fullest extent. And yet, one cannot find a major publication by Husserl that makes no mention of the importance of psychology to the development of his theories of consciousness, even when that role is not explicitly spelled out. But he was also aware that psychological descriptions of our thinking about abstract concepts could take the place of a philosophical examination of the logic that is used for such thinking, or of the language and metaphysical presuppositions that refer to a particular concept in scientific focus. In the context of our psychological descriptions of human experience, some might recognize this issue as the problem of "psychologism" in Husserl's theory of inquiry. For phenomenological psychology, the issue of psychologism represents a problem of establishing validity in our concepts and theories about human consciousness. Ultimately, it is the problem of making judgments about what is indeed a psychological phenomenon.

Husserl delivered a series of lectures in the mid 1920s that delineated the role of psychological inquiry into cognitive mental life as part of his emerging transcendental theory of awareness. Husserl dealt with the issue of psychologism in these lectures in order to move on with the development of his transcendental phenomenological philosophy within a systematic science of essences—which was intended to radicalize all the human sciences toward an intuitive eidetic point of view. Now freed from empirical psychological descriptions by his eidetic depictions of intentional objects versus intentional acts, Husserl's subsequent ontology and ongoing epistemology continued to mark out what he and his followers identified as the transcendental realm or

logical field is to say that transcendental phenomenology in Husserl's tradition focuses on the "ongoing experiencing-of-the-world," where we are capable of reflecting on our own active and passive experiences of living knowingly with others, and upon the meaning of life itself. (Mohanty 1989, 160)

The contingency of personal experience in Husserl's account of transcendental consciousness implies *a priori* categories of universal experience in his methodology. Indeed, students of Husserl's theory of inquiry will encounter expressions of "pure" categories everywhere, such as pure phenomenology, pure consciousness, pure subjectivity, pure Ego, and pure psychology. Pure categories are irreducible primitive concepts that make possible any phenomenological inferences of theoretical constructs. The pure Ego, for example, cannot be reduced in reflections to anything other than our universal subjective way of being human. The irreducible pure Ego is therefore capitalized here in order to indicate its peculiar character of sentient *being* in the fundamental ontology of pure subjectivity. On the other hand, the so-called personal ego could be reduced to the pure Ego's variable way of being human that is distinctly *my own*, and will not be capitalized here as a contingent matter of transcendental subjectivity within a particular region of ontology. In their own areas of subjective experience, the psychological ego could be reduced to the pure Ego's psychosubjectivity, the transcendental ego to the pure Ego's natural attitude, and so on. Pre-existing categories of pure *being* and *doing* provide self-evident propositions about the origin of what appears as contingency might demand in the transcendental register.

In Husserl's methodology, pure categories of concepts epistemologically bifurcate substrates of concepts and derived theoretical constructs. Here, something is said to be bifurcated when it is split off from its origin yet retains elements of its original sense and meaning—much like the branches of a tree are bifurcated from its trunk. Farber (1968, 142) points out that a pure category of meaning represents the essence of a theoretical construct as it finds expression within any conceivable "knowledge-complex." Farber means that a theoretical construct "is said to be possible; and this possibility is guaranteed *a priori* through knowledge of the [pure] conceptual essence." In phenomenological practice, we could have an idea about what something is or might be in the transcendental register when the subject already has some *a priori* experience with the pure category of meaning for that same thing. This is not so different from our ordinary experiences; where for instance, we could recognize something as edible before investigating whether this is the case. In order to recognize a particular concept or construct in the transcendental register, Husserl (1980a, p. 410) must first clarify the pure category of meaning wherein that thing is presented as an instance of a more general or universal concept. For transcendental phenomenology, pure phenomenology provides the *a priori* meaning categories for observations, descriptions, and explanations, versus such things primarily from the empirical standpoint.

In Husserl's tradition of theory and practice, concepts of pure consciousness ground intuitively his concepts of transcendental consciousness. Concepts of pure subjectivity similarly ground concepts of transcendental subjectivity, while concepts of pure psychology ground concepts of transcendental psychology, and so on. Just as important, concepts of pure *being* and *do-*

ing are also intended to ground concepts for any methodology whatsoever in the human sciences. Husserl's metatheoretical use of "pure concepts of concepts" represents our intuitive practice to distinguish an instance of universal eidetic structure for an idea within a particular or individual style of inference. (*see* Farber 1968, 143) This goal is achieved in pre-conceptual experience with an adequate ideation of the essences of those concepts within meaningful forms of individuation and patterns of association. During scientific concept formation, this practice is intended to preclude ambiguity in our theoretical constructions wherein derived concepts are connected for valid conclusions. In our day-to-day unreflective experiences, this practice is often called "insight" during inductive inferences of truth and reality.

Thus grounded in pure psychology, transcendental phenomenological psychology is intended to allow the discipline of psychology to advance along with Husserl's most mature reflections and clarifications of our ordinary experiences of consciousness-formation. I propose that the discipline can do this by focusing on Husserl's descriptions of our judgments and valuations in the cognitive mental life of transcendental consciousness. Moving on in this way means to take to heart Husserl's (1977) last few comments on descriptive psychology during his 1925 lectures on psychological inquiry:

> The actual execution of the indications begun in the lecture would include…a universal doctrine of the structures of individual subjectivity and intersubjectivity. That would be a great work [in the future]. Therefore, I could only project its plan [here], and that would already be much. This [descriptive psychology in the lecture] was thought of as a species of naïve research [since it relies upon deductions from empirical generalizations and universal "external" experience]…. But in the background a purpose can serve a motivating function [for the discipline of psychology, where].. I am an inductive psychologist, but would like to know how the psyche looks "internally." I intend of course [to construct a] "parallel" and altogether inductive research [of genetic inquiry for phenomenological psychology]….
>
> Likewise [in this future work], I can be…interested in personal internality. Here I would have to consider…[that] the personal I has an "internal" life to be disclosed, and a personal self-development. And there I come again upon the demand of a deeper exploration [of non-empirical dimensions]…. Therefore, I could give [here] merely the outline, the presentation of a pure internal psychology…[that leads] then from the psychological reduction to the transcendental phenomenological [structures of conscious awareness]. (p. 179)

In what sense does this background "purpose"—experienced intuitively in traditional practices of empirical psychology—call for a new phenomenological psychology of the "structures of individual subjectivity and intersubjectivity?" How does a descriptive psychology in Husserl's 1925 lec-
dental consciousness? As one of my most controversial arguments, I will

attempt to show throughout this study that phenomenological psychology serves a dual purpose in Husserl's mature theory of inquiry. In the first place, Husserl (1981, 24) was intent during the 1920's on developing a pure "theory of method" for transcendental phenomenology. Husserl wanted to develop the means of phenomenological reduction in the transcendental register as the "method of pure psychology and the presupposition of all its specifically theoretical methods"—that is to say, as a *psychological* reduction. In the second place, Husserl wanted to replicate *as praxis* the essence of mental acts in pure psychology as the "method of access [that] is required" for *entrée* into the phenomenological field of a unified pure and transcendental subjectivity.

I take this to mean that one is to practice Husserl's theory of inquiry (as applied phenomenology) according to the inductive methods that are identified in pure psychology as universal mental acts—where such acts are used by each of us (genetically) in the transcendental register during contingent experiences of consciousness-formation. This interpretation is certainly controversial, but it follows from the notion that Husserl had a rational mind engaged in scientific concept formation and theory construction, and that he proposed a radical praxis that explicitly calls into force the mental life of a phenomenologist in the real world. An equivalent expression would be to say, for example, that behavioral psychologists generally engage in the same behavior as that exhibited by those under study. An alternative to this notion is to suggest that Husserl indeed *had* no mind, and that applications of the phenomenological method proper require no cognitive mental life of judgments and valuations. Finally, it is nothing less than conceit or folly to suppose that any scientist or philosopher has superhuman intellectual skills or mystical abilities that are denied to everyone else during the normal course of events.

Applying the methods of pure psychology not only reveals to reflections what is properly psychological in transcendental consciousness, but by implication it also reveals what is *not* psychological in the phenomenological field. A propadeutic descriptive phenomenological psychology provides access to the pre-existing object-structure and genesis of transcendental consciousness. "So on top of the first 'static' phenomenology," Husserl (1981, 26) writes, "will be constituted in higher levels a dynamic or genetic phenomenology." Transcendental phenomenological psychology is thus a parallel but correlated "act psychology" of object-oriented phenomenology, where its theory of inquiry traces out a genetic course of psychic life throughout Husserl's clarifications of transcendental consciousness.

The Real and the Irreal

Husserl's regressive reflections on the genesis of transcendental consciousness were led to theories of our methods of consciousness-formation in pure psychology, even as he called for a new genetic phenomenological psychology in the transcendental register. One purpose of Husserl's 1925 lectures on psychology, where he seems to have first made this call, was to rid his phenomenological philosophy of the last traces of psychologism in descriptions of objects in conscious awareness. Husserl (1977, 14-15) began these lectures by explaining how the term "descriptive psychology" entered into his struggle against psychologistic practices as far back as the first edition of his 1900-1901 *Logical Investigations*, where phenomenological descriptions were intended to combat "all empiricistic or psychologistic mixing of psychological ingredients of thinking activity into the logical concepts and propositions themselves." In his first publication devoted to phenomenological inquiry, Husserl explains in the *Investigations* that such eidetic things as logical propositions and numbers are objects of potential awareness, just as rocks and trees are objects—except that they are "irreal" (*irreale*), ideal, *a priori* objects, rather than the contingent "actually real" (*reale*) objects of empirical observations.

For Husserl (2001, 42), "the empirical" arises from experience, but it is not therefore that experience itself. He agrees with Kant that only actually real objects *can* be empirically observed with an immediate sense of awareness; but in Husserl's work, both irreal objects and the objects of empirical observations become actually real only when they have been first submitted to our mental acts that make them thus contingently sensible and true. With this orientation toward intentional action versus the intended object to which such action is directed, phenomenologists could observe and describe what one consequently says and does during the lived experience of making objects actually real in conscious awareness. By "lived experience" (*Erlebnis*), Husserl means a phenomenologically reduced unity in consciousness that represents "a real experiential complex, which we (i.e., each man for his own ego) finds in part evidently present, and for the rest [that is not self-evident, we] postulate on good grounds." (p. 205) The subject "lives" an experience immediately when one is conscious of its active content here and now as *my own* experience of self-evident awareness.

Husserl stresses in his 1925 lectures that a proper domain for descriptions of psychological experience is delineated by the activity of thinking about both real and irreal objects. Husserl deliberately avoids mentioning, however, that he once referred to phenomenological inquiry itself as a "descriptive psychology." Husserl (2001) indicated in the first edition of the *Logical Investigations* that phenomenological praxis manages to isolate the pure logic that is revealed when we think about the phenomenon of formal logic. His clarification of an *a priori* pure logic left the contingent mental life of thinking about formal logic to be described as the phenomenological epistemology of how we come to know objects as actually real during theory construction:

> Phenomenology is descriptive psychology. Epistemological criticism is therefore in essence psychology, or at least only capable of being built on a psychological basis. Pure logic therefore also rests on psychology—what then is the point of the whole battle against psychologism? The necessity of *this* sort of psychological foundation of pure logic, i.e. a descriptive one, cannot lead us into error regarding the mutual independence of the two sciences, logic and psychology. For pure description is merely a preparatory step toward theory, not theo-

Even so, the above remarks perhaps reflect Husserl's original but unrecognized intention to use principles of pure psychology as scientific praxis; for he later suggested that it was four years after writing the *Investigations* that he became "self-conscious of its method." (*see* Husserl 1970, §70) This revelation seems to imply that by *doing* phenomenological philosophy Husserl became aware of his own lived experience and *a priori* methods of phenomenological reasoning. When Husserl then broadened his scope of study toward universal examples of cognitive mental life, he realized that he was making a serious error by calling phenomenological epistemology a "descriptive psychology" of our experiences of judgments and valuations.

Husserl seemed to presume in the *Investigations* that we employ distinctive psychological processes for thinking logically in order to grasp formal logic as actually real. Yet there was no indication that there exists something like a "logical" process of judgments and valuations for thinking about formal logic that mirrors that logic itself. More important, both irreal and actually real objects are not psychological activities themselves—meaning, objects of self-knowledge are not descriptive of how we come to know them. Husserl was certainly in error when calling his nascent phenomenology of the objects of consciousness a descriptive psychology. In the 1913 second edition of the *Logical Investigations*, Husserl (2001) perhaps attempted to rectify this error by substituting the following passage for the one quoted above from 1900:

> If *our* sense of phenomenology has been grasped [as a method of inquiry in areas of philosophical interest], and if it has not been given the current interpretation of an ordinary 'descriptive psychology'... then an objection, otherwise justifiable, will fall to the ground, an objection to the effect that all theory of knowledge conceived as a systemic phenomenological clarification of knowledge is built upon [principles of] psychology. On this [wrongful] interpretation pure logic, treated by us as an epistemologically clarified, *philosophical* discipline, must in the end likewise rest upon psychology, if only upon its preliminary descriptive researches into intentional experiences. Why then so much heated resistance to psychologism? (p. 95)

Husserl (2001, 95-6) answered his own question about psychologistic descriptions in philosophical discourse. Although his practice of uncovering irreal objects for clarifications of essential sense and meaning could be described as "psychological" because of its way of proceeding, he is not talking about traditional empirical psychology. Instead, he is referring to a "peculiar 'pure'" psychology of non-empirical qualities that directs one's "contemplation of pure essences." The irreal objects of such contemplation are self-evidently not that contemplation itself—even when knowledge of said objects results in positing something empirically real. By 1913, Husserl's sense of regressive inquiry into the essences of things was considerably advanced from what was being developed in 1900. A silly example here might illustrate what Husserl meant to convey in his revised *Logical Investigations* about naïve practices that rely upon psychologistic descriptions of empirical data for interpretations of both philosophical and psychological phenomena:

One could observe that a cow has occasion to "moo." We might describe a moo in fine phenomenal details of timbre and tone, along with the apparent conditions in which a moo is likely to occur. We could investigate and describe the neurological and anatomical features of a cow, and then infer the physiological characteristics that allow the sound of the moo to be produced. We could go outside the bounds of our empirical data and attempt to interpret what the cow means when it moos, or at least what we think that the cow is intending to communicate. But even so, although we might have cause to believe that we have some intuition into these matters of cow-thinking, we have still done no more than to describe characteristics of the thing that we agree to call a "moo" according to its empirical manifestations within a taxonomy of actually real things. In this case, we must presume in advance that the moo exists as actually real in order to interpret its meaning and the cow's intention to make the sound.

And yet, we have never said what a moo is as an object of interest that has significance beyond its location within an empirical taxonomy that we could sense, amplify theoretically, and measure with our exact technologies. We have never described what is already in agreement between the comportment of a cow and the contemplation of its observer that allows us to call this thing a moo, and not a grunt or a pickle or a toothpick. Husserl's point in 1913 seems to be that empirical psychology addresses as matters of interest only those theoretical objects that have already been "psychologically processed," as it were. It does not, and cannot, describe what is not made actually real within this same process. Any psychological practice or theory of inquiry that relies upon observations of empirical manifestations for experimental manipulations and clarifying descriptions cannot interpret a psychological process according to inductive methods of reasoning. Conclusions for any descriptive psychology of solely empirical matters must instead be deduced according to some contingent philosophical ground.

When psychological studies are thus grounded theoretically in contingent experience, descriptions of concepts and conclusions are presented in agreement with causal presuppositions of what is necessary for something to appear such as it does for observations from a particular ("incommensurate") orienting perspective—that is to say, an extra-psychic cause is usually presupposed for descriptions of processes that result in the empirical manifestations of psychological phenomena. For example, we might rely upon the theoretical ground that a moo is a phenomenon within the "nature" of a cow. However, a descriptive psychology cannot directly infer from empirical data any "natural" characteristics of a psychological process of *mooing*. Indeed, any such process is already gone for observations by the time that its empirical manifestations have come to presence in proper correspondence with its theoretical expectations. Said structures of consciousness are irreal, *a priori* matters that only appear, according to Husserl, within a phenomenological account.

During the same year that the second edition of the *Logical Investiga-*
tions was published, Husserl presented the first of what was intended as a full introduction to his *Ideas Pertaining to a Pure Phenomenology and to a Phenomenological Philosophy*. In what

is traditionally called the *First Book*, Book I, or *Ideas I*, Husserl (1982, §9) describes the presence of distinguishing and identifying "regional ontologies" as eidetic compositions of non-empirical matters that are experienced as one's self-knowledge of something. Here, any formal science—including "the old meaning of psychology" as descriptive of the empirical manifestations of mental life—could be phenomenologically grouped in bracketed meaning-categories according to specific intuitions into the *a priori* ideas of actually real things. The irreal essence of any empirical object of scientific inquiry is then carried over into a corresponding regional category of signifying properties. A regional ontology of signifying properties gives the appearance of a matter of fact for inferences of cause and effect. Consequently, *"any science of matters of fact* (any experiential science) *has essential theoretical foundations in eidetic ontologies."*

Eidetic science deals with ideas rather than solely with realized facts, such as the eidetic sciences of mathematics, logic, and geometry. Husserl's concept of *essence* (*Wesen*) in eidetic science follows Aristotle's meaning of "essence" as that which something cannot lack if it is to be what it *is*. The phenomenological essence of something is its eidetic singular *what-ness*, its original idea. For example, the essence of a moo is a sound made by a cow. The essence of "the psychological" is the activity of mental life. The essence of something is conceptually different from its conditions of existence, its *is-ness* of identity or *being*—put differently, the way that something is *being* what it *is* in thought and speech. A moo is not a toothpick, and a psychological phenomenon is not strictly speaking a biological or chemical entity. We universally grasp these differences intuitively. The difference between *what* something is, and that it indeed *is*, "goes without saying" during our experiences with real things. What goes without saying in ordinary judgments and valuations cannot be verified by empirical practices; instead, they are our metaphysical presuppositions about such categories of things as functions, causality, and shapes.

Presuppositions of *what-ness* and *is-ness* orient the construction of actually real objects during our habitual day-to-day experiences. Reciprocally in this circle of transcendence, one's original experiences with actually real objects provide the intuitive ground for the pre-existence of irreal things in transcendental consciousness. When we sense this reciprocal presence as "a presumptive idea" in imagination (i.e., its *eidos*), we tend to begin our empirical ways of thinking toward an object of the mind. We usually anticipate from this attitude that the essence of an *eidos* and its object has an actually real nature that could be evaluated by inductive methods of reasoning. (*see* Husserl 1973a, §83a) In the normal course of events, the irreality of an enduring *eidos* is our intuitive idea of a specific object, despite whether that object ever gains presence as actually real in its empirical manifestations or is only imagined within a region of eidetic ontology. An eidetic ontology is an *a priori* region of essences where our thoughts are focused pre-conceptually on particular things that could *potentially* come into conscious awareness as actually real.

The discipline of psychology presents a regional ontology of psychological matters in Husserl's science of essences—an eidetic science *itself* that underlies all clarifications of objects and acts. Keep in mind, however, that a pre-theoretical phenomenologically pure psychology of irreal essences is not the same as an empirical theory of psychological experience in the modern (Humean) sense. Rather, when the essence of mental life is described according to its empirical manifestations, it has already become an actually real object from the natural attitude. Husserl (1982, xx) explains in *Ideas I* that any particular manifestation of the psychological experience of mental life is objectified as a matter of fact in ordinary descriptive psychology. Phenomenological psychology is therefore a science of factual matters as well, but only as those matters are intentionally realized as objectified things "in the one spatiotemporal world as the *omnitudo realitatis*." Husserl uses the Kantian term *omnitudo realitatis* to indicate that the fundamental ontology of psychological phenomena encompasses all possible regions of reality that the meaningful human subject intentionally constructs and experiences.

Describing factual representations of the *objects* of psychic life, such as love or fear, is not a psychologistic practice when clarifying a psychological experience of intentional action, such as loving or fearing. In Husserl's science of essences, objects are experienced by means of our intentional acts in cognitive mental life. When we naïvely posit the psychological experience of something to be a matter of fact, we have already experienced the essence of that phenomenon to the extent that its irreality has been transcended into its actually real presence as a conflation of objects and acts—and thus, it has come into awareness within the substrate of all real things that could manifest themselves concretely and empirically. The irreal objects of a regional ontology of psychology entail the *a priori* objects of pure consciousness that we could all experience as elements of sentient life. (*see* Husserl 1982, §65, §76) In this way of *being*, psychological phenomena are not solely irreal, ideal, and *a priori*. They are also things of immediate actual reality that could be sensed intuitively and described by psychologists within an empirical taxonomy of things—*because* psychologists experience (or could ordinarily experience) such things themselves as fact or fantasy in day-to-day pure psychology.

To restate and rephrase Husserl's 1913 position on phenomenological psychology: The objects of empirical psychology point toward our traditional (and thus habitual) practices for thinking about phenomena as concretely real within a regional ontology of psychology. We usually learn in our formal institutions to constitute a psychological phenomenon with reason and evidence as actually real by its empirical manifestations; but in our non-phenomenological naïveté in following this practice, we do not describe the irreal pre-conceptual process of that thinking itself, either for ourselves or for others. Instead, we tend to signal a grasp of mental life by naming as "psychological" historically constructed matters of fact that continue to be observed in both ordinary experience and theoretical reflection. Perhaps we can better understand Husserl's purpose in 1925 for outlining the phenomenological parameters of a descriptive psychology of factual matters—namely, as a defense against charges of psychologism in his philosophical descriptions of pre-conceptual objects of the mind. Yet this approach in his philosophy might also reveals his methodic purpose in calling for a phenomenological psychology transcendental register of pure human consciousness.

Husserl's (1970, §43ff) reflections on the psychic life of transcendental consciousness begin with the "phenomenological-psychological reduction" of our intentional acts of cognition. Here, he initially "leaves open the question of how this reduction stands in relation to the transcendental reduction." Later on, Husserl's mature psychological reduction seems to focus on the active and passive methods in pure psychology by which an object could gain presence as a contingent unity in the transcendental register. Both real and irreal objects are identified in Husserl's propaedeutic regressive phenomenology, where they are presented without psychologistic descriptions in all forms of reduction. That is to say, objects of *what-ness* and *is-ness* are neither cognitive mental acts nor psychological processes, and cannot be properly described as such. In rigorous philosophical reflections, however, the discipline of psychology could itself be seen as a phenomenon of interest. In this case, the practicing psychologist could be described and evaluated as the meaningful human subject within a regional ontology of psychological matters—such as the clinical observer (subject) of the "depressive-prone child" (object). Husserl's descriptions of the discipline of psychology mostly take this philosophical point of view. Indeed, he takes this same point of view toward all scientific disciplines and their respective practitioners.

In the fundamental ontology of psychic life, each of us—philosophers and psychologists alike, in both empirical and non-empirical orientations—makes use of our intuitive methods of pure psychology during activities of consciousness-formation. Husserl (1970, §69) noticed in this relationship that a psychological reduction to one's intentional methods of action on objects is not performed by a descriptive psychology in regressive phenomenology. This is instead a practice for genetic phenomenology in the transcendental register. In regressive phenomenology, descriptions of an object in conscious awareness are meant in part to bracket the subject's pre-existing beliefs about any cultural, historical, or empirical nature of realized phenomena; and in doing so, an eidetic ontology of cognitive mental life is revealed for further reflections on its lived experience. An epistemology of *what-ness* and *is-ness* within a region of psychology in the transcendental register is indeed descriptive of realized facts about psychological experience.

For example, one could grasp the following description given by Piaget (1954) as the epistemology of a fulfilled unity of consciousness for a particular matter of "psychological" fact. The eidetic construction of this unity appears in Piaget's empirical data, "which is natural," by means of a composition of elements referring to the child's cognitive development:

> The formation of the universe [of concrete reality], which seemed accomplished with that of sensori-motor intelligence [by the child between the ages of three and twelve], is continued throughout the development of thought, which is natural, but is continued while seeming at first to repeat itself, before truly progressing to encompass the data of action in a representative system of the totality [of concrete reality]. (p. 380)

20

Piaget's objectifications of psychological experience could be clarified as his grasp of the life-span development of a system of "habitual apperceptions." (*see* Husserl 1973b, §38) Here, the child's original perceptions of concretely real things and their relationships are iterated and extended throughout the transcendental register as intuitive self-knowledge of pregiven things. A descriptive empirical psychology such as Piaget's provides the eidetic ontology and epistemology of the intentional activity to be conscious of something within a construction of actual reality. However, recall that descriptions of objects do not directly reference intentional activities of the subject's thinking about those objects. Instead, traditional psychological descriptions tend to signal what is known to be objective phenomena in non-phenomenological (and therefore already transcended) theoretical discourse. Husserl's psychological reduction in genetic phenomenology isolates this intentional activity as our purely psychological experience with any object whatsoever here and now. In this sense, Piaget saw intuitively in his empirical data what he had already experienced and transcended in consciousness of something universal.

There is the conceptual danger that a descriptive psychology that only names phenomena of mental life according to their empirical manifestations will be understood and presupposed as the complete manifold of conscious awareness. Quite to the contrary, however, transcendental consciousness is composed *seamlessly* of intentional objects, intentional acts, and extra-psychic phenomena in one's sociocultural surroundings. Each description in regressive phenomenology could be given along a finite continuum of one of these elements, but simple descriptions cannot explain the motivation and irreal acts of pure psychology that make the phenomenon of conscious awareness a unified whole thing in the transcendental register. Going beyond the bounds of expository descriptions in regressive phenomenology means that a phenomenologist has likely reverted back to the natural attitude for deductive explanations of the empirical manifestations of a phenomenon. Husserl mentions frequently that the habits of thought for doing empirical inquiry are indeed difficult to overcome, even for phenomenologists. (*see* Husserl 1970, §71)

In his own descriptions of intentional experience, Husserl mostly refers to the exemplary *ways* in pure psychology that humans intentionally comport themselves, rather than to the concrete behavior that could eventually be observed, measured, and experimentally manipulated. Scholarly descriptions of empirical manifestations of psychological phenomena, absent any correlated irreal and *a priori* structures of pure consciousness, tend to follow the habits of thought found in a centuries-old tradition of naïve practices. When Husserl expressed this sentiment in the 1930s, the majority tendency in mainstream psychology was to advance the so-called naturalistic theories that were either behavioristic (e.g., John B. Watson, Edward Thorndike, and Ivan Pavlov) or empiricistic (e.g., Francis Galton, Hermann Von Helmholtz, and G. T. Fechner). Other than the phenomenological perspective, only Sigmund Freud's (Gay 1988, 588ff) psychoanalytic theories and Wilhelm Dilthey's (1977) inquiry into the lived experience of psychological concepts represented

21

Phenomenological Psychology in the Transcendental Register

A new horizon for the discipline of psychology opens up with Husserl's transcendental reduction to the irrealities of ordinary experience. This is indeed the phenomenological reduction to our universal and individual ways of comportment, just as they present themselves for reflections without naïve presuppositions of external cause or objective origins. Under the transcendental reduction, manifestations of the subject's comportment yield to phenomenological-psychological descriptions and explanations of cognitive mental life in the world of human co-existence. Husserl (1970) advises that in order for the pure psychology of this experience to "attain its total horizon" in his theory of inquiry, any phenomenological psychology in the transcendental register should be be practiced as a step-wise series of reflections on the method of phenomenological reduction itself:

> Phenomenological psychology [in the transcendental register] reveals itself…in various steps, because the phenomenological reduction itself—and this is part of its essence [in pure psychology]—could reveal its sense, its inner, necessary requirements, and its scope only in steps. Each step requires new reflections, new considerations, which in turn were possible only through the self-understanding [of the immediate prior step] and the practiced accomplishment of the other steps…. In order to attain its total horizon [as methodical praxis], the phenomenological reduction would require a [so-called] "phenomenology of the phenomenological reduction." (§71)

Here, the word "horizon" refers to a primitive notion in Husserl's theory of inquiry. From the Latin, *pimitivus*, something is said to be primitive in function or form when something else could be derived from it. A primitive notion is not a provable premise in its use, but is instead taken as a necessary presupposition in formal proofs and theory construction. For example, a horizon of curves and angles is a primitive notion for inquiry into shapes and spatial relationships. Similarly, a phenomenological horizon presents the full range of objects and acts within a delimited area of the matter of interest. Each horizon represents in reflections the subject's essential and intuitive (inductive) way of knowing something in general about a particular experience with a phenomenological *eidos*. In Husserl's methodology, an object of the mind must appear originally in reflections within its horizons of potential appearances if it is to be recognized as an identity in subsequent transcendental modifications. Kuhn (1940, 107-8) interprets the meaning of the term *horizon* in Husserl's work as the space of inductive inferences wherein particular instances are transcended toward self-knowledge of the general during a continuous whole thought: "Thus the notion of horizon…stands for the impetus of self-transcendence in which experience is animated." Psychological experience is animated in the transcendental register within the horizon of pure psychology—both in general and in any particular instance.

An "act psychology" in Husserl's mature genetic phenomenology incorporates action-oriented elements within horizons of *being* and *doing*. Clearly, this is not the descriptive psychology that is outlined in his 1925 lectures as "a species of naïve research." In propadeutic reductive reflections, transcendental phenomenologists picture specific mental processes in pure consciousness (such as knowing, remembering, or anticipating) that are intentionally directed toward both irreal and actually real objects—but only those objects that are presented or implied to exist by the meaningful human subject. Once such processes have been adequately described as necessary for the phenomenon as-a-whole to appear in reflections, they could then be set aside within an eidetic analysis of those objects as they come to presence with modifications in the subject's transcendental consciousness. (*see* Husserl 1997, 247)

It seems perhaps that rigorous phenomenologists implicitly practice the psychological reduction as an intuitive and practical method of reasoning within horizons of object-oriented content. Unfortunately, however, the years were not given to Husserl that would have allowed him to develop an explicit practice for employing the psychological reduction as a tool of eidetic reconstruction in applied phenomenology. And so, even the most brilliant students of Husserl's philosophy might have difficulty in seeing a difference in his mature reflections between the irreal objects of the mind in pure consciousness (the so-called *noemata*) and the intentional acts of the mind (the so-called *noeses*) that are intentionally brought to bear (*noetically*) on those objects in the transcendental register.

In Husserl's (1982, §87ff) theory of method, objects of the mind and the mind's intentional activity in pure consciousness are "correlated" such that the actual reality and manifest appearance of a phenomenon could gain presence as a unity in thought and speech. Yet recognizing the difference between correlated objects and acts does not speak to the reason for these differences as Husserl conceptualized them in 1913 for reductive reflections. For some, neither does recognizing a difference between objects of the mind versus the acts of the mind signal the necessity for a psychological reduction in genetic phenomenology—for indeed, as a modality of our irreducible pure Ego, the transcendental ego already represents in Husserl's (1973b, §36) mature theory of elements a "universe of possible forms of subjective processes" whereby objects are contingently present in transcendental consciousness. In Husserl's precise sense, mental processes are thematic *forms* of intentional action amid the various horizons of ego-life (such as thinking or feeling about something), not the cognitive action that realizes an object within these forms (such as judgments and valuations). Mixing the two in reductions is a conceptual error, and describing the mix of a form and its correlated psychological action as an object of the mind represents a psychologistic practice.

Husserl (1973b, §13) wants to make a distinction between objects in pure consciousness and our subjective acts directed toward realizing those objects in the transcendental register. This distinction, however, could be interpreted on the side of phenomenological philosophy as Husserl's way of distinguishing the subjective examination of psychologism in his descriptive the subject's transcendental logic—especially when he sets out to clarify the eidetic ontology of actually real things. (*see e.g.,* Tito 1990, 85f) Just as transcendental objects are not descriptive of transcending acts, neither are said acts descriptive of the logic that is used during such action. Yet Husserl never specified in his 1913 static descriptive phenomenology of *Ideas I* how to reduce a region of "psychological" facts to its underlying eidetic ontology. Neither did he prescribe the means for implementing the psychological reduction in the genetic transcendental phenomenology of *Ideas II* a decade later.

Welton (2000, 267f) seems to pose the crucial question: In order to avoid violating principles of his clarifications of essences, what is Husserl's intuitive practice and content of reflections that keep phenomenological psychology in the realm of a systematic analysis of transcendental consciousness? Husserl does not explain this connection for an eidetic analysis—except at the end of his career with his attempt to describe a "phenomenology of phenomenology" during investigations of our transcendental world-consciousness. When one's awareness of a categorial world of objects and acts is in place *noetically* (including our intersubjective world of human co-existence), the connection between phenomenological philosophy and psychology is to be seen in the transcendental register within the norms and practices of the phenomenological method proper.

During his studies of the phenomenological method proper, Husserl (1997, 213-14) indicated that practices of phenomenological philosophy and phenomenological psychology both apply the eidetic essence of *Psychognosia*—the pure method of phenomenological observation and description first introduced to Husserl by Franz Brentano and practiced intuitively by many scientists for decades before. Because of this connection in praxis, the overall content of psychological reflections in genetic phenomenology represents in Husserl's (Fink 1995, 164) theory of world-constitution the potential for a "reversal of the natural attitude" *by phenomenologists themselves*. The reversal of the content of reflections from contingent psychological experience within the natural world of object-oriented content, to its original conditions of *a priori* pure psychology (that necessarily pre-exist as psychosubjectivity in the transcendental register), is directed toward the "totality of psychic being" here and now. By engaging the psychological reduction in genetic phenomenology, Husserl (Fink 1995) observed in the 1930s, an "infinity of reflections" about psychological experience could be opened up:

> If in…historical fact happened, there took place for the very first time a systematic investigation of psychic life, namely, in the reversal of the natural attitude into the attitude attentive to the constitutive correlation [of psychosubjectivity in the transcendental register], that changes nothing…[of our accomplishments in its parallel object-oriented phenomenology]. Indeed what would have been needed in regard to psychology [for such an investigation] is the decisive will to set as research task the totality of psychic being in its full concreteness, including the infinity of reflections found there and [conducted] in the method of psychological-phenomenological reduction. (p. 164)

By calling for a transcendental phenomenological psychology of the totality of psychic being, including the psychic being of phenomenological reflections and reductions, Husserl (1981, 51) once more reminds phenomenologists that any application of his phenomenological orientation in human science "can take root only in radical reflexion upon the meaning and possibility of its own scheme." The path for phenomenological psychology that follows this metatheoretical stance is the one that is introduced in this book.

The Phenomenological-Psychological Attitude

When Husserl began his academic career at the end of the nineteenth century, philosophy of psychology in Europe was still in its early stages of carving out exactly what "the psychological" means, both in our simple grasp of ordinary experience and as a matter of scientific study. The various paths taken during these early years indeed led to the great diversity of concentration on psychic life that we find in the discipline today. This is as it should be, since psychic life touches upon every motivation and achievement of what we have since come to call the human condition. Yet one common thread for the discipline that has endured from its origins to its applications in today's multiplicity of theoretical and practical interests is that psychologists for the most part still *look for the psychological* in their theories of inquiry. Whether done reflectively or spontaneously, psychologists tend to adopt a so-called psychological attitude as an intuitive ground of pre-conceptual and pre-theoretical grasp of human psychic life.

In the psychological attitude, psychic life is the proper overall theme of focus for psychological studies. This is not so different from any other area of scientific inquiry, where each discipline adopts its own attitude for singling out specific matters of study and application. In the rich flux of diversity for all the sciences, each naïve discipline imagines itself as different according to its own pre-theoretical intuitive grasp of the formal and material properties of something that already *is*. In the early days of modern psychology, the pioneers that we have come to know as the founders of today's discipline were not what we would now usually call psychologists. Rather, they were mostly philosophers who adopted the psychological attitude in order to see the intuitive ground of human experience that lets us isolate distinctively psychological phenomena as matters of inquiry.

Husserl originally thought that adopting the psychological attitude meant that psychic life needed only to be described as "psychological" according to exacting practices of philosophical concept formation and theory construction—where the psychological in human affairs was treated as an object of philosophical reflection that pre-exists within an intuitive taxonomy of real things. (*see* Gurwitsch 1966, xxi) But when developing a praxis that would allow a theme of inquiry to be seen as purely psychological according to its own concepts, Husserl (1970, 294-8) came to realize in the late 1920s, and even more so during the 1930s, that simply describing psychological phenomena as their intuitive objects in a theorized praxis of psychological inquiry does not describe the prior psychic life of that same activity. There is a kind of twin phenomenon of *being* psychological, one might say, involved in the psychological attitude for *seeing* the psychological. Perhaps Husserl's realization of the existence of a parallel but interrelated object-oriented *being* and action-oriented *doing* in human affairs is the genesis of his transcendental phenomenological methodology in its continuing development, as well as the intuitive pre-theoretical ground of Husserl's overall phenomenological attitude.

The intuitive ground of Husserl's phenomenological attitude toward any phenomenon whatsoever generally lies in seeing what is self-evidently an intentional achievement of human imagination and intuition signified by one's expressions of self-knowledge. In methodological terms, the phenomenological attitude represents a phenomenologist's seeing (i.e., "picturing") an object in thought and speech that is obtained by means of the subject's composition of parts and wholes, along with the acts in cognitive mental life that are necessary for the object's gaining presence as a unity of configuration. In Husserl's applied phenomenology, each of us typically intends to make combinations of objects and acts in order to realize the presence of something in conscious awareness. Still, the psychological attitude presents a problem for phenomenological studies in ways that are different from, say, a biological or mathematical attitude for singling out its own proper matter of theoretical interest. The specific problem of psychology is of course that the intuitive ground for singling out the discipline's proper theoretical matter is itself the theoretical matter of psychological inquiry. Put another way, psychologists are themselves *being* psychological when looking for *the* psychological in human affairs—meaning, the problem of self-reference arises. (*see* Fink 1995, §3)

Yet from his phenomenological attitude directed toward the intentional products of human imagination and intuition, Husserl (2001, 11) proposes that there is indeed a psychological area of experience that could be seen in *every* scientific or philosophical achievement—along with its distinctive extra-psychic content that has no mental life of its own. Just as there is a necessary psychological component to realizing an intentional object as a concrete phenomenon, so too is there a psychological component to the abstract concepts and theoretical constructions in our formal theories of inquiry. This observation raises the question as to what could be understood about a seemingly universal psychic life involved in the production of an object of self-knowleldge. In Husserl's 1927 entry on "Phenomenology" for the *Encyclopaedia Britannica*, the intuitive ground for seeing the psychological in any phenomenon of human intellectual achievement is a universal pure psychology that exists in the background depths of thought for everyone. In this article, Husserl (1981, 22) describes the essence of the psychological for both empirical and phenomenological inquiry as the *eidos* of *pure psychology*.

Husserl suggests in his *Britannica* article that the *eidos* of pure psychology represents our pre-conceptual comprehension of the psychological when grasping the idea of psychic life in both its general and specific instances. This is a universal and intuitive pre-theoretical state of affairs that is conceptually opposed to seeing only the empirical manifestations of behavior within an anthropological (i.e., cultural and historical) account of human experience. In this sense, a psychologist's ordinary descriptions of psychological phenomena imply a pure psychology of intentional acts. For example, Churchland's (1990, 36) explanation that "nervous-systems are information-processing machines" implies the author's pre-theoretical grasp of the pure psychology of processing-acts—*in addition* to the non-psychic element of machine-like neurological organization. Husserl (1981, 114) emphasizes in his *Britannica* article that no matter what region of scientific inquiry one cares to look at, no matter what achievements of human imagination and intuition are seen to occur, it is a peculiar characteristic of intentional experience to act psychologically upon the objects that gain presence in awareness as complete and whole realities.

Near the mid-point of his career, Husserl made a so-called transcendental turn in his practices. In doing so, he expanded his range of interest from the universal intuitive ground of pre-theoretical experience for everyone to the production of normative combinations of objects and acts by each of us individually—such as a theorist's intentionally bringing to bear the idea of *process* upon neurological organization. This means that various pre-existing elements of an anticipated actual reality are transcended imaginitively and immediately by this production when an object of the mind comes to presence in conscious awareness as a unified transcendental object. Something said to be "normative" in this context implies an expression of judgments and valuations versus one's simply stating a fact. Husserl calls the issue of describing and explaining the normative production of transcendental objects, "the problem of constitution." From the psychological attitude, constitution *as such* is clearly an action-oriented irreality of pure psychology.

In Husserl's mature transcendental phenomenology, the constitution of transcendental objects is studied as a characteristic of our so-called "absolute consciousness"—that is to say, as our consciousness of the Absolute within the contingent world of human co-existence. Husserl (1982, §44) had earlier clarified the sense of something expressed as "Absolute," not simply as a concept of metaphysical significance, but also as an over-arching totality that includes what humans *can* determine about something by means of our inductive methods of reasoning. (*see also* Hocking 1940, 258) What is said to be absolute thus necessarily includes on a relative basis what humans *cannot* determine about something in the transcendental register. It is self-evident that not all things of conscious awareness could be determined and known as actually real within the bounds of that same contingent experience, any more than someone standing on a street corner could see the entire city.

A transcendental object is nevertheless determinable and familiar to each of us by means of the purely psychological method of grasping something that seems to be already at hand in the world that is commonly talked about: "The 'Absolute' in the phenomenological sense, then," Bruzina (1995, *lvi*) writes, "is…'the comprehensive unity of *the existent as such and the pre-existent…of world and world-origin*.'" Husserl stresses that humans intuitively understand when the boundary is crossed between the determinable and the indeterminable when thinking about something said to be absolutely good, beautiful, true, and so on; in the same worldly manner, perhaps, that each of

an expression of perennial or sacred wisdom. (*see* Boehm 1970, 185 6)

Inasmuch as a constituted objectivity is intuitively grounded in universal experiences with intentional objects, and is actualized by universal acts in pure psychology, a phenomenon (1) gains presence in thought and speech such that (2) it could be recognized by everyone who adopts a similar attitude toward (3) seeing something objective just as it is intended to be seen. These phases represent areas of the transcendental constitution of an object in conscious awareness. When the eiditic content of said phases are oriented in reason by a (say) a biological attitude, biologists see the actual reality of biological *being*, and when oriented by the psychological attitude, psychologists see the actual reality of psychic *being*. From the psychological attitude, we constitute transcendental objects within this same form of self-knowledge in regions of sense and meaning—and then call them "psychological phenomena." From our pre-theoretical intuitive grasp of pure psychology, key concepts provide the original idea or essence of a psychological phenomenon that is at hand for mutual expressions of understanding and extension. Theoretical constructs articulate such constituted phenomena as verifiable and valid objects of inquiry.

However, naïve representations of psychological phenomena are usually of the metaphysically "absolutized" essences of things—not of those essences as they are first presented in pure psychology to be acted upon, and not of the transcending acts that constitute such things as objective phenomena in contingent worldly experience. Some psychologists want to describe our lived experience of existential concepts and metaphysical constructions, but it is self-evident that we do not actively live the contents of philosophical abstractions as the intended products of constitutive experience. The meanings of such irreal content cannot be properly described as concretely real in one's ordinary experiences. Instead, they tend to be described within a so-called transpersonal context of *extra*-ordinary experience that sometimes confuses the transcendental with the metaphysical. Our psychological attitude allows us to see and to describe psychic life as a universal irreality of everyday experience, which is the "highest" mode of ordinary consciousness in Husserl's work. But it is the phenomenological attitude that allows us to see psychological phenomena as intentionally transcended objects of subjective experience.

Even so, one does not usually reflect on psychic life as a subjective experience or as *the* psychological in human affairs. Instead, we tend to focus on the essence of an intentional object rather than on the transcending acts of judgments and valuations that could be described as psychological in the research literature. A descriptive phenomenological psychologist therefore reflects on an already-transcended object of psychic life presented by a research or clinical subject, and then describes the pre-theoretical comprehension of that constituted thing as one's enduring psychological experience with a particular phenomenon. I would suggest that there is nothing in said descriptions of experience that is fundamentally different from straightforward descriptions given by non-psychologists—since *both* are intuitively grounded in our pre-theoretical comprehension of psychic life. Naïve practitioners on the other hand tend to focus on psychic action as a matter of inquiry, but without necessarily recognizing that such intentional acts follow the methods of pure psychology that are intuitively used by all of us.

Only in genetic reflections do we see the psychological as both a universal and contingent practice of consciousness-formation; for as we recall, there is in Husserl's work an eidetic component of psychic life in every region of worldly experience. From its revolutionary breakthrough in 1900, Husserl's studies adopted (at least intuitively) universal acts of judgments and valuations as the means of deep reflection on the pre-theoretical ground of experience referenced by scientists and philosophers. In this context, Farber (1963, 321) observed that "the processes of experience are the means of access to the correlates of experience." This observation perhaps suggests that the norms of practice for Husserl's phenomenological philosophy are found in his theory of method for experiences of pure psychology. Practices of transcendental phenomenological psychology thus reveal the intuitive means by which Husserl's reflections are able to clarify his theory of elements within the composition of an intentional object. This function of pure psychology as intuitive praxis during contingent worldly experience is even more pronounced in phenomenological methodology after Husserl's 1913 transcendental turn.

Husserl often expressed that phenomenological psychology leads him into contingent regions of transcendental phenomenological philosophy. Perhaps Husserl (1970, §56f) means *literally* that his norms for describing objects in transcendental consciousness intuitively follow a pure psychology of judgments and valuations. It is precisely this difference between the means and ends of human reasoning seen in his early studies that later allowed Husserl to use the intentional acts of pure psychology as norms of applied phenomenology. Consequently, Husserl set out in the 1920s to clarify the acts of pure psychology as correlated but parallel to (i.e., independent of) objects of pure consciousness. It was not until nearing the end of his active scholarship that Husserl addressed the status of phenomenological psychology following the transcendental turn: What are the norms of practice in the psychic life of transcendental consciousness, where humans live knowingly as "natural" in the world of human co-existence? For considerations of intuitive praxis, what is the transcendental phenomenological *psychological* attitude?

The subject's sense of the human world (*Umwelt*) is given throughout Husserl's last works as the epistemology of all possible objects that could be constituted in consciousness *of* that world here and now. This is the same determinable and knowable space of things into which an object is intentionally constituted to be actually real and concretely present amid the contingent structures of transcendental consciousness. The horizon of potentials for experience in this world is termed by Husserl (1970, §§35-6), the universal "life-world" (*Lebenswelt*); and within this horizon, the perspective on things where we direct the focus of our thoughts toward living knowingly in the life-world represents our natural attitude toward realizing the factual "nature" of life in general, and of *my life* in particular. An intuitive grasp of the universal life-world as a horizon of *being* and *doing* refers to our pre-eminent transcendental experiences in everyday life and theoretical reflections. Picturing this experience in the psychic life of another—given to reflections as a subjective experience of cognition as existing in the world that is our own—is called the essence of the transcendental phenomenological psychological attitude.

Pre-theoretical Groundwork

There has perhaps always been some dispute among scholars as to whether our natural attitude for the presupposition of an indisputable nature of things could be overcome. Are we able to approach a concrete phenomenon for human-scientific study without presuming that it exists for everyone just as it appears empirically—or at least how we agree that it ought to appear? Are we able to suspend initially all compelling reasons to believe that something exists as actually real beyond its presence in imagination, but without thereby slipping into a kind of deluding rationalism or mysticism? Even today, expressions of the essence and the *being* of our natural attitude represent together an area of controversy in phenomenological philosophy. Yet whether our ordinary presuppositions of actual reality can be completely overcome, there is nevertheless some agreement among phenomenologists that we could at least modify our naïve belief that the obvious appearance of something determines its singular meaning as a phenomenon. We could then begin to modify our natural attitude of law-like assumptions by adopting a more general transcendental attitude, where one focuses strict attention on necessary *patterns* (not appearances) of things that all of us seem to agree truly exist.

One could look for possible patterns of how thing have already come to be, just as they appear to be in their concretely real presence. In Husserl's terms, phenomenological reflections on the sense and meaning of things begin within the "living present" of both an object's immediate appearance and the possible pattern of its coming-into-being here and now. We might then imaginatively leap within reflections from the particular appearances of things to universal patterns of things in the complexity of ordinary experience. The ability to make this kind of association between the particular and the general is an important methodological tool and norm of practice in Husserl's (1982, §112) theory of inquiry. Indeed, this practice was first presented in his 1900-1901 *Logical Investigations* as a qualitative modification of a state of affairs for scientific study. (*see* Husserl 2001, 258) Husserl's so-called imaginative free variation of a particular theory, belief, or opinion, according to its normative pattern of intentionally composed sense and meaning, allows him to "neutralize" his own natural attitude toward causal relationships for whatever is presented by another as an object of self-knowledge.

From the strict perspective of Husserl's phenomenological attitude, one cannot spontaneously picture for theory construction any empirical manifestations of actually real objects. These are the kinds of objects that we presume to exist and come to expect from the natural attitude. From Husserl's rigorous transcendental phenomenological attitude, one cannot picture as pregiven even the existence of the world that comprises all natural reality. Husserl can originally see only an irreal pattern of eidetic composition that may or may not succeed in coming to presence as actually real in conscious awareness. Husserl must be given compelling epistemological and ontological evidence that the meaningful human subject achieves this success. Phenomenologists are able to modify their own natural attitude, and follow along with Husserl's clarifications of epistemological and ontological evidence, because irreal patterns of eidetic composition exist wherever we choose to look for them—including within our ordinary presuppositions of the nature of things.

For example, there is an irreal pattern to the constitution in consciousness of the concrete appearance and actual reality of a glass of water: There must first be the distinctive ideas of the existence of water and of a glass—i.e., their eidetic ontologies of *what-ness* and *is-ness*. Before we could speak of a glass having been filled with water, both must have been in proper juxtaposition for filling according to their original ideas. Water must be liquid and a glass must have an opening—i.e., their epistemologies of *sense*. In Husserl's methodology, the subject intends to "see" or picture *this* water in *this* glass according to their pre-existing universal essences within a fundamental ontology of "being-sense." The regional ontology of the idea of a glass of water is the being-sense of what we tend to call "a glass of water" in ordinary experience. Husserl does not mean that it is somehow wrong to think of a glass of water solely as the particular thing of material properties that we call a "glass of water." Each of us lives with particular things, both material and spiritual, and we are continuously surrounded by particular things in the world that is commonly talked about. Each of us knows our own world of actual reality by its particular things; and indeed, *my life* is a particular thing that is constituted in consciousness to be my own. But the sheer appearances of constituted things do not immediately reveal the rich patterns of thought that seem to support such appearances.

The term "constitution" sometimes signifies that an objectivity (i.e., whatever is seen and experienced as *not* subjective) typically gains presence as a fact of reality in its phenomenal appearance. At the same time, the term also signifies that the coming-into-presence of the appearance of something is just as experientially real. It is a fact of reality for example that I live in Pittsburgh, just as it is a fact that I know that I live in Pittsburgh. But first in constitutive experience, I am now thinking about where I live as a matter of factual reality. This same individual and temporal relationship holds for the psychological experience of constitution whether the object in conscious awareness happens to be (say) a table during apperceptions of something physical, an imaginative abstraction such as the geographical Pittsburgh, or the belief in one's own factual existence. The multiplicity of Husserl's use of the term "constitution" reflects the multiplicity of the ways that objectivities gains presence as actually real within an intentional structure of consciousness. Perhaps the closest that Husserl (1970, §49) comes to a simple explanation of phenomenological constitution is given to psychologists as "a structure of meaning formed by [our intentional acts] out of elementary intentionalities."

Husserl might be criticized for ignoring the aesthetic value of particular things, and for thereby focusing on the so-called technical reality of human consciousness. There is indeed a danger that thinking and communicating from the phenomenological attitude could become ponderous when trying to account for the various reduced strata of a structure of awareness. Husserl's (2001, 143) "technical realism" shows itself by his attempts to clarify constitu-

ness counts as real (*real*) just as much as what is 'outside' of it." Another

31

danger to avoid is in thinking that evaluations of just one mental process in pure psychology could exhaust explanations of constitutive life for a pre-existing idea; since as Husserl (1982, §114) warns, "…a mental process is from the outset a position [toward]…a plurality of potential positions [on an *eidos*]." Students of Husserl's phenomenology could keep in mind that he aims at overall clarifications of the *instrumental* production of conscious awareness—including, and perhaps foremost, our "technical" characteristics of choice and motivation during intentional experiences with the universal phenomenological method of consciousness-formation.

"Phenomenological method" is no mere jargon term in Husserl's theory of inquiry. Neither is its idea naïvely grasped as ordinary research technique. Rather, the term denotes a way of thinking in pure consciousness for structuring essential elements of sense and meaning with reason and evidence. This way of thinking is indeed the universal method of pure psychology that is experienced *prior* to any phenomenological methodology, and is thus its intuitive ground. (*see* Cairns 1940, 3) We all use this method of consciousness-formation, both intuitively and sometimes with deliberate praxis, in order to constitute awareness of phenomenal reality. When this experience is seen in our practices of scientific judgments and valuations, the "technology" of traditional reasoning is revealed to reflections (*see* Husserl 2001, §11) In its essence as *techné* ("practiced artfully"), the phenomenological method is what we *do* in order to be conscious of something by means of our eidetic intuitions and insight. (*see* Husserl 1982, §26; 1970, §57)

The phenomenological method proper is articulated in Husserl's methodology as a pre-theoretical "method of methods" for intentional activities of correlated *being* and *doing* during consciousness-formation. Clarifications of these activities tend to begin with reflections from the phenomenological attitude directed toward the (usually empirical) epistemology of something experienced by another. Here, the subject's expressed or implied knowledge, belief, or opinion represents the sense of an already-realized object in constitutive life. Husserl then reorients this epistemology toward the enduring essence of an intentional object in reduced levels of pure consciousness. He does this in order to clarify the constituted phenomenon's "peculiarly" single eidetic ontology of being-sense that pre-exists all transcendental modifications. Given this sequence, scholars should not be misled into thinking that Husserl's clarifications of issues pertaining to human consciousness are directly comparable to theories that are principally associated with those who do not take his perspective on applications of the phenomenological method proper.

It is a *mistake*—an egregious error in thinking—to suppose that the clarified concepts and practices of Husserl's theory of inquiry have a direct one-to-one epistemological relationship with such things that find their place solely in the natural world of sheer appearances of objective truth and actual reality. Much of the confusion arising from interpretations of Husserl's phenomenological philosophy, particularly as it relates to phenomenological psychology, is the direct result of not recognizing that Husserl is using his own eidetic intuition and insights into the universal and a-historical phenomenological methods of especially Franz Brentano, Immanuel Kant, René Descartes, and Wilhelm Dilthey. Husserl does not criticize these theorists so much as he clarifies their presented eidetic ontologies as exemplary patterns of universal consciousness-formation. In its essence as a metatheory of inquiry for all the human sciences, Husserl's phenomenological praxis provides a way to reflect rigorously upon the subject's intentionally bestowed sense and conferred meaning for both an *a priori* world of human co-existence and the contingent things that are seen to reside there.

By calling his psychological studies "phenomenological," Husserl incorporates two primitive concepts from his philosophy, *Phenomenon* and *Logos*. *Phenomenon* signifies the Greek verb, *phainein*, "to show itself," while *Logos* is treated as the goal-oriented conceptual frame for what shows itself as reality in thought and speech. Indeed, a constituted object gains presence in awareness because of the synthesis of *phainein* and *logos* in cognitive mental life. (*see* Husserl 173b, §17) The meaning of "phenomenological psychology" thus refers to inquiry into the *Logos* of the *Psyche*—the goal-oriented conceptual frame of the phenomenological method proper. (*see* Husserl 2006, §29) Here, the psyche acts upon objects and constructs reality by means of cognitions in both pure and transcendental consciousness. This is a pre-theoretical and non-empirical perspective that does not rule out psychological studies of such things as affective conduct, cognitive development, or social relationships, for these are all teleological goals of the psyche. From the Greek, *telos* (= completion or end), a teleological goal implies an intentional purpose to the psyche's activities in mental life. At the same time, neither does this perspective rule out the psychological study of brain chemistry, physiology, or anatomy as the immediate environment wherein the psyche's intentions are played out within the bounds and meaning of our physical bodies in pure subjectivity.

In Husserl's (1982, §57) work, "pure subjectivity" denotes the "ray of regard" for the phenomenological method proper in both phenomenological philosophy and its parallel psychology. Pure subjectivity is the intuitive *way* in which the synthesis of *phainein* and *logos* is directed toward its actualization in conscious awareness. According to this trajectory in universal mental processes, the phenomenological method is rigorously applied in Husserl's methodology as a norm of praxis for genetic reflections in the same spatiotemporal order as the subject's constitutive life is directed within a "stream of pure consciousness." Here, pure subjectivity includes as a goal of the psyche the actualization of our "solipsistic" subjectivity, where nothing but one's own real existence is presented to consciousness. But pure subjectivity also includes our transcendental subjectivity, where the real existence of others is presented to consciousness as well during intersubjective relationships. In all cases of ordinary experience, the concept of *pure subjectivity* represents the subject's simultaneous perspective on the irrealities of one's own existence and on things of actual reality in the world that is commonly talked about.

Our constituting activities typically entail a pre-conceptual norm of practice where we bring an object of the mind to presence in first solipsistic and then intersubjective structures of consciousness. By means of this cognitive practice, we constitute subjective sense and meaning from our own perspective on things in the living present. Effecting one's preferred and habitual

acts in cognitive mental life, in order for an objectivity to be in consciousness amid a construction of actual reality, is our universal phenomenological method of constitution. When we constitute the presence of an intentional object in awareness, each single mental process of pure subjectivity—such as an imminent process of willing, reasoning, or feeling in pure consciousness—consists of multiple psychological processes of contingent judging- and valuing-acts directed toward elements of that object. In both spontaneous judgments and theoretical reflections, humans intend to actualize the *logos* of the *psyche* in transcendental consciousness by psychological processes of cognitive acts and passive acceptance. The ray of regard in ordinary cognitive mental life is to construct the reality of one's thoughts within the life-world of all potential realities for living as "natural"—but knowing rationally all the while that this world is not solely of one's own making.

It perhaps takes a measure of courage in Husserl's work to appropriate the notion that conscious awareness exists contingently for each of us in order to provide an adequate dimension of reality and certainty in our lives. Husserl's philosophy challenges our presuppositions for belief in the actual realities constructed by humans as being infinite, accidental, or entirely unanticipated. With his clarifications of our constitution and self-knowledge of an intentional object, Husserl intends to cut out such presuppositions for grasping the presence of things in human consciousness. This intention is articulated in his methodology as the "phenomenological *epoché*," and practiced as a rigorous application of non-empirial thinking and pictorial reasoning. Under the *epoché*, actual reality (as opposed to the irreality of potential or possible reality) is seen by phenomenologists to be a constructed reality; and intentional objects in conscious awareness are composed in cognitive mental life to be just as they are intended to appear in the universal life-world of human imagination and achievements.

With Husserl's (1982, §§10ff) use of the *epoché*, an intentional object is not merely the actually real thing that gains presence in consciousness as something concrete in its appearance—since it is also that object *as it is intended* to be seen in thought and speech. Fantasies and illusions are thus also intentional objects in pre-conceptual experience. An intentional object is nevertheless *the* singular irreal object of thought that is indeed the object of the mind in both solipsistic experience and contingent structures of transcendental consciousness. In its essence, an intentional object remains constant throughout all phases and stages of reality construction during consciousness-formation. For a simple example, we might recognize someone on the street but fail to recollect her name: "Oh, I know her, she works over there and has a daughter named Mary. But what *is* her name?" The woman's name is the intentional object that becomes actually real when it is remembered or otherwise grasped. Said object is then expressed in fulfilled thought and speech within its construction of irreal sense and meaning: "Of course, her name is Martha." When it finally gains presence in awareness as factually real, the woman's name refers to one's attention to a constituted objectivity of nominative identity. Husserl (§37) describes the relationship between a pre-conceptual intentional object and a subsequently "seized upon" referential

34

object of attention as signifying a pre-existing structure of consciousness.

Husserl's phenomenological attitude and system of reductions call for a transcendental theory of consciousness—given as a cognitive synthesis of intentional objects and constitutive acts—rather than simply for a psycho-physical theory of perceptual awareness. The actual reality of an apple, for instance, is constructed in thoughts and experienced by each of us as more than a combination of color, texture, taste, and smell. Despite naïve theories of synesthetic multi-sensory experience to the contrary, we cannot in actual reality bite into an apple's color or bake its smell. Rather, during the normal course of events, sensory elements of the objectivity called "apple" are intentionally transcended as individual things during one's experiences of (say) eating or baking. It is self-evident that the idea of an apple does not endure in daily life as a collection of multi-sensory data in pre-conceptual experience. Neither does the idea become actually real according to our verbal reasoning about the word "apple." Instead, the idea endures into actual reality as the intended transcendental object that we find in its practical use. An apple is indeed experienced in awareness as more than its constituent elements due to the "soulish" action of pure psychology.

Husserl's Psychology with a Soul

Husserl's (1982, §85) notion of "psychology with a soul" is a pure psychology of the human spirit of autonomy and agency in the world of real life—put another way, it is the "*noetic stratum*" of "*phenomenological being*" when human intentionality is brought to bear upon an object of the mind. Husserl thus makes a distinction between the irreality of our spirit-life and our corporeal-life of bodily existence. From this perspective, a universal human spirit shows itself by such things as our anticipating something, or believing in something, or passively letting something be. The primitive notion of a human spirit is first seen within the horizon of ontology as the essential motivating element of *soul* (*Seele*) in constitutive life. The term "soul" signifies the being and sense of the idea of *mind* in the life-world of everyday things and their causal relationships, the world that is experienced as one's "naïve natural world" of all potential "natural" realities. One such reality is the presence of other humans as similar souls of affective intentionalities during intersubjective relationships. The minds of others, then, are typically believed to be similar to our own minds, where the subject's own mind is seen by Husserl (1973b, §44) to be one's "spiritual ownness" in pure psychology.

Perhaps in keeping with his "principle of all principles," Husserl's (1973b, §44) applied transcendental phenomenology also investigates the mental life of a person among other persons—meaning, the intersubjectivity experienced in one's personal lifeworld (*eine persönliche Lebenswelt*). This experience is seen in rigorous reflections as the pure Ego in the midst of its contingent worldly surroundings (*der Außenwelt*); where typically, the *logos* of the psyche is fulfilled with the objectification of one's spirit-life and corporeal-life

in a mutually objectified world, where we are individuals rather than merely members of an animal species, phenomenological psychology could be easily contrasted with a naïve psychology of objectified "personhood." A non-phenomenological orientation toward objectified experience indeed seems unable to uncover our intentional encounters with the communal spirit and irreal relationship of human-among-humans. Still, a universal human spirit of autonomy and agency motivates both active and passive constitutive life in one's personal lifeworld when we attempt to actualize our life-goals, both sacred and secular. Such goals are realized by means of our intentional judging- and valuing-acts in cognitive mental life, along with our passive acceptance of communal interactions. (*see* Husserl 1973b, §44, §58)

Practices of transcendental phenomenological psychology are meant to disclose the cognitive action that is motivated by the human spirit throughout all reduced phases of mental life—the action that continues, then, up to the highest level of lived experience during the construction of a unity of awareness in one's personal lifeworld. Theoretically grounded in Husserl's theory of method, transcendental phenomenological psychology is therefore an integral part of Husserl's mature but incomplete science of essences that focuses on life-world experiences, a part that is seen as inquiry into the cognitive mental life of persons amid the full range of pure subjectivity. In the context of our transcendental methods of constitution, Husserl (Fink 1995) explains that references to a "theory of method" entail the function of cognitions. One might say that "method" is *what we do* in order to fulfill the *logos* of the psyche in "soulish" cognitive mental life:

> The concept "theory of method" has a certain ambiguity the basis of which lies in a diverse, multifarious use of the concept "method." For example, one understands by method in a completely superficial sense the arrangements, practices, etc. of *research technique*…. Another time it means rather the <activity of cognition as actually exercised and as> *dispositional*. Or by method (way, approach) one understands <not that which one finds by directing one's look at> cognizing, but <at its> "what," viz., the *most general basic insights* into the thematic region [of *what* cognitions are intended to *do*]…. The *transcendental* concept of method of course designates primarily a "what" of cognition (<and> not an arrangement of <merely> cognitive practices!). (§4, with Husserl's marginal notations)

Husserl's references to the phenomenological method point toward a clarification of the *eidos* of *method* in constitutive life—which is, namely, the idea of the pure Ego enacting consciousness by means of cognitions. Husserl's theory of method delineates instances of psychological experience with this *eidos* as an intentional way of comportment; and thus, it is the theoretical ground and rationale for inquiry into the psychic life of the phenomenological method proper. By using the term "givenness" with regard to *method*, Husserl signifies the form or category in which the content of an active idea is encountered by the phenomenological method of reasoning. The givenness of something in pre-conceptual experience represents one's grasping or "noticing" the object in pure subjectivity that one intends to constitute in awareness. This state of affairs implies that the contingent givenness conditions of transcendental consciousness are intentional on the part of the pure Ego. The givenness of something by means of cognitions is therefore a necessary part of the phenomenological method of consciousness-formation when anticipating its fulfillment in the transcendental register. By inference of such conditions of pre-conceptual experience, the "what" of cognitions is given to genetic reflections under the psychological *epoché* and reduction as the transcending action of the psychological ego in one's personal lifeworld.

The psychological *epoché* is a variation of the phenomenological method of *epoché* for pictorial reasoning and non-empirical thinking, where all else but psychic life is bracketed in reflections. Husserl (1982, §136) explains that the psychological *epoché* discloses the potential for our universal methods and motivation to constitute a rational affective unity as the content of conscious awareness—although the meaningful human subject might indeed fail in this intention. Under the psychological *epoché*, the psychological reduction represents the pure Ego's so-called mind's eye method of "seeing" and acting upon the essences and their relationships that make up the deep structure of transcendental consciousness. This structure already exists in pure consciousness as correlated elements necessary for the presence of a unity of configuration in the transcendental register. Such essences, however, are clarified in Husserl's theory of elements, not in his theory of method where we find the acts and practices of pure psychology. (*see* Fink 1995, §2 *et passim*) Elements are things of simple perception and higher-level apperception that have been retained (or not) during the constitution of an intentional object. Under the psychological *epoché*, "elements" are objects of the mind.

The psychological reduction also reveals the psychological ego as the "performing ego" of immediate psychological experience in genetic reflections. Here, the psychological ego represents the pure Ego's psychosubjectivity in the transcendental register—that is to say, the subject's transcended spirit-life of pure psychology in the world that is commonly talked about. Husserl (1973a, §11) points out that the psychological ego typically engages in acts of "retrogression" on pre-existing elements during constitutive life. Because of the psychological ego's acting upon the *pregivenness* of elements, the essence of an intentional object endures as a presumptive unity throughout its transcendental modifications. One such action of the psychological ego is to "see" (as an *act* of ideation) the retained elements of an *eidos*, which are then given to constitutive life by the transcendental ego's "picturing" (as an intentional *form* of ideation) the anticipated composition of those elements. The transcendental ego generally represents that region of pre-conceptual experience where we notice the sense and meaning of irreal objects from the natural attitude, even as we anticipate that those objects will gain presence in transcendental consciousness as fully composed unities in thought and speech. The psychological ego is affectively motivated to fulfill this prior anticipation.

In response to this "soulish" motivation in spirit-life, the psychological ego constitutes the *ennui* of an intentional object as it appears in the transcendental ego's form of ideation so that *this* object is constituted and not another. The psychological ego's composing-acts amid the complex ego-life of transcendental subjectivity present to reflections the givenness of the pure Ego's intentionality in the transcendental register. Seen under the psychological *epoché* as habitual comportment during the normal course of events, a pre-conceptual object is composed of its elements of ideation by the psychological ego in order for it to be what it *is* in transcendental consciousness. When composing elements of an intentional object, cognitive acts of mostly judging and valuing are carried out in psychological processes according to norms of practice for constituting conscious awareness of something actually real—and because of these pre-existing conditions, every concrete thing in conceptual space is a transcendental object. The appearance of the world of concrete phenomena implies the pre-existence of intentional objects in pure consciousness upon which the psychological ego has already acted, and continues to act in such a world. The psychological reduction discloses both the successes and failures of cognitions with regard to an intentional object and its enduring *eidos* in the world that is commonly talked about.

Since transcending acts are only indicated in Husserl's work by the presence of our transcendental objects of life-world experience, a regressive inquiry into the origins of such achievements is called for. Regressive inquiry provides epistemological and ontological evidence of the genesis of a transcendental object during pre-conceptual activities; and in doing so, implies the pre-existence of pure psychology in the subject's transcendental constitutive life. Husserl (1973a, §11) describes our transcendence of the irreality of pure psychology as "the subjectivity whose operations of sense have made the world which is pregiven to us what it is, namely, *our* world."

The subject's self-knowledge of *our* world does not happen unless it begins with a grasp of the universal life-world in its imminant pregivenness (*Vorgegebenheit*) to consciousness-formation. Here, the pure Ego's transcendental sense of the external world is experienced as a correlate of one's enduring personal lifeworld—which is the substrate of the life-world that indexes elements of other ego-subjects that pre-exist in the world that is at hand for *me* and *mine*. With this pre-givenness of *sense*, the phenomenon of *my life* is present as the subject's transcended pure subjectivity amid the intersubjective world. (*see* Husserl 1973a, §11) Transcendental objects are typically positioned by the psychological ego in order to be experienced in this same constructed and constituted world of purely subjective origins.

The norm of practice in Husserl's work for observing and explaining transcended pure subjectivity finds its intuitive ground (*Boden* = literally "the earth," the genesis from which life is supported and springs forth) in his theories of ego-life. Instances of the pure Ego's transcendence of pure subjectivity are at least implicitly mentioned or implied as necessary throughout phenomenological philosophy from nearly its inception. Yet the transcending acts of the psychological ego are finally revealed for interpretations only in Husserl's (Fink 1995, 180) mature "phenomenology of phenomenology" as part of his transcendental theory of method for genetic inquiry. Here, focus of genetic reflections under the psychological *epoché* is on the cognitive mental life of the pure Ego's world-consciousness—but only as the will of the psyche is played out by the psychological ego in co-existence with other ego-subjects in the world that is commonly talked about. The affectively motivated cognitive action of the psychological ego is indeed the essential and decisive connection between Husserl's (1970, §58) transcendental theory of consciousness and the discipline of psychology. Consequently, the alliance between psychology and transcendental philosophy demands totally new practices for both disciplines. (*see* Husserl 1973b, §20)

Husserl once again seems to call for a phenomenological psychology of transcendental constitution, only now he is more explicit as to its origin; which is, namely, a pure psychology that is internal to constitutive life, both individually and in groups. The pure psychology of human consciousness is irreal and immanent, rather than solely contingent within a regional ontology of empirical manifestations. By implication, transcendental phenomenological psychology is intended to observe our free variation of pure psychology throughout pure and transcendental subjectivity—and more generally, to observe the will of the psyche that shows itself as intentional cognitive action during consciousness-formation. In sharpest contrast with Husserl's (1982, §85) references to a psychology of constituted phenomena as objective matters of fact (i.e., a "psychology without soul"), transcendental phenomenological psychology is concerned with the structuring of subjective experience that is both *a priori* and contingent. In all of its imaginative forms used to see the sprit-life of human autonomy and agency, transcendental phenomenological psychology is psychology *with* a soul.

The Phenomenological Field of Actionality

In the pure psychology of transcendental subjectivity, the psychological ego is the bifurcated ego-subject "I" of *I-act* during the constitution of a rational affective unity. (*see* Fink 1995, 187) Here, in the living present of consciousness-formation, sensory data, memories, and irrealities of every sort are transcended as individual elements by the psychological ego within a so called field of actionality. The phenomenological field of intentional action delimits human spirit-life throughout every region and horizon of pure consciousness, including regional ontologies of being-sense in the conceptual space of theoretical discourse. Husserl's complete transcendental theory of consciousness relies implicitly on interpretations of the acts of the psychological ego for clarifications of not only the sense and meaning of what is constituted both individually and collectively, but also for what was originally intended and anticipated in pure subjectivity to be a fully composed unity in thought and speech. Yet despite their intuitive presence in transcendental subjectivity, transcending acts of the psychological ego are only seen under the psychological *epoché* and reduction by means of a reconstructive genetic phenomenology.

In genetic phenomenology, the totality of all possible human comportment makes up a field of actionality in pure consciousness, including as a potential every intentional action and non-action directed toward (or away from) some object of the mind. The psychological ego indeed conducts its transcending acts as a free-will agent of contingent experience within this field of pure subjectivity. With the psychological reduction in genetic phenomenology, intentional acts of the psychological ego are seen to permeate one's awareness as a flowing stream of unity (*Abschattende*) throughout the horizons of epistemology, ontology, and metaphysics—from pre-conceptual to conceptual space—outward toward the immediate level of constructed reality that is experienced in one's personal lifeworld. A phenomenological field of action represents the spatiality of intentional experience where the psychological ego *lives* in cognitive mental life according to Husserl's theory of method.

Although the intentional acts and essential functions of the psychological ego are intuitively grounded in the methods of pure psychology, the delimiting modes of active and passive actionality for the subject's methods of transcendental world-constitution have not been fully evaluated and clarified in Husserl's system of ego-life. Still, during the constitution in consciousness of the world of humanity in all its richest forms of expression, we know that Husserl (Fink 1995, 181-7) meant to articulate our transcendental methods of constitution within the structures of pure consciousness as *themselves* providing a limiting horizon of actionality. Pure consciousness is indeed the universal human consciousness that pre-exists *per se* as a thing-in-it-self (*Ding an sich*) in constitutive life. Pure consciousness is therefore the intuitive ground (*Boden*) of transcendental consciousness in both Husserl's theory of elements for compositions of a unity of awareness, and in his correlated theory of method where we find the constituting-acts of the psychological ego.

In Husserl's post-1920s transcendental phenomenology, pure consciousness is the most radical, fundamental, and original "inner life" of conscious awareness. The concept of *pure consciousness* under the psychological *epoché* represents the pure Ego's experience of insight into an anticipated reality that is implicit during the psychological ego's every action and non-action. With each transcending act of the psychological ego, as a norm of practice during the normal course of events, I assert to myself—and could usually assert to others—that something in fact truly exists. The certainty of our intuitive grasp of truth and existence within the eidetic structures of pure consciousness genetically pre-exists all possible validation of an object of knowledge that is intended to come into being for (subjectively) *me myself* and (intersubjectively) "for everyone." Husserl (Fink 1995, §3) suggests that universal methods of transcendental constitution are peculiar to our human agency in spirit-life for composing a rational whole thought in one's naïve natural world. Because of its intentional function to constitute consciousness of a world of humans among humans with acts of transcendence, the psychological ego indeed separates the human species from beasts of the field.

During our day-to-day experiences in the transcendental register—where memories, expectations, and certainty already exist in the life-world of all possible realities for living as "natural"—the psychological ego constitutes an intentional object to be a rational affective parts/whole unity in conscious awareness. Within this phenomenological field of action, anything in imagination that could be posited or asserted as *being* in pure consciousness has its own potential for presence as actually real in transcendental consciousness. Throughout its necessary phases of parts/whole grouping in this field, the

40

flowing movement of a potential rational affective unity is seen under the psychological *epoché* and reduction to be a genetic sequence of transcending acts by the psychological ego. During this flow of intentional action in cognitive mental life, a constructed unity of elements becomes an actually real object in thought and speech, where the presence of something is originally posited in pure subjectivity. Then genetically, we each modify the now pre-existing and pregiven intentional object with the belief and anticipation that others could recognize it *as* an actual reality. Although it is cognitively modified in order to represent an objective matter within a community of others, one's transcendental consciousness-of-something is typically fashioned in order to exist simultaneously as *my own* within a personal lifeworld of immediate experience.

Transcendental Idealism and Phenomenological Psychology

Husserl's notion of cognitive mental life amid a phenomenological field of intentional action is theoretically grounded in his philosophy of transcendental idealism. (*see* Husserl 1970, §26) Since Kant's 1787 *Critique of Pure Reason*, transcendental idealism has been a tenet of the Continental School of philosophy—where in general, the causal and spatial relationships of natural things exist in thought and speech by means of one's own mental processes. As a characteristic tradition of the Continental School, Kant's work represents both a philosophical thesis and a universal way of thinking. (*see* Heidegger 1997, 1-5) In Husserl's (1970, §28) version of transcendental idealism, "all of us (even I who am now philosophizing) consciously have our existence" such that the "semblance" (*Schein* = likeness or resemblance) of irreal matters— seen as the sense and meaning of intentional objects, and constituted in co-existence with other ego-subjects—is the consequence of one's own mental processes directed toward actualizing the givenness of pre-conceptual experience with an enduring *eidos*. Irreal and actually real things are thus experienced as similar but not the same in Husserl's transcendental idealism. Rather, the idealized semblance of irreality is intentionally constituted in awareness and experienced as actually real in the world that is commonly talked about.

Broad conceptual differences between Descartes's (naïve), Kant's (regressive), Hegel's (historical), Husserl's (genetic), and Heidegger's (existential) transcendental idealism are issues in the Continental School that will not be addressed here. One might notice, however that Fink's (1995, §12) section on "'Phenomenology' as transcendental idealism" represents Husserl's position when given from the phenomenological attitude. Otherwise, those who attempt to advance Husserl's philosophy could perhaps fail to distinguish our worldly objects of thought (posited by the ego of transcendental subjectivity) from our correlated but parallel intentional acts for constructing the semblance of reality for those same objects (enacted by the ego of psychological subjectivity). The concept of *transcendental consciousness* makes no sense in transcendental idealism without the human spirit in pure psychology that motivates our intentional acts in mental life to constitute the semblance of an ideal reali-

plishments can be understood only in terms of the activity that accomplishes

41

them." His phenomenological philosophy of transcendental idealism, Husserl continues, is one such accomplishment of the human sprit.

In Husserl's transcendental idealism and its system of ego-life, the essence of the transcendental ego is referenced by the subject's transcendence of solipsistic subjectivity into the natural world of immediate intersubjective experience. (*see* Fink 1995, 164-5) On the other hand, the psychological ego refers to manifestations of the *a priori* essence of pure psychology transcended within a regional ontology of psychological phenomena. (*see* Husserl 1982, §54) Here, the psychological ego represents all potential manifestations of the immediate spirit-life of psychic being in transcendental consciousness. When practicing psychology from the natural attitude, intentional acts of the psychological ego are what we naïvely posit as the observable manifestations of the *semblance* of ideal mental life when humans are being "psychological." In genetic reconstructions of a constituted phenomenon, including one's consciousness of overt behavior in empirical accounts, the psychological ego *lives* under the psychological reduction in its first-person experience of acting upon elements of an anticipated actually real object that is intended to have a similar appearance to everyone. In this sense, the psychological ego is seen in reflections as the *way* we experience mental life in the world that is commonly talked about; and in this sense as well, the psychological ego is the properly reduced subjective experience of psychic being in the transcendental register.

Husserl (1973b, §11) suggests that the psychological ego enacts the transcendental ego's naïve form of ideation for transcendental consciousness of one's "self" in a world of common semblance. This is the same world of intersubjective experience lived by each of us in the normal course of events, consisting of similar idealized forms of reality, causality, and relationships of essences. One's ordinary intersubjective experiences *invariantly* include the pure Ego's pre-conceptual experiences of human co-existence. Lived as both irreal and actual in the transcendental register, these experiences in their totality are represented by the existential concept of *being-in-the-world*. (*see* Husserl 1983, §1) From the perspective of the psychological attitude, being-in-the-world is accomplished by means of cognitions. The psychological ego is therefore the performing ego of immediate psychic being-in-the-world—meaning, the psychosubjectivity and active agency in one's personal lifeworld. (*see* Fink 1995, 164) In this way of *being* and *doing*, the psychological ego endures throughout constitutive life as the unity of intentional acts that constitute the subject's self-knowledge and self-objectification of *my life*.

However, seeing the intentional acts of the psychological ego is not sufficient for a complete explanation of the phenomenon of human consciousness; and certainly, phenomenological psychology cannot account for what remains of the human condition outside the determinable boundaries of pure consciousness, for this is the domain of studies devoted to metaphysics or to theology. Witchcraft, magic, and pseudo-science also address issues of the indeterminable in human affairs. The domain of inquiry for transcendental phenomenological psychology is restricted by Husserl's theory of method and is found primarily in his genetic reconstructive phenomenology of transcendental world-consciousness. Transcendental phenomenological psychology cannot evaluate by itself any object during its constitution in conscious awareness for one simple reason—namely, the objects of transcendental constitution enjoy no immediate mental life of their own. It is therefore an error to suppose that just any phenomenological concept or theory pertaining to human consciousness is "psychological" in Husserl's transcendental idealism.

In addition to representations of ego-life, Husserl's philosophical concepts in the transcendental register mostly refer to partial and whole objects of the mind among the *a priori* and contingent horizons, along with their empirical and metaphysical manifestations from the perspective of our natural attitude. Husserl's purely psychological concepts, on the other hand, refer to intentional cognitive acts upon those objects *within* his system of ego-life. Phenomenological psychology thus stands alone in comparison with any other theoretical psychology, such as psychoanalysis, analytical psychology, transpersonal psychology, existential psychology, and mainstream cognitive science. Yet despite its unique character, the path of development for phenomenological psychology diverged during portions of Husserl's active scholarship, and most especially in the years following his death in 1938.

Other Theoretical Approaches

Kockelmans (1973) provides a useful exposition of divergences within the phenomenological movement in psychology. Written over three decades ago but pertinent still, his analysis is theoretically grounded in the meaning of psychology as presented in Husserl's 1925 lectures on the essence of the discipline amid a regional ontology of traditional practices. I have done no less than to single out these lectures as the beginning of real advancements for phenomenological psychology, and I understand easily how Kockelmans would choose to expand upon the two primary paths that diverge from Husserl's original praxis—namely, hermeneutic and dialectic techniques in the existential register. Furthermore, I am entirely sympathetic with Kockelmans's choosing to follow the hermeneutic technique for his own interpretations of psychological phenomena. I did the same myself for many years. However, I have since come to believe that phenomenological psychology has a new alternative for realizing Husserl's (2006, §29) original intentions; and that is, his implicit directions for an eidetic transcendental phenomenological psychology. The existential register is but a "stage of the way" for this alternative.

Discussion here of the approaches identified by Kockelmans will be mostly in terms of Husserl's struggle to maintain a rigorous tradition of scientific practices. Because of this tradition, Husserl's transcendental phenomenological philosophy has demonstrated throughout the years its effectiveness for appropriation, advancement, and extensions in applications to the seemingly infinite range of issues pertaining to the idea of human existence. In Husserl's (Fink 1995, 169) mature fundamental ontology, the essence of human existence (*menschliches Dasein*) is represented by the transcendental "'humanization' [of] nature and of man himself." The existential world of humanity that coexists in pure consciousness with the spirit of communalization, and that is pregiven for each of us in ordinary psychological experience and cognitive development as the world of common semblance, is embraced by Husserl's (1970, §59) concept of the "life-world (the 'world for us all') [that] is identical with the world that can be commonly talked about."

The world we commonly talk about is typically one's own transcendentally constructed and constituted personal lifeworld. Said world is pregiven in the living present of consciousness-formation when we grasp our most fundamental existential relationships within the horizon of ontology here and now. In this way, the semblance of one's personal lifeworld exists categorially with similarities and differences to others in the universal life-world that is at hand for all of us. During any single moment under the *epoché*, our personal lifeworld is represented in part by one's immediate experience of psychic being. It is self-evident in daily life that humans could notice similarities and differences between the world at large and the psychological events of the phenomenon of *my life*. Each of us could intuitively and spontaneously grasp a condition of similarity-and-difference in familiar things of all sorts—for indeed, we have already preconstituted an object of similarity-and-difference in the world of common semblance so as to recognize the existential *Other* in relation to *me myself* and *mine*. One's personal lifeworld represents a transcended *sense* of human existence; it is our intersubjective "being-in-the-world."

In the fundamental ontology of one's personal lifeworld, my life is *mine* while their life is *theirs*. (Husserl 1973b, 30) This, too, is intuitively self-evident. Yet it could be intuitively self-evident as well that each expressed "life" during our intersubjective relationships of my-life-with-their-life represents one's apprehension of a universal similarity of bodies and souls. Our certainty of particular differences in the midst of a universal similarity in all human life is the *eidos* for the experience of one's personal lifeworld and perhaps the genesis of our ethical comportment: "The surrounding life-worlds [of other persons] are relative to the various cultures but have a *universal structure*." (Bernet, Kern, and Marbach 1993, 228) The universal structure of human consciousness includes those absolute things of existential significance that are indeterminable by our acts in one's personal lifeworld, but that nevertheless intentionally enter into our judgments and valuations within the horizon of metaphysics as what goes without saying in the "world for us all."

In Husserl's (1970, 303) transcendental theory of method, when intuitive self-evidence of reality is presupposed as the existence of something, then that *something* is grasped as "genuinely true" in subsequent valuations and judgments. For example, since my hand is actually real, as I do believe, then it's true that it will still exist even when it is in a glove and out sight; and when I think about it, it's likely that your hand is just as real as mine. Husserl calls the gathering of truth from intuitive self-evidence the normative practice of a "Galilean worldview." This orientation is indeed directed toward believing something typical about the existence of things in transcendental consciousness. With our intentional acts of grasping what seems to be objectively real in one's surroundings, as well as with our naïve practices in philosophy and science for positing matters of fact, we intend to achieve along with Galileo the genuine truth of an intentional object according to our metaphysical presuppositions of a pre-existing world that is familiar to everyone and typical for all:

Precisely in this way we see that, universally, things and their occurrences do not arbitrarily appear and run their course but are *bound* a priori by this style, by the invariant form of the intuitable world. In other words, through a *universal causal regulation, all that is together in the world* has a universal immediate or mediate way of *belonging together*; through this the world is not merely a totality [*Allheit*], but an all-encompassing unity [*Alleiheit*], a *whole* [that is dependent upon the *a priori* causality of worldview maintenance]....

This universal causal style of the intuitively given surrounding world makes possible hypotheses, inductions, predictions about the unknowns of its present, its past, and its future. In the life of pre-scientific knowing [i.e., when grasping the sense of something day-to-day] we remain, however, in the sphere of the approximate, [and] the typical [since the approximate and the typical pre-exist in the causal regulation of an intuitive worldview and participate in its ongoing maintenance]. (§9.b)

As part of Husserl's (Fink 1995, §11, marginal note 374) theory of transcendental world-constitution—wherein a personal lifeworld is seen to gain presence in the background of conscious awareness—the essence of our worldview toward the human condition is the "totality of humans living with one another in open, finite mediation, existing [*daseiender*] for one another, having experiences, thinking, acting with one another. As living in the world that is existent for them, they are aware of the existent world and also of themselves as living in it and as existent in the world with a body and a soul."

Besides Husserl, the most influential phenomenological philosophers of the twentieth century who dwell upon the question of what it means to be human-in-the-world, individually and collectively, are Martin Heidegger, Jean-Paul Sartre, and Maurice Merleau-Ponty. Each takes a divergent path from Husserl's eidetic praxis and fundamental ontology in order to establish an alternative conceptual ground for phenomenological inquiry. Heidegger (1927) reduced Husserl's basic subject-matter from the knowing subject to the non-reducible human existent. In doing so, he moved the theoretical ground of phenomenological evidence for the content of human consciousness from an intuitive eidetic epistemology of *sense* to a historical ontology of *Being*—both authentic (i.e., concerned with one's subjective potential) and inauthentic (i.e., concerned with the presence of others).

Heidegger's turn in focus from the eidetic to the existential established long-standing principles of hermeneutic interpretations of both the universal essences and contingent experiences of psychic life. Kisiel (1996) provides the following description of this technique of phenomenological interpretation in the existential register, where Heidegger seems to rely on Wilhelm Dilthey's concept of a human capacity to imagine one's existence as a historical matter within a continuous world of intellectual achievements—meaning, within an existential anthropology. With this perspective on time and place, Heidegger does not recognize our intuitive ideation of the life-world as the immanent locus of *being* and *doing* in the transcendental register:

Heidegger will point to a nonintuitive form of access that hermeneutics calls understanding, a certain familiarity that life already has of itself and that phenomenology needs only to repeat. This spontaneous experience of experience, this doubling of experience, this streaming return of experiencing life upon already experienced life is the immanent historicity of life [itself]....Thus, the response to the question of accessibility [to eidetic intuitions] is at once an answer to the objection against the expressibility of immediate experience: *Verstehen* [i.e., the phenomenon of understanding matters of existence]. (p. 46)

Bruzina (1995, *x-xi*) records that Georg Misch analyzed the rift between Husserl and Heidegger in 1929, and reported that Heidegger was then the leading representative of phenomenological philosophy in the public eye. Furthermore, with his focus on a historical understanding of human existence in the world (*Dasein*), Heidegger was seen to be more closely aligned with Dilthey's popular philosophical anthropology. Husserl (Welton 2000, 228) wrote back to Misch saying, "the 'a-historical' Husserl had to take distance from history only for a short time." Husserl believed that philosophy and history are concerned with two different objects of theoretical focus—for each, respectively, the ideas and the constructed facts of human existence. The two are closely related in the manner that they show themselves as contents of conscious awareness, but there is nevertheless a qualitative difference between their methods of constitution. (*see* Natanson 1973, 52) It was Husserl's view that an epistemologically validated a-historical means of interpretation of these methods must be developed before inquiry into either historical or ontological matters begins. Husserl's mature approach toward phenomenological psychology hinges on this view that favors an epistemology of intentional action in his theory of method.

It is certainly the case that facts of human existence are composed in a calculus for judging and valuing the true meaning of things, and it is also the case that a history of such truth-seeking could be constructed. Each historical fact could be evaluated and affirmed or rejected in light of immediate insight and understanding; yet at the time that a matter was calculated to be true in the past, it too was being either affirmed or rejected in light of contemporary conditions. In the spirit-life of human existence, the idea of seeking truth is lived out within a calculus for the construction of facts here and now. Even when we take a mediating historical perspective on this experience, the idea of seeking truth lives on as a universal psychological experience—only now, Husserl (1970, §15) points out, our truth-seeking is sedimented intersubjectively over the historical time of inter-generationally constructed facts about objectified human achievements. In this manner of understanding what it means to be "in the world," what endures historically is the "reawakened" will of individuals to seek the truth whenever its necessity arises—and *not* some factual matter taken naïvely as a "surviving goal" of objectifying historical processes or metaphysical presuppositions about human existence.

Still, Husserl (Fink 1995, §2) decided after Misch's report that a systematic phenomenological theory of human consciousness requires a so-called generative logico-historical approach for interpretations of the intellectual achievements enjoyed by persons and groups. This approach was to provide a constructive "transcendental dialectic" of the "beginning and end" of both individual and inter-generational world-constitution. Farber (1968, 570) explains that there were two choices for Husserl in this approach: either adopt the naïve practice of looking back at a history of facts about the human world, "or to undertake the phenomenological 'genetic' method, which is devoted to 'intentional' analysis." In genetic phenomenology, metaphysical presuppositions of the existence and spirit of humanity in historical accounts are generated by individual achievements of similar essential meanings. Such action occurs during the sedimented lived experience of an enduring inter-generational goal. A so-called generative phenomenology of this goal not only means to explain the step-wise development of an idea from its genesis to its most mature level of lived experience, but it also means that this genetic sequence is intentional at every developmental and historical stage or phase in which it appears.

Husserl (Steinbock 1996, 257ff) wanted generative phenomenology to lead his science of essences beyond simple descriptions of historical origins and genealogical sequences. Generative phenomenology was intended to go even beyond the metaphysics of a universal life-world for grasping the sense and meaning of the living present. However, Husserl's praxis for generative phenomenology does not appear in either a published work or a single manuscript. Husserl (1982, §78, §122, §125) simply describes phenomenological "generation" (*Erzeugung*) as the "production" (*Produktion*) of subjective processes of spontaneous thought within the mediating presence of others. Leading clues for methods of generative phenomenology are nevertheless found wherever Husserl's reflections lead to questions of the inter-generational givenness of an intentional object. As examples in the philosophical literature of what Husserl meant by speaking of the generation of an idea over historical time, an implicit generative phenomenological method perhaps shows in the works of van den Berg (1975), Foucault (1977), and Deleuze (1994).

These authors introduce a radical historicity to subjective meanings of objective cultural content for prevailing inter-generational goals. The co-occurring individual and communal achievements directed toward this goal represent the flow of an intentional object in the living present of spontaneous thought from one generation to the next. A historical psychology is expressed by these theorists in ways that Husserl never completed in his phenomenology of world-consciousness—for as we recall, he was still calling for a psychology that would reflect the transcendental turn in the phenomenological method proper. Instead, Husserl's (1964a, §33) notion of simultaneous spatial and temporal essences finds a place in his (Fink 1995, §9) mature work as the synthesis of the transcendental ego's transcended objects and the psychological ego's transcending acts. One's apprehension of this synthesis indeed represents an experience of psychological consciousness. Psychological consciousness is the mental sphere of pure consciousness, where we grasp elements of irreality and actuality as an affective unity. (*see* Husserl 1982, §76)

Yet despite its incomplete status, an important area of Husserl's phenomenology of world-constitution was to develop, as a so-called transcendental dialectic, a genetic system of explanations for the beginning and end of constitutive life itself. As a student of both Husserl and Heidegger, Czech philosopher Jan Patočka (1996) poses the crucial question of meaning for the term "dialectics" as it pertains to the *being* of consciousness experienced by us individually, collectively, and historically:

> Dialectics is the theory of objective conflicts, tensions, contradictions. The "being" of a thing is contradictory [when objectified in historical accounts of collective activity]. Consequently, so is consciousness…. The important point now is that being human cannot be reduced to consciousness and its structures [during historical reproductions of life]. We need to transcend consciousness [as an objectified thing] in order to reach being. But what is being?… If we show that it is necessary to transcend individual consciousness [in order to avoid contradictions in historical accounts], does that already show us just what is that primordial being which consciousness reflects? [That is to say, does it not show that individual consciousness of objective things in the historical reproduction of life transcends subjective relations of conflicts, tensions, and contradictions?] (p. 145)

In terms of a dialectical technique for phenomenological interpretations of the interaction between (subjective) individual and (objectified) collective manifestations of human consciousness, Jean-Paul Sartre (1994) chose a middle path between Husserl's eidetics and Heidegger's historicism. Sartre stresses that our human capacity to transcend pregiven historical presuppositions and objectifications implies a fundamental freedom to choose one's own situatedness *as* an existent within a pre-existing world of others. Most generally, our working-out the dialectics of that freedom at the existential level of pure consciousness represents one's mental life of *choice* between authenticity and inauthenticity in social relationships. Here, authenticity refers to a finite human existence whose possibilities are made worldly by the inescapable "facticity" of being born into one's social and cultural surroundings. Inauthentic existence is experienced when we take refuge in "the realm of convention where one unquestioningly accepts as absolutes the prevailing values of the group in which one finds oneself." (Barnes 1969, 18)

Within this broad philosophical context, Sartre's approach to psychology seems to focus on a matter of choosing for or against something already objective in his phenomenology of facticity—rather than upon any intentional acts in psychological processes that constitute transcendental consciousness of both the authentic and the inauthentic, along with their subjective conflicts and intersubjective resolutions. Indeed, the ontology associated with this matter of choice is situated, not with our intentional judgments and valuations of the dialectical being of things, but rather within a "magical" world of emotions. (Sartre 1976, 90-1) Whereas for Husserl a particular emotion or mood (*Gemut*) seems to posit one's consciousness of an affectively significant *eidos* in structures of self-knowledge, emotions are treated in Sartre's existential analysis as authentic ways of understanding matters of existence that are correlated but nevertheless independent of the inauthentic world. For Sartre, one's consciousness of either authentic or inauthentic *Being* is a modality of *Verstehen* in Heidegger's sense of being-in-the-world.

Husserl's eidetic analysis of intentional experience demonstrates to Sartre the philosophical truth of authentic human existence, where we understand and respond affectively to possibilities in the manifest world as a consequence of our choices regarding factical life. However, according to Sartre, Husserl's reflections on the realization of inauthentic human existence (i.e., on our natural attitude) reveal only an impersonal and objectified transcendental logical *being* for subjectively real living persons. Since logic neither understands nor feels, the idea of authenticity is missing ("negated") for a dialectical synthesis in Husserl's account of world-constitution; and therefore, in his account of transcendental consciousness as well. Indeed, at the existential level of understanding, Husserl's transcendental logic of inauthentic life (as represented by the transcendental ego) means *nothing* for either the truth of one's authentic experience of worldly existence, or for the meaning and *being* of human existence (*Dasein*) within a self-constituted world. There is no possible dialectic of intentional action between the irreality of authentic existence and the metaphysical absoluteness of what is quite literally a *nothingness* in actual reality—we can only choose to accept or to reject such prevailing conditions.

Yet despite his protests to the contrary, Sartre presumes a naïve Cartesian duality of metaphysical opposites for existential interpretations of our "external" worldly experiences—where one could be either a "thing" as a static entity or a "no-thing" as an unrelieved emptiness. By reflecting on such experiences that regressively aim toward the existential register, he thus avoids a *synthesis* of their ontic differences in the transcendental register. Sartre (1957, 50) does this in order to posit the independent "nature" of inauthentic existence during a dialectic of reason, both in his own philosophy and for interpretations of Husserl's theory of consciousness. The experience of awareness and its psychic life are therefore viewed in Sartre's work from the natural attitude of metaphysical certainty, which is already a transcendental attitude toward authenticity. By rendering our understanding of authentic existence as the simple contrast of inauthentic factical life, Sartre presents a naturalized existential ontology of human consciousness that requires no explicit transcendental turn in his methodology. Kirkpatrick and Williams (1957) explain some of Sartre's differences with Husserl in the transcendental register:

> Thus, with no transcendental ego or contents to clutter up consciousness, phenomenology, or the reflexive study of consciousness, becomes directly occupied with human existence in its concrete relations to the world, with the nature of man as a consciousness of things, of himself, and of other selves. It is precisely such a phenomenological description of human existence in its "situation-in-the-world" —"phenomenological ontology" as the subtitle of *L'Etre et le Néant* [*Being and Nothingness*] proclaims—that constitutes the goal of Sartre's existentialism, as contrasted to the more logical and abstract purposes of Husserlian phenomenology. (pp. 25-6)

Maurice Merleau-Ponty (1964) argues that human consciousness could never be as transparent as either Sartre or Husserl proposes. Neither, according to Merleau-Ponty (1968, 115), could the historical human existent be as easily understood as Heidegger proclaims. Furthermore, "what one might consider to be 'psychology' ([as expounded in Merleau-Ponty's influential 1962 publication] *Phenomenology of Perception*) is in fact ontology." (p. 176) In Merleau-Ponty's ontology of transcendental consciousness, there will always remain a great wealth of unsynthesized meaning for the concept of *being-in-the-world*, since consciousness and perception of the world are but single aspects of a universal human behavior in this state of natural *Being*. It would be best then, according to Merleau-Ponty, to clarify the meaning of a particular human behavior within an existential analysis of its *Gestalt* or form of stimulus during the dialectical synthesis of "internal" consciousness and "external" perception. Merleau-Ponty wants to describe what already exists for the sentient subject of perceptual experience before that subject intentionally takes up a position of self-consciousness within pregiven social and cultural structures of a so-called embodied existence.

Merleau-Ponty (1968, 77) reasons that what already exists for descriptions at the existential level of human behavior—that "makes the notions of value and meaning come to life," and supports "a certain kind of knowledge and truth"—is a "spontaneous organization beyond the distinction between activity and passivity, of which the visible patterns of experience are the symbol [of intentionality]." An eidetic account of human consciousness, his argument goes, is simply an epistemological control of obscure processes of behavior in Husserl's transcendental philosophy and Gestalt-like phenomenological theory of perception:

> In other words, I believe that to give weight to his eidetic intuition and to distinguish it sharply from verbal concepts [of Hegelian philosophy], Husserl was really seeking, largely unknown to himself, a notion like that of the Gestaltists—the notion of an order of meaning which does not result from the application of spiritual [i.e., psychic] activity to an external matter. (p. 77)

Husserl's eidetic clarifications of transcendental consciousness nevertheless provide Merleau-Ponty with "ontological" evidence of a spontaneous embodiment of everyday life. It might be argued, however, that Merleau-Ponty probably misinterpreted Husserl's phenomenological epistemology of embodied existence. Reflections on the "analytic Body" of a dialectical relationship between thematic human behavior, and the language that describes said behavior, represents Merleau-Ponty's (1968, 175-9) "indirect method" of access to an existential ontology of human consciousness—given as an embodied "vertical" history of meaning and being. In Husserl's (1980a, §42) work, expressions of an embodied existence point toward our metaphysical presuppositions of a spatiotemporally ordered world that we naïvely believe to be the *sui generis* reality of the "convergence of causality and contingency" for the true nature of things. Embodied things exist in thoughts, not as "Gestalt-like perceptions," but because we intend for them to exist as analogies with the sense of one's own corporeal-being-in-the-world—including, for example, the analogy of Merleau-Ponty's embodied "vertical" (Marxian) history with the essence of universal human behavior.

It has been suggested (Edie 1964, xvii note 10) that Merleau-Ponty's direction in phenomenological studies "has no basis in Husserl at all." Furthermore, Natanson (1973, 79) warns that "Husserl's thought is given [only] a dialectical placement as a point of departure and return for Merleau-Ponty's own ruminations...[that] strikes at the philosophic core of phenomenology." As a former student of Merleau-Ponty's at the elite *École Normale Supérieure*, Foucault (Miller 1993, 41) characterizes Merleau-Ponty's phenomenological philosophy as "an anthropological understanding of concrete man that would combine a Marxist view of history with an existential outlook on the free human being." Despite their differences in practices and interpretations, however, the phenomenological philosophies of Husserl, Heidegger, Sartre, and Merleau-Ponty nevertheless address ontological, epistemological, and metaphysical facets of the same world of psychological experience that all of us tend to enjoy. But even so, Embree (1993) offers a piquant observation of the difference between Husserl's dialectical transcendental phenomenology and the subsequent turn toward an existential analysis that finds currency in today's phenomenological psychology:

> No competent reader can...fail to comprehend (a) that Husserl's [phenomenological philosophy] was from about 1905 through to the end of his life a transcendental philosophy, and (b) that Husserl's focus was in the philosophy of science. Existential phenomenology is not transcendental and, although not lacking in interest in science theory, is more concerned with human existence [than with human consciousness]. (p. xi)

A Psychology of Consciousness Versus a Philosophy of Existence

When existential arguments arise solely from within the horizon of metaphysics in order to be posited as objectively true, they could be seen in phenomenological reflections as fulfilling a norm of "reifying" apperceptions in the transcendental register. (*see* de Boer 1978, 395) This norm might well mirror a radical human motivation in conceptual space to bring to life what goes without saying as objectified matters in the world of common semblance. Yet during our unreflective moments in daily life, as a matter of anticpation in preconceptual experience, an intentional object is *supposed* to exist as genuine and correct by itself according to its conferred meaning and bestowed sense—independent of any further judgments and valuations of its worldly existence. Each of us tends to become habituated to a norm of truth-seeking in our spontaneous thoughts, even as we indeed look for what is supposed to exist as actually real in the world that is commonly talked about.

Under the psychological *epoché*, whatever is not pregiven by intuitive self-evidence in the living present does not matter to the psychological ego for consciousness-formation. Only what *is* in existence for the transcendental ego's form of ideation matters here and now during typical life-world experience (*see* Husserl 1970, §50). What goes without saying for the pure Ego is then structured in the horizon of metaphysics according to idealized forms of embodied spatiotemporal dimensions for apperceived elements. Said dimensions are already correlated in the horizon of ontology, and already deemed likely to be in the world according to one's social and cultural surroundings. The subject's "ego-pole" of transcending interactions between solipsism and intersubjectivity is constructed as a synthesis of such apperceived elements.

The transcendental ego's ideation of retained elements for an intentional object—including its embodied dimensions—is typically "retrogressed" along the subject's ego-pole of subjective experience. An ideation of elements is then transformed by transcendence into a mental formation of cognitive action for the constitution of *this* objective reality as genuinely true from the natural attitude—"genuinely true," that is, according to its epistemological representations of subjective *sense*. Theorists who rely on inferences of existential relationships for deductions of truth, or on an epistemology of embodiment for deductions of actual reality, fail to bracket their own metaphysical presuppositions about an objective "nature" of truth and reality.

The existential concept of *Verstehen* is not synonymous with consciousness in Husserl's work despite its conflation of meaning in naïve philosophical discourse. Rather, the concept is interpreted as one's apprehension and subsequent self-knowledge of worldly experience. (*see* Farber 1968, 235) During our worldly experiences of daily life and theoretical reflections, mental processes aim intuitively at achieving the norm of genuine truth for pre-existing things. In Husserl's (1982, §39) phenomenology of reason, whatever *is* in the living present for this norm excludes one's consciousness of what *is-not*. Indeed, this rational exclusion of possibilities that do not matter thematically here and now is characteristic of the horizon of our natural attitude.

As a norm of practice in the living present, the psychological ego excludes the existential register as a prior genuine truth ("in itself") when the transcendental ego's form of ideation directs its transcending acts toward grasping the ontic pregivenness of what is *supposed* to be genuinely true ("for itself"). (Husserl 1973b, §35) During the spontaneous immediacy of psychological experience, the exclusion of what does not matter for constitutive life is a mode of comportment for the psychological ego within its background of actionality. (*see* Husserl 1977, 50) It is precisely this rational exclusion of pre-existing irreality in the transcendental register that could be interpreted as existential *nothingness* within the horizon of metaphysics; since of course, the actual reality of what "goes without saying" from the natural attitude does not exist immediately in the world that is commonly talked about.

When following Husserl's (1970, 398) lead for studies in the transcendental register, a phenomenologist brackets the subject's metaphysical presuppositions of pre-existing things given from the natural attitude—including any naïve concepts pertaining to the "existential nature" of mental life. A transcendental phenomenologist, in effect, makes the human psyche and the world constituted in consciousness, respectively, the subject and the overall object of psychological experience. Whatever then exists according to intuitive self-evidence in one's personal lifeworld represents an intentionally predicated object for transcendental phenomenological psychology. In all cases of intuitive self-evidence of what truely exists "in the world" for everyone, the (subject-predicate-object) matter that *is* in transcendental consciousness is a correlate of the irreal intersubjective state of affairs called, "my life with their life." The phenomenological *eidos* of *my-life-with-their-life* presents for genetic reflections the psychological theme and dialectic of a synthesized rational affective unity of similarity-and-difference for *me myself* as an intentional object.

In Husserl's (1973b, §42) theory of method for this dialectic, whatever is *not* an element of *me myself* in the living-present profile of ego-life is "fashioned" and posited to be an element of one's "alter" ego-life. By these actions, the pure Ego observes and comes to know itself intuitively as its own embodied (i.e., non-spiritual) mode of "my being-as-ego." This performance is indeed necessary in one's naïve natural world—necessary, so that it goes without saying that I exist as objectively real. The factical elements of "my being-as-ego" are grouped in mental processes of thinking and feeling, where they are synthesized in psychological processes by means of such valuations as *pleasing*, *abhorrent*, or *passable* during intersubjective relationships. The psychological ego is thus directed by the intentions of the pure Ego within the *a priori* and contingent horizons, and motivated affectively in pure psychology, to construct an eidetic affair of similarities and differences of essential element in order to "harmonized and fit together…the unity of one total actuality" in the world of co-existence and common semblance. (Husserl 1977, 44)

During one's day-to-day experiences in this world of idealized and absolutized factical life, conscious awareness is partly structured by our metaphysical presuppositions of truth about the universal life-world. (*see* Husserl 1970, §34a.f) The psychological ego's ordering of elements for what is believed to be true from such partial pregivenness leads constitutive experience back toward those particular things retained within a horizon of contingent possibilities for realizing *my life* as a rational affective unity. Elements in this horizon include such pre-existing things of spirit-life that the meaningful subject experiences as basic trust, hopes, commitments, and fears. (Gurwitsch 1974, 12) Phenomenological reflections on these elements of so-called authentic experience are similarly led back to existential concepts and their developmental origins, but only insofar as they are directed in the living present during the immediate experience of constitutive life.

In this regard, Husserl (Fink 1995, §3 note 31) warns phenomenologists that attempts to describe an "exhaustive" process of cognitive "iterations" of retrogression directed toward the genetic antecedents of conscious awareness—including its existential elements—are "senseless from the start." Thinking in endless returning to the past is not how we typically go about constituting awareness and constructing actual reality for something in one's personal lifeworld. Instead, each cognitive iteration and reiteration represents the pure Ego's knowing and living a psychological theme of actionality in the living present. Cognitive mental life is directed into the temporal past of pure existence for *this* intentional object alone as it appears and is acted upon as contingency demands. Past experience with something similar to this object, perhaps retained in memory as a pre-existing analogous element of action, represents a pregiven experience with an object of the mind that is believed to exist as true here and now. Indeed, we tend *not* to remember in conceptual space what does not endure as truly existing in the living-present profile of consciousness-formation. (*see* Husserl 1964a, §26)

By trying to account for all possible cognitions of a phenomenon, focus of reflections could be directed away from singularly necessary intentional acts that lead to the subject's constitution of *this* object and not another. In this case, the radical ("pure") psychological basis of cognitions is sometimes lost for inferences, since the pre-conceptual irreal acts of the psychological ego are excluded from reflections on the "external" manifestations of cognitive skills. Lycan (1990) provides an explanation of how some scholars seem to abandon inductive inferences of subjective psychic life in their theories of cognitions—especially when such theories are conceived and find evidence of truth from the natural attitude toward objectified "semantical features":

> A key point to note is that intentional or representational features are semantical features; beliefs are true, or false; they entail or imply other beliefs; they are (it seems) composed of concepts and depend for their truth on a match between their internal structures and the way the world is; in particular their "aboutness" is very naturally regarded as a matter of mental referring. Some…have taken this semanticity of beliefs as a strong clue to the nature of intentionality itself, suggesting that beliefs and thoughts have their intentionality in virtue of properties they share with other semantically characterized items, the sentences of public natural languages. (p. 277)

The "sentences of public natural languages" are clearly neither intentional acts nor analogous in sense and meaning to such acts in cognitive mental life—but instead, they are unified objects of the mind. Yet when cognitive psychologists construct their theories from the natural attitude toward such objectified and absolutized things, the phenomenon of cognition is itself given as an objectification of particular skills and competencies over against the Husserlian concept of our subjective acts of *knowing*. Indeed, cognitive acts in the transcendental register are mostly judging- and valuing-acts within a mental process of *knowing* in pure psychology. Anticipating something to be objectively real and true pre-exists in the living present of a naïve psychologist's experiences of mental life; and therefore, the idea of cognition *as such* is pregiven to constitutive life as an objective psychological phenomenon rather than as universal subjective experience. With its thematic focus of *aboutness* on the transcendental ego's form of ideation for the objectifications of life, the psychological ego of a naïve psychologist cannot but act to constitute self-knowledge of cognitive mental life to be the objectification of human *knowing*.

The pure Ego's turn of regard outward from pre-existing elements during consciousness-formation—including existential, solipsistic, and previously objectified things in linguistic constructions—begins with an intentional act of "Ego-advertence." This universal act of pure psychology also signals a reorientation in Husserl's (1970, §58) phenomenological studies to its intersubjective phase in the transcendental register. A propadeutic regressive phenomenology now ends in Husserl's (Fink 1995, §§7f) mature theory of inquiry in order to begin a genetic reconstruction of the subject's transcendental consciousness of an intentional object—where constitutive life is directed toward awareness of objectivities in the world that is commonly talked about. When adopting the psychological attitude toward this phase of action in the phenomenological method proper, phenomenologists intend to see the spirit-life of transcendental subjectivity in one's personal lifeworld.

As a universal mode of comportment in pure subjectivity, naïve psychologists experience as well a transcendental reorientation during the constitution of one's self-knowledge of objectified psychological phenomena. Kagen and Segal (1992) give the following example of the transcendental turn for psychologists in a textbook for beginning students—where the turn of regard proceeds from focus on "yourself," to embodied categories of objectified historical "people":

> More than any other subject you are ever likely to study, psychology is about a topic that should be of interest to you. It is about yourself. The field embodies an effort to answer the kinds of questions you have doubtless often asked about your own makeup and behavior—questions that surely must have puzzled our ancestors for countless generations.
>
> The questions addressed by psychology are endless—and endlessly fascinating: Were you born the way you are or did you get that way? And if so, how? Are you the master of your fate or a helpless pawn of your environment? Can you change if you want to? What accounts for the differences within the human species? Why are some people so quick to learn, others so slow? Why do some people crumble in the face of everyday stress, while others can overcome even seemingly devastating crises?…Why do some people appear to be perfectly sane and rational, while others behave in ways that are regarded as strange and abnormal? (pp. 3-4)

One aim of this book is to give psychologists a direction and opportunity to think deeply about what "the psychological" means no matter where one's interests might lie within the discipline. In keeping with Husserl's tradition to respect the beliefs and concerns of non-phenomenologists, the work presented here is not meant to advocate any single or totalizing approach for research or clinical application. Neither is it implied that all members of the discipline are capable of grasping principles of transcendental phenomenological psychology in theory and practice—or indeed, that they would even be inclinded to do so. Rather, this introduction is intended to be a beginning inquiry into the meaningful human subject's plurality of psychological experiences when one is knowingly conscious of something. "And that would already be much," Husserl might say.

2.

Uncovering Husserl

The Student Years

Edmund Gustav Albrecht Husserl was born on April 8, 1859 in the ancient Moravian town of Prostějov (Prossnitz) in what is now the Czech Republic. Since Moravia was then part of the Austrian Empire, Husserl was an Austrian by birth. Welch (1941, *xiii-xxiv*) reports that having finished his elementary education at the age of ten, Husserl was sent to Vienna to enter secondary school. Described as a "sleepyhead" by his fellow students because of his pensive moods, he nevertheless qualified for entrance into a university. Husserl spent the years from 1876 to 1878 at the University of Leipzig, where he attended courses in physics, mathematics, and astronomy. At Leipzig, Husserl befriended Thomás Masaryk, who is today celebrated as the first president of Czechoslovakia. According to Moran (2000, 67), Masaryk persuaded Husserl to take a course in modern philosophy that included reviews of Descartes, Leibnitz, and the British empiricists. He also attended lectures in philosophy given by Wilhelm Wundt—a developer of the view that phenomena of human experience cannot be understood except through the structure of their interrelations. Wundt is perhaps best known as the creator of the first school of inquiry devoted to psychology.

Wundt apparently failed to excite young Edmund's interest in the further study of either philosophy or psychology; for in 1878 owing to his aptitude in mathematics, Husserl transferred to the Friedrich Wilhelm University of Berlin. In Berlin, Husserl had the rare opportunity for a nineteen year-old of studying with three of the foremost mathematicians of the day: Leopold Kronecker, Eduard Kummer, and Karl Weierstrass. Under the influence of these three, Husserl became intrigued with the concept of the arithmatization of mathematics. For example, how do we turn logical rules of mathematical inference into the practice of counting integral numbers? No doubt Husserl received from these mathematicians a remarkable training in the rigorous study of abstract concepts. Yet while they were stimulating the imagination of Husserl the mathematician, Friedrich Paulsen was perhaps instilling in him a desire to study philosophical issues of reasoning and the question of human consciousness.

Paulsen was professor of pedagogy and a leading scholar of Kant's philosophy during Husserl's student years. Even while positing that human consciousness exists as our will to live (*Zielstrebigkeit*) independent of all forms of reasoning, Paulson nevertheless challenged Husserl to reformulate traditional theories of volition in terms of their practical methods. He undoubtedly also directed Husserl's early thinking into areas that were destined to prove productive during the development of his phenomenological philosophy—such things as Paulsen's view that our so-called natural disposition responds to demands not only from physical sensation, but also from the moral and ethical environment in which we ordinarily find ourselves. As a former pupil of G.T. Fechner, Paulsen reformulated Fechner's work on psychophysical properties of awareness, and developed in Husserl's classes his own theories of panpsychism—the Greek anthropic principle where the physical presence of all parts of matter results from interactions with human consciousness.

Although Husserl was focusing his attention increasingly on philosophy, he nevertheless transferred in 1881 to the University of Vienna in order to finish his mathematical studies. He believed that earning an Austrian degree might improve his chances of employment. (*see* Moran 2000, 68) In October 1882, having studied elliptical functions with Leo Königsberger, Husserl received his doctorate at the age of twenty-four. His dissertation, entitled "Contributions to the Theory of the Calculus of Variations," was an impressive work that one could think of as the mathematization of geometrical measurement. Weierstrass had first aroused Husserl's interest in formal methods of calculus for topological features in the summer of 1879. In 1882, in consideration of their mutual interests in the radical foundations of mathematics, Weierstrass invited Husserl to Berlin to act as his assistant. Due to illness, however, Weierstrass took leave in the winter of 1883, and Husserl quickly volunteered his services to the Austrian military for a year—"presumably to gain a period of reflection on his future career." (p. 69)

When Husserl ended his military service in Vienna in 1884, he not only became re-acquainted with Masaryk, who was then on the philosophical faculty at the university, but he also found the department captivated by Franz Brentano, a former priest and the university's most popular professor. In 1869, the Catholic Liberal Party of Germany adopted as principles of education certain arguments supporting the dogma of papal infallibility that seemed to go against the teachings of Aquinas. As the result of Brentano's opposition to these principles, he not only relinquished his professorship at the Catholic University of Würzburg, but he was also forced to withdraw from the priesthood. He retired officially from the university in 1873. In the following year, Brentano published his major work, *Psychology from an Empirical Standpoint*, and was invited to Vienna as professor of philosophy. During his years at Vienna, Brentano continued to be an influential figure throughout the emergence of psychology as a discipline, even while his personal life became an object of gossip. In 1880 he wanted to marry, although Austrian law forbade this of an ex-priest. Brentano therefore went to Leipzig to escape this regulation, resumed his German citizenship, married, and returned to the University of Vienna—but as a *Privatdozent*, the equivalent of a university lecturer.

While working on his dissertation, Husserl had gone to hear the expriest who was arousing such keen interest in a philosophy of psychology. Focusing on Aristotle's work, Brentano was then developing the notion that mental life is a succession of intentional states of consciousness, rather than passive physiological functions. No scientific account of the mind could be given, Brentano claimed, except as an epistemology of human intentionality in the perception of our natural world. In opposition to Wundt, Brentano taught that the primary scientific principle of psychology is not experimentation but rather close observation. Nothing within a structure of consciousness could be properly evaluated experimentally unless and until the elements of that structure are presented for observations as phenomena themselves. Designed to be an analogy with the most radical practices of natural science, Brentano called his inquiry into the "inner life" of consciousness a "phenomenognosis." Husserl was so favorably impressed by Brentano that he welcomed the opportunity to study with him after completing his military service—and presumably after having decided on the direction of his future career.

According to Brentano's theory of consciousness, something similar to scientific methods is found in our ordinary experiences of problem solving as well. Every decision, Brentano maintained, every emotion, every desire and inclination begins with a mental act of presenting something that is to be accepted or rejected, liked or disliked, desired or avoided, and so on. In the act of presenting an object to consciousness we intend to make such choices. Although it bothered Husserl (1964a, §6) that Brentano did not address the (psychologistic) problem of differentiating a mental act from the object of that act—such as perceiving the perceived—he always accepted Brentano's (Welch 1941, 3) principle that "the *act* of intending, not the intended object, is that which is to be investigated by psychology." Brentano's philosophical psychology is primarily the study of intentional mental phenomena: the acts and functions of human sentient life which leaves out of consideration any possible physiological genesis of such phenomena, along with the physical dimensions of whatever is intentionally presented to consciousness. In Brentano's phenomenognosis, these latter considerations belong within the domain of an empirical descriptive psychology, rather than with the "pure" *a priori* psychology of mental phenomena and of consciousness itself.

From 1884 to 1886, Husserl not only ardently pursued the study of philosophy under Brentano, but he also enjoyed a close personal relationship with his famous teacher. Throughout his lifetime, although he moved away from many of Brentano's core precepts, Husserl never failed to acknowledge his debt of gratitude for Brentano's early influence, both personal and professional. It was during his post-doctoral days with Brentano that Husserl became persuaded of the value of Bernard Bolzano's philosophy of science. Bolzano (1972) introduced a view of what it means to do science rigorously in its application, an issue that Husserl certainly took to heart. The ontology that supports every epistemology in science, according to Bolzano, needs to be examined by a precise methodology without presuming in advance what that ontology might be. Husserl (1970, §34e) remarked that this concept influenced him deeply in the years ahead. Bolzano likewise introduced to Husserl such philosophical doctrines as a proposition-in-itself, an idea-in-itself, and of truth-in-itself. Husserl (2001, 68) was to use these doctrines in developing a "logical 'theory of elements'" for his constructions of phenomenological concepts pertaining to "the thing itself" in pure consciousness.

Bolzano's theory of scientific practices bolstered Brentano's division of inquiry into a pure philosophical psychology of mental acts, and a separate descriptive psychology of the empirical manifestations and consequences of said acts. In Brentano's and then Husserl's view, mental acts are directed outside the mind, and are the means by which we make sentient contact with the material world. By extension and analogy, we thus make contact with those things that are already posited to *be* in that world. Such contact through one's perceptions, judgments, and emotions form the basis of any psychology, yet such contact by itself is not sufficiently universal for empirical generalizations in the real world (versus our experimental constructions)—for indeed, the necessity for any particular intentional action is contingent on the environment in which consciousness-formation occurs. In Brentano's philosophy, however, philosophical clarifications of universal mental phenomena provide a basis in certainty for scientific knowledge of human consciousness itself, along with its descriptive psychology of empirical manifestations.

With Brentano's Cartesian approach toward concept formation and theory construction, scientific knowledge derived from philosophical clarifications is knowledge of something that is evident and therefore true, or is at least highly probable. Whatever is then immediately evident in strict and rigorous study provides the *a priori* "Archimedean" points for inquiry and arguments in all the sciences. The manner in which Brentano linked philosophy and science was an enduring inspiration to Husserl; and indeed, throughout Husserl's (1965a, 71ff) subsequent career, phenomenological philosophy was intended to be above all "scientific" (*wissenschaftlich*). Husserl understood this to mean that a phenomenologist must constantly bear in mind the need for strict discipline in practices, and must rigidly adhere to prior concepts and principles. Although Husserl was perhaps moderately interested in the way that Paulsen and Wundt viewed the relationship between science and philosophy, their emphasis was more on the biological sciences. Brentano on the other hand was writing about psychology and lecturing on logic.

On the advice of Brentano in 1886 (*see* Welch 1941, 5), Husserl went to the University of Halle in Germany as a post-doctoral assistant under Carl Stumpf. Here, Husserl obtained not only his teaching certificate in philosophy, but also a thorough grounding in contemporary psychology. Stumpf was another former student and life-long friend of Brentano's; and similarly to Brentano, Stumpf taught an "act psychology" rather than Wundt's psychology of the structural content of human consciousness. Working with the phenomenon of how we perceive specific tonal and atonal qualities of sound when listening to music, Stumpf devised conceptualizations and experiments that purported to show that we intentionally group elements of pure tone in order to perceive the whole chord quality of the musical content. What Stumpf had originally labeled as his "psychology of sound," he later called a work of *Phänomenologie* in the tradition of Brentano's method of phenomenognosis.

Stumpf's inquiry into the psychology of sound was meant to be a "pre-scientific" study (*Vorwissenschaftlich*) of day-to-day perception that would provide *entrée* into a state of affairs essential to universal human consciousness. It was understood thus to be propaedeutic to both a philosophy of perception and to any theories of psychological response to physical stimuli. Stumpf instilled in Husserl (2001, 167f) the idea that sentient contact between mental phenomena and external physical stimuli could be observed as an experience of perception that is itself a subjective act of intentional experience. Along with Husserl, Stumpf is considered to be a co-founder of contemporary phenomenology and an inspiration to Gestalt psychologists. On the sixth of July 1887, Husserl became a *Privatdozent* under Stumpf in the philosophical faculty at Halle. The start of his academic career was not devoted directly to phenomenological philosophy, however, but rather to the eidetic basis of mathematics. Husserl's (2003) first publication at Halle in 1891, *Philosophie der Arithmetik (Philosophy of Arithmetic)*, was nevertheless dedicated to Brentano, since Husserl adopted his methodology for an analysis of parts and wholes.

Husserl's Nascent Phenomenology:
Psychologism, Historicism, and the Epoché

During the formation of Western psychology as the independent discipline we recognize today, there was a dispute in Germany about what direction the new discipline was to take. As Husserl took up his teaching duties at Halle in the late 1880s, one could imagine that an important question was: "Is psychology primarily a science of explanatory theories about the (perhaps physical) mind as part of the natural world, or is it primarily a scientific way of comprehending the (perhaps metaphysical) psyche as the animating spirit or soul of humanity?" The only thing that seemed to be in agreement was that the new discipline was to be a science. If psychology were to become an explanatory science of physical properties, something occurring in nature, its methodology could then be modeled on those of the natural sciences of physics, biology, and chemistry. On the other hand, if it were to become a science with practices designed to understand the presence and mental activities of the human psyche, then theories already presented in such eidetic sciences as formal logic, mathematics, and geometry might be profitably modeled.

Husserl did not seem to be concerned with the direction of an emerging discipline of psychology, however, as he began to develop his own approach to philosophy. Husserl was becoming known at Halle for criticizing the German philosophical environment as a "murky vapor of idealistic or better mystical pseudophilosophy." (Smith and Smith 1995, 5) Publication of his *Philosophy of Arithmetic* in 1891 provoked a negative reaction from the founder of analytic philosophy, Gottlob Frege, who (some say unfairly) attacked the book for identifying the logic of mathematical inference as a variation of everyday practical judgments. Perhaps more important, Paul Natorp criticized Husserl from his neo-Kantian position for presuming that any form of subjective knowledge represents no more than the mirroring of realities or entities that refer to the contents of conscious awareness. (*see* Husserl 2001, 208) This critique began a life-long relationship of correspondence between Natorp and Husserl, where throughout the years Natorp seems to have somewhat fulfilled the role of Husserl's interpreter of Kant's epistemology.

Yet even as his popularity grew at Halle, Husserl (Moran 2000, 73-4) became increasingly dissatisfied with human-scientific theories that blindly followed traditional practices—although he admittedly had no good alternatives to offer: "He found himself at the lecture podium expounding the epistemological ideas of his contemporaries, and he realized he himself had nothing to say." In order to clarify his position toward philosophy as a human science in Bolzano's sense of rigorous praxis, Husserl began working on the *Logische Untersuchungen (Logical Investigations)*, which was published in two volumes during 1900-1901. Borrowing topics from the *Philosophy of Arithmetic*, Husserl meant for the *Investigations* to present a rejection of unexamined skepticism and relativism as legitimate practices of scientific analysis. Instead, Husserl argued, the laws and rules of pure logic provide a basis for critique of the so-called theoretical connections that constitute the validity of a particular scientific concept or construct. This focus raised the question as to how a scientist's consciousness of an "ideal lawfulness" for logical operations could become a methodological rule for doing science. Husserl concluded that no matter what the factual matter of scientific inquiry happens to be, pure logical forms of elementary things and their relationships are transformed by mental acts into norms and rules for systematic theory construction.

By making this determination, Husserl implicitly cast his lot with those who wanted psychology to move in the direction of other eidetic sciences in order to understand the human psyche as an animating property of ordinary experience and scientific praxis; and with this determination, he began his career-long struggle with the problem of psychologism. Psychologism is the general thesis that objective "laws of logic" are reducible to descriptive facts about how the mind works in subjective psychological processes. The logical premise, for example, that two objects cannot occupy the same space at the same time does not directly refer to anything objective in descriptions of actual events, for we must choose to posit this relationship and its truth conditions according to subjective self-knowledge of *space* and *time*. "Choosing to posit" implies a subjective psychological origin to this premise. What we presume to be universally objective concepts of truth and reality surface in a philosophy of mind as only relative states in theories that rely upon psychologistic descriptions of objective matters. Consequently, things that hold logically for *our* minds might not hold for different logics and different minds.

This is an epistemological issue for Husserl that seems to begin with the Aristotelian principle that we cannot think in any way but according to "forms of thought." Here, said forms "predicate" (= assert as a concretely real presence) the existence of things in universal and absolute categories of meaning—and indeed, everyone is potentially capable of apprehending such categories or forms. If this were not the case, according to Aristotle, then there would be no difference in thought, for example, between substantial things and spiritual things. Otherwise, Aristotle believed, there would be no difference in thought between sound and sight, humans and beasts, or you and me. In most scientific theories there could be an implicit position of strong psychologism, where formal logic (as the logic of forms wherein, say, "p and not-p" is a contradiction) is believed to be descriptive of the prepredicative mental processes where we do and indeed must think. There could also be a weak psychologism, where descriptions of formal logic are believed to prescribe mental processes for how we *ought* to think. And there could be an anti-psychologism, where forms of logic are independent of any descriptions of our subjective mental processes within such forms.

Corresponding respectively to these positions, (1) either objective forms of logical relationships cause our subjective psychological processes to be such as they are in mental life, or (2) our subjective psychological processes depend upon objective forms of logical relationships for causal matters, or else (3) there is no direct causal relationship between a logical form and the psychological processes used within each form. Taking one of these positions for theoretical matters seems to be decisive for logicians and methodologists in the human sciences—since either a logical relationship has its origins as a still-to-be-determined psychological phenomenon, or else explanations of psychological phenomena depend upon developing the logic of forms for evaluations of the significance of their active content. Husserl's descriptions of objective forms of logical relationhips in his *Philosophy of Arithmetic* indeed carried overtones of weak psychologism after having studied with Weierstrass, Brentano, and Stumpf. (de Boer 1978, 19f)

In Husserl's (Mohanty 1995, 47-8) early non-phenomenological studies, a precise decription of any philosophical or scientific concept would include its psychological origins in mental life. Husserl believed that every fully conceived concept consists of "presentations" (*Vorstellungen*) of two independent forms of thought: an intuitive form (sometimes called, "authentic") and a symbolic form (sometimes called, "inauthentic"). In Husserl's original non-phenomenological theory of consciousness, each of us reasons by means of objective and logical forms of relationships within universal psychological processes. More reminiscent perhaps of Wundt's structuralism than of Brentano's notion of intentionality, abstract phenomena such as the idea of numbers in Husserl's philosophy of arithmetic have their origins in psychological processes; but the actual denotative numbers and number systems that we invent and use symbolically refer back to one's intuition into pre-existing objective logical relationships. Reasoning *as such* in Husserl's early work is the spontaneous application of universal psychological processes of abstraction, combination, and reflection on or toward realizing the objective forms of time and space that already exist symbolically in one's thoughts.

Between publication of his *Philosophy of Arithmetic* and the second edition of the *Logical Investigations*, Husserl's arguments began a movement away from even weak psychologistic descriptions of human consciousness. Husserl eventually asserted the universality of two different forms of thought: a logic of calculus and a calculus of logic. A logic of calculus is a way to think about something categorially—typically, as a categorical fact. A calculus of logic, on the other hand, is how we predicate that same thing in conscious awareness when given prior categories as conditions for judgments and valuations. For example, counting is a logic of calculus for knowing the number of things, while grouping is a calculus of logic for counting. Thinking of my friend's face is a logic of calculus for recognizing her, while recollecting her features is a calculus of logic for thinking about her face. A logic of calculus could include any number of necessary calculi for positing a contingent matter of fact. However, a logic of calculus and a calculus of logic are conceptually independent of any psychological processes for their potential use—meaning, they are both objects of the mind that may or may not be acted upon in any particular instance of predication. Yet when they *are* acted upon, it is intentional on the part of the reasoning actor. This theory of step-wise categorial thinking is perhaps the basis of Husserl's methodology for genetic phenomenology.

Throughout Husserl's (1982, §§2f) work, a predicated "fact" does not exist as an unquestionable objective truth or reality according to a universal logic of forms. Rather, what we call a fact is present in consciousness as a factual "matter" (*Sache*) within an intentionally constructed "matter of factualness" (*Tatsache*). Before something *is* a concrete fact in thought and speech, it is first meant and intended to be a concrete fact in conscious awareness. In order to fulfill this intention, a calculus of judgments and valuations is chosen and either acted upon or passively accepted. This choice is itself part of one's logic of calculus for realizing a matter of fact in conscious awareness. When exercising our ordinary inductive intuition, the meaning of something objective is believed to be a factual matter when fulfilled within a chosen calculus of logic that is potentially at hand for everyone. Its meaning is a matter of fact as to how and in what categorial form something *is* objectively real and true.

One might claim as a fact, for example, "Her hair is brown." What is predicated here is the objectively real color of her hair within a range of hues believed to be at hand for perceptions, not the subjective matter itself—which is, "Excluding all other colors, I believe that her hair is brown." Subjective experience is only implied and presupposed when predicating a state of affairs in a calculus of logic, even while psychological processes construct a matter of factualness for what is posited to be objectively real and contingently true. When something might prove *not* to be objectively real according to subsequent judgments, one's meaning is nevertheless subjectively real in its predicating logic of calculus. For instance, we could all agree that there is no such objectively real thing as a round square, yet the meaning even of such an absurdity is subjectively real in a logical semantics of one's choosing. Consequently, we could all understand what is meant by a "round square" when the term is used in a logic of calculus to predicate an illogical state of affairs. Strictly speaking, a matter of factualness in Husserl's work does not represent or describe an objectively real thing outside of its logic of calculus.

Humans intuitively understand predications of factual reality, since a constructed matter of factualness points toward an *injunction* for constituting objectively real things in conscious awareness. That is to say, something is "ordered" or "instructed" to come to presence in awareness as factually real by means of a universal logic of calculus for reality construction. Essential elements of a logic of calculus for factual matters—including the calculi we choose for contingencies of "this case"—are much like the ingredients of a recipe that is an injunction for a cake, or like a musical score that is an injunction for a symphony. One could describe a cake as an objectively real thing from its appearance, but not its flavor in the finished product. One could, however, describe the ingredients of a recipe such that an original flavor might be reproduced. An original flavor is the ideal flavor for each of us according to the calculus of logic for *this* cake, where we are all aiming at a flavor that is similar enough to be recognized as approximately the same. The recipe is a matter of fact during our day-to-day experiences, acting to bake the cake is factually real, and the cake as it is produced is an objectively real thing. Furthermore, something like an original flavor could be potentially experienced by each of us in this matter of factualness about something ideal.

Perhaps another way to grasp these distinctions is with Husserl's categorial descriptions of denotative cardinal numbers and symbolically real numbers. Here, each category is an element within a transcendental logic of calculus used for quantifying actually real things. During our day-to-day experiences with such things, cardinal numbers from one to ten are used in a calculus for counting. As a normative rule, there cannot be any numbers but these in their symbolic representations, with zero representing the absence of a cardinal number. In Husserl's (1973a, §96b) mature reflections on objects of the mind, cardinal numbers denote categories of qualities that have a one-to-one relationship to one another. This relationship holds no matter what the quantities of things in each category happens to be when calculating the number of things, since a cardinal number is infinitely regressible as the division of a whole. A transcendental logic of calculus for quantifying things is an *idealizing* form of reasoning—meaning, we intentionally look for ideal numerical categories when we count according to the calculus that leads to the symbolic representations of cardinal numbers in thought and speech.

We are usually taught and come to believe that numerical categories ideally exist as real within a calculus that is at hand for counting. As a rational norm of practice, we need only to replicate pregiven categories in our acts of counting when we make passive use of this calculus, just as it is learned and generally practiced by everyone. Cardinal numbers and their symbols are thus intentionally idealized in our logic of calculus as actually real things themselves when we count, and each of us will indeed come up with one such number just as we intend—even if we miscount. When we count things and think about the ideal number "three," for example, the object in its calculus is *not* about (say) the numerical category "five." The elementary laws of relationships in the calculus for counting "three" already have adequate meaning for the category "three" in one's logic of calculus. *This* meaning of "three" is adequate for the practice of counting, since the category of "three" is believed to be valid for the fact of "three" in one's intuition into counting experience. A calculus of "three" is not intuitively valid for the fact of any other cardinal number according to one's ordinary experiences with actually real things.

Naïve scientific practices reflect a transcendental logic of calculus that is potentially at hand for everyone—where presupposed laws and axioms are passively applied in ideal categories of symbolic meaning. These symbolic things are then constituted as actually real with the application of a system of norms for categorizing according to a tradition of reality construction. Here, the term "norm" denotes a standard of achievement for thinking activities. We generally call a system of norms for categorizing things in logical forms of eidetic relationships a "methodology" for scientific reasoning. Sometimes we call this system in ordinary experience our intuitive "common sense." Husserl (2001, 23-7) wanted to distinguish early on between two kinds of norms and their typical calculi found in both our scientific methodologies and ordinary inductive intuitions. First, there are those norms that could be characterized as "mere species" or "traditions" for scientific or philosophical arguments. Each norm of this kind has its own content of an active idea that differs as an object of the mind from one case to another in formal-logical studies.

One could easily think of norms of the first kind as reflecting pre-existing epistemological interests for judgments and valuations, such as with a particular school of thought or with a particular vocation. Our intentional use of these norms could be observed empirically in historical descriptions of objectified things, as well as in contemporary scientific discourse about factual matters. Another kind of norm, Husserl (2001, 26) continues, "regulates" or "fixes" our use of the first kind when we attempt to achieve a "universal practical aim" within an *a priori* system of "apodictic connections." This norm "tells us on what basic standard or basic value all normativization must be conducted." Husserl adopts here the use of the Greek term, *apodeiktikos*, in order to refer to something that is necessarily certain and thus true. This second kind of norm could only be seen within theoretical reflections of what is self-evidently real and true for each "mere species" of norms of the first kind.

In his *Logical Investigations*, Husserl (2001, 26) calls the norm that aims at indisputable conclusions the "basic norm" of both scientific inquiry and ordinary experience. He means that we already possess adequate certainty as to where our system of norms will lead within a calculus of one's choosing, at least in terms of idealized outcomes. For example, if we want to measure and add up the total degrees of angle for a triangle, we are already certain from previous experience that the triangle has at most three angles to be measured. We would never expect to find more than three angles within the ideal dimensions of a triangle. In both day-to-day living and theoretical reflections, apodictic certainty in a calculus of logic can in no way be seen as problematic for a rational system of norms. For instance, I am apodictically certain that my left hand is at the end of my left arm. I am also apodictically certain that enzymes are made up of proteins. Apodictic certainty is one's self-evident certainty of something that "goes without saying" during normative comportment.

Husserl (1973b, §9) once again takes up the issue of apodictic certainty in his later transcendental phenomenology as essential to his theory of conscious awareness—but he has to allow that this matter of certainty was not well understood in the *Logical Investigations*. Indeed, he felt that the principle of apodicticity should have been applied more rigorously against the principle of "relativism." (Bachelard 1968, 103) In Husserl's first attempts to formulate his phenomenological philosophy, the issue of our capacity for obtaining certain knowledge dealt with reasoning in the conceptual space of theoretical discourse—a calculus of objective things where we aim to be certain of its idealized outcome, independent of any subjective mental processes and personal contingencies in pre-conceptual space. That is to say, the calculus for *doing* formal logic was already accepted as an objective matter of certain knowledge in the *Investigations*. Being certain of conclusions within a calculus of logic, however, does not speak to the range and limits of what is to be observed and accepted as evidence of one's realization of that certainty according to a calculus of contingent experience. How then do we come to have apodictic certainty of our own thoughts as factual matters in order to speak of them?

Husserl (1973b, §9) points to Descartes's famous dictum, "I think therefore I am," as perhaps the best example in the philosophical literature of naïve apodicticity within a transcendental logic of calculus. Yet in order for

Descartes to gain apodictic evidence of the fact that he is thinking, he doubts that very fact—since as Descartes imagined, he could be fooled into believing that he is thinking by some "evil demon." Because Descartes could doubt that he thinks, the argument goes, he must nevertheless be thinking even as he doubts. It is self-evident that Descartes is apodictically certain of the existence of *doubt as such* in the transcendental register. Evidence of Descartes's certainty that "I am" as the idealized outcome in his algebraic calculus is thus contingent on his intention and relative to his ability to doubt within his transcendental logic of calculus for knowing the existence of things.

Sometimes with our normative comportment—perhaps with maturation, most of the time—relative evidence of truth and reality is adequate for constructing a state of affairs where we could know something as ideally true and factually real. Descartes had no apodictic evidence in his calculus, for example, to suppose that if he were to doubt that he thinks, he would thus *in fact* be thinking. This means, too, that Descartes's transcendental logic of calculus provides no injunction to produce doubt itself as an idealized outcome of thinking. Instead, doubt is presupposed as objectively real according to the basic norm that regulates where his algebra will lead. By extension, anticipating apodictic certainty in the conceptual space of our logical constructions, even when faced with the possibility of contingent doubt in its pre-conceptual calculus, is a typical goal of reasoning when oriented by our naïve natural attitude toward realizing ideal things in conscious awareness.

Husserl (1973b, §63) characterizes much of the *Logical Investigations* as his "*first stage of phenomenology*—a stage which in its own manner is…*infected with a certain naïveté (the naïveté of apodicticity)*." For "the only thing I can posit in absolute apodicticity" is that I exist, that "I am." (§60) Still, in his first work devoted to phenomenological inquiry, Husserl delivered notice to the discipline of philosophy, and to human science in general, that he intended to overturn traditional practices that repeated what he believed to be fundamental errors in concept formation and theory construction. Husserl returned again and again throughout the years to principles first set down in the *Investigations* in order to develop his own system of phenomenological norms. This work in all of its revisions continued to guide Husserl's career-long reflections on both our universal experiences with the phenomenological method of reasoning and on its possible application as human-scientific praxis.

Moran (2000, 75-6) reports that despite its initial lackluster acceptance by the academic community, publication of the first volume of the *Logical Investigations* influenced the Prussian ministry of education to appoint Husserl "Professor Extraordinarius" at Göttingen University. His appointment in September 1901 succeeded against objections by the philosophical faculty, but seems to have been made in hopes of obtaining a fruitful collaboration between Husserl and the university's world-renowned mathematician, David Hilbert. As Husserl took up his duties at Göttingen, however, he abandoned his mathematical studies with growing confidence that his new theory of inquiry in the human sciences would gain wide acceptance from mainstream philosophy. During the sixteen years of his tenure at Göttingen, Husserl targeted especially for acceptance the school of neo-Kantian scholarship found in the works of Paul Natorp, Heinrich Rickert, and Ernst Cassirer.

One of Husserl's first interests in neo-Kantian scholarship dealt with Kant's (1965, A106f) explanations of transcendental psychology as the experience of "transcendental apperception." Along with Kant (*see* Scruton 1982, 57), Husserl noticed that there is a "gap" between our *sense* that we are conscious of something, and our knowledge of *what* we are consciously aware. Husserl intended to address this gap as "the problem of constitution." He meant *specifically* the constitution of subjective self-knowledge of objectively real things—but only as such things are predicated with apodictic evidence during one's use and application of an idealizing logic of calculus. Beginning around 1913, the problem of our constitution of an object in awareness presented the "central point of view" for the universal function of mental life. This point of view is expressed throughout Husserl's (1982, §86) developing philosophy as the "quintessence" of the human spirit when knowing something actually real and objectively true. Furthermore, "this point of view of function [i.e., of acting in spirit and reason] is the central one for phenomenology; the investigations radiating from it suitably comprise the whole phenomenological sphere, and finally *all* phenomenological analyses."

Husserl (1977, 57f) later argued that traditional psychology could describe the empirical manifestations of a transcendental unity of apperception—while the methodology of his *Investigations* could be used to clarify the subject's method of "ideation" for those same manifestations. During our typical experiences of apperception, an ideation "pictures" the relative "pole of direction" for constituting activities in a logic of calculus; and thereby, the pure Ego sees in the living present and orients constitutive life toward what is already intended as an ideal outcome in conscious awareness. Yet there is no mention here of the method of constitution for a synthesized unity in Kant's sense of transcendental psychology. It was not until Husserl's (1964c, 31) Paris lectures in 1929, when he turned to his modification of Descartes's method of reflecting on apodictic evidence within a transcendental logic of calculus, that he gives the hint of an intentional method for the constitution of a unity of apperception: Transcendental consciousness is *my* consciousness, where "all that exists for me exists…as the intentional objectivity of my *cogitationes* [i.e., of my own subjective cognitive acts]." One's *cogitationes* of contingent judgments and valuations indeed operate within a transcendental logic of calculus for synthesizing a unity of apperception for symbolic representations of objective reality.

Husserl's work in the 1920s makes an important connection for clarifications of our methods of consciousness-formation between Descartes's way of reflection, Kant's transcendental unity of apperception, and Brentano's act psychology. This connection is perhaps first represented in Husserl's theories of consciousness by his references to a universal human agency within an active mental life. During typical activities of consciousness-formation, our peculiar human spirit of intentional choice and affective motivation is played out in pure subjectivity as the experience of psychic being—wherein by apperception we know that we are indeed conscious of something. Husserl (1964c, 31) explains in his 1929 Paris lectures that a characteristic of ordinary mental life is the intention to actualize a unity of apperception that is constituted with apodictic certainty. These lectures provide an introduction to Husserl's (1973b) *Cartesian Meditations*, which was published two years later.

In this latter work, Husserl not only presents Brentano's act psychology as *entrée* into clarifications of the constitution of a transcendental unity of apperception, but he also articulates his clarification of Descartes's approach to the purely subjective character of constitution in the transcendental register. That is to say, he presents Descartes's (now parenthesized) method of reflection on the *being* and *doing* of pure subjectivity for Brentano's (now parenthesized) act psychology of transcendental subjectivity. Husserl uses his own genetic phenomenology of intentionality in order to reveal the objects that are acted upon by universal *cogitationes* in order to be consciously aware of something. These steps reveal Husserl's transcendental theory of method as arising from "the case of a pure 'internal psychology'" (Husserl 1973b, §20)—the "case" that leads him into principles of transcendental phenomenology.

One is reminded that Husserl (1977, 179) referred to a similarly subjective "internal psychology" at the conclusion of his 1925 lectures on the essence of psychology as a human science. One is reminded, as well, that during the later development of his philosophy, Husserl (1970, §69) prescribed the phenomenological-psychological reduction as praxis for a parallel transcendental phenomenological psychology that would bracket all non-psychic irreality in mental life—thus leaving in isolation the intentional object in its pure and transcendental representations for a genetic phenomenology of world-consciousness. Even though a phenomenological psychology in the transcendental register that he called for throughout the years was never realized, Husserl began working as early as 1905 in Göttingen on a propadeutic regressive phenomenology of our day-to-day experiences with both universal objects in pure consciousness and universal mental acts in pure psychology.

However, the direction that Husserl was to take during his investigations of our constructed world of intentional acts and constituted objects was importantly shaped by Georg Misch's (1930) analysis of a widespread misunderstanding between Husserl's treatment of transcendental subjectivity—clarified in part as the experience of our natural attitude—and the so-called lived experience of natural things that form the basis of Wilhelm Dilthey's human science of personal existence. (*see* Bruzina 1995, *xii*) Husserl (Welton 2000, 228) wrote to Misch (who in 1917 had succeeded Husserl's post at Göttingen) to say that he had always enjoyed a longstanding "'inner commonality' [*innere Gemeinsamkeit*]" with Dilthey's theories of the "objectifications of life"—meaning, with Dilthey's implicit representations of a transcendental ego. While describing the psychic lived experience of intentional sense formations for objectified things, Husserl (1977) fondly relates in 1925 the beginning of his involvement with Dilthey's philosophy:

> Brentano was never willing to recognize [the methodology of the *Investigations*] as the mature execution of his idea [of phenomenognosis]; he then, secluding himself in his own intellectual circle, refused to go along in the new directions, quite differently from Dilthey who recei-

ved the *Logical Investigations* with great joy and saw in them a first concrete execution of his [1894] *"Ideen zu einer beschreibenden und zergliedernden Psychologie"* [*Ideas Concerning a Descriptive and Analytical Psychology*], even though they had arisen without any relation to his writings…. Dilthey always laid the greatest weight upon this coincidence of our investigations, in spite of essentially different points of departure, and in his old age he took up [questions of psychic life and its methods] once again with sheer youthful enthusiasm in his investigations in the theory of the sociocultural sciences…. The result was the last and most beautiful of his writings on this subject—from which he was unfortunately taken by death. (pp. 24-5)

Husserl's best-known reference to Dilthey's work comes in 1911 during the Göttingen years with his article, "Philosophy as a Rigorous Science." On Heinrich Rickert's invitation, Husserl (1965a, 71-174) was attempting here to resolve misunderstandings about his studies vis-à-vis dogmatic tendencies of theory construction in mainstream German philosophy. Philosophical praxis, Husserl believed, should enable discovery and surprise, not doctrinal narrow-mindedness. In this article, co-edited by Husserl and published in the first edition of Rickert's journal *Logos*, the schools of "naturalism" and "historicism" were targeted in order to carve out a distinctive role for his theory of inquiry. McCormick (1981, 162) writes that the first dogmatic tendency seen by Husserl in human science "is the error of reducing all phenomena to physical states, whereas the second is the error of reducing all phenomena to particulars." Rather than grasping such reductions as praxis, "phenomenology is proposed as a philosophical inquiry into the invariant (and therefore nonhistoricist) features of pure (and therefore nonphysical) consciousness."

Husserl's (1965a, 98f) exemplar of dogmatic naturalism in his *Logos* article is the modern psychology that began with John Locke's seventeenth-century empiricism. Psychological phenomena are reduced in naturalistic accounts to those physical states that could be represented factually by such expressions as "perception," "imagination," or "recollection." Today, these terms would include "neural networks" and "hemispheric brain functions." That's all well and good as normative practice, according to Husserl, as long as a descriptive language and the positing of facts enjoy a prior validity for the concepts they represent in theory construction. This argument means, for example, that perception of something physical does not simply *happen* to the psychological subject. Instead, the psychological subject intentionally perceives something physical. However, this intention is self-evidently not a physical thing itself. Sometimes naturalized psychological phenomena cannot be properly reduced to their immediate physical expressions, since their presented typology or morphology might be the result of an enduring development of the empirical manifestations of an underlying a-historical or non-physical matter—such as a matter of religious experience, or the experience of cognitive development. Husserl argues in his *Logos* article that a phenomenological analysis could provide concept validity in terms of indisputable arguments about the essential meaning of any human-scientific concept whatsoever.

It makes no sense, for example, to speak of the empirical manifestations of a "spiritual being" such as a wish, yearning, or hope that animates our lives. Yet such "soulish" things of human experience have an intelligible structure of meaning and motivation that endures in daily life. The question of how something that is not originally given empirically, but could still be apperceived and experienced as actually real, is a fundamental question for Husserl's (1980a, §41) mature philosophy. On this question hinges "the opposition between *nature* and the *world of the spirit*, between the natural sciences and the human sciences.... Our entire worldview is determined, essentially and fundamentally, by the clarity of these distinctions." Ricoeur (1967, 37) describes these distinctions in Husserl's work as correlated parts of our constructions of reality for Nature in its totality *(die gesamte Realität)*. All that we could posit as natural in this totality is constituted as either "material nature" or "psychic nature." Here, Ricoeur (p. 51) mentions that Husserl understands the sense of "soul," not merely as a metaphysical abstraction, but also as an order of reality construction for what is essentially material or psychic. Despite the importance to phenomenological psychology of Husserl's use of the terms "spirit" and "soul," a brief explanation of them might suffice:

When we intend to constitute something actually real in conscious awareness, we are self-evidently motivated to do so. We might then reach out for something, listen for something, taste something, wonder about something, and so on. These subjective acts of autonomy and agency are conceptually opposed to our involuntary organic responses to physical stimuli; and indeed, they represent our spirit-life of intentionality as we make sentient contact with something "external" in our lives. Thus motivated to take some action, we construct a pre-conceptual state of essences and relationships for what we intend to constitute. When the regulating norm for this activity is to actualize the nature of things, such essential states could include a construction of reality for the intended-to thing as either material nature or psychic nature in the transcendental register. The material nature of something is typically constituted from the natural attitude as a concrete object amid the conceptual space of physical things—while the psychic nature of something is constituted as self-knowledge of that same object in one's naïve natural world.

Our self-knowledge of Nature is apodictic knowledge in the same sense that Descartes did not doubt that he doubted. The idea of Nature in its totality therefore encompasses all contingencies of an objective natural world. The psychic nature of knowledge in this totality is not a concrete thing of empirical dimensions, but rather is experienced as *my thoughts* with certainty that I am aware of something "natural." That *something* in the living present is an object of the mind that we intend to constitute as more or less of material nature or of psychic nature by means of a contingent transcendental logic of calculus. For example, we might see something but not know what it is, or we might imagine something but not have the skill or ability to express it. Usually, however, we constitute the nature of things with apodictic certainty along a polar continuum of irreality and actual reality within the bounds of what is determinable of Nature in its totality here and now. The entire constellation of reality construction represents the psychic order of constitutive life, while the experience of this order refers to activities of the human soul.

From the psychological attitude, Husserl's concept of the *soul* represents human intentionality at work in absolute consciousness—i.e., that part of pure consciousness delimited by our cognitions of truth and reality. Here, one's soul is experienced as the will of the psyche, which is the fundamental element of *motivation* in a logic of calculus for constituting both material and psychic nature. (*see* Husserl 1980a §56f) Generally speaking, the human soul is the intellectuality of the species during consciousness-formation. During our unreflective moments, the essence of one's soul is spontaneously seized upon as one's habitual norms of sentient *being*; that is to say, the norm for being self-consciously aware of something. We tend to grasp this pre-conceptual activity as a unity, which is then experience as *my* idea about that same thing. (*see* Husserl 1982, §83) When we think of the human soul in its non-theological sense, we usually speak of mental life from the natural attitude.

During the normal course of events, the essence of an *eidos* is grasped as either material nature or psychic nature, or some combination thereof within a psychic order of action. Husserl (1982, §83) points out that one's ideation of an intentional object exhibits "a series of modes of givenness" in pure subjectivity. Said givenness changes according to the "determinedness of the surroundings" during contingent constitutive activities. The psychic order of transcendental constitution typically demands both an essential idea as the content of conscious awareness, and a pregiven context or intentional form for intending to that idea with autonomy and agency. Our ordinary method of consciousness-formation in the transcendental register is to order and constitute an original idea in the midst of an environment of pre-existing sense and meaning—or else, an unconstituted idea is sometimes experienced as one's intuition into something immanent in the psychic order. (§3) Most generally, something said to be immanent is persistently "inside" a psychic order, such as a necessary before-and-after relationship, the mood of passivity, or one's will to construct reality. The experience of immanence, too, is part of the spirit-life of our human soul.

When a history of reality construction and ideation is approached in the manner of a natural science, looking perhaps for the presence of immutable laws of Nature, then the study lays claim to objectivity in order to explain the human sprit as a natural thing. Although the spirit-life of intentionality has not been reduced to a physical state as in naturalistic theories of psychological phenomena, the human spirit is nevertheless presented as a matter of fact in historicistic epistemologies according to the objective words (such as "wish") that are naïvely presumed to stand for historical events of subjective experience (such as *wishing*). Inquiry into the events of sprit-life that animate our every motive, mood, and action of *being* is often called "metaphysics." A history of the human spirit in accounts of the truth and reality of *being* is called a "metaphysical historicism." Husserl's (1965a, 122) exemplar of metaphysical historicism in his *Logos* article was Dilthey's anthropological philosophy of *Weltanschauung*—our general worldview toward objective "historical" truth and reality. *Weltanschauung* "can include every kind of social unity, ultimately the unity of the individual itself and also every kind of cultural formation."

The metaphysical historicism of Dilthey's *Weltanschauung* philosophy, Husserl (1965a, 122) writes, "takes its position in the factual sphere of the empirical life of the spirit." As represented by our accomplishments in the arts, religion, and technologies, according to Husserl, the empirical manifestations of human spirit-life enjoy a certain enduring historical character in presentations of continuous matters of fact. Manifestations, expressions, and references to that historical character could be studied according to its durability within individual experience, as well as within pervasive structures of social and cultural institutions. This is precisely the social-scientific domain for interpretations of factual matters that delimits the discipline of history. However, the construct validity for conclusions and terminologies grounded in an epistemology of metaphysical historicism is in question for scientific theories of empirical dimensions. Whatever is represented as factual in contemporary discourse by the word "wish," for example, might have been something called a "curse" in the past, and might be called a "hope" in the future.

Even so, whatever is meant by the lived experience of the event called "wishing" in historicistic accounts could be grasped as the metaphysical presupposition of a factual matter when given as a theoretical construct; and no doubt we could validate and know intuitively from our experiences of wishing what is meant and presupposed by the word "wish" as an objective thing. But the concept of a universal spirit-life of *wishing* amid a general historical worldview could not be validated by an empirical method of induction without presupposing an invariant "nature" of a wish for individuals and groups. Neither can the presuppositions of a worldview be observed empirically. Something as soulish as a wish or a worldview can only be apprehended by us within the horizon of metaphysics such that its existence goes without saying as a predicated matter of apodictic certainty—*before* it is ever grasped as a matter of fact in naïve historical records. From Husserl's (1965a, 126) a-historical perspective, metaphysical concepts can only be validated beginning with the phenomenological practice of reductions to the intuitive essences and ideas of our individual and communal spirit-life—including of course, such things for scientists and philosophers in their respective worldviews.

When Husserl came to this conclusion in his Göttingen years, he was not only beginning to take notice of problems relating to evidence and validation in the phenomenological method of reasoning, but he also wanted to incorporate in his nascent philosophy certain intuitive methods of concept formation given by the so-called School of Graz. This group was centered on the work of another of Brentano's former students, Alexius Meinong; and like Brentano, Meinong wanted to establish psychology as a separate discipline that would not contradict philosophical concepts of the mind or of human consciousness. Meinong set up a laboratory for experimental psychology in Graz, Austria in order to investigate the principle of intentionality as it might show itself during manifestations of empirical reality. He concluded that we *can* have in mind an object that does not exist empirically here and now, such as a "golden mountain," but that could nevertheless be represented contingently in thought and speech *as if* it were empirically real.

Meinong's "golden mountain" is constituted by means of a predicating calculus for apperceptions of elements that are already in one's memory of empirical things. Similarly perhaps, Descartes's expression of "I think" in its calculus is a contingent element for the empirical manifestations of "I am." During the psychic order of this sort of calculus, the pure Ego first posits a grouping of elements to be the object's empirical dimensions. Those dimensions are then retained and composed as elements of analogous qualities for a matter in categorial thought and speech. Here, the transition from irreality to actual reality occurs according to a transcendental logic for constructing empirical evidence for an eidetic affair of similar essences. Today, however, what is of concern for philosophers in this area of transcending analogies is to obtain objective knowledge of non-existing things that could be posited as empirically real by one's choice of word-meaning—rather than by one's choice of a contingent calculus of validated sense and meaning. (*see* Sainsbury 1995, 86-7) Controversy regarding the words that we use in order to refer to the irreality of non-empirical things was also prevalent during Husserl's Göttingen tenure.

When Husserl published the second edition of the *Logical Investigations* in 1913, he drafted a new preface for that work in order to clear up certain fundamental misunderstandings about his philosophy and its theoretical limits. Although the draft was not published in its entirety, Husserl (1975) made a point to say explicitly that his theory of inquiry is not in any way to be taken as merely an analysis of the formal logic of word-meanings:

> I shall attack right here the discussion of yet another misunderstanding that is again hard to comprehend—hard to comprehend for any one who knows the present work in its context. It appears to have become almost a slogan (especially since it has entered into the accounts intended for beginners) that phenomenology...[is] "a somewhat differentiated analysis of the meaning of words".... Whoever has read only the introduction (to the first edition [of the *Logical Investigations*]) and then some sizeable portions of the work must surely over and over again have hit upon the fact that phenomenology is spoken of in an incomparably broader area, that analyses are carried out...on many sorts of experience-types that [only] occasionally occur in connection with verbal phenomena. (pp. 49-50)

By the time that Husserl wrote the above passage, he had already formulated his theory of the phenomenological reduction in order to see the so-called sphere of immanence when one is conscious of something. The sphere of immanence is the "inner life" of absolute consciousness that is studied without any presuppositions that could be given by naïve concepts of linguistic representation, principles of formal logic, or empirically validated knowledge. Application of the phenomenological reduction in Husserl's work is the fundamental means of gaining access to the sphere of immanence in both pure and transcendental consciousness. "For this reason," Husserl (1982, §33) explains, "we shall, on most occasions, speak of *phenomenological reductions* (but also, with reference to their collective unity [as a method of reasoning regarding parts and wholes], we shall speak of *the* phenomenological reduction) and, accordingly, from an epistemological point of view [toward both *a priori* and contingent knowledge], we shall refer to transcendental reductions. It should be added that these terms and *all* our others must be understood exclusively in the senses that *our* expositions prescribe for them and not in any other which history or the terminological habits of the reader may suggest."

With his reductions of conscious awareness to its sphere of immanence, Husserl's methodology relies on Kant's (Allison 1983, 137f) philosophy to posit a unity of consciousness that requires that we have an everyday familiarity with absolute consciousness. In the tradition of Continental philosophy, Husserl means to indicate by "transcendental reductions" that his applications of the phenomenological method proper uncover knowledge of not only what we intend in absolute consciousness, but also what we *do* in the midst of contingent truth and reality—namely, think within the determinable bounds of pure consciousness in the transcendental register. Here, "pure consciousness" is how Husserl (1982, §33) refers "in a broadest sense" to the intentional structure of all possible mental activity and all possible objects that could be constituted by means of cognitions within a logic of calculus—where now, that logic could include any number of contingent calculi.

In order to apply the phenomenological reduction properly in any of its modes of praxis, however, and in order to withhold all presuppositions of sense, meaning, and certainty, a phenomenologist must first exercise the phenomenological *epoché*. Husserl's (1982, §31) use of the term "*epoché*" is derived from the Greek, ἐποχή, signifying one's withholding or suspension of judgments. In pre-Socratic Greek philosophy (Copleston 1985, 408-9), the *epoché* is a method of reasoning that relies upon one's doubting the judgments of others; and as a habitual norm of practice, doubting is a way of life for philosophical skeptics. Descartes also used the Greek *epoché*, according to Husserl (1982, §31), but only to begin his philosophical meditations—leading then to judgments that were intuitively grounded in pregiven conditions of apodictic certainty. Husserl on his part understands and accepts the Greek skeptic's use of the *epoché* as a non-empirical way of thinking, and does indeed disbelieve the validity of objective truth and reality as representing the *a priori* pure consciousness that is self-evident when judgments are made here and now.

Yet Husserl does not adopt the Greek *epoché* as an invariant mode of skepticism. Neither does he follow Descartes in using the *epoché* only at the beginning of reflections. Instead, the *epoché* is applied continuously as the means for suspending a *phenomenologist's* own prior belief in the existence and meaning of the active content of any judgment made by the *subject*. Making a judgment is an irreal matter of apodictic certainty, whereas *what* we judge to be actually real and true is a contingent matter of subjective experience. We are therefore less certain of the outcomes of our judgments than we are that we have indeed made a judgment. With this premise, the *epoché* is used throughout the entirety of Husserl's reductions to the essences of both the acts of judging and the contents of judgments; and with this practice, Husserl suspends all representations of objective truth and knowledge from his own judgments without rejecting such things in the constitutive life of another.

Exercising the *epoché* is Husserl's prescribed means of suspending a phenomenologist's naïve belief in contingent empirical reality. At the same time, no reasonable skeptic can doubt that the subject indeed grasps the sense and meaning of something when expressing self-knowledge of a state of affairs—even when that expression refers to purely subjective experience or to logically non-existent things. The phenomenological *epoché* and reduction represent together an orientation where presuppositions of validity for a given matter are put out of play for reflections on both an intentional object and any cognitive action taken upon that object here and now. In its essence under the *epoché*, the phenomenological reduction is a norm of practice in Husserl methodology that enables him to apprehend the apodictic character and eidetic structure of pure and transcendental consciousness. The phenomenological reduction thus provides neutral access to the immanent sphere and intentional activities of consciousness-formation. (*see* Husserl 1982, §50)

A Critique of Cognitions:
Rationale for the Phenomenological Reduction

There is a clear division between Husserl's norms of practice in the *Logical Investigations* and his later science of essences with its transcendental reduction and theory of method. Yet Husserl's (1973a, §43) phenomenoloigcal reflections have consistently been directed toward a constituted object and its correlated constitutive acts, all within a "relation of connections" that structures the complexity of pure human consciousness. In the pure subjectivity of this structure, a relationship of objects and acts represents an intentional construction of actual reality for things that matter to us individually and collectively. Things that matter universally include such irrealities as *ideas, sensibility,* and *understanding.* (Husserl 1970, §25) These things are contrasted in Husserl's fundamental ontology and epistemology of transcendental subjectivity with one's own ideas, one's own sensibility, and one's own understanding that exist contingently for each of us.

In Husserl's theory of inquiry during the 1930s, when the being-sense of something that matters as one's own is composed and constituted for an object in transcendental consciousness, its active idea could be traced back in regressive reflections to its irreal origins as an *eidos* in pure consciousness. That same *eidos* and its modifications could then be genetically retraced in constitutive experience—as a normative extension of sense (*Sinn*) from this genesis—to its presence in conscious awareness as an actually real objectivity of intersubjective significance. The subject's transcendental consciousness-of-something is reconstructed in this manner, and is thus clarified in sense and meaning just as it is lived in the contingent world of human co-existence.

But in 1906, Husserl (Nakhnikian 1964, xiii) underwent a crisis in confidence about his investigations into human consciousness. He was having doubts about both the importance of his phenomenological studies and the direction that this work might take in order to gain wider acceptance. And so, from April 26 to May 2, 1907, Husserl delivered five lectures to his students at Göttingen in order to introduce some of the ideas that would guide his work to the end of his days. His philosophy, in effect, was beginning its systematic turn from pure to transcendental phenomenology.

These lectures represent an important advance for phenomenological studies (and especially for phenomenological psychology), an advance that in practice had already begun at the conclusion of the first edition of the *Logical Investigations*. Husserl's emerging grasp of the phenomenological method proper as fundamental human experience was centered in the *Investigations* on universal objects in order to clarify the very essence of what is produced in pure consciousness. In the 1907 spring lectures for an overview of his new approach, however, Husserl (1964b, 1) signaled his intention that from then on his theory of inquiry was also to be a study of the cognitive methods of reduction in the tradition of Continental Philosophy—since "the critique of cognition" by reductions to essential judgments and valuations is the method used by Hegel and Kant during their own reflections on human consciousness.

A critique of cognitions is used throughout Husserl's succeeding investigations in order to apply the phenomenological method of reduction to essences and relationships of essences, all within a unity of awareness here and now—but only with evidence that the subject could be knowingly conscious of parts and wholes. Hegel and Kant provide such evidence in their own studies; where by means of their cognitive methods of intuitive praxis, even while rejecting charges of mysticism (*see* Henrich 2003, 65), they both apply the method of eidetic *seeing* toward reduced elements of consciousness-formation. Husserl (1964b) outlines the following beginning steps for this application in his 1907 lectures on *The Idea of Phenomenology*:

1. Adopt the phenomenological attitude toward reflections *on* things just as they are presented, as opposed to one's "natural" thinking *about* things, such as we tend to do in empirical science and everyday life. (p. 1)

2. Abstract a phenomenological "field" of intentional experience with those things themselves, where cognitions in general are available for inferences and interpretations. (p. 2)

3. Develop instrumental means of practice for inferences and interpretations according to the methods of cognition that are seen within the abstracted phenomenological field. (pp. 2-5)

4. Reduce the phenomenological field to essences and relationships of essences in order to arrive at focus upon a grouping of elements that do not depend for their presence in consciousness on introspective psychological "feelings" or on the positing of pre-existing metaphysical absolutes. (pp. 5-7)

5. Meditatively "inspect" these grouped and correlated compositions in order to differentiate between what is seen as original unities of meaning and the cognitive action that occurs in order for those unities to reference the appearance of phenomenal reality. (pp. 8-12)

Husserl does not doubt that something posited as real is intended to be known *as* real, even if it could be logically refuted. Furthermore, when something is said to exist, it exists as an object of the mind for cognitive judgments and valuations. In *The Idea of Phenomenology*, Husserl (1964b) describes his approach for clarifying the phenomenon of human consciousness as partly a critique of cognitions that instrumentally employs a phenomenological realism for essential elements and universal ideas. By following this approach, Husserl indeed avoids psychologistic descriptions of real objects as realizing-acts during reductions of a unity of configuration. In the tradition of the Continental School, where a thesis is also a methodical way of proceeding, Husserl established in 1907 certain enduring norms for applying the universal phenomenological method of reduction as a radical practice of scientific reasoning.

Specifically, Husserl (1964b, 46) prescribes a rigorous practice for human science that must wait for meanings of a phenomenon to emerge from reduced levels of experience. Intended meanings emerge, not as restatements of pregiven matters in historical or cultural records, but as the result of a universal method in cognitive mental life for conferring meanings on objects. By employing the phenomenological reduction, Husserl (p. 53) also establishes the theoretical basis for his regressions to pre-existing intentional objects—where intentional objects are irreal temporal antecedents of phenomenal reality that must be built up by cognitions. "Cognition" means nothing more than the categorial way of expressing the formal concept of *knowing* when one is conscious of something, rather than any specific knowledge or skill that is acquired by or for such action. (p. 7) A phenomenological study of cognitive mental life is a study of our intentional experiences of *knowing* by means of one's judgments and valuations throughout the reduced levels of an eidetic structure of awareness.

In order to grasp the development and necessary modifications of Husserl's theory of inquiry beyond 1907, one perhaps needs to understand no more than the above five steps of reduction and their rationale as fundamental human experience during consciousness-formation. On the other hand, as one might suspect, if these rigorous practices are not well understood as generally guiding Husserl's studies, even the best students of his work might become lost in its procedures to solve philosophical problems of knowing the essence of things. One might then fail to notice that non-physiological consciousness occurs as the consequence of intentional cognitive action in reduced levels of our pre conceptual performances of *knowing*. In this light, Husserl (1964b, 1) is concerned with clarifying the praxis of *applied phenomenology* during our experiences with observations and interpretations of phenomenological data. Initiated by Kant as a purely mental (*geistige*) approach to inquiry, applied phenomenology is the scientific application of the universal phenomenological method of reasoning. (*see* Heidegger 1997, §4 and Husserl 1970, §28, §57; 1982, §76; 2001, §3)

In all of his publications and most of his manuscripts since 1906 that deal with the problem of human consciousness and its method of constitution, Husserl was consistent in presenting the following procedural style of reduction for applied phenomenology:

1. *Re-present* the natural attitude of the pure Ego toward a matter of interest under the phenomenological *epoché*, expressed in first-person terms of "I," "one," "me," "we," and "us" in its worldly horizon here and now.

2. *Observe* from the phenomenological attitude what could be seen as intentional experience within a field of constituted objects and constructed realities presented by another.

3. *Prescribe* eidetic inferences and reflective abstractions for reduced levels of the phenomenological field in order to see the elements and cognitive action directed in the living present toward realizing the essence of an original idea in thought and speech.

4. *Interpret* this same essence in terms of what the pure Ego, *I*, would necessarily experience in order to achieve consciousness of the original idea as a constituted objectivity in its eidetic structure of actual reality.

5. *Evaluate and Clarify* an experience of conscious awareness by reconstructing the constitutive life of the pure Ego in terms of the composed elements and cognitive action intended to fulfill *this* objectivity within *this* eidetic structure of reality according to *this* series of performances in ego-life.

With its "official" introduction to the philosophical community, Husserl (1982, §32) refers to applications of the phenomenological reduction under the *epoché* as together the practice of "bracketing" (*Einklammerung*)—as an act of epistemic exclusion—and then of "parenthesizing" (*Einschieben*)—as an act of ontic clarification—the sense and meaning of objects and acts expressed from the natural attitude. From the perspective of our natural attitude, we tend to believe as unquestionable matters of fact the reality and natural cause for everything seen to exist as material or psychic within an intentionally absolutized Nature. Husserl's (1970, §57) applied phenomenology eventually follows the neo-Kantian lead in making a "Copernican turn" from Hegel's phenomenology of historically given absolutes in order to achieve "once and for all a systematic transcendental philosophy…by means of a radical liberation from all scientific and pre-scientific traditions." For Husserl, the free human spirit of pure subjectivity is the center around which the phenomenal world is conceived according to the inherent will of the species. Husserl (1982, §32) is emphatic that applied phenomenology cannot be done properly from the natural attitude of theoretical reflection.

Applications of the phenomenological method of reduction imaginatively situate a phenomenologist's point of view "inside" the objectified and idealized appearance of a matter of fact given from the natural attitude—that is to say, within its eidetic structure. In order for conceptualizations to be thus inside the living-present depths of a constituted objectivity, elements of a matter of fact are imagined to be enclosed within their own eidetic spaces of essences. What is immediately present is the so-called residue of *a priori* pure consciousness that remains when necessary universals are, so to say, "decanted" for reflections by bracketing the presented and implied contingent elements of a particular *eidos*. Such contingencies are determinable only in *this* instance of the subject's use of the phenomenological method of reasoning in cognitive mental life. In anticipation of one's transcendental consciousness-of-something, *this* is the reduced region of pure subjectivity seen in phenomenological reflections without presuppositions as to its content here and now.

When positioning reflections on the subject's consciousness of something by bracketing its constructed and constituted appearance, Husserl is able to see an intentional object's irreal pre-existence under the *epoché*. As a method of scientific reasoning, Husserl's application of the phenomenological reduction obviates George Berkeley's warning in his 1710 *Principles of Human Know-*

ledge not to commit the error of *phenomenalism*. Berkeley (Grayling 1995) spells out the difference between seeing phenomenal things and his naïve notion of phenomenology as two levels of observation for something immediately present, where phenomenalism is an "existential trap" for empiricists:

> The phenomenal level concerns the things we encounter in ordinary experience—books and trees—while the phenomenological level concerns facts about sensory experience considered strictly from the viewpoint of the experiencer's apprehension of sensible qualities. Given this distinction...we can say that at the phenomenological level what are immediately perceived are colours and textures, while at the phenomenal level what are perceived are books and trees. The latter consists wholly of the former, and it is only if one disregards the distinction of levels that one might fall into the mistake of thinking [i.e., the mistake of phenomenalism] that when one perceives a book, one perceives redness and smoothness *and* a book, as if the book were something additional to the sensible qualities constituting it. (p. 515)

Husserl's phenomenological reductions and bracketing allow the conceptualization of *both* levels of experience in pure consciousness—the concrete actual appearance and the irreal sensible qualities of an object—to come into reflections simultaneously. Each bracketed level could also come into focus individually without excluding the other as an element within the total configuration and eidetic structure of conscious awareness. Those same reduced elements of anticipated appearance and intended sense could then be parenthesized for clarifications, along with their unity of configuration here and now. For example, imagine that the ordinary experience of phenomenological reduction occurs in your field of vision while driving a car. There are perceptions of things in your peripheral vision that cannot be ignored; but for the moment, attention is focused on (say) a pothole in the road ahead. When you express your attentive focus while driving you might speak of the pothole and of what that object means for your judgments and decisions, such as turning the car's wheels. You might then notice from your peripheral vision whether and when it is safe to do so.

In this case of the phenomenological method of reasoning, expressing your awareness of the pothole signifies your intentions in the living present, where your idea is (post-phenomenologically, actually and factually) to avoid the hazard, and simultaneously (pre-phenomenologically, irreally and ideally) to survive on the road ahead. This matter of reduction and bracketing points toward a transcendental logic of calculus for transitions from the irreal to the actual during a flow of reasoning from pre-conceptual to conceptual space. Thinking about turning the steering wheel is a practical cognitive activity within a calculus that posits causality to the perception of things according to the "internal relations" of time and place. In Husserl's applied phenomenology (Mulligan 1995, 211), this means according to the relations of *dependence and distance* (*Abstand* and *Abhängigkeit*) when making judgments and decisions about something in the world that is commonly talked about. When you anticipate turning the wheel, the pothole is cognitively "closer," as it were, to your attentive focus than any other possible element. Your immediate experience of cognitive mental life is thus centered here and now (i.e., reduced and bracketed) on avoiding the pothole ahead.

A phenomenologist of course has the same cognitive capabilities within a shared phenomenal world. But a phenomenologist in Husserl's tradition attempts to use our skills of apperceiving dependence and distance during the practice of a rigorous theory of inquiry—specifically, during the reduction of intentional experience for a clarification of the essence of an active idea in conscious awareness. It might be obvious from its rationale, and from the above example as well, that applying the phenomenological reduction as praxis depends for coherence mostly on the subject's rational comportment in cognitive mental life. The presumption that persons could think and act rationally is essential to Husserl's work. He also presumes that there is such a thing as subjective self-knowledge when someone purports to know something objective by rational means of inference. These notions in Husserl's methodology not only prove convenient for descriptions of intentional experience in reduced levels of consciousness-formation, but they also provide an epistemological basis for examinations of our communal interactions.

Even so, rational comportment is not inevitable for persons or groups. We are not always reasonable in our judgments, and seeing an all too human "non-reason" is commonplace in Husserl's work. Still, each of us could usually recognize what would count in theoretical discourse as rational comportment. The salient assumption in Husserl's system of reductions is that humans—whether knowingly and deliberately, or simply habitually—are capable of being rational in judgments and valuations when we choose to be. And when we *do* so choose, the intentionality of human consciousness stands out in relief for reflective descriptions and clarifying evaluations. For example, when we are working on a math problem or giving directions on how to get from here to there, our thinking seems to slow down as we gather our thoughts from reduced levels in order to make them coherent and understandable. We usually have a goal in mind when being rational, and we usually intend to realize that goal to some satisfaction for ourselves and for others.

Being rational means that in the spirit-life of intending something to *be* in thought and speech, we are purposefully committed to the constitution of an actually real object beginning from reduced levels of experience. Rational comportment is indeed a way of *being* and *doing* during the normal course of events that we humans willingly choose as free agents throughout cognitive mental life. When thinking rationally, a constructed reality represents in reflections the ontological consequence of a commitment to meaning in our judgments and valuations—where actually real things gain presence in thought and speech because we want to realize the potential of epistemological sense for this same pregiven meaning here and now. Our ability to think rationally in both reduced and realized levels of consciousness is an essential quality of what it means to be human, and Husserl intended in his developing philosophy to replicate this ability as a norm of scientific practice within a revolutionary theory of inquiry.

The Göttingen Years and a Question of Praxis

During Husserl's Göttingen years, the sheer excitement of grasping the phenomenological method of reasoning as scientific practice attracted a collection of devoted followers that came to be known as the "Göttingen Circle" of phenomenologists. What drew the Göttingen Circle together was its main interest in finding ways to describe the essences of things by means of further applications of the phenomenological reduction. The most outstanding members of the Circle were Fritz Kaufmann, Winthrop Bell, Roman Ingarden, Alexander Koyrè, Edith Stein, and Hedwig Conrad-Martius. Much of the worldwide momentum in popularity for Husserl's early philosophy could be traced back to the work of these members in expanding the scope of matters for phenomenological inquiry. The basic research text of the Circle was the *Logical Investigations*, and they took that work just as Husserl intended—namely, as the rudiments of his phenomenological methodology. Edith Stein (1986) tells of her first meeting with Husserl in 1903:

> Neither striking nor overwhelming, his external appearance was rather of an elegant professorial type. His height was average; his bearing, dignified; his head, handsome and impressive. His speech at once betrayed his Austrian birth…. His serene amiability also had something of old Vienna about it. He had just completed his fifty-fourth birthday….
>
> He called the new students to come up to him one by one. When he mentioned my name, he said…"How much of my work have you read?"
>
> "The *Logische Untersuchungen*." ["The *Logical Investigations*," I said.]
>
> "All of *Logische Untersuchungen*?" he asked me.
>
> "Volume Two—all of it."
>
> "All of Volume Two? Why, that's a heroic achievement!" he said, smiling. With that, I was accepted. (pp. 249-50)

Following publication of the *Investigations*, Husserl was immersed in a frenzy of activity in order to develop a systematic means of seeing such theoretical distinctions as he had already presented as necessary for conscious awareness. Husserl (1956) took on the specific tasks after 1904 of researching a detailed phenomenology of reason with regard to the concepts of perception, "abstract objectlessness" (i.e., the experience of pre-conceptual apprehension which was later dropped as an intentional method of reasoning), time, and the thing that presents itself from the natural attitude as an object of rational thought. Husserl had in mind the production of a three-part compilation of this research under the organizing title of *The Ideas* (*Ideen*). Mohanty (1995) reports that this compilation was to be presented as follows:

> Book I: A general introduction to phenomenology, consisting of fundamental methodological considerations and analysis of pure consciousness.

Book II: Problems connected with the relation of phenomenology to the natural sciences, to psychology and the human sciences, and to all a priori sciences [such as epistemology, ontology and metaphysics].

Book III: A concluding discussion of the ideas of philosophy grounded in phenomenology, as a precondition of all metaphysics. (p. 62)

Husserl tentatively outlined the course of research for Book I in the second volume of the *Investigations* with his four divisions of theoretical space seen in scientific concept-formation: (1) pre-scientific space, i.e., unreflective everyday life; (2) pure geometry, i.e., *a priori* spatial relations; (3) pure logic, i.e., applied geometry of ideal categories; and (4) the space of metaphysics, i.e., presuppositions of objective reality, apodictic certainty, and absolute truth. Intended perhaps as part of his "principle of all principles" for inquiry into the subject's ("peculiar") pre-conceptual experiences of consciousness-formation, intuition of essences (*Anschauung*) occurs in this same order in Husserl's (1982, §24 *et passim*) *Ideas I*. Following this sequence for reflective abstractions is indeed the praxis for making the turn from regressive to genetic phenomenology. The methodological status of geometrical and logical space was fairly well established in the *Investigations*, leaving only pre-scientific and metaphysical space to be later clarified in expressions of conscious awareness.

In pre-scientific space, phenomenologists are confronted exclusively with the "surface" appearances of things from the natural attitude. The correlated difference-and-identity of an object is already apperceived as the actually real semblance of something in symbolic representations and in predications of factual matters. This means that the inside plane of immanence for the pre-conceptual space of irreal objects is opaque for phenomenological descriptions and explanations. The pre-scientific space of actually real things is an unreduced horizon of post-phenomenological phenomena; and so, the eidetic structure of conscious awareness is not immediately revealed to reflections. Still, human intentionality cannot be manifested in pre-scientific space without immanent mental processes of sentient *being* and *doing*. (*see* Husserl 1982, §85) Indeed, the presence of our natural attitude itself implies that there is at least one intentional mental process that correlates reduced elements of sense and meaning as a unity of configuration in pre-scientific space.

Moreover, there are at least *two* phases for each single mental process of correlation within a system of apperceptions—*because* there are two kinds of action involved in this experience during the normal course of events. Throughout an immanent psychic order intended to achieve a teleological goal, we see first in genetic sequence the elements of an original idea that Husserl (1982, §85) calls the "Data" of specific sensual qualities, such as roughness. As a norm of practice, these elements are retained and composed by the subject in what Husserl refers to as meaningful categories of "*hyle*," such as texture. Derived from the Greek word for the cause of things, the term *hyle* is used by Husserl to reference the meanings of both real sensation and "phantom" impressions during pre-conceptual performances of stimulus response. Each sensory datum in its category of meaning is an element of the irreal object that is seized upon here and now—what Husserl sometimes refers to as the "*noema*," the immediate object of the mind.

At the start of the pure Ego's structuring of immanence in pure consciousness, grasping now that something is in the living present of constitutive life, a non-intentional (i.e., organic, physiological) modality of a mental process of perception presents an irreal object of singular sense for retention within a system of apperceptions. And then, rising up and out "noematically," a second but now intentional modality of this same process seizes upon further apperceptions of evidence, truth, and self-knowledge of that object. This latter phase requires contingent judgments and valuations in multiple psychological processes of cognitive action in the transcendental register—all the while aiming intuitively at realizing an intentional object as a phenomenon-as-a-whole in awareness. As a result of this universal method of consciousness-formation, an intentional object is constituted in pre-scientific space as one's consciousness of something from the natural attitude.

Human intentionality in the living present is the character and title of that aiming toward unity for any mental process whatsoever, no matter whether that process eventually succeeds or finally fails. According to Husserl's (1981, 22-4) comments in his 1927 *Encyclopaedia Britannica* article, he had in mind something like the pre-empirical manifestations of cognitive mental life that would fulfill our intentions for conscious awareness in pre-scientific space. The full potential for these manifestations is typically seen with the method of *epoché* as an experience of pure psychology within a regional ontology of empirical generalities. One of the first tasks for Husserl's (1982, §§411) emerging transcendental phenomenological philosophy was to propose the means by which a phenomenologist might be in the conceptual position to see the forces at play when the immanence of irreality, and the immediate experience of actual reality, are joined together as a "synthesis of identity" by mental processes of cognitive action. This expression implies that mental processes involving judgments and valuations modify the ultimate expression of conscious awareness in pre-scientific space.

Husserl (1964a, §16, §37) concluded around 1905 that consciousness in the plane of actual reality is the same consciousness as in the plane of irreality—excepting, of course, any possible organic changes in mentation during the flow of reasoning from pre-conceptual to conceptual space. There seemed therefore to be no need in 1913 for separate reductions of the immanent and actualized profiles of consciousness in pre-scientific space; since during the normal course of events, there is but one consciousness of a single object during a temporal succession of phases in constitutive life. There is a *oneness* about the experience of human consciousness that carries a unity of meaning within its enduring structure of essences and relationships of essences. This intentionally structured unity serves to correlate both planes or phases of irreality and actual reality for some one thing in apperceptive experience. When an intentional object is presented by the subject for reflections amid a structure of unity in conscious awareness, space *as such* is imaginatively varied during a phenomenologist's own intuition of essences by employing the method of bracketing—just as it is in one's ordinary experiences during apperceptions of parts and wholes. For rigorous reductions of parts/whole dependence and distance, a phenomenologist's thematic focus is relative to the intentional object when its essence has different profiles of irreality and actual reality.

What then was Husserl to make of *time* during the temporal succession and psychic order of changing profiles in a structure of pure consciousness? As a fundamental human experience, the phenomenological method proper indeed seems relative to moments of either irreality or actual reality. If so, then conscious awareness is time-relative and time-dependent. Reality *as such* is therefore time-contingent. Yet when the irreal episodes of perceiving and thinking are methodically bracketed into moments of a temporal unity in the sphere of immanence (i.e., here and now), those episodes represent what Husserl (1982, §19) calls the real things themselves in pre-conceptual activities of consciousness-formation. Such things are necessarily propadeutic to constituting the transcendental "nature of things" within the conceptual space of post-phenomenological phenomena. Two questions for Husserl's phenomenology of reason seem to follow: How is an irreal entity such as the idea of time objectified for representations by the reasoning subject in pre-conceptual space? And, how is our reasoning in space and time to be seen?

In the winter semester of 1904-1905, Husserl began a five-year series of lectures at Göttingen, entitled "Important Points from the Phenomenology and Theory of Knowledge," dealing in part with our constitution of objective time. Out of those lectures nearly twenty years later, Husserl's (1964a, §§2ff) practice of *seeing* intentional structures within genetic divisions of a unity of consciousness was developed as a series of reflections on our lived experience of *time* here and now. Brough (1981) reports that Husserl began his lectures in 1905 by discussing what is central for the phenomenological perspective in order to see the "internal time-consciousness" of intentional experience:

> He commences with the notion that time-consciousness exemplifies that most general structure of conscious life, intentionality. This assumed, the phenomenologist in performing the reduction of epoche attempts to describe...the manner in which temporal objects appear through the time-constituting acts which constitute them as experiences of temporal objectivity. (p. 272)

Exemplification is a primitive notion for its derivative terms used in Husserl's methodology. "To exemplify" means semantically to denominate an example that signifies a specimen or instance that is typical of a group, set, or category of which it forms a part or is a member. An example thus presents to reflections a repeatable and consistent spatial pattern for one's attention to a single thing. (*see* Welton 2000, 378f) From the phenomenological attitude, an exemplification directs attention toward the meaning of its representation within a plurality of expressions, where each example is correlated pre-conceptually to be an objectification of irreality. This pattern of the subject's attention shows itself as a temporal succession of cognitive action within the sphere of immanence for apperceptions of *sense*. However, an example that is presented in conceptual space as the subject's objectification of irreality might not be univocally expressed because of contingent factical matters such as culture, language, skill, and experience. Nevertheless, our consciousness of the meaning of any example points toward the spatiotemporal pattern of its attention as an intentional object in thought and speech. Despite all other possibilities, *this* is one's attentive focus here and now. Our grasp of spatiotemporality within the universal phenomenological method of reasoning exemplifies the most general structure of the living present—namely, intentionality.

There is an irreal (sometimes provisional or partial) core structure "inside," as it were, the overall flux and changing profiles of pure consciousness. This immanent structure of essences and their relationships is typically preserved in time-consciousness as the eidetic memory of a pattern of correlates in pre-conceptual experience. Said structure is then repeated and constructively followed as an intuitive trajectory for constituting a unity of being-sense for an intentional object. In order for the temporal pattern of an eidetic structure to be repeated and preserved in constitutive life, there must indeed be the memory of previous experience with an *eidos* that coincides with one's intentions in the living present. That is to say, there must be the retention of essential elements of the pregiven *eidos* from pre-conceptual performances to conceptual reasoning when we present that *eidos* by exemplification with all of its subsequent modifications. Our eidetic memory is the retention of a pattern of experience with an *eidos* amid the flux of pure consciousness—whatever one's contingent self-knowledge and understanding of that pattern happens to be here and now. Not every participating structure of the whole pattern is completely determined by the subject's memory of previous experience, however, since the temporal "spread" of an *eidos* is never met in spatial isolation during consciousness-formation. (Gurwitsch 1974, 87)

In the normal course of events, we adapt our natural attitude to a particular intellectual environment in which the active idea is now in play. We then accommodate and assimilate a new actual reality for something according to agreements with retained elements of its pregiven *eidos*—just as in pure mathematics new theorems may be generated from the old. In order for a temporal pattern of repetition and preservation to be constructed during consciousness-formation, there must be a carrying-over of retained elements of the *eidos* into the future. Husserl (1964a, §24) calls this intentional act (from the Latin, *protensio*) a "protension in recollection." He means that every "constitutive process is animated by [acts of] protention" that intercept (*auffangen*) the infinite givenness of the *eidos* in pre-conceptual space; and therefore, we tend to recollect only what we intend to carry over into the future. Only that retained part of an *eidos* which matters in the living-present profile of one's consciousness-of-something is held constant and preserved into actual reality. Expressions of the actual reality of our memories are thus usually incomplete *re*-collections of elements belonging to a finite phenomenological *eidos* in the midst of its contingent structures of awareness here and now.

Essential elements of an *eidos* are combined by acts of retention and protension when constituting an intentional object in conscious awareness. One's memories of irreal and actually real things co-exist simultaneously during this experience as correlates within the internal time-consciousness of our everyday reasoning and theoretical reflections. Later on, Husserl (1973a, 179) described the associative linkage of modes of reality in one's internal time-consciousness as being intuitively grounded by a unity of elements that is "passively constituted in advance, a unity in 'sub-consciousness.'" Such so-called passive associations of unity "rise up" in pre-conceptual performances in order to "vivify" previous experience as one's ordinary reproductive memory in rational comportment. In the 1913 *Ideas I* of his planned three-part treatise at Göttingen, Husserl's (1982, §§136ff) reflections on the rational comportment of humans generate his phenomenology of reason.

Husserl's own practice of reflecting on exemplifications of non-physiological consciousness was perhaps intended to be analogous with his sense of the phenomenological concept of *human reasoning*—which is, generally, acting out the noetics of cognitive mental life. The word "noetics" is derived from the Greek, *nóēsis*, meaning the operations of *nous*. Husserl adopts the term's Middle Platonic sense in his methodology, where *nous* is one's way of thinking intellectually as opposed to one's physical sensations, and where *nous* includes our "internal" intuition as well as our "external" discursive knowledge. Husserl's (1982, §145) use of the term "noetics" ("in the pregnant sense" of being fruitful for one's intentions) could be grasped as the potential for achieving conscious awareness by means of our cognitive judging- and valuing-acts. That is to say, something could gain presence in thought and speech by an operation of *nous*. As a correlate of the subject's cognitive action to be conscious of something, the presence of noetic structure represents intuitive evidence of *cause* to believe in the existence of whatever is achieved during consciousness-formation—when that achievement is indeed the consequence of one's own judgments and valuations. By an operaion of *nous*, we could each think and say, "Here's the reason I believe this is real and true."

Such so-called reason-as-evidence allows us to continue building up something in thoughts rationally during consciousness-formation, even as we reduce possibilities in a normative logic of calculus for some one thing to mean in actual reality what it is essentially intended to mean. Reason-as-evidence is treated in Husserl's (1982, §140) phenomenology of reason as the concept of *validation*, where either "possibility coincides with actuality" or else it does not. There are various necessary properties or attributes of an intentional object that are grasped by each of us in order for a cognitive correlation of reason to be achieved during constitutive life. Clarifications of these properties serve as Husserl's "theory of elements." An "element" is the way that Husserl seems to refer to what varies independently as a pre-conceptual or conceptual entity, but that is nevertheless necessary *in this instance* of non-physiological consciousness itself. One such element is an immediate sensory perception. Another might be represented by the concept of *belief*, or perhaps as a pre-conceptual relationship of similarity between things.

A cognitive correlate of reason is an intentionally unified grouping, combination, or composition of elements that finds sufficient evidence for its durability in constitutive life. Composed elements in this construction are dependent to a whole thought and immanent within representations of a constituted objectivity. Husserl's (Fink 1995, §4) transcendental theory of method for this correlating activity represents in practice a "mirroring" of the way we tend to experience his theory of elements in processes of noematic action. Rigorous reconstructions of the phenomenological method of this experience are meant to bring into reflections the immanent plane of the (fully correlated, now transcendental) phenomenon of conscious awareness. An intentional object in the transcendental register is presented for evaluations of its method of constitution as the end product of cognitive action that is experienced as peculiarly *my own*. Said action joins ("synthesizes") Husserl's theory of elements with his transcendental theory of method for reflections on the intentional act-object structure of human consciousness.

The idea of an intentional synthesis of elements, objects, and acts in the living-present profile of conscious awareness is "the central one" for Husserl's (1982, §86f) pure phenomenology and pure psychology. Indeed, this synthesis represents the subject's intuitive experience of self-knowledge here and now. The question of genesis for this and similar experiences runs throughout Husserl's work, both as to the origins of consciousness-formation when it shows itself for reflections, and as to the proper beginnings for rigorous practices of phenomenological inquiry. It is a vital principle for applications of the *epoché*, for example, that a constituted phenomenon has sense and meaning only within the bounds that it was originally synthesized by another. Since the subject presents an epistemology of intentional experience that is grasped as one's own "legitimating source of cognitions," a so-called foundational criterion of objective knowledge is not to be seen in Husserl's work.

For instance, unlike Freud's (1959b, 98) foundational metapsychology of the unconscious that "produces effects…that finally penetrate to consciousness," a previously realized state in Husserl's theory of consciousness could intentionally "pass away" in one's internal time-consciousness of habitual comportment in pre-scientific space. Perhaps the predominant force in human psychic life is one's habitual patterns of consciousness-formation, which may or may not coincide with Freud's descriptions of the unconscious during any single moment of expression. In Husserl's transcendental phenomenology, whatever is prior to constitutive life in the living present must be intentionally retained in eidetic memory as pre-existing in order for it to have its affects on operations of *nous* here and now. Yet despite such differences in conceptualization, Husserl was continually frustrated by what he saw to be a lack of mainstream understanding that his phenomenological methodology represented a radical departure from those of foundational human science.

Husserl's praxis is indeed easily misunderstood when approached as traditional orthodoxy. For the most part Husserl not only presents his clarifications of the phenomenological method proper from the phenomenological attitude, but he also tends to present his key concepts and practices from this perspective as well. For the most part, too, his methodology articulates our subjective expressions of universal norms for grasping an original idea, and then of bringing that idea to fruition as actually real in thought and speech. Husserl always cared how elements of sense and meaning are established in pre-conceptual and pre-linguistic performances, although much of his terminology for one's mind being "busied" with such things tends to be vague and provisional. Husserl's initial descriptions of elements seem to be intended to give practitioners of applied phenomenology something to grasp intuitively as an idea being played out in constitutive life. His terminology, Husserl (1982) explains, then becomes further detailed and delimiting as that original idea becomes more explicit in rigorous reflections:

> Therefore we can only count on definitive terminologies at a very advanced stage of development…. It is an error and basically absurd to apply extrinsic and formal criteria of a logic of terminology to scientific expositions which are just emerging and to demand terminologies of the sort which fix the concluding results…at the beginning. For the beginning, any expression is good…. Clarity does not exclude a certain halo of indeterminateness. Its further determinations or clarifications is precisely the further task…. [Those who] demand "definitions" as in the "exact" sciences or who believe that they can easily get along in a non-intuitive scientific thinking and thereby advance phenomenology with phenomenological concepts acquired from rough analyses of a couple of examples and which they assume to be fixed, are but beginners who have not yet even grasped the essence of [applied] phenomenology and the [fundamental] method essentially and necessarily required of it. (§84)

Despite the above sentiment, Husserl (1982, xxii) claims that his early definitive use of the term "idea" follows Kant's concept of *idea* as a synthesis of *a priori* and contingent elements that have no basis in the everyday world. According to this "supremely important concept," ideas are the means by which we think in categories that have no existence outside the immanence of mental life. When we objectify an idea, it is then experienced in its finite "thing-appearance" rather than in its noumenal quality of seemingly infinite givenness. (*see* Husserl 1964a, §43) Even so, Husserl (1973a, §38) believed that Kant treated the synthesis of elements in consciousness as an objective phenomenon rather than as an intentional method of consciousness-formation— and thus failed to notice that reasoning in irreal categories is an operation of *nous* in pure subjectivity. One must therefore, Husserl (1970, §30) insisted, "quite systematically inquire back into those things taken for granted" by Kant as principles of transcendental psychology. Husserl intended to disclose by *epoché* the "unspoken ground" of Kant's concept of *idea* that is "hidden in respect to its deeper mediating functions" of synthesis during consciousness-formation. That is to say, he intended to clarify Kant's concepts of *idea* and *synthesis* as a pre-conceptual relationship of essences in pure psychology.

Husserl (1970, §30) concluded that Kant's account of *idea* and *synthesis* incorporated Kant's own fear and skepticism toward anything that is *not* "a part of nature." The *eidos* of *idea* in Kant's "mythical concept-formation" is described by Husserl as the intentionality of "mental being in its absolute ultimate peculiarity and of that which has come to be in and through the mind." Yet since Kant's did not refute "the inadequacy of the psychology of his day" that posited an empirical "nature" of the noumenal qualities of an idea, his explanation of human reasoning during synthesis displays an "opaqueness of the distinction between transcendental subjectivity and soul." (§31) Husserl mentioned that it was not an error for Kant's methodology to "pass through psychology" in order to reveal everyday life as the lived experience of transcendental consciousness; but in doing so, Kant unknowingly "naturalized" the human mind and mental life—parenthesized in psychic life respectively as our human soul of autonomy and agency, and as our motivating spirit that pre-exists in pure reason—as a psychology that displays no inherent intentionality for human reasoning to exist at all.

Husserl nevertheless followed Kant's practice of passing through psychology in order to reveal the transcendental structures of pure consciousness. The *eidos* of *synthesis* is lived by each of us within these structures as an immanent logic of calculus when making the judgments necessary to achieve self-evident knowledge of something here and now. (*see* Husserl 1973a, §89) More fundamentally, Husserl's clarification of Kant's concept of *synthesis* discloses the universal phenomenological method of synthesis for a rational affective unity in conscious awareness. By implication of the correlation of objects and acts in the transcendental register, the *eidos* of *synthesis* is seen in Husserl's theory of method as the way we achieve consciousness of an intentional object by cognitive acts of transcendence. Furthermore, Husserl refers to Kant's idea of synthesis as the *eidos* of the methodic practice for clarifying his theory of elements in the transcendental register. The contingent quality of Kant's concept of *synthesis* represents the experience of transcendental consciousness as itself an aesthetic matter from the natural attitude. (*see* pp. 351-64)

The Early Freiburg Years and a Question of the Transcendental

Perhaps in response to his lectures on a phenomenologically modified Kantian philosophy, Husserl was called to the University of Freiburg *im Breisgau* in 1916 to replace Heinrich Rickert as chairman of its philosophy department. Despite Husserl's attempts at collaboration, Rickert was by then a leading neo-Kantian opponent of Husserl's Göttingen phenomenology. During the next twelve years, Husserl tried to resolve mainstream doubts as to his various philosophical positions by clarifying further the phenomenological method of reasoning as fundamental human experience. Husserl advanced this effort by formalizing phenomenological methodology—as applied phenomenology in the Continental tradition—to be a way of mirroring in *praxis* the methods of rational thinking seen in norms of scientific practice. In Husserl's applied phenomenology at Freiburg during the 1920s, rational human comportment is seen to be intentional in whatever transcendency of expression it might appear. "In this way," Husserl (1973a, §8) writes, "a *transcendence of sense* clings to every particular apperception" when one is consciously aware of something.

In 1916, however, Germany was still at war, and Husserl was suffering deeply the recent combat death of his son at Verdun. Most of Husserl's student assistants at Freiburg were on the front lines or interned, leaving "The Master" (Stein 1986, 254) largely to his own devices for revising a manuscript for Book II of the *Ideas*. Husserl believed only three years before that his three-part *Ideas* would revolutionize human science by theoretically grounding it within a systematic phenomenological philosophy of transcendental idealism. Now that promise seemed not so certain. Although Husserl never completed Book II of the *Ideas*, he continued to update it throughout his Freiburg tenure with his ongoing reflections regarding the transcendental constitution of our natural world. Unfinished sections of his manuscript that discussed the metaphysical presuppositions that provide the conceptual foundations of naïve philosophical and scientific practices were finally published posthumously as Book III of the *Ideas*. (Husserl 1980b)

Husserl intended during his years at Freiburg to give transcendental phenomenology its own voice of self-evidence in scientific discourse; and with this intention, his work advanced phenomenological philosophy by giving it a new goal to reach by rigorous application of the phenomenological method proper. Whether we take "method" to mean one's ordinary way of going about achieving something, Husserl believed, or whether such ways are formalized in a scientific methodology, a method *as such* always has something at least implicitly to be aimed at for its conclusions. The aim of Husserl's theory of inquiry since 1913 has been partly to clarify the role of metaphysics in providing immanent conditions of transcendence for every philosophy and science. And so, in Husserl's early Freiburg years, parenthesizing metaphysical presuppositions as presentational objects was to be a theoretical goal of his studies in the transcendental register. Husserl proposed that metaphysical presuppositions and their accompaning certainties are constituted in consciousness similarly as any other intentional object. This direction is consistent with norms first set down in Husserl's (2001) *Logical Investigations*:

> Its task is to pin down and to test the untested, for the most part not even noticed, yet very significant metaphysical presuppositions are, e.g., that an external world exists, that it is spread out in space and time, its space being, as regards its mathematical character, three-dimensional and Euclidean, and its time a one-dimensional rectilinear manifold; that all process is subject to the causal principle, etc. These presuppositions, all to be found in the framework of Aristotle's First Philosophy, are at present ranked under the quite unsuitable rubric of 'epistemology' [rather than metaphysics]. (p. 16)

Generally speaking with regard to psychic life among the *a priori* horizons, in epistemology we *know* something with adequate evidence while in metaphysics we *presume* something on good grounds. When Husserl refers to metaphysics he means those things of experience that cannot be verified by empirical methods—such things, for example, as the human spirit of choosing to construct the reality for a science of material nature. Positing the true nature of things on good grounds implies that the methods of natural scientists correlate knowledge with value in the horizon of metaphysics. When striving for "good" natural science by building upon this correlate, we are typically motivated in pure psychology to act with self-responsibility for moral and ethical conduct in formal methodologies. However, we cannot verify the

Good that begins and sustains with certainty any natural-scientific inquiry by its own rational means of inference; we can only speculate and presuppose qualities of the Good when evaluating our claims to objective knowledge.

Speculations, presuppositions, and certainties of what is good, true, or even real underlie the study of metaphysical experience, yet they do not rise to the level of attention in naïve scientific practices—they simply go without saying in our theoretical judgments. Tito (1990) noticed that in all three books of the *Ideas*, Husserl described metaphysical properties of scientific discourse as denoting either necessary presuppositions or mere speculations:

> On the one hand, he means by metaphysical [those] claims that concern true Being, genuine value, genuine knowledge, and so forth, claims that are based on descriptive analyses [of necessary presuppositions]. On the other hand, he uses the term in a pejorative sense to refer to claims that are but speculative portrayals of those ultimate dimensions of the world and experience—in other words, to refer to speculation [in scientific epistemologies] as opposed to descriptions [of metaphysical principles pertaining to Being, value, knowledge, and so forth]. (p. xxxvi)

Much of Husserl's early research at Freiburg was directed toward the metaphysical presuppositions of naturalism and historicism, the issues outlined in his 1911 *Logos* article for radicalizing practices of theory construction in the human sciences. Husserl's growing familiarity with Dilthey's naturalistic metaphysics surely brought much to bear on his own thinking toward the ultimate goals of transcendental phenomenology philosophy. In the "Dilthey-Husserl Correspondence" between these philosophers, Husserl (1981, 205) acknowledged, "there are no serious differences whatsoever between us." Indeed, Husserl (1980a, §§49f) intended sometime during his tenure at Freiburg to parenthesize the essence of Dilthey's *Weltanschauungen* (= universal elements of a natural worldview) as the lived experience of constituting consciousness of one's naïve natural world. But in order to do so, his philosophy required a transcendental turn in its methodology. Partly in response to this need, Husserl enacted a modification of his *praxis* that "involved 'suspension' of our natural attitude toward the world…in order to uncover the peculiar act-object structure" of transcendental subjectivity. (Moran 2000, 173)

Husserl intended to clarify the phenomenon of transcendence within the spatiotemporal structure of the natural world—meaning, within the intentionally embodied structure of ordered space and time that goes without saying as a metaphysical presupposition. The nature of things is naïvely presumed to exist within this structure, but without adequate evidence in immediate experience for believing so. The transcendental turn in Husserl's philosophy began with his reflective meditations on the mental life of pure consciousness—*before* our metaphysical presuppositions of space and time could be constituted and expressed as matters of fact or mere speculation in the transcendental register. Given as presentational objects, however, metaphysical presuppositions are not psychological phenomena. Instead, they are objects of the mind that are acted upon as essential elements during the ordinary structuring of transcendental consciousness. Moran (2000) seems to imply that Husserl started the transcendental turn in his methodology by bracketing any naïve metaphysical presuppositions about objective psychological phenomena that already existed as primitive assumptions in his system of ego-life:

> Husserl was beginning to have misgivings about the extent to which his new phenomenology could…be equated with the descriptive psychology of the Brentano-Stumpf variety. Though he had overcome psychologism [by separating objects and acts in pure phenomenology], Husserl came to believe that he was still trapped in a kind of naturalism regarding the nature of mental acts [as objective phenomena versus subjective operations of *nous*]…. Husserl was also uncomfortable with the way he had ignored the role of the ego as synthesising our mental experiences into a single life in the *Logical Investigations*, because he had followed Brentano's more or less Humean treatment of the ego as a bundle of [discrete acts versus the pure Ego's psychosubjectivity when constructing an eidetic unity]…. Now he recognised the need to focus on the unifying factor [of synthesis] underlying the temporal spread of consciousness. (pp. 136-8)

Husserl's turn from descriptions of our awareness of static irreal objects in the *Investigations* to an implicit genetic phenomenology of the pure Ego's constitution of a unified transcendental consciousness in *Ideas I*—that was intended later to include our metaphysical correlations of objectivity and certainty in *Ideas II*—did not sit well with his closest disciples from the Göttingen Circle. Stein (1986) explains why:

> The *Logisich Untersuchungen* had caused a sensation primarily because it appeared to be a radical departure from critical idealism which had a Kantian and neo-Kantian stamp. It was considered a "new scholasticism" because it turned attention away from the "subject" and toward "things" themselves…. However, the *Ideas* included some expressions which sounded very much as though their Master wished to return to idealism. Nor could his oral interpretation dispel our misgivings. It was the beginning of that development which led Husserl to see, more and more, in what he called "transcendental idealism" (which was not to be confused with the transcendental idealism of the Kantian schools) the actual nucleus of his philosophy and to devote all his energies to its establishment. This was a path on which, to his sorrow as well as their own, his earlier Göttingen students could not follow him. (p. 250)

A key feature of Husserl's new direction was that with the transcendental turn comes the "Copernican turn." Here, the main focus of rigorous reductions is on the pure subjectivity of intentional experience versus the constituted things themselves. Perhaps for the Göttingen Circle, this practice fixes the universal phenomenological method of reasoning in the realm of relative possibilities rather than with certain knowledge. Presented as his theory of the transcendental register of pure consciousness, the main idea of Husserl's (1982, §§47f) early transcendental idealism could be described this way: There is a self-evident (ontological and epistemological) difference between pre-existing phenomena of irreality that have no appearances that could be immediately perceived, and those same phenomena during apperceptions of objective reality. Elements of the former are transcended as individual things of sense and meaning in order to construct and constitute awareness of the latter. For example, we could see a flushed face and measure a substantially increased heart rate, but we cannot directly observe any correlated objective phenomenon of anger in the experiencing actor. Yet something we call "anger" nevertheless exists as an intelligible object for each of us in the transcendental register, and this same object could be described as actually real according to its phenomenal manifestations of a flushed face, and so on.

What we intend to see and experience usually *seems* the same to us precisely as we have come to expect, or else we perceive a difference based upon a lack of semblance. The negative reaction of the Göttingen Circle to Husserl's new approach might be an example of this latter experience. More generally, however, the semblance of a phenomenon refers to the transcended sense of a deeper-lying meaning that exists simultaneously with its phenomenal manifestations. We tend to apperceive immediate appearances as idealizations of the semblance of irreal things; and in this way, we transcend the simple sensation and solipsistic sense of something in pure consciousness. We complete these acts of transcendence so as to constitute the object of conscious awareness to be actually real in the world of common semblance. We usually think about both the pure and transcendental registers of consciousness as without question one and the same—although it is intuitively self-evident, for instance, that a flushed face and an increased heart rate do not by themselves signify *anger* as a concept for scientific epistemologies. Neither do these things necessarily mean that we are angry. What then does allow a phenomenon such as anger to be seen with certainty as actually real in ordinary experience and theoretical reflections? What are the "good grounds" of human experience for such presuppositions in the world of common semblance?

The constitution of idealized and objectified things is the underlying theme for reflections in *Ideas II*. Out of the thinking that went into this work prior to 1929, Husserl's transcendental-phenomenological idealism arose. The various *entrées* for Husserl's (1980a, Epilogue, 416) reflections in Book II are the metaphysical presuppositions that typically go unquestioned in the natural attitude. Yet evaluations of the constitution of a transcendental object do not begin from the phenomenological attitude toward a purely metaphysical presence in thought and speech. Instead, Husserl's practices in the transcendental register begin with that object as given from the natural attitude of the pure Ego, with all of its constructions of actual reality and pre-conceptions of causality already in place. From the perspective of our natural attitude, a transcendental object enjoys the apodictic certainty of existence according to a metaphysical presupposition of its true nature. At the beginning of propadeutic reflections on a constituted objectivity, potentials for expressions of (epistemological) sense, (ontological) meaning, and (metaphysical) certitude have already been intentionally modified during pre-conceptual performances.

Why would clarifications of the subject's transcendental consciousness of something start with an intentional object's presented material or psychic "nature," rather than with its ontology of meaning or epistemology of self-knowledge? Husserl (1970, 305f) perhaps reasons that a metaphysical Nature is not grasped as "natural" in ordinary experience. There are no spatiotemporal coordinates or a beginning and end to an absolutized and idealized Nature from the natural attitude. Instead, the essence of Nature is an "ordering principle" in constitutive life that "is independent of all worldly, all natural being." (Husserl 1982, §51) The nature of things is a correlate of consciousness in the natural attitude, not its cause. Our naïve attitude toward the nature of things is thus already bracketed for the moment when we reflect on metaphysical phenomena of human spirit- and corporeal-life experienced by *me myself*—such as our presuppositions of universal wants and needs. This moment is enough within the circle of transcendence, however, to provide methodological *entrée* into the immanent sphere of transcendental consciousness.

As a motivated belief or opinion about what matters here and now, a metaphysically correlated object is constituted in the cognitive mental life of our so-called inner-psychological intuition. When we reflect on something that is presumed to matter to *me myself*, or on what goes without saying for everyone, an intentional object stands out *affectively* from a field of potential realities in pure consciousness. In this manner of comportment, we are "being psychological" in judgments and valuations; and for this reason, Husserl (1980a, Epilogue, 416) approached the problem of constitution of a metaphysically presented object in *Ideas II* by "passing through" the pure psychology of affective inner experience. The term "affective inner experience" refers in this context to our intentional ways of genetic constitution throughout the *a priori* and contingent horizons. Since subjective ways of constitution are circumscribed by Husserl's system of ego-life, the subject's affective inner experience points toward the full complexity of constitutive life for the pure Ego.

In Husserl's (1982, §§35f) systematic "egology," the pure Ego is the *I* of Descartes's "I am" in the transcendental register, and the *I* of "I think" within intentional mental processes of pure psychology. Various modalities of ego-life co-exist during consciousness-formation as contingent possibilities for being aware of something with adequate evidence or on otherwise good grounds. The pure Ego cannot be reduced to any other sense or meaning in this system, for it is purely one's potential for subjective experience. Indeed, before intentional experience is ever reoriented to the transcendental register, the pure Ego is a solipsistic entity that exists only for itself in pure consciousness. However, the pure Ego (representing the essence of what it means to be subjectively human) typically "awakens" to its immediate surroundings and becomes attentive to the possibilities of experiencing whatever is *Other* to its solipsistic existence. In this same moment, an intentional object comes into ontic being as a possible correlate of the universal life-world, and the potential for its transcendence presents itself in pure subjectivity.

The bifurcated transcendental ego is now the subject to an object that is at hand for judgments and valuations in the living present. Here, the pure Ego's pre-conceptual performance of consciousness-formation is a subjective experience of transcendence, and "the thing itself" in pure consciousness is an anticipated subject-predicate-object state of affairs. Although a pre-conceptual intentional object with its metaphysical presuppositions of causality and certainty may not be fully formed as the actually real thing we encounter in ordinary experience, all of the necessary pregiven and at-hand elements are nevertheless in place, retained in pure subjectivity in order to fulfill one's intentions of thinking about something actually real in the world that is commonly talked about. We usually intend to constitute the presence of actually real things that matter for *me myself* such that their appearances could go without saying "for everyone" in eidetic structures of common semblance. Such structures typically include retained elements of the pre-existing life-world of naturalized things that one has already experienced in the world for us all. Husserl (1980a, Epilogue, 416) describes the fulfillment of this intention as actualizing what is already "accessible" in pure subjectivity. Something that pre-exists affectively in solipsistic subjectivity provides ontic validity of its accessibility for transcendental subjectivity—even when we don't know *why* something pregiven sometimes goes without saying.

Our Natural Attitude and the Life-World

Husserl (1982, §§27f) noticed that when the pure Ego attends to its surroundings in pure subjectivity, that space of experience becomes the active field of sense perceptions and affects. From our solipsistic perspective on what is other than the *I* of the apodictic *I am*, whatever we perceive as different from one's subjective place in time exists affectively and cognitively in valuations as *Other* to the pure Ego. (§39) In this construction, the *eidos* of *the world for us all* is typically pregiven in transcendental constitutive life as a presumption of "alien" otherness, and then grasped as the otherness of common semblance to the pure Ego's enduring solipsistic subjectivity: "I wouldn't do that myself, it's completely alien to my nature." Or else: "Yes, that's just like me." The essence of worldly common semblance points toward one's ongoing grasp of Nature in its totality, including its contingent dimensions of actual reality and presuppositions of causality correlated in the horizon of metaphysics. The irreal relationship between solipsism and the otherness of things thus pre-exists for constituting awareness of an object during life-world experiences here and now. A potential for the coming-into-being of our natural attitude is therefore already at hand at the origins of transcendental consciousness.

When I naïvely reflect on what is believed to be an instance of objective reality, pre-conceptual structures of otherness come into my solipsistic world. At this genesis of consciousness-formation in the transcendental register, there is now a potential for constituting self-knowledge of the genuine and true nature of an intentional object—along with the potential for moral and ethical comportment directed toward objectified things in general. (see Husserl 1973b, §64) By means of a predicating injunction correlated in the horizon of metaphysics, one could then construct a matter of fact for something "natural" that goes without saying in the world of common semblance. Apodictic certainty of the nature of things is intuitively grounded in the metaphysics of an absolute Nature, and a pregiven sense of the natural world is ordered in thought and speech according to this principle. As Husserl (1982, §28) phrases it, "Living along naturally, I live continually in this fundamental form of 'active' ['*aktuellen*'] living" from the natural perspective. The natural attitude is indeed the transcendental ego's perspective on the objective reality and absolute truth of both a physical and spiritual nature. (*see* Cairns 1976, 83)

An exemplary expression of the natural attitude is one's absolute belief in the material nature of transcendental objects, which are not by themselves absolute things of (say) Goodness, Beauty or Truth. Rather, transcendental objects are intentionally constituted things, but constituted in order and in such a fashion that we could experience them as rational affective unities within a pre-conceived world of absolute qualities. (*see* Husserl 1980a, Epilogue, 416) From our normative natural attitude toward judgments and valuations, our corporeal-life as an animate organism, and our spirit-life as a human surrounded by an actively living Nature, are both preconstituted as elements of affective significance—meaning, elements of body and soul *matter immanently* to the pure Ego for correlations in the transcendental register. Metaphysical presuppositions of an actively living Nature are of an absolute life that goes without saying in the seemingly infiite world of human co-existence, although we know intuitively that nothing in nature is solely of one's own making. Still, one's life as a whole is intended and anticipated to be constituted as an intersubjective objectivity within this same space of experience, since the absolute quality of *my life* now matters to the pure Ego.

Husserl (1980a, p. 417n1; 2006, p. 93) had not yet arrived at this conclusion at Göttingen, however, mainly because he had not completed his transcendental theory of consciousness in light of our intersubjective relationships of empathy (*Einfülung*). Intersubjective structures of a natural worldview are built up in empathy during one's life-span cognitive development in a world of common semblance—specifically, the common semblance of transcendental objects. Indeed, Husserl (1982, §51) worried in 1913 that "in the face of our philosophical poverty… we are vainly fatiguing ourselves" when trying to grasp the sense of things given from the natural atttude. Yet by 1929, Husserl (1980a, §62 note 1) had parenthesized the metaphysics of Dilthey's *Weltanschauung* philosophy, reducing its essence to our presuppositions about the so-called nature of human spirit-life. Anticipated in his 1911 *Logos* article, Husserl (1965a, 122) calls these presuppositions the "spiritual formation" for living a natural worldview. In its fullest extension, consciousness-formation of a metaphysical Nature includes worldview correlates for all potential forms of natural life, including the form that is constructed in empathy to be *my own*.

Elements of transcendental consciousness that are given to constitutive life with the conferred meaning of one's corporeal-life and spirit-life in the natural world represent our achievements of transcending the essence of life itself in solipsistic subjectivity. The essence of life itself pre-exist as pregiven during consciousness-formation, and typically agrees (by correlation) with our presuppositions of an absolute First Cause for actually real things. All through the *a priori* horizons here and now, when the essence of living naturally is, so to say, "breathed" into the pure Ego of apodictic certainty that *I am*, the transcendental ego then comes into (ontic) being as the (epistemic) manifestations of one's life in the (metaphysically) naturalized world. The transcendental ego represents the way that each of us is in one's naïve natural world that is "disclosed to me in my own life." (Husserl 1980a, Epilogue, 416-17) *My own life* is pre-conceived to endure as a substrate of the *eidos* of *pure life*.

Although he refers in various publications and manuscripts to conjugates of human life (such as ego-life and life-processes, versus a philosophy of life), Husserl (1980a, pp. 405ff) seems to mention only in the Epilogue to *Ideas II* his concept of *pure life* as the metaphysical ground of our intersubjective life-world—the universal world of real life wherein the transcendental ego lives out its presuppositions and natural attitude toward transcendental objects. Husserl's (1970, §28f) notion of the life-world was clarified during his later years as an unexpressed presupposition of "Kantian thinking," and published incomplete and posthumously in *The Crisis of European Sciences*. Husserl (Gurwitsch 1966, 397-447) cautions in his 1935 Vienna lecture that theoretical "occurrences" of the life-world (*Lebenswelt*), such as its mathematization or experimental manipulations, are not to be taken as evidence of either its genesis or its constitutive ground in the human world itself (*Urwelt*). Neither do expressions of an epistemology of the life-world provide evidence of more than the metaphysics of our ordinary world of day-to-day experience (*Umwelt*).

The *Urwelt* and the *Umwelt* represent eidetic categories of our predicated "cultural world" in Husserl's *Lebenswelt* philosophy. (*see* Gurwitsch 1974, 17f) These forms contain grouped elements of the *eidos* of being-in-the-world during consciousness-formation of our intersubjective relationships and communal interactions. Pure life, corporeal-life, and spirit-life are the pertinent irreducible distinctions for transcendental consciousness in *Ideas II*, and the life-world is a correlate of these fundamental categories in the horizon of metaphysics. I mention this now in order to emphasize that Husserl seems to intend his use of the term "life-world" to be an epistemological distinction of the *sense* of our natural attitude itself, just as it is experienced by each of us as something that goes without saying—but *not* as an ontic clarification of the theoretical ground for anything that could be constituted as actually real in conscious awareness. This is germane since much of today's phenomenological psychology relies upon an epistemology of the life-world as evidence of mental life in the transcendental register, perhaps without recognizing that Husserl is speaking in terms of metaphysics and not psychology.

Husserl on his part avoided the problem of mental life and psychological experience in the transcendental register during his early Freiburg years, mostly by focusing on the ego-function of the "self" from the natural attitude toward issues of sprit and reason. One's self, Husserl (1973a, §92) suggests, represents a "*fundamental concept of a region* [of consciousness that] *cannot be converted into another by variation*." One's self is the idea and totality of all that is *my own* in the transcendental register, and cannot be otherwise in the world that is commonly talked about. The *eidos* of *self* is experienced as an object from the natural attitude; and by implication, one's self is an expression of the spirit-life of living naturally. Yet this is not a direct reference to the psychological ego. As a norm of practice in the *Ideen*, the pure Ego is epistemologically bifurcated in Husserl's "knowledge-complex" into modes of (1) its irreducible existence as a living entity of subjective experience, and (2) its naïve existence in the life-world as the transcendental ego. Yet Husserl never mentions a similarly bifurcated (3) psychological ego of spirit-life. Book I is concerned with psychology as a regional ontology for eidetic inquiry, not with our psychological ego-life. In Book II, the psychological ego is only implicitly represented by the "psychological ego-idea" that "leads [reflections]…into the sphere of immanence" for a transcendental object. (Husserl, 1980a, 128-39)

Perhaps by way of explaining a lack of reference to the psychological ego in the *Ideen*, Husserl (1973b, §11) mentions in 1930 that the psychological ego does not usually appear in object-oriented phenomenology. More specifically, the psychological ego does not appear as a presentational object under the *epoché* of our natural attitude. Expressions of the natural attitude point toward a position-taking "attentional formation" on an intentional object by the transcendental ego. (Husserl 1982, §92) The psychological ego does not appear as an epistemological distinction in the life-world because we do not grasp the natural existence of the pure Ego's psychosubjectivity as something objective. From the natural attitude, one pays attention instead to *me* as an objective thing, or to *my self* as its objectified correlate. In methodological terms, there is no directly observable psychosubjectivity in the life-world, since all psychic acts are already completed in the *a priori* and contingent horizons. Consequently, there is no valid construct of a psychological ego that is directly experienced in either the *Urwelt* or the *Umwelt*. Furthermore, without engaging our naïve metaphysical presuppositions and naturalized epistemologies about psychic life, there is no psychological ego to be seen and described solely in reflections on what is called in theoretical discourse, "*the* life-world."

Only with Husserl's genetic reconstruction of fulfilled intentionality, as an act psychology in Brentano's sense, does the psychological ego come to the fore in phenomenological reflections. Throughout the unity of Husserl's system of ego-life, the pure Ego is the apodictic *I am* of *a priori* experience. The transcendental ego is the contingent "*I am* a natural being." But the psychological ego is neither of these. The ego-life of the psyche is, "I act in cognitive mental life just as *I am* in pure subjectivity." Following the transcendental turn from solipsism to our intersubjective relationships, the ego-life of psychosubjectivity is, "I act as being in the world that is commonly talked about." Husserl (Fink 1995, 164) explains that the psychological ego acts in the transcendental register of pure psychology as the agency of the transcendental ego's natural attitude by manifesting the will and autonomy of the psyche in transcendental consciousness. When the psyche and its intentional acts are transcended in accordance with one's natural perspective toward the objectifications of sprit-life, the pure Ego's psychosubjectivity is seen in reflections as the subject's naïve expressions of mental life here and now.

In genetic phenomenology, the subject's consciousness-of-something is reconstructed and clarified in the precise temporal order as it is constituted from pre-predicative to predicative experience throughout a flow of reasoning from pre-conceptual to conceptual space. (*see* Husserl, 1973a, §54) In the midst of this order during consciousness-formation, one's psychic life typically gains presence as an object with the same essence of pure life as our spirit-life and corporeal-life are constituted in the natural world. We could then speak from the natural attitude of one's mind, spirit, and body as objective things co-existing with other objective things—instead of (more precisely) a synthetical unity that has already been transcended and elapsed in pure subjectivity. Every material phenomenon in the natural world is a correlate of the region of reality given by the transcendental ego, and we make that correlate actually real with psychological processes of objectifying-acts. A fulfilled correlate is then usually referred to as a constituted "objectivity" in Husserl's (1982, §87) theory of consciousness. Sometimes Husserl (§145) calls the essence of an objectivity its *noema*—meaning, the immediate object of *nous* in "rational concatenations" of elements during a psychic order of constitution.

Yet Husserl's early transcendental idealism lacked demonstrations of our methods for bringing deeper lying essences in pre-conceptual performances to the surface of immediate predicative experience. Only then, it seemed, could pre-existing irrealities be met in reflections with evidence that they truly exist in one's naïve natural world. It could indeed be seen in applied phenomenology that elements of an intentional object have already been composed for some matter when that object is presented as a rational affective unity in thought and speech. Yet Husserl cannot experience any intuitive reason-as-evidence for an actually real object according to his cognitive operations of *nous* under the *epoché*—as he would do with his habitual judgments within his own worldly horizon of material things. That is to say, as Husserl would do from the natural attitude. From his phenomenological attitude, Husserl (1982, §18) sees instead, "'ideas,' 'essences,' [and] 'cognition of essences,' [that] are denied by empiricism." "But to judge rationally or scientifically about things," Husserl continues, "signifies to conform *to the things themselves* or to go from words and opinions [given by the transcendental ego] back to the things themselves [given by the pure Ego], to consult them in their self-givenness [as *my own* by another] and to set aside all prejudices alien to them." (§19)

The phenomenological subject would not typically say, for example, "Noon is an abstracted interval within a collection of twelve equal temporal moments of infinite possible regression, whose reality is constructed to be the actual hour when the sun passes the local meridian." While all of this might be the case in theoretical reflections, the *eidos* of *noon* is experienced generally and naturally in spontaneous thought and speech as "the time" when something occurs—such as both hands of the clock being straight up, or as the occasion for lunch. The expression "twelve equal temporal moments" does not enter into accounts of ordinary experience with the object of *nous* we call "noon." Still, each of us in our natural attitude notices that most things *do* occur regularly within a particular succession of before-and-after moments. The idea of noticing a temporal sequence represents Husserl's (1964a, §§8f) phenomenological *eidos* for his theory of internal time-consciousness, where our intentionality regarding spatiotemporal relationships is revealed to reflections.

Even so, how is a phenomenologist to see a relationship of ideas and essences as things themselves necessary for conscious awareness when given from the natural attitude? There can be no prior judgments under the *epoché* as to cause for the presence of an actually real object, since such cause must still be determined with epistemological and ontological evidence. All that Husserl could initially infer with the method of *epoché* is that a constituted objectivity exists in consciousness here and now with reason and evidence as the consequence of the subject's intentions to make it so. Given this intention, when a phenomenologist wants to reduce something to its pre-existing essence as an object of *nous*, one could imagine that correlations of sense and meaning have already been carried out on an *eidos* by mental acts in pure psychology.

For example, upon reflection of a presented belief in the duality of mind and body (in the sense given from Descartes's natural attitude toward thinking and being), there exists no straightforward evidence of actual reality for this belief, and therefore no implied validation of its matter of factualness. We cannot directly experience our body as something fundamental; we can only think *about* the body as a transcendental object of corporeal properties. This holds as well for grasping the mind as one's spiritual ownness during psychological experiences of (say) willing, feeling, and acting. Nevertheless, predication of a duality for corporeal- and spirit-life transcends their common essence of pure life. This kind of transcendence is ordinarily accomplished by our use of intentional acts of "non-reason" during pre-conceptual performances of consciousness-formation. (*see* Husserl 1982, §145)

With an intentional act of non-reason, constitution proceeds in the conceptual space of our natural attitude without benefit of immediate reason-as-evidence for necessary elements—just as Descartes's algegraic meditations on thinking and existence proceed without direct evidence of an "evil demon." In this example of Descartes's predicative experience, acts of transcendence by non-reason disclose to reflections the co-presence of his objectifications of the preconceived ideas of both an irreal mind of psychological significance and a biological body of organic substance. Each of these ideas already existed in his eidetic memory as differentiated states of pre-predicative experience with the essence of life itself. Husserl (1981, 238f) describes the pre-existence of corporeal-life in a 1931 manuscript as the experience of one's body during its functioning as the kinaesthetic "center point" (*Stillkinaesthese*), or "null-point" (*Null-Oder*) of ordinary consciousness-formation. As a correlate of the pure Ego's *a priori* experiences, this pre-conceptual center provides a spatiotemporal orientation in the living present for the essence of pure life in the world that is commonly talked about.

Directed by this orientation in one's naïve natural world, a state of pre-existence for pure life is typically apperceived during relationships of empathy as either the physical reality of corporeal existence or as the extra-physical reality of spiritual existence. Stein (2000, 1) advises that clarifications of empathetic relationships involve two necessary areas of investigation: the first refers to "causality and motivation—operating together within one sentient subject with a sensuous-mental essence. The second investigation broadens the consideration from [solipsistic] isolated sentient individual to [intersubjective] super-individual realities." The experience of empathy is the way in reason and non-reason that our corporeal- and spirit-life of solipsistic subjectivity enters into the intersubjective world of individual and communal interactions. The subject's presented self-knowledge of empathetic relationships represents one's natural attitude toward human co-existence.

Beginning from his Göttingen years, Husserl (1982, §145) makes use of our expressions of normative non-reason as *entrée* into a mutually constructed reality during empathetic relationships—including the non-reason given in passive relationships of linguistic empathy. (*see* Husserl 1970, 358-62) Applications of human non-reason find a place throughout Husserl's (1982, §70) reflections on the eidetic ontology of our natural attitude as his imaginative "feigning" ["*Fiktion*"] means of reduction. In a similar fashion, for example, Gazzaniga (1992, 121) naïvely feigns the "interpretive function" of brain networks when positing the natural reality of the mind. Feigning is a vital element of the universal phenomenological method of non-reason, and feigning is therefore a valid practice in Husserl's methodology—just as it is in every eidetic science and ordinary practice that makes use of a constructed symbolic order of sense for signifying references to a deeper lying order of meaning. Indeed, for all of us, feigning *as if* is a rational method of reality construction.

A phenomenologist is usually first presented with an objectivity given in rational thought and speech from the natural attitude. Rational thought implies by necessity a pre-existing matter of judgments and valuations in cognitive mental life—where elements of a pregiven *eidos* have already been retained in the constitutive life of transcendental subjectivity. As an operation of *nous*, those elements have been cognitively correlated with evidence of their existence within the horizon of one's worldly experiences and intersubjective relationships. When necessary elements of conscious awareness are composed as a rational affective unity with the appearance of common semblance in one's sociocultural surroundings, then a naïve *what-ness* represents the subject's intelligibility of an *eidos* in the transcendental register. Absent indications to the contrary, our achievements in cognitive mental life that constitute transcendental objectivities are presumed by Husserl (1982, §6) to mean what they are essentially intended to mean from the natural attitude, just as they are given as actually real and objectively true within a region of eidetic ontology.

Within its region of sense and meaning, an achievement of conscious awareness is documented by Husserl (1982, §§6-10) as an "eidetic affair-complex" for observations of its intentionally composed unity in thought and speech. Seen under the *epoché* in the transcendental register, consciousness-formation is typically directed by means of a logic of calculus for constructing an affair-complex for an object of actual reality and idealized dimensions. Because of this orientation, an affair-complex mirrors the pure Ego's transcendental logic and all contingent calculi for constituting awareness of something in one's naïve natural world. Despite all such pre-conceptual contingencies, potentially everything—every element, method, sense, and meaning—that is necessary for an intentional object to gain presence as one's transcendental consciousness of something is already at hand and pre-existing within an eidetic affair-complex. Clearly, a phenomenologist does not want to mask such things by one's own prior correlations of reason—hence Husserl's continual use of the *epoché* from solipsism to intersubjectivity.

Husserl (1982, §§98ff) also stresses that if immanent properties of an intentional object are to be seen in expressions of transcendental subjectivity, it is against a phenomenologist's interests to ignore or to discount any correlation of reason presented from the natural attitude. It serves no purpose of phenomenological inquiry—indeed it is "childishness" (*Kinderei*)—to be critical of the subject's naïve consciousness-of-something until its immanent qualities are clarified. Because of the intentional acts of another, a "central point of view" for intuitive evidence of actual reality has already been established from among a seemingly endless possibility of historical and imaginative perspectives. This view is that of the pure Ego in the transcendental register—the *I* within its finite horizon of potentialities for transcendental experience in both active and passive counterpart to its *Other*. According to a phenomenologist's intentions to disclose human reasoning and its consequences, there is no reason-as-evidence after the *epoché* to doubt the validity of this constructed view of things in the world that is commonly talked about.

Eidetic Affairness

A transcendental phenomenologist is neutral toward the appearance of an objectivity presented from the natural attitude. (*see* Husserl 1950, §8) A phenomenologist is neutral, however, only with regard to the givenness of an intentional object that provides methodological *entrée* for propaedeutic reductions to its distinctive elements and correlations within an eidetic affair-complex. All else is bracketed during clarifications of an active idea under the *epoché*. For example, the size of a shoe does not make it any more or less a shoe in reflections; and so, size is not necessary for grasping the eidetic structure and essence of *shoe* when presented as an idealized objectivity. Here, the *eidos* of *size* is rigorously set aside ("bracketed") within the reduced affair-complex for the subject's consciousness of *shoe*—since during the specific moment of a regressive phenomenological inquiry into the essence of *shoe*, size is not a salient element of the intentional object.

In order to recognize (literally, to *re*-cognize) the constitutive activities of another, a genetic phenomenologist actively pursues (i.e., "varies imaginatively") the intentional methods by which elements of an *eidos* must necessarily have been pregiven to thought and speech with reason and evidence. A phenomenologist then documents this transcended pregivenness in eidetic categories as the pure Ego's prior apprehension of bestowed sense. The contents of these categories are seen in regressive phenomenology to be grouped around a core "pure sense" of respectively the existential *I* and *Other*. This practice follows the pure Ego's internal time-consciousness and psychic order of constitution for essential elements of an intentional object. A composition of unity for these categories—presented to reflections as the subject's self-knowledge, belief, or opinion about a single idea—implies in Husserl's (1973a, §38) theory of empathy that its expression exists for observation as a consequence of the pure Ego's use of a transcendental logic of calculus. A logic of calculus for constituting the presence of an object in awareness with sense and meaning pre-exists in the living present as a norm of practice for the universal phenomenological method of reasoning.

That is to say (partly by way of explaining the implication of a transcendental logic in the phenomenological method proper), an eidetic affair-complex in the transcendental register is the intended outcome of an empathetic relationship between the subject who expresses a belief, knowledge, or opinion from the natural attitude, and the observing transcendental phenomenologist, or anyone else for that matter—*because* the subject intends and anticipates this state of affairs to be so when presenting such expressions within idealized dimensions of common semblance. Furthermore, we employ a logic of calculus for linguistic empathy in pre-conceptual cognitive mental life in order to express an idea's sensible meaning to one's self and to others. A "sensible meaning" is the idealized correlate of sense and meaning raised to the level of signification in conceptual space. (*see* Husserl 1982, §124) When oriented by the natural attitude, each of us habitually makes use of a norm of empathy during our spatiotemporal structuring of an eidetic affair-complex. One simple eidetic variation of a grouped ("$\oplus$") affair-complex for the pure Ego's intentional experience with the *eidos* of *shoe* could be given as follows when the subject presents the belief and calculus that, "this is my shoe":

$$((I=[[\text{myself}]\oplus[\{\text{here}\}\oplus\{\text{is}=\text{have/own mine}\}]])$$
$$\oplus(Other-[[\text{shoe}]\cup[\{\text{there}\}\oplus\{\text{is foot cover}\}]]))$$

Symbolic notation in Husserl's methodology provides the means for documentation of eidetic constructions, not the means for reflections on essential sense and meaning. For reflections on epistemology, the above terms document a group-theoretical syntactical concatenation of the elements for a unitary structure of *I* and *Other*. Ontologically, this structure represents an intentionally composed order of correlated sense and meaning for *what* the *eidos* of *shoe* is to the pure Ego, *I*, and *how* it is *Other*. As a normative calculus of transcendental logic, this concatenation represents and documents one's belief, opinion, or self-knowledge of something potentially whole within a particular arrangement of necessary elements. Here, a concatenation of elements is composed within contingent structures of an affair-complex in anticipation of its unity. Consequently, we believe and have an opinion about something when we seize elements of its *eidos* in rational concatenations—and reciprocally, we have already grasped the idea of something when we predicate a belief or opinion according to the transcendental logic of its constituent elements.

A concatenation of elements is intended by the pure Ego to achieve adequate sense and meaning for knowing but one thing according to a relationship of dependence and distance to another thing, such as the relationship of a part-to-a-part. This arrangement also includes any pertinent relationship of *otherness* between my own things and those things apperceived as *not* my own in the transcendental register. Arranging and modifying bestowed sense and conferred meaning with these intentions directed toward *I* and *Other* is what we do in cognitive mental life when achieving conscious awareness of something in one's personal lifeworld. (*see* Fink 1995, §11) These intentional arrangements and modifications are given to reflection as "expressible constructs" within a transcendental logic of calculus for a unity of configuration. During the pure Ego's performances in its bifurcated role of the "phenomenologizing ego" of transcendental world-constitution (§11.a), we tend to experience a vague affective grasping of the semblance of something irreal when arranging and modifying sense and meaning within a pre-linguistic and pre-conceptual eidetic affair-complex—all this so that the appearance of a transcendental object could be situated in the world for us all.

The Later Freiburg Years and a Question of Renewal

Anticipating a unity of sense and meaning is the lived experience of our motivation in spirit-life to reach out from the immediate perception of things in order to construct the actual reality for an intentional object. During the composition of an eidetic affair-complex, the psychological ego responds to this motivation in pure psychology with transcending acts throughout the course of consciousness-formation. The phenomenon of conscious awareness and its eidetic structures of intentional experience—including the constitutive action of the psychological ego in cognitive mental life—is to be characterized according to Husserl (1973a, §7) as "transcendental" in this sense of reaching out from necessary and essential beginnings. Husserl's tenure at the University of Freiburg could also be described as reaching out from such beginnings, and perhaps most of Husserl's reaching-out during his last years of academic duties was motivated by the influence of Freiburg's most famous student of phenomenological philosophy, Martin Heidegger.

When he replaced Heinrich Rickert as chairman in 1916, Husserl was among the most eminent philosophers of his day. Upon his arrival, Husserl called Edith Stein from Halle to aid him in the editing of his manuscripts at Freiburg; and a year later, Stein received a doctorate *summa cum laude* with her dissertation, *On the Problem of Empathy* (Stein 1989). Prior to Husserl's arrival, Heidegger had been Rickert's student in neo-Kantian philosophy as well as his academic assistant. In this capacity he obtained his "habilitation" certificate in order to begin teaching, although he had not yet done so. Husserl later retained him in that same role of assistant when Heidegger returned to the department in 1918 following a stint in military service. Stein (1986) recalls her first meeting with Heidegger at Husserl's Freiburg home:

> I liked Heidegger very much that evening. As long as there was no mention of philosophy, he was quiet and unassuming; but as soon as a philosophical question popped up he was very animated…. He had gotten his habilitation while Rickert was still there, and Husserl had taken him over [as assistant in academic duties] from his predecessor. Heidegger held his inaugural lecture only after Husserl was in Freiburg. It contained unmistakable digs at phenomenology. (p. 409)

But even so, Stein (1986) continues, "the Master" did not seem to notice Heidegger's early "digs" as anything of mounting significance, busy as he was in organizing his own uncertain future:

> [Husserl] had complained about being unable to make any headway with his work. He had made an outline of the second part of his *Ideen*…at the [same] time he wrote the first part in 1912. After that first part had appeared in 1913, he had been pressed to give priority to getting out a new edition of the *Logische Untersuchungen* since the old edition was out of print. Then had come the outbreak of the war, the death of his son Wolfgang, and the move to Freiburg. All of this had torn him from concentration on his work, and he had trouble finding his way back. He was unable to decipher the outline [for Book II of the *Ideas*] he had then written in pencil and in tiny shorthand; his vision was no longer good enough. (p. 409)

Also, the student body at Freiburg following the end of World War I showed a profound difference in philosophical interests than did Husserl's earlier students at Göttingen. There was a general feeling that Western civilization was in a severe decline that could only find its so-called renewal amid a more universal understanding of what it means to be human. For many, Husserl's work seemed to provide the only alternative for such renewal in opposition to the existential angst and spiritual questioning found in the philosophies of Nietzsche and Kierkegaard. Yet others greeted Husserl's emphasis on the eidetic analysis of pure consciousness as a failed scientific rationalism. Science has its limits, they argued, and one of those limits is its inability to explain what it means to be human. Husserl responded that phenomenological inquiry could instead revive a sense of purpose that had been lost in philosophy, and could moreover renew the ideals of the study of the spirit of humanity that was now in want of recovery in all the human sciences.

One recollects, for example, that Henri Poincaré (Sahakian 1968, 245), the brilliant mathematician and leading light of Positive philosophy in Husserl's early academic development, expressed that scientific theories represent a scientist's hope to arrive at coherent conclusions that might then benefit all of mankind. Husserl believed that a phenomenological theory of inquiry for uncovering the essence of spirit-life, such as with Poincaré's hope for his own theories, would provide moral and ethical support to the so-called exact (i.e., experimentally controlled and mathematized) sciences of growing popularity. In 1923, Husserl contributed an article entitled, "Renewal: Its Problem and Method" to the Japanese philosophical journal *Kaizo-La rekonstruyo* in his attempt to welcome that community of scholars to the ideals of European Enlightenment—along with a warning against the failure of Enlightenment's "surface rationalism." (*see* Natanson 1973, 167) We find in this article perhaps the best example of Husserl's (1981) pent up disgust with the prevailing intellectual and political environment of post-war Western civilization:

[We are] free-willing subjects who are actively engaged in our surrounding world, constantly involved in shaping it. Whether we want
to or not, whether it is right or wrong, we act in this way. Could we
not also act rationally? Do not rationality and efficiency stand within
our powers? The pessimists and the supporters of "*realpolitik*" will, of
course, protest that these are chimerical goals. If the idea of the individual shaping his personal life according to a life of reason is an un-
attainable ideal, then how are we supposed to undertake a similar task
for community life [*Gemeinschaftsleben*], national life, and indeed, for all
of Western mankind? (p. 326)

Husserl continues to say in his *Kaizo* article that natural science is rich
with data of facts that are meant to explain our surrounding world, and enjoys
an almost limitless technology for gathering more facts. But how can human
science aspire to a similar ideal level of rationality without likewise merely explaining the facts of the material world? The essence of human science for
Husserl is not to describe and explain the human condition as an epistemology of a factual nature. Instead, Husserl (1981, 326f) believes that human science is meant to investigate the human spirit of truth-seeking—the "pure logos"
of rationality—that supports individual achievements in the establishment and
explaining of intuitive "paradigms" of "spiritual reality." The radical difference in essences between the natural and human sciences self-evidently calls
for radical differences between their methodologies as well. Although the natural sciences already have intersubjective means of long-standing practices
for arriving at rational explanations of empirical reality, an intersubjective system of judgments according to universal norms of practice for truth-seeking
is missing for the human sciences. They therefore tend to be non-intuitive,
and are thus lacking in the human spirit of autonomy and agency.

Human science, Husserl (1981, 328) explains, is "hindered by naturalistic practices" from realizing its essence as a unified science of the human
spirit. He now intends to "bring us closer to the peculiar methodological character of what we have previously called the missing science for which our
[transcendental] analyses are striving." In his emerging transcendental theory
of method, Husserl describes our human spirit-life made worldly as an affectively motivated "self-contained life of consciousness" during intersubjective
relationships. Belonging to such relationships "are the distinctions of rational
and irrational [forms of connection for ego-subjects], of [one's spiritual ownness when] thinking, valuing, and willing 'rightly' or 'wrongly.'" (p. 329)
Husserl signals his intention in the *Kaizo* article to formulate a new science of
essences for what it means to be human—namely, a "*mathesis* of spirit and of
humanity" that would clarify the pure principles of the spirit-life of persons
and groups. The human spirit of transcendence by means of our judgments
and valuations is now to be mirrored in Husserl's applied phenomenology.

Husserl is perhaps referring here to his (Husserl 1982, §59; 2006, 195)
study of Leibnitz's monadic *mathesis universalis* (i.e., formal ontology) of logically self-sufficient truths. In order to see the dynamic spirit of intersubjectivity
(versus the solipsism of a passive state of pre-existence), presuppositions of

logical cause for manifestations of spirit-life are now to be bracketed by means of the transcendental *epoché*—just as *any* logic of natural induction is bracketed as ontological necessity in applied phenomenology. Sometime before 1929, Husserl subtitled the edited section in *Ideas I* where naïve presuppositions of logical cause within our normative judgments are excluded from principles of spirit-life as "The Norm of Phenomenology." (*see* Husserl 1982, §59 note 12) But not all transcendencies can be excluded, Husserl notes in this section, if anything is to be left of the transcendental register. Clearly, for instance, transcendental objects cannot be excluded from clarifications of unity in object-oriented phenomenology. Instead, reductive and genetic focus is to be on the norms of practice by which an *eidos* is transcended and then experienced contingently during empthetic relationships and communal interactions—rational or non-rational, right or wrong.

For Husserl (1973b, §44), the spirit-life of personal experience cannot be excluded from a complete investigation of transcendental consciousness. It follows that the transcendental register of pure psychology cannot be excluded as well. Husserl thus implicitly calls for a transcendental phenomenological psychology of the human soul made worldly in personal experience. Indeed, it is a norm of practice when adopting the phenomenological attitude toward personal things (such as one's "lived body") to see the day-to-day ego-life of the human spirit, just as it determines its own realities according to its own choices in pure psychology—all within its own naïve self-contained "monadic" life of conscious awareness. In the wake of a worldwide economic and political upheaval that followed the Great War, Husserl envisioned a heady future for transcendental phenomenology. This promise attracted a new group of students to Husserl's lectures at Freiburg: Hans-Georg Gadamer, Aron Gurwitsch, Ludwig Landgrebe, Alfred Schutz, Herbert Marcuse, and Eugen Fink all from Germany, along with Dorion Cairns and Marvin Farber from the United States. Each of these persons would become well known philosophers in their own right during the years ahead.

Consistent with the aims of his *Kaizo* article, Husserl began a series of lectures in 1923 in order to present his vision of a phenomenological movement of renewal in the human sciences. In the first of these lectures, entitled "First Philosophy," Husserl (1965b, §9) disclosed his plan to redeem "in a higher sense the truth of the radical subjectivism of the skeptical tradition"—meaning, he intended to uncover the norms of "transcendental subjectivism" in the phenomenological method proper. Husserl's ultimate purpose, it seems, was to apply those universal norms to the practice of transcendental *epoché* in the world that is commonly talked about. In effect, the Greek *epoché* was to be clarified as scientific praxis. (*see* Moran 2000, 148-52) The skeptic's lack of commitment to an assertion that could be opposed by another possible assertion carrying equal weight could itself provide a way of thinking for phenomenological reflections in the transcendental register. By taking the skeptic's radical point of view as *entrée* into deeper levels of what it means to be uncommitted in judgments, the intentional experience of *judging* might then stand out in relief under the transcendental *epoché* and reduction.

When objectified principles of logic are excluded by *epoché* as evidence of eidetic variation during judgments and valuations, what stands out in reflections is one's personal transcendental subjectivity of contingent experience—where all possible assertions are *not* weighted equally. In the moment of our constitution of an intentional object in the transcendental register, immediate apperception is privileged for asserting the actual reality of an *eidos* in one's naïve natural world. The so-called privileging attitude of transcendental subjectivity represents our will to seek the truth of matters in the midst of one's variable sociocultural surroundings. This universal attitude is indeed representative of human spirit-life during the construction of actual reality in the world of human co-existence—along with the contingent things that are seen to reside there. Under the transcendental *epoché*, when the transcendental ego privileges immediate apperception, a phenomenologist brackets any other pre-existence for the intentional object. What remains outside of these brackets of other eidetic elements includes the intentional object and the intentional acts of transcendental subjectivity.

Under the transcendental *epoché*, Husserl (1980a, §19) brackets all naïve predications of psychological phenomena by setting aside historical descriptions of both the intentional and non-intentional (psycho-physiological) acts of the mind. This practice is necessary for object-oriented reflections in the transcendental register, since such descriptions have already been correlated within the horizon of metaphysics to be culture-bound and naturalized prior to becoming fully conceived matters of fact. He also avoids any psychologistic tendencies for descriptions of the transcendental objects naïvely called "psychological phenomena" with this rigorous bracketing. Husserl (1977) once again takes up the issues of historicistic and psychologistic practices during his 1925 lectures on psychology:

> In the nineteenth century, psychology received a new, great, even splendid, impetus. The impulse came from leading German physiologists and physicists...and was especially expedited by the organizing power of Wundt. There sprang up a psychology intimately connected with natural science and especially with physiology, to which it was faithfully adapted as to the nature of its method. Indeed, psychology seemed actually to be on a par with exact physics.... (p. 2)

In this part of the lecture, Husserl describes some traditional norms for doing psychology as an objective science of nature. In order to clarify psychology as a discipline in the human sciences, he begins by employing the reduction of radical skepticism upon such norms as intentional *methods* of practice. In doing so, Husserl (1977) brackets any historical understanding of logical cause for what are in fact—through mathematical and experimental manipulations—the empirical manifestations of the *eidos* of *mental life*. These matters of fact typically stand as psychological phenomena in psychologistic descriptions of the nature of things, even though our presuppositions of either the logical or natural cause for the presence of these matters are self-evidently not psychological phenomena themselves:

And yet it could come to pass that a very radical skepticism could be directed against this psychology—surely successful in a certain manner—such as could never be directed against the exact science of nature [by their own methods of practice].... (p. 3)

Husserl (1977) makes the point that an "exact science of nature" does not reveal individual subjectivity—including any "organizing" judgments by its practitioners and their rationale. He is now parenthesizing by means of the transcendental *epoché* and reduction the practices of traditional psychology as constituted naturalistic prejudices within a logical system of "psychic facts." Due to its methods for constructing naturalized explanations of the mind, empirical psychology in Wundt's tradition is "blind" to the subjective character of an active mental life that underlies all human psychological experience:

This skeptical critique [by transcendental *epoché*] turns toward nothing less than the entire methodology of this psychology insofar as it ever raised the claim...to explain the facts of the life of mind mentally, and that is, psychologically. Indeed, this skepticism, in its later, matured form [of reduction], even turns toward the...method of establishing psychic facts as psychological, which means: [clarifying the methods for] not simply making experimental facts apparent as facts, but analyzing them in explicit internal experience [for individuals], [and] further subsuming them under concepts which express the structural essential species of these facts as psychic [phenomena themselves].... The new psychology [influenced by Wundt, however, is]...blind to the unique essential species of psychic life, blind to all essential forms specific to mentality as an intentionally active subjectivity, constituting mental formations and also cultural community. (p. 3)

Husserl does not intend to describe explanatory practices for phenomenological psychology in the tradition of the exact natural sciences. Neither does he intend to validate any naïve concepts of psychological phenomena for transcendental phenomenology. Instead, Husserl wants to clarify by *epoché* the essence of thinking about mental life that is exemplified in naturalistic methodologies—and thereby to reveal the a-historical spirit-life of psychology as a human science. Reminiscent of comments in his *Logos* article, and perhaps given as its parallel, Husserl presents in his 1925 lectures a bracketed psychology (consisting of descriptions of the normative practices for doing psychology) in preparation for its phenomenological clarification within a systematic science of essences. Yet how are such naturalistic practices to be reduced and bracketed in order to let the intentional mental acts of psychologists show themselves independently of historical accounts? Husserl's (1977) response is to clarify by transcendental *epoché* and reduction Wilhelm Dilthey's exemplary "descriptive and analytic" psychology of the human mind:

In the year 1894, in the midst of a time which was filled with exaggerated hopes in the new psychology, a time which expected of it simultaneously an exact grounding of the socio-cultural sciences and a reform of logic, theory of knowledge, and all specifically philosophical sciences, W. Dilthey…[presented] the first assault against this naturalistic psychology.… [Dilthey] seeks to show in comprehensive presentations that over against this "explanatory" or "constructive" psychology, as he expresses himself, there is need of a "descriptive and analytic" psychology, the idea of which he attempts to sketch extensively in a continuing critique of experimental psychology.… [On] the basis of [historical] experience it projects hypothetical substructions of causal nexus which are not experienced [in real life] and of hypothetical laws referring to them. But this entire procedure is completely inappropriate to the essence of the psychic [in human science].… This procedure has a sense and a necessity in natural science; for it rests [conceptually] upon external experience which gives us nature as merely spatial mutual externality, while the objective nexus of universal causality which provide regulative unity for this mere mutual externality are not also given in immediate intuitiveness. But [the *essence* of Dilthey's descriptive] psychology and consequently all sociocultural sciences refer to the one mental nexus universally given by internal experience [*innere Erfahrung*]. (pp. 3-5)

Any historical view on mental life will certainly afford explanations of human experience with *something*, yet such expressions are intelligible only within our mutually constructed "external" world (*der Außenwelt*). Historical explanations are typically given as objective matters of sociocultural significance in the transcendental register, but they are neither directly nor necessarily validated by principles of causality that are experienced immediately by individuals. Instead, historical explanations of natural cause point toward an enduring sense of an objective spatial nature in daily life. This experience is regulated by a norm of sociocultural tradition in order to function as a mediating unity during our mutual explanations of the appearances of things. Following this norm, Dilthey's descriptive theme is represented by explanations of gathering facts about the mind in accordance with its appearance in historical accounts. His intentional object is therefore not the mind *as such* in psychological descriptions, but rather the lived experience of gathering facts *about* the mind.

The practices of traditional psychologists are described by Dilthey as "psychological" experiences with temporal "substructions" of causal nexus (i.e., necessary connections) and their objective "laws" of association. Such connections of causality pre-exist as "hypothetical" presuppositions of "external" things from one historical moment to another. The idea of mental life is therefore naturalized by such psychologists within the horizon of metaphysics as dependent on natural law—and consequently, Locke's notion of the mind as *tabula rasa* in nature endures for naïve descriptions of psychological experience. (*see* Husserl 1970, §11) Dilthey in effect describes a norm for doing psychology as the activity of gathering facts about the empirical manifestations of mental life within the law-like prejudices of a natural worldview. This is indeed what Dilthey sees from his natural attitude.

And yet, Husserl (1977, 5) continues, Dilthey's "descriptive and analytic psychology" could stand as the exemplar of truth-seeking that is evidenced by psychologists who follow traditional practices of empirical inquiry. In naturalized explanations of the mind, expressions of psychological experience represent metaphysical presuppositions of spatially continuous and temporally infinite characteristics of impersonal, objectified and idealized, mental life—although one's personal experiences are neither spatially continuous nor temporally infinite in real life (even experimentally). But before such external manifestations of contingent spatiotemporal substructions could be seen (because a calculus of contingency implies a prior goal), there is always an "internal" experience enjoyed universally and a-historically by each psychologist—namely, a pre-existing mental nexus that is lived as one's experience of pure psychology. The essence of pure psychology is what Dilthey *sees intuitively* in a psychologist's mental life of gathering practices and truth-seeking.

In the context of renewal in the human sciences, Dilthey's intuition provides Husserl (1977) with a theory of method for the "internal experience" of psychic life, lived as a monad-like unity in transcendental consciousness:

> Internal experience gives no mere mutual externality; it knows no separation of parts consisting of self-sufficient elements. It knows only internally interwoven states, interwoven in the unity of one all-inclusive nexus....The living life streams on continually [in pure psychology] and it not only is, it is lived [*erlebt*] and at every time [there is] a notice, a pondering, a valuing, etc., [that life itself] can be directed toward [a unity of interwoven states]. But they themselves are merely new pulses of this life [in pure psychology], not external to it, but taking place in it as moments, as lived experience making its appearance in life and directed toward life becoming singlely prominent in the unbroken unity of one life and lived experience....
>
> [That] psychic life is not merely given externally and as mutual [i.e., sociocultural] externality, but is given in its nexus [of psychic acts in a spiritual formation of pure psychology], given by self-knowledge [of one's own life], by internal experience [with personal things], constitutes the basic difference between psychological knowledge and the knowledge of nature [in naïve "psychological" descriptions]. (p. 5)

Husserl continued to stress the need for a phenomenological clarification of human science in a series of lectures between 1926 and 1929. Most notable for psychology were Husserl's lectures in Amsterdam on April 22 and 29, 1928. In Amsterdam, Husserl (1997, 213f) resumed from where he left off in his 1925 lectures by tracing out phenomenological psychology's "parallel" a-historical role according to his new transcendental perspective. Yet by explicitly bracketing historical explanations as eidetic evidence for the essence of any phenomenon whatsoever, the Amsterdam lectures signaled a clear break with Heidegger on the direction that the phenomenological movement was to take. Friction between these two powerful and brilliant philosophers had been building up to a breaking point for over a decade.

Moran (2000, 85) reports that beginning in his Freiburg lecture courses, Heidegger was blatantly critical of Husserl's transcendental idealism, perhaps especially for modifying Dilthey's *Weltanschauung* philosophy as historical descriptions of a universal human spirit. Specifically, Heidegger believed that Husserl failed to account for historical influences when focusing on the contingencies of human consciousness in the transcendental register. Heidegger also made light of Husserl's practice of transcendental reduction whereby transcendental subjectivity is identified as the pure Ego's natural attitude in pure subjectivity. Most important for psychology, Heidegger disagreed that emphasis should be placed on our intentional acts of cognition versus an ontology of practical living experience. Schürmann (1990) presents the following concise explanation of Heidegger's continuing opposition to Husserl's transcendental phenomenology:

> By methodically falling back on the *cogito* [i.e., by clarifying reasoning as transcendence and pure subjectivity as fundamental ontology], the phenomenology of transcendental subjectivity accomplishes a step backward that leads from the immediately and naturally given world to the world given for and by consciousness. Everything that 'is', and notably the object of intentionality, is in consciousness, present to consciousness. To be is [merely] to be represented....
>
> Heidegger turns away from this phenomenology of transcendental consciousness in three stages: first, by passing to existential phenomenology as fundamental ontology, then by passing to the phenomenology of historical *aletheia* [i.e., all possible experiences of truth], and lastly by attempting a topology of the 'event' [i.e., the making-present of historical temporality during the conjunction of *Being* and being-in-the-world]. [Heidegger's] metamorphosis of phenomenological transcendentalism leads to the replacement of the 'subject' by Dasein [i.e., that *Being* concerned with truth and existence]. (pp. 68-9)

As long as Husserl's philosophy remained the product of intuitive reflections on the universal phenomenological method of reasoning and on our universal practices of truth-seeking, Heidegger seemed to have no objections. But possibly from Heidegger's point of view, as soon as Husserl began to approach a metaphysical content of human consciousness with his methodology, such as the spirit of humanity or presuppositions of human existence as the idealized semblance of pre-conceptual irreality, then Husserl's transcendental phenomenology became a philosophy of the meaning of *Being* in the natural attitude—that was not then theoretically grounded within an existential anthropology of "I-Man" in the world. Yet Husserl seemed oblivious to a growing embarrassment of criticism from his young assistant, and continued to support and promote Heidegger in the department. Despite what Husserl saw to be a lack of scientific rigor in its practices, he viewed Heidegger's work as representing the future growth and continuation of phenomenological ideals. Welton (2000, 123) mentions that Husserl thought of Heidegger as "the best" in a new generation of phenomenologists, and followed his stellar

career at the University of Marburg between 1924 and the time that he succeeded Husserl at Freiburg in 1928 as if it were his own.

In 1927, Husserl was asked by the *Encyclopaedia Britannica* to write its
entry on "Phenomenology." Husserl invited Heidegger to collaborate, but the
partnership proved to be anything but congenial. The two were so opposed as
to the article's direction that Heidegger's contribution was eventually dropped
from publication. Husserl's own text was cut to fit into a limited space and
sometimes even paraphrased. There is speculation that not only did Husserl
never recommend the entry's reading as a fitting example of his work, but also that in apparent disgust he never read the published article at all. According to Spiegelberg's (1981, 19) interpretations, the *Britannica* translation even
"reverses the order" of phenomenological philosophy and pure psychology in
Husserl's methodology.

Yet perhaps the best evidence for interpretations of what Husserl intended to say in the *Britannica* article about an *a priori* phenomenological psychology was given in his 1928 Amsterdam lectures. Husserl seems to respond
in these lectures to many of the critical charges that Heidegger leveled against
his transcendental phenomenology; and indeed, the notes and text of the Amsterdam lectures represent part of the fifth (though not final) draft of the *Britannica* article that was meant to introduce Husserl's theory of inquiry to a
worldwide audience the year before. (*see* Palmer 1997, 199) The differences
between phenomenological psychology and philosophy are spelled out in
greater length and depth in these lectures, and the issue of priority in
Husserl's methodology is cleared up as well. Here is how Husserl (1997) began his Amsterdam lectures in the spirit of renewal:

> At the turn of the century as philosophy and psychology struggled for
> a rigorously scientific method, there arose what was at once a new
> science…both of philosophical and psychological research. The new
> science was called phenomenology because it, or its new method [ra-
> ther, was the one] which individual natural scientists and psycholo-
> gists had previously demanded and practiced [intuitively since the
> middle of the previous century]. The sense of this method in men
> like [physicist Ernst] Mach and [physiologist Ewald] Hering lay in a
> reaction against the threatening groundlessness of theorizing in the
> exact natural sciences. It was [also] the reaction against a mode of
> theorizing in mathematical speculations and concept-forming which
> is distant from [eidetic] intuition, a theorizing which accomplished
> neither clarity with insight, in any legitimate sense, nor the production
> of theories [that could be intuitively comprehended].
>
> Parallel to this we find in certain psychologists, and first in [Franz]
> Brentano, a systematic effort to create a rigorously scientific psycho-
> logy on the basis of pure internal experience and the rigorous de-
> scription of its data (*Psychognosia*) [i.e., the *eidos* of Brentano's method
> of phenomenognosis—*see* Welch 1941, 3-5, 280].… In the further
> course of development…[a theory of inquiry based on pure internal
> experience] presents us with a double sense of its meaning: on the

one hand, as psychological phenomenology, which is to serve as the radical science fundamental to [an intuitive grasp of] psychology; on the other hand, as transcendental phenomenology…that is, of being the philosophical science of the [eidetic] sources from which philosophy [itself intuitively] springs. (pp. 213-14)

On this first day of lecture, Husserl presents a psychology that shares the same mental life of "pure internal experience" as his transcendental philosophy—which is, namely, applications of the method of *Psychognosia* for eidetic *seeing*. He means that there is an intuitive radical method of observation and interpretation of human-scientific data for both phenomenological philosophers and psychologists, where this universal method is applied with respect to the subjective content of each separate area of focus. With the method of *Psychognosia*, both disciplines share an encompassing phenomenological attitude within their "parallel" areas of eidetic inquiry. Even so, what is Husserl's (1997) idea for a psychology that is directed by the phenomenological attitude toward seeing the subject's inner life of pure consciousness? It is nothing less than a science of the essence of mental life, "purely as such":

[It] is clear that investigation into the purely mental is…in some measure possible…. How otherwise is one to attain rigorously scientific concepts of the mental in terms of its own [extra-physical] essence and without regard to all its concrete interwovenness with the physical? If we reflect on the fact that to these concepts there must also necessarily belong concepts which encompass the universal and necessary eidetic form of the mental in its ownmost essential character (which are concerned with all of that without which something like the mental would simply not be thinkable) then there opens up the prospect of a possible a priori science of essences belonging to the mental purely as such. We take this as our guiding idea. (p. 216)

Husserl suggests that there is a pre-existing and pregiven mental region of pure consciousness that intuitively grounds our possibilities and guides our practicalities for arriving at the truth of anything in science and philosophy. Such is the case with every endeavor in our sprit-life of truth-seeking. We all tend to grasp intuitively, for example, something of the eidetic properties of gravity during one's pre-conceptual activities of consciousness-formation. Our enduring sense of the idea of gravity is one of our truest senses; and so it is said, we build our houses with the ceilings up and the floors down. If we are to think of the mind at all, not as something organic that displays no mental life of its own, but in terms of its extra-physical essence, then there must surely be an *a priori* region of conscious awareness that guides us similarly as does our ordinary understanding of the idea of gravity. Pure psychology literally *re*-presents to every psychologist the essence of mental life for all of us, but before that life is interwoven with the contingent concrete world and the physical things that are seen to reside there.

It serves little purpose for rigorous practices, however, to say that a "pure internal experience" already exists for scientific concept formation and theory construction without the proper means for seeing such apriority. Husserl (1997, 216-18) therefore recounts in his Amsterdam lectures the norm of practice for seeing pre-conceptual experience by the method of *Psychognosia*. Here, a phenomenologist in Husserl's tradition attempts to observe the "authentic eidetic truths in apodictic insight only from out of their original sources in intuition." This means that a phenomenologist must have available a source of intuitive (not only discursive) experience from another that is representative of a search for truth about an original idea with the goal of apodictic certainty. In effect, a phenomenologist reflects on our so-called reflective attitude toward the particularities of life itself. Husserl (1983, §78) noticed more than a decade earlier that the reflective attitude is an altered state of ordinary consciousness. The phenomenological attitude of reflection *on* reflection is, in the stronger case, an even "more" altered state of ordinary consciousness when applying the eidetic method of *Psychognosia*.

In his remarks to the Amsterdam audience, Husserl (1997, 213-16) wondered if a state of reflective attitude is a property of life for all animate organisms, or if this is a peculiar capacity of the human species alone. Even today we do not know with certainty if so-called brute animals are capable of reflecting on distinctive categories of reality. Yet we know from experience that humans *are* typically capable of making this distinction, and we do this by focusing attention on what is extra-physical in our lives. We also tend to focus on what is extra-physical in the lives of others during our empathetic relationships. Each instance of non-physiological consciousness in the transcendental register entails an original *eidos* that is carried over from *a priori* to contingent experience, even as that same idea intentionally moves through states of irreality to actual reality With Husserl's rigorous application of the method of *Psychognosia* for eidetic *seeing*, "consciousness-of" is what shows itself as the overall content of phenomenological reflections—just as it does during our ordinary reflections on a unique idea in different levels of reality. Being conscious of something "is the essential character of mental life in the full sense of the word, and is thus inseparable from [pure principles of psychology]." (p. 217)

When we reflect from the natural attitude on extra-physical things (such a belief or opinion), our thoughts are led to the already-objectified experiences of psychic life, including perhaps the experience of reflecting in this moment. But when phenomenologists reflect *on* naïve reflections, and upon the subjective "*I*" that is reflecting here and now, what appears initially is neither the purely intuitive ego of extra-physical reality nor the mental process of reflection itself. Appearing instead are the presented objects of the mind, including our objectified acts of being conscious of something affective, such as loving or fearing. At this level of reduction, what appears is an epistemology of the content of reflections, composed of the subject and the object of conscious awareness—the eidetic *what-ness* that is revealed by the intuitive method of *Psychognosia*. In this way of proceeding, applications of *Psychognosia* also reveal "the necessary eidetic form of the mental in its own most essential character (which are concerned with all of that without which something like the mental would simply not be thinkable)." (Husserl 1997, 216)

We naïvely tend to see objectifications of mental life as experiences that are similar for each of us, but not precisely the same for everyone. And when we think about *the* mind, we do not focus on something that is constructed in mental processes to be an experience that is contingently *my own*. Instead, we direct our psychic life of consciousness-formation from the natural attitude toward its object-oriented content—namely, toward an intentional object in the transcendental register, and the transcendental ego as the objectification of *me myself*. Yet in Husserl's Amsterdam lectures, and in his *Britannica* article as well, there is no evidence that would support an epistemology of something like a psychological ego that would carry out such objectifying processes during ordinary experience—*because* Husserl wanted to isolate and clarify by *epoché* the *a priori* pre-conceptual essence of human consciousness that makes it possible for us to think of the mind at all. That is to say, he was attempting to introduce pure psychology into the transcendental register.

At this stage of development for phenomenological psychology, Husserl can perhaps do no more than to suggest a transcendental relationship of essences between pure psychology and an object of the mind. Due to the so-called ontological *nothingness* of pure psychology during our life-world experiences with actually real things, what Fink calls the problem of "meontics" in phenomenological methodology (*see* Bruzina 1995, *lv-lvii*), Husserl cannot directly reflect on the ontology of mental processes that do not appear with epistemological evidence in the transcendental register—since there is thus no neutral *entrée* to their irreal pre-existence. Even when such processes are intuitively pregiven as principles of pure psychology during applications of *Psychognosia* (*see* Brentano 1995, 3), they remain within a pre-conceptual region of the extraphysical, never to be actualized in conceptual space. This is perhaps one reason that the distinction of a psychological ego does not appear in Husserl's 1925 lectures on the essence of psychology as a human science.

In the 1930s, however, as an alternative to naïve psychologistic practices, Husserl (Fink 1995, 188-9) focused on what appears by means of eidetic *seeing* to the reflecting ego. What generally shows itself is the pure Ego's "progressive world-experience" with essences and their relationships. It is here that the ego-life of the "pure soul" appears in regions of the extra-physical. In effect, Husserl applied the psychological *epoché* for reflections on the eidetic pregivenness of pure psychology during life-world experiences—where mental processes pre-exist as a "flux of becoming" in pure consciousness. In Husserl's (p. 164) transcendental theory of method, this flux is "enworlded" as the pure Ego's psychosubjectivity in the transcendental register and represented by the bifurcated psychological ego in processes of noematic action.

After his 1928 Amsterdam lectures on the radicalization and renewal of psychology, Husserl barely mentions this region of pre-conceptual experience for phenomenological psychology until his remarks on a proposed "phenomenology of phenomenology" at the end of his active scholarship. Husserl (Fink 1995, 166) anticipated in these remarks that phenomenological psychologists would "set as research task the totality of psychic being in its full concreteness" under the psychological *epoché* and reduction.

Husserl's Last Years

Beginning in the late 1920s and continuing throughout the end of his days, Husserl worked to produce a systematic organization of his methodology as an applied transcendental phenomenology. He retired in 1928, and felt free then to devote his energies to developing his theory of inquiry such that it would be firmly established as a rigorous discipline within a renewal of the human sciences. To this end, Husserl (1969) completed *Formal and Transcendental Logic* in 1929 (after its text lay dormant for more than eight years) in order to clarify the transcendental logical structures of intentionality during genetic phases of constitution. He had just published this book when Husserl (1964c) wrote out the draft of his Paris lectures on seeing the intersubjective structures of consciousness as the irrealities of transcendental subjectivity that are peculiarly *my own*. This work was then expanded and published in France as his (Husserl 1973b) *Cartesian Meditations*. Portions of this book—characterized as "German Meditations" on world-consciousness—were to form the basis of a transcendental theory of method in subsequent publications.

Still, Husserl began to worry in the 1930s that he was running out of time to complete what had now become his life's work to establish phenomenological philosophy as the very model of a scientific discipline. Part of this foreboding came from those students and associates closest to him who went off in their own directions of interest, but without taking along Husserl's rigorous praxis for applied phenomenology. Moran (2000) reports that when Husserl retired as chairman of philosophy at Freiburg on March 31, 1928, being appointed Professor Emeritus, Heidegger was his handpicked successor despite their apparent differences in orientation and practices:

> Heidegger had Husserl's full support (against some opposition in the Faculty), succeeding even over Husserl's more senior [former] student Alexander Pfänder, who had been teaching at Munich for many years, and also the prominent Neo-Kantian, Ernst Cassirer. Later, in 1931, Husserl wrote a letter to Pfänder acknowledging his "blindness" in not seeing through Heidegger, but pointing out that Heidegger had been an excellent assistant and had followed the later development of Husserl's transcendental phenomenology, which, in his opinion none of his earlier Munich followers had done.... In the summer of 1929 Heidegger presented a copy of *Being and Time* and of *Kant and the Problem of Metaphysics* to Husserl, who finally found time to carefully read and annotate them. Husserl was shocked by the extent of Heidegger's departure from his phenomenology. (pp. 85-6)

Husserl's "Munich followers" was a group of phenomenologists at the University of Munich that grew to prominence under the leadership of Alexander Pfänder during the 1920s and 1930s. Stein (1986, 509 note 227) records that Pfänder "was in Husserl's opinion 'our most substantial worker' in the evolving phenomenology of the 1920s." The Munich Group practiced what Welton (2000, 68-9) calls a "categorial phenomenology" that "imposes a twofold restriction upon the analysis of the field of experience." The first restriction is "limited to a generally classificatory analysis of types of mental acts and experiences that would belong to a theory of knowledge." This analysis provides the second restriction of "a typology of acts in relation to varying fields of objects, and finally to the various a priori disciplines forming our regional and formal ontologies." The result "is that conscious life is viewed as a correlational intentional structure, precisely that kind of structure that can be unfolded by an analysis of the necessary conditions of knowledge."

With this approach, the Munich Group took its inspiration almost entirely from the *Logical Investigations*, and did not follow the implicit transcendental turn of Husserl's methodology in *Ideas I*. However, when a phenomenologist *does* follow as praxis the transcendental turn in the phenomenological method proper, and thereby moves from regressive to genetic reflections, pure categories of sense and meaning are seen to be intentionally transcended by synthesis as contingency might demand. Each synthesis is experienced personally in the transcendental register as a constructed unity of awareness that is constituted to be experienced similarly by everyone. In effect, pure phenomenology is itself transcended in Husserl's mature methodology. Still, a phenomenological approach to inquiry could indeed become an intuitive "categorial phenomenology" in Welton's sense—given that we are taught to reason in thematic categories, and given Husserl's early emphasis on modifying Aristotle's forms of thought as objects of the mind in the *Investigations*.

The school of pure categorial phenomenology at Munich began its "new scholasticsm" as early as the first publication of the *Logical Investigations*. This informal group, formed under the influence of psychologist Theodor Lipps (who introduced the concept of *empathy* to Husserl), included as early members not only Pfänder, but also Johannes Daubert, Adolf Reinach, and Max Scheler. Daubert and Reinach were both killed during the First World War, and Pfänder eventually replaced Lipps as leader of the group. Despite their lack of interest in transcendental phenomenology, Husserl was nevertheless enthusiastic in his support of the Munich Group for more than twenty years. Reinach was especially highly regarded, and would have been groomed to be Husserl's successor had he not met with an early death.

Husserl (Fink 1995, 191) intended in the years ahead for a community of transcendental phenomenologists "to have an effect upon their fellow men [in human science], training [them] into phenomenology, and then out of phenomenology laying down norms for human beings as a whole (keeping constantly in mind the distant horizon of non-phenomenologists) and in accord with those norms endeavoring to train them in a new humanity." But in the late 1930s, Husserl began to consider himself, as Moran (2000) reports, a "leader without followers":

> Husserl spent his last years attempting to rescue the true meaning of the science of phenomenology from Heidegger who had turned it into anthropology, just as earlier Scheler had weakened it into a form of life philosophy…. Husserl was acutely aware that he had no genuine successor…and that the scientific conception of phenomenology

118

which he had promoted had now dissipated into many separate styles of enquiry in many diverse areas. For better or worse, phenomenology in Germany in the 1930s and 1940s came to be associated with the name of Martin Heidegger, and after the war, in France, with the existential phenomenology of Sartre and Merleau-Ponty (pp. 89-90)

Husserl's lofty vision of a human-scientific community of phenomenologists was never realized. Whereas the First World War seemed to present an opportunity for the phenomenological spirit of renewal in science and philosophy, the Second threatened that same spirit's ruin for decades to come. Tragically for the phenomenological movement worldwide, and for Husserl personally, the National Socialist German Worker's Party came to power in 1933, the same year that Heidegger was named the *Rektor* (= headmaster or director) of the University of Freiburg. As a Party member and the *Rektor* of a state university, Heidegger countersigned a new law calling for the establishment of a permanent civil service whose composition would exclude all non-Aryans. This exclusion meant that Husserl being of Jewish parentage was stripped of his position as Professor Emeritus.

Husserl was subsequently banned from pubishing, his license to teach was revoked, his philosophy was officially condemned, his German citizenship was taken away, and he was finally restricted to travel only within Nazi-controlled boundaries. For advocating a universal human rationality found intuitively in all races and creeds, Husserl's phenomenology was suppressed throughout Europe and beyond. Some of Husserl's loyal followers, including Edith Stein, were later imprisoned and executed. Because Husserl was forbidden to teach or to publish, he was forced to develop his most advanced theories of transcendental phenomenology through personal correspondences and in public lectures.

One of these lectures, "Philosophy in the Crisis of European Humanity," was delivered in Vienna in May 1935. Notes and texts for this lecture later formed part of Husserl's (1970) posthumous publication, *The Crisis of European Sciences*. The *Krisis*, as this publication is traditionally referred to, was originally intended by Husserl to be an expanded work of five books that would present his systematic approach to a phenomenological science of essences. But Husserl died of pleurisy on April 28, 1938, and parts of the beginning for what he hoped to be his greatest academic achievement were split up and edited into two books: the *Krisis*, and *Experience and Judgment* (Husserl 1973a). On the day of Husserl's funeral, Heidegger was "sick in bed" and so could not attend to pay his last respects. That day signals the end of the phenomenological movement as it had been under Edmund Husserl's strong influence and personal example of rigorous science.

3.

Phenomenological Epistemology and Ontology

Eidetic Structures of Sense and Meaning

After his retirement in 1928, Husserl (Carr 1970, *xv-xvii*) updated many of his earlier publications, manuscripts, and working notes in light of advances in object-oriented phenomenology. More often, though, he addressed each topic anew, looking ahead for applications of his transcendental theory of method in order to explain the oneness of conscious awareness as a complex unity of (1) an intentional object, (2) cognitive action in mental life, and (3) the actual reality that we construct in daily life. Husserl (Fink 1995, §5) cautioned in the 1930s not to read all of his previous works as if they were the results of reductions to a pure theory of elements or to a pure theory of method; and certainly, phenomenological psychology and its relationship to transcendental idealism had never been adequately worked out. Yet by the end of his career Husserl had come far enough in developing his transcendental phenomenology and its parallel phenomenological psychology, together within a revolutionary eidetic science of essences, in order to indicate his intentions and means for further evaluations of the phenomenon of human consciousness.

Focus of this chapter is on the two principal areas in Husserl's theory of inquiry that make up the "foundation of the ground" for transcendental phenomenological psychology—namely, the epistemology and ontology of constitutive life during our pre-conceptual performances of consciousness-formation. The first area was developed as the theme of bestowing sense (*Sinn*) on an intentional object; the latter was thematized as conferring meaning (*Bedeutung*) on that same object in anticipation of expressing "the meant" (*Vermeintes*) in conceptual space. Transcendental phenomenological psychology is theoretically grounded in the pure psychology of these actions and their methods of fulfillment. Yet my remarks here are not solely expository within these horizons of pure subjectivity. Since much of Husserl's methodology requires that his readers assume the perspective of the phenomenological attitude, I will follow his example of reflecting on both an ongoing epistemology and a clarified ontology of our activities of consciousness-formation. For an adequate grasp of later portions of his philosophy, Husserl (Fink 1995, §11 note 384) requires that his readers be capable of attending to concepts and practices from the transcendental attitude, since the pure Ego's transcendental reorientation is already reflected in his own remarks.

In Husserl's science of essences, phenomenological epistemology represents the possibility in pre-conceptual experience for knowing the essence of something categorially (i.e., its thematic *what-ness*), even as his fundamental ontology represents that essence's place within a singular category of identity or existence (i.e., its thematic *is-ness*). Eidetic categories of *what-ness* and *is-ness* are formed and filled during activities of consciousness-formation with the active content of an *eidos* according to that idea's intentionally bestowed sense and conferred meaning. It is a conceptual error to take a presentational object of material ontology to be Husserl's clarified fundamental ontology of an object's irreal essence within a hierarchy of meaningfulness. It is equally an error to take an expression of phenomenological epistemology to be only an object of knowledge within a naïve construction of intelligibility. In order to position remarks for speaking of psychological experience within the horizons of epistemology and ontology, I will be mostly concerned with those horizons in genetic phenomenology, where the psychological ego appears as the performing ego of bestowed sense and conferred meaning.

An object is constituted in consciousness amid a construction of actual reality for the sense and meaning of an enduring *eidos*. Here, an object's bestowed sense is the singular *what-ness* for something that already *is* within the flux of pure consciousness. In the midst of this flux, an object typically gains presence in the transcendental register with reason and evidence as contingency demands here and now. Composing a sense of true being as it is bestowed upon an intentional object represent the eidetic structuring of a form of realization for *this* meaning and not another. Structuring a form of anticipated actual reality for what is intended to come into presence as factual in thought and speech is how we ordinarily bestow sense upon an intentional object. We usually intend in the living present, and are motivated affectively in pure psychology, to make an object of the mind intelligible in the world that is commonly talked about. Such action varies in kind and adequacy for both rational and non-rational comportment when structuring parts and wholes by means of the universal phenomenological method of reasoning.

The eidetic structure of awareness entails a grouping of elements that maintains a thematic identity of sense and meaning for a particular *eidos* in constitutive life. Said construction is seen from the phenomenological perspective to be a pre-conceptual calculus of *what-ness* and *is-ness* that could be documented in conceptual space as logical, grammatical, geometrical, or mathematical structure. When built up by means of a system of normative practices, eidetic structure gives a pregiven and sometimes purely metaphysical point of view on an anticipated outcome in transcendental consciousness. A phenomenologist could recognize a predicated actual reality within this structure by its expression as being rational, axiological, practical, metaphorical, and so on, in its epistemological sense of valuing and presenting to reflections the meaningfulness of an intentional object. Husserl leaves open for exemplary cases of experience whether a presentational object displays the Kantian transcendental structure of a fulfilled unity of apperception. It is absurd to suppose that the subject's every utterance or mode of comportment demonstrates the character of intelligibility.

However, in all cases of our expressions of extra-physical consciousness (such as willing, thinking, or feeling), eidetic structure provides epistemological evidence for, and confirmation of, phenomenological interpretations of the sense and meaning of an intentionally constituted objectivity. Throughout the *a priori* and contingent horizons of eidetic structure, a presentational object exemplifies an original idea in universal experiences of pure consciousness that are peculiarly my own—even when an object of the mind is not yet fully constituted as an intelligible unity. Elements of an intentional object might indeed remain unrealized in an eidetic affair-complex, and then experienced as a "certain halo of indeterminateness" about an object in conceptual space: "You know," one might say, "I'm not really sure, but…." Within its epistemological limits of intelligibility, an intentional object already has adequate meaning as a reduced entity in Husserl's (2006, 133) theory of the transcendental register of pre-conceptual experience.

When presented as one's naïve self-knowledge of something, the subject's expressions offer a "mundane" (*weltlich*, i.e., non-phenomenological) description of a matter of fact given from within the horizon of epistemology. (*see* Gurwitsch 1966, 89-90) A matter of fact in its construction of intelligibility points toward a pre-conceptual injunction to bestow sense and to confer meaning on an *eidos* here and now. In its structure of bestowed sense, for example, a mundane descriptive psychology provides *entrée* for evaluations of a psychologist's self-knowledge of the *eidos* of *mental life*—both universal and in the instance of "this case." Something said to be universal signifies something potentially experienced by all of us; and in phenomenological reflections, universals are usually seen in modes of typicality in the world that is commonly talked about. Husserl's 1913 revision of the *Logical Investigations* could partly be seen as an epistemology of universal cognitive mental life in his effort to bracket (for a clarification of pure logic) what was explained later that year in *Ideas I* to be a regional ontology of psychic life. The essence of this region was clarified in Husserl's 1925 lectures on psychology as seeking the truth of pure psychology with apperceptions of empirical evidence in the natural world.

By eschewing a mundane orientation in his work, Husserl's theory of inquiry has never been naïvely epistemological according to traditional practices of simply providing definitions. Instead, Husserl wants to radicalize scientific and philosophical *doxa* (i.e., "of-necessity" beliefs and opinions) in order to present an ongoing epistemology of *knowing*. The essence of *epistēmē*, given by Husserl (1970, §5) as the *eidos* of *knowing*, represents the spirit-life and universal goal of pure reason that shows itself in the cognitive mental life of transcendental consciousness. Still, Husserl's use of the word "transcendence" and its derivative terminology are perhaps confusing in several areas of his early epistemology in the *Investigations*. They are only minimally less so in later publications. Husserl (Fink 1995, §5) suggests that a naïve interpretation of the phenomenological *epoché* in the horizon of epistemology is one source of this confusion—where it is difficult to see that nothing whatsoever is rejected as untrue or false for any conceived expression of prior knowledge in the phenomenological field. Rather, such expressions of truth-seeking are set aside in reflections as intended outcomes within their regions of subjective content.

Grasping the intelligibility of transcendental experience under the *epoché* hinges on seeing the correlation of a transcended object and a transcending act within a unity of eidetic structure. Indeed, an object exists such as it does in thought and speech because of one's prior actions in cognitive mental life to make it so. All my knowledge of an objectivity is grounded in the most radical ("pure") sense of what is available and lasting for *me myself*, even as I intend to bring my own subjective knowledge-of-something into presence within a pre-existing objectified world. Human spirit-life includes our intention to seize upon the essence something that is already partially pregiven by pre-existing eidetic structure—such as particular physical properties of material objects that are partially pregiven by our intuitive familiarity with physical things in general. (*see* Husserl 1982, §10) The pregivenness of things during consciousness-formation presents a problem of method in Husserl's phenomenological epistemology of pre-conceptual experience.

Husserl's "Basic Questions of Epistemology"

We construct categories and relationships for the irreal essences of things during pre-conceptual performances of consciousness-formation, and then believe that we know something actually real when we constitute the unity of those essences with reason and evidence. This is perhaps one way to understand Husserl's (19703a, §9) epistemology of apperception in his theory of method. But how is a once-constituted object able to be perceived still later, and then literally *re*-cognized as pre-existing objective knowledge enjoyed by everyone in conceptual space? This higher-level apperception in transcendental subjectivity points toward one of the "basic questions of epistemology" in Husserl's (2001, 89) theory of conscious awareness. This question cannot be answered immediately, however, since its response requires both Husserl's eidetic and transcendental reductions of an intentional object. Its answer indeed represents the full complexity of constitutive activities for *knowing* during the subject's experience of pure consciousness.

Still, a review of phenomenological epistemology from the psychological attitude, given as the problem of human *knowing*, could begin with Husserl's theory of perception—a theory of both intentional acts and their accompanying intentional objects. Husserl's theory of perception was continuously updated throughout his studies of consciousness-formation; and in nearly every area since 1913, Husserl describes a pre-conceptual burst of cognitive action beginning from the perception of immediate sensory data, leading up to our most complex levels of apperception. In his later works, Husserl's theory of perception discloses the various horizons of potential for knowing something within extended eidetic structures of *sense* in the transcendental register. Yet during our intersubjective relationships of empathy wherein we constitute a rational affective unity in the world of human co-existence—only one horizon of self-knowledge is purely epistemological during our pre-conceptual experiences of *knowing*.

A meaningful grouping of elements gains presence as a unity amid an epistemological horizon of pre-conceptual *sense*. Here, the grouping represents in reflections the *what-ness* of an intentional object's fulfilled anticipation and realization of something objective. When a grouping of elements for an *eidos* is fulfilled in transcendental consciousness, one could express its sense by saying, for example, "The price of apples is ninety-nine cents a pound," or even, "Schizoaffective psychosis tends toward remission without permanent defect, but is prone to recur." Within its parts/whole overlay of *sense*, the horizon of epistemology includes strata of intelligibility in both pre-conceptual and conceptual space. The horizon of epistemology in Husserl's methodology thus delimits the phenomenological field for evaluations of a configuration of unity during the subject's activities of consciousness-formation.

In the normal course of events, one's self-knowledge of something in the transcendental register is intended to be objective knowledge for everyone in the world of co-existence and common semblance. Therefore, during regressive reflections on a presented object of self-knowledge, the epistemological horizon is the first to appear under the eidetic reduction. The last "pure" *a priori* horizon to appear genetically in reflections is the horizon of metaphysics. It is self-evident that correlations for presuppositions of certainty come last in transcendental constitutive life—since something must pre-exist for us to recognize and be certain of its presence here and now. Recall that correlated elements of *certainty* and *sense* provide regressive *entrée* into the meaning of an intentional object in the sociocultural world. These same correlations in conceptual space also close the transcendental circle of constitutive life for reconstructive phenomenology in the transcendental register.

When oriented by our natural attitude toward philosophical and scientific practices, as well as toward our day-to-day experiences of thinking, willing, and feeling, we typically have certain doxic presuppositions about the existence and pregivenness of irrealities in one's naïve natural world. Such things are finally expressed from the horizon of metaphysics, but their sense and meaning are pregiven within the horizons of epistemology and ontology. If the horizon of metaphysics appears before the horizon of epistemology in regressive reflections, interpretations of a system of apperceptions tend to be directed toward an existentialism of perceptual experience rather than toward a clarification of the subject's self-knowledge of an intentional object. (*see* Gurwitsch 1966, 91-3) This practice is an error in Husserl's methodology, since the pure Ego's apodictic self-knowledge is then ambiguous in reflections as to *what* goes without saying in the transcendental register—either an *eidos* within its *a priori* horizons, or any number of contingent correlations.

Cognitive correlations in transcendental consciousness, including our normative extensions of objectification and idealization during intersubjective relationships, are axiologically grounded within (i.e., valued according to) what has already been grasped in the solipsistic register of pure human consciousness—such as a pre-existing sense of time and place, or the pregivenness of one's own body. Our metaphysical presuppositions of what goes without saying are constructed by one's own transcending acts, both rationally and nonrationally. More specifically, by those acts of apperception directed toward pre-existing and pregiven elements deemed necessary for awareness here and now. Husserl never clarified a phenomenology of reason within the horizon of metaphysics, although he had planned to do so with a "Seventh Cartesian Meditation." (*see* Bruzina 1995, xvi) Therefore, one cannot anticipate precisely here either Husserl's rigorous praxis for a transcendental phenomenological psychology within the horizon of metaphysics, or of a fundamental ontology of metaphysical presuppositions in transcendental constitutive life.

Yet we know that a doxic presupposition of *absoluteness* for a pre-existing intentional form of eidetic structure shows itself within this final horizon of metaphysics as what Husserl (1970, §6) calls "a latent orientation toward reason"—meaning, an enduring pre-conceptual "drive" or "urge" for constituting what one intends to know with apodictic certainty. And we know, too, that a doxic presupposition is composed with greater or lesser degree of evidence in order to grasp the contingent sense of an intentional object in one's naïve natural world. (*see* Husserl 1973a, §65) Indeed, naïve presuppositions of the absolute and infinite duration of a metaphysical Nature characterize apperceptions of everyday evidence for our constructed realities. In the normal course of events, a meaningful sense of infinite *absoluteness* is apperceived within the horizon of metaphysics as a correlate of the idealized things and relationships that we encounter habitually in the world of common semblance. It seems reasonable that similar presuppositions are given in mundane science and philosophy as matters of factualness.

Presuppositions of actual reality typically exist apodictically in the transcendental register without question of an intentional object's epistemic *what-ness*—because a pregiven sense of metaphysical *absoluteness* is correlated and *re*-cognized in predicative experience as a truly existing matter of fact about data of apperception. Ever present in the psychic order for this state of affairs, between simple perception and higher-level apperceptions and at greater depths of reflection yet, there is the horizon of ontology for conferring meaning on the appearance and presence of an intentional object. Here in the horizon of ontology, a metaphysically oriented *absoluteness* for something in immediate perception could be cognitively correlated with a pre-existing eidetic form and content of epistemic *what-ness*. We usually do this during apperceptive experience when anticipating the realization of a pregiven meaning of an intentional object as *this* meaning and not another. A singular meaning is originally presented and preconstituted in the horizon of ontology, and is only subsequently correlated as necessary in the horizons of epistemology and metaphysics as the subject's apodictic sense of something here and now.

Metaphysically correlated knowledge-claims point toward one's pre conceptual orientation in the living present for typical transcending acts of *knowing*. As presentational objects, presuppositions of absoluteness and certitude go without saying in the natural attitude as pre-existing things; and as injunctions for judgments and valuations, they tend to be categorized as epistemology in naïve theoretical discourse. During the flow of reasoning from pre-conceptual to conceptual space, however, the essence of epistemology is independent and neutral *vis-à-vis* the essence of metaphysics, just as both are independent and neutral regarding the essence of pure psychology. Even so, elements of perceptual experience could be grouped as a composition of sense and meaning in the horizon of ontology. Here, pre-existing elements in the horizons of epistemology and metaphysics, each individually or combined with others in anticipation of unity, could be correlated within an ontic affair-complex of meaningfulness for an intentional object. The horizon of ontology indeed represents the "center core" of conscious awareness and self-knowledge for any intentional object whatsoever in pure consciousness.

The subject's references to the sensible meaning of something in the horizon of epistemology provide access to that very core of fundamental meaning in propaedeutic regressive reflections. In subsequent genetic reflections, beginning from this origin of ontic givenness, the psychological *epoché* and reduction disclose the cognitive action that groups the sense and meaning of an object within each *a priori* and contingent region of realized being-sense. During the genetic temporal spread of transcendental consciousness, the pure Ego's psychic order of constitution proceeds step-wise within and between the horizons of epistemology, ontology, and metaphysics.

But for now under the eidetic reduction in regressive phenomenology, we will look at a second basic epistemological question in Husserl's theory of consciousness: What *is* such "stuff" of a perceptual act and its perceived object that is seen throughout the various horizons of constitutive life? Quite simply, the stuff of perceptual experience represents the human potential for self-knowledge of something within bounds of what is determinable here and now. Under the eidetic reduction in the epistemological horizon of pure consciousness, a potential for the coming-to-presence of one's knowledge-of-something exists in pure subjectivity as perceptions of unarticulated sensory data—from the Latin, *sensorium*, denoting mental responses to external stimuli. Indeed, all potentials for the phenomenon of non-physiological consciousness exist within pre-conceptual experiences with sensory data.

Husserl (1982, §97) stresses that perception is the "really inherent moment of consciousness"—meaning, perceiving sensory stuff as mental stimuli is typically the genesis and initial eidetic form of intentional experience during every phase of constitution and reality construction. Grasping sensory data as objects to be acted upon "animates" mental life with a committed bestowing of sense on all subsequent extensions of this original givenness in pure consciousness. (§85) Yet the *possibility* of this potential for awareness is not itself a constituted object *per se*. Within its infinite range of likelihood, a possibility *as such* is not a thing to be known as actually real in a world of objective things, although the *probability* of something could usually be presumed as an idealized outcome of constitutive life. (*see* Weyl 1940, 289-95) Perhaps our best intuitive grasp of the possibility for anything whatsoever is given by our choices within a calculus of logic for an ideal outcome of expressible and sensible meaning. One might say that the possibility of conscious awareness is lived in the spirit-life of *hope* and *anticipation*.

When bound in anticipation by the epistemological horizon of bestowed sense, immediate perceptual experience is an intentional experience of *knowing what* the objects and acts within a pre-existing "external" world is *about*. Under the eidetic reduction, this universal experience of *knowing* and its psychological theme of *aboutness* point reflections toward one's norms of practice in the cognitive mental life of pure consciousness. (*see* Husserl 1982, §44) As a metatheoretical concept of concepts, pure consciousness represents a complexity of human comportment for transcending raw sensory data in every horizon and category of potential knowledge-of-something. "Consciousness is ruled by norms in every genus," Husserl (§145) notices—for otherwise, conscious awareness would not be an intentional experience.

As a matter of agency seen under the *epoché*, the pure Ego seems to wonder, "What is the sense of this thing that is perceived?" This third basic epistemological question points toward our ordinary pre-conceptual experiences of apperception—a purely subjective response to sensory data that is the genesis of one's psychological consciousness of a rational affective unity. Such data are only later assigned higher-level intellectual and affective significance; and indeed, our most primitive intuitions are about the stuff of apperceptions. Before we have words to describe our bestowed sense on something, at greater depths of experience than where we find language-use, our apperceptions have already modified an original potential for knowing something in extended structures of pure consciousess. Cognitions of *sense* are thus delimited at the beginning and throughout constitutive life.

Husserl (1973a, §23) explains that when our anticipation of grasping elements of an *eidos* is fulfilled by apperception as a parts/whole potential, we have achieved the "simple apprehension" of an intentional object. While still pre-conceptual and not yet fully formed with reason and evidence, simple apprehension "is in no wise a single datum, but exhibits in itself a multiplicity of structures in which it constitutes itself as an immanent temporal unity." During successive modifications of an original apperception, simple apprehension is the initiating "moment" of psychic life within a "flowing unity of activity."

Husserl (1982, §23) also points out that in the midst of this cognitive activity, an experience of apperception remains the "still-in-grasp" unity of an original perceiving-act and its perceived object. Throughout all delimiting horizons and contingent modifications, a correlated unity of *this* particular object and *this* particular act endures in the living present as an immanent "coincidence with itself" in extended structures of a built-up system of apperceptions. Here, acts of retaining-in-grasp a correlate of one's original experience with an *eidos* are directed in a mental process by its intentional function to constitute ontic *being* (i.e., a meaningful *is-ness*). Said acts are first intended to "see" the essence of an *eidos* in pre-conceptual constitutive life. A subsequent unity of identity and coincidence typically arises from a system of apperceptions to represent the fulfilled intelligibility of one's transcendental consciousness of an intentional object. Acting in this modality with this intention is itself a universal norm of cognitive mental life in pure psychology.

Husserl's (1977, 41f) descriptions of the pure psychology of perceptual experience are of our initial grasp of something at the beginning of a built-up system of apperceptions. Generally speaking, Husserl's (1973b, §50) anti-psychologistic notion of primitive perception means the following: Whatever is *there* in the perceptual field—and thus (nonthetically) "external" to one's (thetic) "internal" purely subjective focus *here*—"perceptually motivates something else being there too." Perception of something motivates humans to confer meaning and to bestow sense upon that very thing. By this simple function of apprehension of potential sense and meaning, I know intuitively that I am indeed perceiving something. Only then does an intentional object proceed to its fulfilled intelligibility of bestowed sense within the epistemological horizon of pure consciousness. In later phases of this system, the transcendence of particular sensory data is retained in eidetic memory and repeated in more complex cognitive operations during intersubjective relationships.

Apperceived elements of material things in extended structures of pure consciousness, including apperceptions of bodily existence and organic functions, point regressive reflections toward the pure Ego's kinaesthetic center point of anticipated objective reality. One might say that the soon-to-be-transcended intentional object is "embodied" in one's thoughts with our acts of apperception and apprehension at this center of reality construction. Intentional embodiment typically actualizes an at-hand object in agreement with pregiven spatial and temporal dimensions of our apperceived external world (*der Außenwelt*). Said world includes pre-existing objectified things, such as the common semblance of objectified corporeality. This means that the idea of an objective Body is the determinable material substrate of an absolutized Nature in the horizon of metaphysics. Bestowing a sense of embodiment on our immediate experiences of the natural world is described by Husserl (1973a, §29) as a parts/whole "function" in higher-level apperceptions of spatiotemporality. An intentional object is only then directed amid a pre-conceptual system of apperceptions into other spheres of possible self-knowledge of the idealized spatial and temporal dimensions for something in awareness—where now, that *something* has an element of embodiment in referential expressions of *sense*.

Embodiment

Much of Husserl's mature reflections could be brought to bear on the problem of everyday *knowing* in the transcendental register. (*see* e.g., Husserl 1970, §12; 1973a, §68) Surprisingly, perhaps, this area includes the different presuppositions and orientations in the discipline of psychology between (1) a natural-scientific approach, (2) a naïve human-scientific approach, and (3) Husserl's phenomenological psychology of human consciousness. These differences are played out among the horizons of metaphysics, epistemology, and ontology; and within these horizons, the *eidos* of *embodiment* points toward the construction of intelligibility for psychological concepts in general. In light of its potential for misunderstanding, Husserl's theory of embodiment might be examined more closely as the intentional way we go about knowing the objective "nature" of things—including both their appearances and lived experiences in the world that is commonly talked about.

Husserl meant for phenomenological psychology to be distinctive according to its differences with a centuries-old tradition of practices. Traditional psychology not only tends to confuse metaphysics for epistemology even today, but also remains bound to the "misconstructions and misinterpretations" of constituted objectivities versus subjective acts of constitution (*see* Husserl 2001, 89). Husserl (1970, §58) points out that one of the original tasks set for the pioneers of modern psychology in Europe was to explain us humans as unitary psyches or souls that could be divided into two strata of an inner mental life of subjective spiritual properties, and an external material life of objective physical properties. Yet in order to determine a durable unity of reality for each stratum in the natural world, the original idea of the human psyche as the spirit-life of the species was metaphysically embodied in philosophical and scientific methodologies. The objectified psyche was then presumed to be an actually real thing of naturalized spatiotemporal dimensions consisting of internal psychological phenomena and external biological phenomena. In this construction, "the mind is what the brain *does*."

Interpreting manifestations of mental life as analogs of embodied objects in the natural world is certainly one way to appropriate the original task set for early psychologists. But in this traditional fashion of truth-seeking, a purely subjective structure of intentional experience is objectified by inference of the true nature of things in a world of common semblance. (*see* Husserl 1970, §59) When this metaphysical view of embodied reality is naïvely grasped as certain knowledge necessary for theory construction (i.e., as epistemology), then our human agency, the peculiar spirit of intentionality that animates our every perception and judgment in mental life, is then *re*-cognized in higher-level apperceptions as an objectified empirical thing. Husserl does not mean to imply that there is no such *eidos* as "the empirical," or that inquiry grounded in experience with material things has no validity—just that it is valid only for seeing the manifestations of an embodied reality that is intentionally constructed to exist within a similarly constructed natural world.

Husserl (1970, 271) mentions in his 1935 Vienna lecture that the spirit-life of human intentionality and truth-seeking is hidden from us by our own naïve attitude toward scientific practices and their metaphysical prejudices. In particular, human intentionality is ruled out in favor of natural causality within a natural-scientific approach to psychic life wherein psychological experience is described solely by its empirical manifestations of physical presence. The spirit-life of human intentionality, however, must exist in the empirical approach to truth-seeking as a matter of necessity. It is self-evident, for example, that if a physiological psychologist becomes aware of the actual reality of embodied mental life, then that psychologist must intend for mental life to be thus real as something embodied. The same would hold true, of course, for the naturalized intentional objects of biologists, chemists, and physicists. The idea of our human soul, given in part by Husserl (1982, §39) as our transcendence of mere physical existence, remains an unarticulated but necessary presupposition for naïve practitioners within their various philosophical and scientific methodologies. Consequently, presuppositions of such "soulish" transcendence also go without saying during our intersubjective relationship and communal interaction—for, indeed, how could physical things by themselves ever be intersubjective or communal?

With normal cognitive development and typical maturation, each of us habitually adopts a naïve attitude toward the metaphysical totality and intelligibility of all that *is* for us, probably *has been*, and perhaps ever *will be*. From our natural attitude we experience routines in familiar surroundings with the persons that we usually already know. We do not need to consider strict natural laws of cause and effect in ordinary experience, or a mathematical and logical precision that might exist in theoretical reflections about material things. We tend to live practically within this spontaneous totality. When we want to single out something to think about rationally as a matter of salience or importance, rather than as something of passing awareness, we intentionally abstract by judging-acts of dependence and difference what it is that interests us the most. We then construct what could be seen under the eidetic reduction to be an affair complex of elements for that same matter within the flux of potential for knowing something concretely real here and now.

As a norm of practice for things that matter to the pure Ego, we grasp an eidetic affair-complex simply and originally, in existentially reduced terms of *I* and *Other*. We then repeat the configuration of this complex and its logic of calculus for acts of apperception when gathering elements of sense and meaning for an intentional object. In the transcendental register of this flow of reasoning, a pre-existing affair-complex is valued and pregiven to the psychological ego as a form of ideation for what is to be constituted—where now, that form is intelligible and meaningful in the living present for subsequent validating apperceptions. An intentional form of ideation is iterated pre-conceptually and experienced as one's ordinary intuition during constructions of truth and reality, even as the form itself is modified to be in accord with one's contingent worldly experiences. An intentional form of ideation is typically pre-constituted in this psychic order by the function of our cognitive acts of *abstracting* and *valuing* elements necessary for living knowingly as "natural." Consequently, *this* intentional form for *this* object of the mind is pregiven in conceptual space, just in the manner that it stands out from its original ground of potential for realization in one's naïve natural world.

During the pure Ego's contingent worldly experiences, a pre-existing eidetic affair-complex is meant to endure as a unity of configuration in its spatiotemporal thetic and non-thetic givenness to consciousness-formation. In higher-level apperceptions of common semblance, we repeat this intentional function of apprehension of a unity by abstracting things of interest with feelings comparable to those already experienced during daily life—mostly with the affects correlated with belief and certainty when recognizing familiar persons and commonplace objects. We notice intuitively in the living present what affects us in pre-existence as potential unities for abstractions and cognitions. Husserl (1970, §9) is explicit that this activity of apperceptive apprehension represents the universal norm of cognitive mental life that ex-emplifies the essence of normal praxis. This is indeed the lived experience of our typical everyday psychic being; and for each of us, this is the normal course of events for the phenomenological method of reasoning during our day-to-day comportment and theoretical reflections.

When following this regulating norm in the *a priori* and contingent horizons, natural-scientific psychologists abstract physical things from the natural world, while naïve human-scientific psychologists abstract what is believed to be an objective human nature. Both practices represent normative modes (i.e., habitual fashions) for embodying an eidetic affair-complex in theoretical constructions. This activity points toward a pre-existing grasp of spatiotemporality in the horizon of metaphysics—where the *eidos* of *embodiment* is located for correlations of sense and meaning at the pre-conceptual center of reality construction. An intentional object thus becomes a correlate of embodiment, and is then constituted and used practically during the conduct of formal inquiry: (1) Natural-scientific psychology typically studies the psyche in its familiar and presupposed embodied modality of objective materiality. (2) Naïve human-scientific psychology tends to study the psyche in its modality of familiar and presupposed comportment toward an embodied existence. However, (3) Husserl's (1982, §16) practices abstract from the pure psychology of mental life only such presupposed "formal-logical laws and eidetic universalities" of embodiment that retain "allusions to Kant's critique of reason" in the horizon of epistemology. Embodiment *as such* is our intentional experience of knowing spatiotemporal dimensions as actually real and objectively true.

It is a conceptual error, Husserl (1970, §63) warns, to pursue a "naturalized" psychology as a unity of matter and form, where an "inner" subjective experience of *mind* is studied solely with the means for determining one's "outer" experience of *body*. For then, the pure psychology of reason and evidence in the horizon of epistemology—which is itself a horizon of practices for inductive inferences of spatiotemporality in scientific methodologies—becomes instead a *metaphysical naturalism* for deductive inferences about an embodied "nature" of the psyche. Metaphysical naturalism represents a limited view of reality, where only bodies have inferable and analogous extensions in space and time; not the psyche as interpreted mental life, and not the human spirit as our animate agency. With a naïve naturalistic approach toward the study of psychological experience, everything is seen to have a spatial body of empirical dimensions, or at least what could be extended as such under rules of general causality. (p. 315)

An expressed or implied presupposition of embodied reality presents an intentional form of calculus leading toward one's pre-conceptual apprehension of a naturalistic abstraction. The intelligibility of this form is fulfilled in apperceptive experience according to such material stuff of concrete dimensions that could be transcended spontaneously in one's naïve natural world—for example, as the simple apperception of a body of water, or of a body of work, or of one's own physical body. Intentional forms of spatial dimensions of embodiment, and the intelligibility of their retained elemental contents in temporal duration, change according to principles of the so-called lawful nature of things in the horizon of metaphysics. The nature of embodied things goes without saying in mundane thought and speech as something absolute and objective, and could ordinarily be inferred and experienced directly with one's habitual norms of practice in the natural world. As a result of such intentional action, the totality of all that exists actually and factually, both for one's self and for others during our intersubjective relationships and communal interactions, is spontaneously constituted in conscious awareness by analogy with pre-existing embodied spatial things.

Embodied things pre-exist in the transcendental register as pregiven spatial unities of objectified temporality consisting of minutes, units, ages, and so on. (*see* Husserl 1970, 316) That is to say, embodied things are historical and cultural in the pre-scientific conceptual space of everyday life. It is well known, for example, that linear perspective in art was invented during the Renaissance. The directing of a viewer's eye by embodied lines and planes only appears in Western art, "or art so deeply influenced by western art that it has lost its own special character." (Van Doren 1991, 129) Objects of immediate apperception are typically directed in mental life to become *truthful* correlates of a presupposed self-sufficient and historically embodied world. Here, a world of extended material properties exists in transcendental consciousness according to one's cultural and scientifically determinable true form of a spatiotemporal nature. The intentional directing of pre-conceptual performances toward the embodied nature of the psyche represents the spirit-life of traditional truth-seeking toward the surrounding cultural world and the objective place of psychic life within it. Yet the a-historical and enduring truth about the relationship between corporeal- and spirit-life is never given by embodied psychological phenomena—which is, that the physical Body has no soul, but rather the soul has a physical Body. (*see* Husserl 1980a, 366-7; 2006, 160)

However, truthful principles about objective psychic life are deducible by natural-science psychologists according to presupposed psychophysical laws that have already determined the embodied nature of mental life. Such laws in their naturalistic abstractions are then experienced in conceptual space as intuitively valid for theory construction. A similar calculus for positing what truly exists for everyone is retained and repeated in naïve theoretical reflections during our intersubjective and communal interactions. Husserl (1970, §57) concludes that such "mostly Kantian" metaphysics for presuppositions of embodied existence dictate that the human spirit of autonomy has duration in naturalistic methodologies only as an objectified thing. The human soul thus has neither meaning nor intelligibility as individual subjectivity or as one's spiritual ownness in a world consisting only of historically objectified realities. (*see* pp. 315-16) Husserl's clarification of our experiences with the *eidos* of *embodiment* directs phenomenological reflections back to a basic epistemological question in the *Logical Investigations* regarding the potential for objective knowledge. One could now ask, "What makes something 'objective' in our thoughts during consciousness-formation?"

More precisely for phenomenological psychology, "How do we objectify intentional objects such that they are constituted to be the embodied things we typically recognize as actually real and true in the natural world?" This question follows a turn of regard in cognitive mental life, where perhaps a proper response requires Husserl's transcendental *epoché* and reduction—for indeed, *the* natural world, including its structures of meaningfulness, its necessary presuppositions, its constructed realities, and its intelligibility, comes to presence as a unity in awareness as a correlate of transcendental constitutive life. Throughout the duration of consciousness-formation, a unity of sense and meaning remains a psychological theme of apprehension and apperception for an objectified intentional object in the world of common semblance.

The Transcendental Experience of Intelligibility

Whatever the subject says or implies to be objectively real is seen under the *epoché* and eidetic reduction to be the correlate of a transcended object and all necessary transcending acts—all this within a flow of reasoning from pre-conceptual to conceptual space. Here, elements of an object of anticipated self-knowledge are pregiven to the performing ego of constitutive life by means of a form of ideation; and according to this form, the object is then transcended further in higher-level apperceptions of particular sense and meaning. As a teleological goal in this system of apperceptions, where every eidetic system in psychic life is characterized as intentional on the part of the pure Ego, the intelligibility of an intentional object is constructed with reason and evidence of common semblance in the world that is commonly talked about. A transcendental dialectic of reasoning takes place among the various horizons of constitutive life—coming to conclusion, then, within the horizon of metaphysics wherein the intentional object is correlated with apodictic certainty as an embodied configuration of unity. Genetic reconstructions of this performance begin in the horizons of ontology and epistemology with the transcendental *epoché*, practiced as a radical skepticism of the subject's apperceptive experiences when presented from the natural attitude.

A transcendental phenomenologist wants to see the ongoing and enduring intelligibility of an intentional object during a dialectic of reasoning, starting from its solipsistic origins and continuing on into the subject's intersubjective relationships. One of the first things to show itself under the transcendental *epoché* is a transcending-act in pure psychology that runs throughout the *a priori* horizons. Husserl (1982, §37) calls this act "a particular 'objectifying' turn" of an intentional object into the structural features of a pregiven world of objective reality. It is easily seen that Husserl's practice is to "pass through" pure psychology as fundamental human experience in order to reveal the transcendental structures of pure human consciousness.

The subject's "accomplishment" of intelligibility in the horizon of epistemology is Husserl's *entrée* into a regressive phenomenology of conferred meaning in the horizon of ontology. During a genetic phenomenological reconstruction of consciousness-formation beginning from this ontic origin, something that shows itself as an intelligible object under the transcendental *epoché* and reduction has already appeared under the eidetic reduction of one's signifying expressions of an active idea. Here, an accomplishment of intelligibility shows itself as the "still-in-grasp" essence of an *eidos* throughout all modifications in its dialectic of reasoning—including those modifications in the horizon of metaphysics. Here, too, Husserl (1970, §47) sees under the transcendental reduction that the unambiguous essence of an idea endures in apperceptive experience from its genesis in solipsistic subjectivity into its intersubjective constitution as a transcendental object. A world of concrete phenomena and objective reality would not be intelligible to one's self and to others except for an inner structure of intentionality for bestowing sense on conferred meanings according to this psychic order. Under the transcendental *epoché* and reduction, Husserl is "inquiring consistently and exclusively after the…world's manner of givenness" to transcendental consciousness.

Husserl seems to suggest that one purpose of the *eidetic* reduction in the transcendental register is to see the enduring "what" of constitution, while one purpose of the *transcendental* reduction is to see its intentional "way"—that is to say, to see both the universal and contingent givenness of an intentional object to consciousness-formation. Our apperceptions in the transcendental register are intended to achieve intelligibility for an intentional object, no matter whether that intention ever succeed or finally fails. Yet with one's anticipation of intelligibility—for the first time in reflections—the transcendental ego makes its appearance in Husserl's knowledge complex as the pure Ego's experience of living knowingly in the world of human co-existence and common semblance. All elements of objects and acts are now at hand within a reconstructive genetic phenomenology for clarifications of the "what" and the "way" of conscious awareness; and the transcendental turn is thus accomplished for both philosophy and psychology in Husserl's theory of inquiry.

Because of our pre-conceptual transcending-acts of *valuation* in pure psychology, an intentional object gains presence as what Husserl (1982, §37) calls, "the full intentional Object"—put otherwise, as the objectified intentional object of constructed intelligibility. Whatever is then expressed by the subject as objectively real presents to reflections an "intentional correlate of the valuing act" within the epistemological horizon of transcendental subjectivity. We typically value an object in this horizon by determining it for judgments as having (say) practical utility for expressing a pregiven meaning, or (perhaps) normative significance for reality construction, or (maybe) predominantly affective content. What we value about an intentional object in all cases and horizons of transcendental constitutive life is the enduring essence of what one intends and anticipates to be constituted in consciousness of something intelligible. This pre-conceptual action is how we literally "make sense" of things in thought and speech during the normal course of events.

Due to our on-going valuing-acts during apperceptive performances, an *eidos* endures into fruition as a unity of configuration in its anticipation to become a fully realized intentional object—rather than to remain an unintelligible multiform composition of elements in pure subjectivity that I might not express to myself or to others. For example, in an affair-complex that includes the valuing-act of loving something, we seize upon the elements of an intentional object that in anticipation one believes could be loved by *me myself*. In the same affair-complex that includes the valuing-act for self-knowledge of that object, we seize upon the elements that we intend to know. In the case of objectifying an intentional object, we seize upon the elements of what we value and intend to grasp as an objective thing for everyone. And so, when I construct this concatenation of apperceived elements into a unity of configuration, I could constitute awareness of something objective that I believe others might similarly know and love.

When an intentional object is deemed intelligible in the world of common semblance, the pure Ego's logic of calculus includes those valuations and judgments that enable its eidetic structure to tend toward a unity of configuration. In the living present for this anticipated unity, the pure psychological field represents the horizon of all potential action on elements in cognitive mental life here and now. This is the domain of the pure Ego's psychosubjectivity, given to regressive reflections as universal psychic being. The constitution of an intentional object is fulfilled by the action and nonaction of the pure Ego's psychosubjectivity, which is then given to genetic reflections as the psychological ego. Under the transcendental reduction in the horizon of epistemology, references to the psychological ego signify the intelligibility of our rational and nonrational acts of comportment when being "psychological"—as opposed to something extra-psychic that lacks the spirit-life of autonomy and agency (such as a neurological "machine" of embodied dimensions). In both active and passive modes of intentional action, in both pure and transcendental consciousness, the *eidos* of *actionality* exemplifies the essence of cognitive mental life that Husserl calls, "consciousness-of."

The essence of being conscious of something thus pre-exists as a potential for action in constitutive life, where this potential is described by Husserl (1973b, 29) as a *dynamis* in the spirit-life of pure psychology. Dynamic action turns the opportunity for consciousness of an intentional object into an *entelecheia* (= a complete reality in its fulfillment) of intelligibility and meaningfulness. An unfulfilled, not yet actualized, intentional object represents only the potential for conscious awareness. If some matter is to be fully realized as a rational affective unity in transcendental consciousness—*and it might not be*—then further action must be taken in cognitive mental life. In the case of constituting one's "truthful" self-knowledge of something, further objectifying acts of valuation are anticipated by the pure Ego within a transcendentally mediated eidetic affair-complex. Without such subsequent action there is usually not enough reason-as-evidence for certainty in rational valuations of one's self-knowledge of something: "I don't know if it's true or not, that's just what I feel," or else, "I don't know *what* I mean."

Husserl (1982, §145) noticed that sometimes in naïve reflections there is something there that calls to us "like a mystic voice from a better world: Here is the truth." But a mystical voice of intuition from the horizon of metaphysics can neither confirm nor disconfirm anything objective during rational comportment. Our spirit-life of truth-seeking cannot by itself provide evidence of one's own constituted objective knowledge-of-something. In the pure psychology of seeking the truth of an intentional object, we might indeed have the sense of conjecture or speculation about something objective, just as it is intended, along with its correlated affect of anticipation in pure psychology. "It could happen," one might say. But this too is not adequate epistemological or ontological evidence of an objective reality, and our sense and feelings about something are then prone to ambiguity as to its meaning. In most cases of our constructions of intelligibility, the answer to a call in transcendental spirit-life for adequate evidence of objective truth and actual reality is found during one's intersubjective relationships of empathy.

In relationships of empathy, each of us has a spontaneous and pre-given sense of what it means for something to be objectively true and actually real, and we usually enjoy the feeling that others share such meaningful sense. If for no other reason, it seems, we share what appear to be similar experiences during our day-to-day living. We tend to use the words "subjective" and "objective" quite loosely in naïve reflections on this experience, where my own subjective sense of something and its mutually shared objectification are fairly indistinguishable. In any event, we suppose, differences in *sense* could be brought into proper correspondence with some further thinking on the matter—*if* it matters. When something does matter to us affectively, we could notice that there is a difference in intelligibility between my own subjective sense of something, and what could be valued and judged as objective for all of us. As a pre-conceptual matter of apperception, we then abstract that difference in anticipation of further actionality during our intersubjective constructions of intelligibility. (*see* Husserl 2006, 133)

The cognitive action whereby we abstract differences in relationships of empathy provide *entrées* for Husserl's (1973a, §64) clarifications of norms for gaining self-knowledge of objectified things. One's self-knowledge of such things is sustained by our constructions of actual reality here and now; but first, an affair-complex must be modified in order to include the potential for the presence of actual reality in the conceptual space of common semblance—a reality that is simultaneously subjective in its origins and objective in its contents of intelligibility. The potential for knowing something as actually real and objectively true is pregiven in solipsistic subjectivity and fulfilled intersubjectively within a flow of reasoning from pre-conceptual to conceptual space. This same potential is realized in the transcendental register by an act in mental life that adjusts the intuitive position of the pure Ego within a system of apperceptions. The intentional function of this transcending act of synthesis is to modify ("re-orient") the spatiotemporality of an intentional object's affair-complex into the unambiguous "one time" of sense and meaning—a moment usually experienced as the irreal essence of *now*. An affair-complex, Husserl (1973a, §38) explains, is composed in this way to coincide in essential features with the pregiven "oneness" of pre-conceptual experience in pure subjectivity; and by this action, the anticipated intellibility of an intentional object becomes situated *here* for judgments in the living present.

An intentional object is subquently carried over into our contingent experiences of transcendental subjectivity, where it is typically constituted as a unity with the appearance of objective reality. Husserl (1982, §22) is well aware that his approach to the concept of *reality* is criticized for what is characterized as its "Platonic realism." However, he posits a reality for such "non-things" as ideas and essences because they are presented as actualized objects of the mind in the natural attitude. Indeed, Husserl's so-called platonizing serves to disclose the presence of such things in constitutive life that are already positioned within an intentional construction of intelligibility. Still, phenomenological realism in Husserl's methodology is simply a "matter of 'grammatical hypostatization.'" His instrumental use of Platonic realism is emphatically not intended to be construed as a matter of "metaphysical hypostatization"—where the naïve intelligibility of something metaphysical tends to be realized as a concrete thing according to the language that is used to describe that thing as objectively real.

It is perhaps worth noting that the problem of "hypostasis," along with what makes up hypostasized knowledge in the world that is commonly talked about, has been controversial to this day. A hypostasized object could be thought of as something that has no pre-conceptual evidence or ground of support for its intelligibility. From the natural attitude, we only *suppose* the existence of such support when referring to something objectively true. It goes without saying, we naïvely tend to believe, that something presupposed as concretely real in conceptual space is objectively true whenever it might appear for judgments and valuations. Husserl (1973a, §52) suggests that for blatant examples of metaphysical hypostatization we need only look to modern physicists who rely upon the "unknown cause of appearances" for descriptions of physical things. From the phenomenological attitude, on the other hand, the reality of presentational objects is the self-evident reality of their being imagined, followed by the reality of their being constituted in conscious awareness, and the subsequent reality of our expressions about them to one's self and to others. Those who fail to grasp Husserl's instrumental use of a presentational object as regressive *entrée* into its eidetic pre-existence and underlying sense and meaning have no proper understanding of his methodology. (*see* Fink 1995, §11)

During the genetic succession of reality construction for an intentional object, beginning from its imagination to its appearance as actually real in conscious awareness, there is a temporal flow of before-and-after underlying irreality of the essence of something that is anticipated to become an intelligible object. This pre-conceptual flow of the ("before") epistemic ground of *knowing,* and its anticipated ("after") fulfillment of self-knowledge, discloses the manner in which the *eidos* of *reality* is correlated in transcendental consciousness. (*see* Husserl 1973a, §64) One's ordinary experience of reality, Husserl (1970, §55) suggests, "stands within the sphere of self-evidence…[and from the natural attitude,] any attempt to inquire behind it would be absurd." Yet under the transcendental reduction, all forms of reality comprise the "interlaced" (*verflochten*) commonality of spatiotemporality during our lived experience of the constitution of an intelligible object of self-knowledge. (*see* Husserl 1973a, §29) One's ordinary *sense* of actual reality is thus an intentional outcome of constitutive experience in the transcendental register.

The psychological ego's iterating activities of before-and-after reality construction disclose the pure Ego's pre-conceptual form of givenness for an intentional object here and now. With the phenomenological method of reasoning, a form of givenness is intuitively grasped by the performing ego in order to *re*-present the intentional object's spatiotemporal form of anticipated intelligibility and meaningfulness during any single moment of consciousness-formation. Something *re*-presented in the transcendental register is therefore pre-existing and pregiven within the flow of a psychic order of constitution. The pure Ego's internal time-consciousness of this flow is the immanent *time* of the living present for psychic life—the *when* of cognitions. Once imagined by the subject and now phenomenologically "real" (*Reel*), an original idea is retained as the origin of cognitive action on necessary elements. Something purely subjective that retains its place in time and space points regressive reflections toward the singular core essence of a phenomenological *eidos*.

The term "core essence" refers to an element that Husserl (1982, §131) calls "the pure determinable X" of an intentional object. A core essence does not vary as the bearer of sense and meaning in any form of givenness to intelligibility. For example, the core essence of a moo will never be more fundamental than a sound made by a cow, even when we write the word "moo." For another example, the *eidos* of *shirt* is judged to be actually real during the normal course of events because of a durable underlying core essence of openings for head, arms, and body within a system of apperceptions—even if additional elements of utility, color, size, or shape are retained during consciousness-formation. The spatiality of a singular core essence is centered and unmoved within its eidetic affair-complex, where it temporally pre-exists any modifications of its *eidos* in perceptual experience, transcendental objecti-fication, or constructed reality. Yet because of our genetic modifications of an object of the mind, the spatiotemporal configuration of any number of other retained elements varies during the composition of a dynamic affair-complex for a core essence and its eidetic relationships.

The internal time-consciousness of simple and higher-level appercep-tions follows a psychic order in the living present that is directed iteratively back-and-forth by apprehended differences in duration of the elemental rela-tionships of an original idea. (*see* Husserl 1964a, §10) During a dialectical syn-thesis of conscious awareness, beginning from the solipsistic register of one's fundamental existential relationships, a psychic order persists as an immanent temporality for the singular core essence of an intentional object. Here, a pre-given element of dependence and difference is apperceived with the greatest clarity of givenness in pre-conceptual experience, even as that element is ab-stracted for further transcending acts of correlation with other elements of contingent experience. Whatever endures through its iterations from imagina-tion to actualization within the *a priori* and contingent horizons has already been experienced for some (albeit, sometimes very small) time as the potential for an intentional object to be intelligible in the transcendental register.

In Husserl's (1982, §136) phenomenology of reason, spatiotemporal givenness points toward something in apperceptive experience that is at hand for cognitions of intelligibility. That *something* could be seen under the *epoché* ("in the broadest sense"of *seeing*) as the potential for the pure Ego's apprehen-sion of a rational affective unity. An intentional unity of irreality and actuality is the essence and lived experience of psychological consciousness—where said potential could be referenced by saying to one's self, for example, "I can see it, but what is it?" During our pre-conceptual performances to fulfill a po-tential for awareness, the psychological ego follows the pure Ego's internal time-consciousness of the duration of necessary elements for an *eidos* within an affair-complex's ongoing eidetic composition. In the example of pregiven-ness to consciousness-formation just presented as "I can see it...", the psycho-logical ego is composing elements of an affair-complex for the singular core essence of an *eidos* according to the logic of calculus for grasping the intelligi-bility of the still-vague intentional object "it."

During higher-level apperceptions of objectivity within a calculus of intelligibility, some elements of "it" will be retained and some will elapse dur-ing a temporal order of constitution. According one's judgments in this men-tal process of reasoning, we might then say, "I don't quite get it." When further necessary elements have been composed within a purely subjective ei-detic affair-complex for the core essence of "it," that complex is transcended intersubjectively during the same mental process: "Oh, I understand *that*. Doesn't everyone?" With our spirit-life and motivation to know something intelligible as objectified self-knowledge, each element necessary for the structure of an affair-complex has its own pregiven irreality during the tempo-rality of intentional action in the living present. Each element is thus retained during pre-conceptual performances as necessity demands for contingent ex-periences with "everyone." This state of affairs points toward a synthesis of unity for the *a priori* and contingent elements of a transcendental object.

And yet, each pre-conceptual element by itself is not and never will be actually real. Instead, each temporally modified affair-complex for a singular core essence is pregiven with the sense of a *composition* of unified elements here and now. An intentional object is apprehended by the pure Ego as the potential for something that could be known as actually real, but only as a whole thing within the horizon of epistemology. (*see* Husserl 1973b, §70) For example, we do not spontaneously judge something to be a tree solely according to the shape of its trunk, since that same shape could be an element of a post or a column. If we claim, "It is a tree," the signified irreal "it" is the so-called quidditive content of a judgment that continues to exist within an "internal horizon" for one's inductive inferences of *why* or *how* "it" is a tree. (§8) Husserl mentions that sometimes the core essence of *it* "is enough" for intelligibility in conceptual space. As vague as it might be in terms of sense and meaning, *it* is a singular thing of anticipated unity in pure consciousness. *It* is real in some form of reality construction in the living present beginning from the original presentation of an idea in one's imagination. In the midst of a mental formation of transcendence, *it* continues thus real for judgments throughout an immanent psychic order of cognitive action.

Husserl (1964a, §8) describes the pure psychology of internal time-consciousness within any mental formation as the "living production" of reality during consciousness-formation. An order of action and non-action in a mental formation of objects and acts is typically directed in the living present toward an eidetic composition's fulfilled appearance of an actually real object. Here, a constituted objectivity is indeed meant to be intelligible as a whole thing. We could then, for instance, *re*-cognize the *eidos* of *tree* in conceptual space as an intelligible object, not only from the retained shape of its trunk but also by its configuration of branches and by the shadow that it casts. A mental formation of iterated cognitive action and non-action is intuitively valid for psychological inquiry—since this is the expression of psychic life in the horizon of epistemology whereby the pure Ego achieves its goals of intelligibility and self-knowledge of an object of the mind.

Under the eidetic reduction, Husserl (1970, §49) writes, the horizon of epistemology gives the "temporal mode of the present; [where] this mode points toward its horizons [of both *a priori* and contingent experience]." Phenomenological horizons indeed set the limits of one's consciousness of something here and now. Husserl (1982, §79) explains that each horizon presents a range of potential rational and non-rational comportment directed toward intelligibility—beginning from what is assigned and restricted to beasts, and continuing on to what could be assigned and restricted to God. Here, each horizon is pregiven to consciousness-formation as an overall delimitation of what could exist within a relationship of *I* and *Other*. Not only are there horizons for elements of sense and meaning, but as we have seen there is also a purely psychological horizon for the retention-elapse-anticipation of necessary elements throughout the day-to-day "flux of consciousness."

When composing elements of an intentional object in the midst of this flux, there is also a horizon that delineates the potential for our cognitions of the *eidos* of *space*. In the horizon of space, Husserl (1982, §72) points out, there are a "*finite number of concepts and propositions* derivable in a given case" from every other horizon of experience—including the horizons of epistemology, metaphysics, ontology, and pure psychology. The spatiality of an object's pregivenness is seen under the *epoché* to be delimited as either thetically *here*— from the Greek, *thetos*, meaning laid down in place—or nonthetically *not-here*. Something potentionally intelligible and meaningful that is *not-here* is *there* in the spatiality of action in the living present. Typically given to consciousness-formation by the pure Ego's internal time-consciousness for particular events of pure and contingent experience, the temporality of awareness is a finite matter within the horizon of space. An intelligible world of actually real things thus gains presence as a "definite manifold" of spatiotemporal strata of essences and their here/there relationships in the transcendental register. In Husserl's work, the eidetic structure of geometry best "documents" the subject's cognitions of the *eidos* of *space* in the phenomenological field.

The *eidos* of *space* presents the horizon for a delimited plurality of elements that could be grouped and composed as correlates of a common essence—composed, that is, such that they gain presence as a unity of sense and meaning. (*see* Husserl 1982, §86) In Husserl's (1970, §62) descriptions of pure consciousness, the highest genus of common prior essence is life itself, which is played out in the spatiality of transcendental consciousness as the pregivenness of corporeal- and spirit-life. For example, I tend not to think of my hand *here* in the space of things when I reach for a glass of water. Yet the essence of *my hand* is nonthetically *there* for action in the living present, where it pre-exists as a correlate of unity for the intelligibility of *reaching*. Also, a shape of irreality that pre-exists *there* in solipsistic structures could be retained *here* within spatial formations of actual reality as contingency demands in the transcendental register. Moreover, each element within a spatiotemporal unity of thetic givenness could be transcended individually in temporal duration; for instance, as corporeal-life is embodied as a physical thing for everyone, and as spirit-life represents the extra-physical everywhere. These experiences support the notion that the givenness of corporeal- and spirit-life is intuitively *pregiven* in the sphere of immanence by the irreducible element of *pure life* in time and space.

In the midst of a complex manifold of here/there givenness, each of us could usually constitute an objectivity in transcendental consciousness as a correlate of (a) the pure Ego's intuitive grasp of parts and wholes in the sphere of immanence, and (b) the internal time-consciousness of before-and-after configurations for essential elements. In the living-present profile of an eidetic affair-complex, the idea of a common essence for retained elements of intelligibility and meaningfulness, and the idea of a manifold of finite spatiotemporal strata wherein contitutive life takes place, together anticipate (as the potential for correlations) a (synthetic) transcendental unity of awareness. When we grasp an object's composition as a unity of elements among the *a priori* and contingent horizons, that object is then constituted within the manifold-as-a-whole by correlations with the *eidos* of *space*. Husserl's methodology means to articulate each modality of constitutive experience as together a spatiotemporal unity of intelligibility and meaningfulness.

Naïve expressions of intelligibility and meaningfulness direct reflections toward life-world experiences of *being* and *doing*. (*see* Husserl 1973b, §58) Within the epistemic horizon of such things, the concept of *life-world* points to our constructions of reality that are oriented to one's self-knowledge of the world of Nature—a world seen under the *epoché* to be composed of embodied objects and transcended pure subjectivity. Here, the transcendental ego's grasp of intelligibility and meaningfulness for something at hand represents the pure Ego's being-sense for a transcendental object. When fulfilling the intentional function to compose a unity of common essence amid a plurality of elements, necessary elements of solipsistic and transcendental subjectivity are thematically grouped so as to construct a "synthetical unity" for (say) the transcendental object experienced as *my life*. (*see* Husserl 1982, §86)

Each pregiven unity of being-sense typically resides *there*, in the "background" of spontaneous thought. However, as needs might arise *here* for consciousness-formation, salient elements of life-world experience are abstracted in order to construct one's *personal* lifeworld as an intelligible unity of configuration within its own internal horizon—meaning, we compose a unity of experiences that are retained as *my own*. This pre-conceptual eidetic structure is given by protension to constitutive life by what Husserl (1977, 32) calls our "psychological subjectivity" in the living present. Cognitive acts in psychological processes group elements for both what is anticipated in personal experience and what is believed to exist as actually real and objectively present here and now. *My life* thus exists as an intelligible object in spatiotemporal relationships with what is pregiven in the life-world as intelligible for everyone—namely, objective knowledge of embodied corporeal-life, and objective knowledge of the sprit-life enjoyed by all of us. The psychological ego is included in the background of this experience as the manifestation of our human agency for intentional mental acts in one's personal lifeworld.

For as long as the pure Ego's active agency endures from solipsistic to transcendental subjectivity during life-world experience, the psychological ego shows itself within all substrates of ego-life as one's "personal ego." (*see* Husserl 1973b, §32) The intelligibility of one's personal lifeworld is built up in eidetic compositions partly to provide adequate evidence for the presupposition of prior common essence for the experience of *my life* in co-existence with others. The objectification of *my life* is represented in thought and speech by the unity of one's lived experience with this presupposition of unity and its intelligibility. Our ordinary belief in a common essence of human existence typically includes the spatiotemporal dimensions of idealized semblance for every intentional form that includes a fundamental relationship of *I* and *Other*.

In 1913, however, Husserl (1982, §150) remarked that "the profoundest phenomenological sense" of the *eidos* of *space*—along with the idea of a personal manifold of intentionality and psychic being—had not been fully grasped in his work as our intuitive sense of spatiality. Perhaps the best thing to do, Husserl mentioned at the time, is to clarify those phenomena "in which space is intuitively presented and is 'constituted' as the unity of appearances" for an intelligible object. Yet despite Husserl's early pessimism, he noticed that each of us comes to know the natural world as a unity of objective reality by means of our acts of valuation in pure psychology. The motivating affective spirit of these acts in the living present means to have such a world in thought and speech—but only as it is constituted amid the temporally finite and spatially enclosed objectifications of *my life*. *Me-in-my-world* is a correlate of unity during this contingent experience in the transcendental register.

Husserl (1981, 224) outlined the finite horizon for the construction and constitution of this correlate in his 1934 manuscript on "the origin of the spatiality of nature." He explains in this manuscript that during life-span experiences with transcendental objects, the subject's awareness of worldly existence is typically correlated in the horizon of space for cognitions of pregiven objective things and their mutual relationships here and now. The sense of *my life* within this horizson represents the contingent space of experience that is peculiarly *my own*—where in cognitive mental life, "I 'conceive'" the intelligibility of objective things for *me myself* with the meaning of my being an objective thing in spatial relationships with other objective things.

In Husserl's (Fink 1995, 182) theory of world-consciousness, a world of objective things is seen to be "the totality of real things as existent actualities." This totality—this spatiotemporal manifold that always and already surrounds each of us in one's naïve natural world—represents a built-up horizon of immediate potential for *my life* to gain presence as an objectified unity in conceptual space. We achieve this unity by transcending one's fundamental (multi-form) sense of *I* and *Other* in the transcendental register. (*see* Husserl 1973a, 34) During the normal course of events, we spontaneously transcend the pre-existing *being* and *doing* of solipsistic subjectivity in the world of human co-existence; and with this transcendence, the fundamental relationship of our intersubjective experience of (the unity-form) "'I' *with* 'Other'" comes to hand (*here*) within the spatial horizon for what is actually real and objectively true. In this way of intentional action, our intersubjective experience of being-in-the-world is the lived experience of objectified human co-existence.

Because of the psychological ego's objectifying acts, not only is the potential for objective knowledge realized as an intelligible unity, but *my life* becomes objectively real as well. The objectification of *me myself* thus co-exists with other objectified things, and my so-called worldly sense is therefore my being-sense in all horizons that delimit my being an individual existent in the midst of a plurality of existents. Along with its nonthetic correlations for worldly things retained *there* during consciousness-formation, the core essence of *the* world (just as *any* core essence) does not change in the transcendental register—even as a plurality of objectified elements expands in greater length and depth of maturation in their embodied givenness to contingent experience. Instead, as Husserl (Fink 1995, 192) points out, one's consciousness of *my life* as an intelligible object *here* changes as it is "brought to givenness in its very self" of passive acceptance of the objectified world of common semblance. Each naïve reference to an objective world of human co-existence, or to what is signified when we think and speak of a universal human nature, point reconstructive reflections toward the pregivenness of conferred meaning on *me myself* as a real existent—along with the totality of all real things (*der realen Dinge*) that are meaningful in one's life. (§9)

The Horizon of Ontology

It perhaps seems counter-intuitive that the subject's expressions of self-knowledge (rather than a semantics of meaning) provide *entrées* for examinations of constitutive life within the horizon of ontology. Yet it is on the core essence of an object of potential self-knowledge that meaning is conferred in this horizon, making that essence immanently meaningful for correlations in all other horizons. It consequently matters to the pure Ego that *this* set of correlated elements is to represent the being-sense of *this eidos* in thought and speech. Since the lived experience of something meaningful is grounded by a pre-existing meaning found in the horizon of ontology, conferred meaning is an enduring substrate of "the meant" during the changing profiles of pure and transcendental consciousness. (*see* Husserl 1982, §95) Husserl's fundamental ontology is a parenthesized and clarified ontology of experience within this horizon; and indeed, Husserl uses mundane ontology "as transcendental theme" for reconstructing the constitutive life of something deemed to be meaningful in conscious awareness. (*see* Fink 1995, §11 note 384)

A transcendental theme of consciousness-formation typically presents to reflections the subject's unique course of inductions whereby the pure Ego posits the meaning of something actually real in referential expressions. One could say within a transcendental theme, for example, "We're all doing a good job here," or "Birds of a feather flock together," or "Psychology accepts that people remember events and truths, that they categorize objects, that they draw inferences, [and] that they act on beliefs and preferences." (Burge 1996, 377) A naïve predication as to the meaning and being of an intentional object provides regressive *entrée* into Husserl's fundamental ontology of pre-existing being-sense for *this eidos* and not another. Just as pure psychology is intuitively pregiven in thoughts of mental life, so too is fundamental ontology intuitively pregiven for inquiry into the meaning and being of what truly exists. A description of what Husserl refers to as a mundane ontology of formal properties is provided by Blackburn (1994):

> ["Ontology" is] derived from the Greek word for being, but [it is also] a 17th–century coinage for the branch of metaphysics that concerns itself with what exists.... [There] have existed many *a priori* arguments that the world must contain things of one kind or another.... Philosophers characteristically charge each other with reifying things improperly, and in the history of philosophy every kind of thing will at one time or another have been thought to be the fictitious result of an ontological mistake. (pp. 269-70)

In Husserl's work, fundamental ontology is clearly not a "branch of metaphysics," since an argument or belief about the existence of something is self-evidently not that thing itself. Rather, "fundamental ontology" refers to the radical sense of ontology, the *a priori* experience when one is conscious of something meaningful and truly existing. As part of the motivating spirit-life of spontaneous thought, there is a fundamental, intuitive, desire for the possibility of something to exist with meaning in every anticipated structure of pure and transcendental consciousness. The ontic boundary of a pre-existing structure of meaning represents Husserl's (Fink 1995, 182) universal "horizon of horizons" for realization of an intentional object in constitutive life. That is to say, the potential for being conscious of something that truly exists pre-exists the language that we use in order to express the actuality of that thing's being-sense to one's self and to others. It is easily seen that Husserl's (2006, 44n.13) ontology holds to the doctrine that the cognition of possibilities must precede the cognition of actualities. For example, we seize upon the essence of *redness* before we ever apprehend that the meaning of *red* could be grasped as a visual perception, and before an intentional object is ever cognitively correlated to be actually red as a fulfilled objectivity in conscious awareness.

Every moment of intentional experience, every enduring culture, every science and philosophy, presents more than a naïve ontology of existence with our expressions of what is meant. With each human intellectual accomplishment there is a fundamental irreducible organization of elemental relationships that pre-exists for thinking meaningfully about an object of the mind. Husserl's phenomenological ontology is not only explained in his theories of constitution as conferred meaning on an intentional object; it is also demonstrated in applications of the phenomenological method of reasoning, where phenomenologists could experience the tacit presentation of an originally given meaningfulness for something in our lives. Ontological categories and their relationships, including correlations of metaphysical presuppositions of certainty, are intelligible with the method of *epoché* only in the context of the cognitive action that confers meanings on objects. It is by will of our human agency alone that we are capable of making such conferring-acts in the ontic horizon of ordinary experience and theoretical reflections.

Ontic conferring-acts are universal elements of *choice* in the pure psychology of intentional experience. One such ontic conferring-act, for example, is to think and say a similar meaning in its intentional form to others as to one's self within a single transcendental theme. Another is to posit the meaning of something such that its form of ideation is not contradicted by apperceptive experience. In the world of human co-existence, the horizon of ontology delimits the transcendental logic that we use during apperceptive experience when grasping the meanings of objectively real things as being here for all of us. Meanings of intentional objects then gain presence in thought and speech, rationally and non-rationally, with studied reasoning and spontaneous fantasy, only because of the pre-existing logic of calculus for having them here in *this* form of ontic being. When we experience conscious awareness within a region of worldly intelligibility, Husserl's fundamental ontology represents the origin and intuitive ground in the living present of what is grasped as fulfilled sense and meaning—for indeed, fundamental ontology represents the genesis of one's being-sense here and now.

Some irreal things pre-exist with meaning at the genesis of our psychological consciousness of a rational affective unity, and are therefore already at hand during the normal course of events for valuations and judgments in transcendental constitutive life. For instance, with regard to its geometrical properties, the element of *triangle* in a logic of calculus does not depend for its presence on anything posited in formal ontology. Each of us usually grasps the meaning of the *eidos* of *triangle* during pre-conceptual experience even before we learn what to call it. In the pre-scientific space of actually real things, the meaning signified by the word "triangle" is then determined by one's prior act of conferring on this irreality either a pre-existing meaning of three things together or of a solid shape having three sides. Either (or both) of these relationships could be correlated with contingent elements within the horizon of ontology, and then pregiven as an intentional form for the word that signifies the meaningfulness of *triangle* here and now. Both categories of meaning thus pre-exist our learning and practical use of the word "triangle," and both pre-exist any transcendental modification of its *eidos* in the conceptual space of mundane speech—even when "the meant" refers to a romantic entanglement.

Under the transcendental *epoché*, conferring-acts are, so to say, "hidden" from the subject's spontaneous grasp; since within the organizing horizon of space, the focus of the performing ego is instead on the meaning of an anticipated objectivity within its eidetic affair-complex—although the intentional act must have indeed occurred. In this sense of thematic focus in the living present, we bracket our irreal mental life of cognitive action amid the spatiotemporality of constitutive life. Husserl's object-oriented methodology similarly brackets pure psychology for evaluations of the core essence of an intentional object within the horizon of ontology. Nevertheless, the abstracted grammar and syntax of fulfilled ontic conferring-acts provide *entrée* into a series of regressive reductions to both the elements and intentional mental acts of pure and transcendental consciousness. The pure psychology of this state of affairs includes those cognitive operations and norms of practice in the horizon of ontology that maintain the meaningfulness of constituted objectivities and constructed actual realities.

Consequently under the psychological *epoché*, interpretations of cognitive mental life within the horizon of ontology help to clarify the genetic constitution of an intentional object—not as a random or accidental grouping of elements, but as the unity that gains presence out of a plurality because of our acts in pure psychology to confer meanings on objects of the mind. Delimited by the ontic horizon for an anticipated meaningfulness during consciousness-formation, one's thoughts and cognitive operations of *nous* subsequently turn outward from what had been previously and inwardly *me and mine* in solipsistic subjectivity. Beginning from within the horizon of ontology, during a so-called zig-zagging iterative movement of intentional activity between Husserl's phenomenology of reason and his theory of pure psychology, applied transcendental phenomenological psychology could direct genetic reflections into the transcendental register of pure human consciousness.

A Phenomenological Psychology of Ontic Experience

While discussing elements of world-consciousness we experience during the ego life of transcendental subjectivity—versus the field of pure subjectivity that provides its intuitive ground—Husserl appended a summary comment to

145

Eugen Fink's (1995) *Sixth Cartesian Meditation* that includes his reflections on consciousness-formation within the horizon of ontology. In collaboration with Fink, Husserl addresses in this publication an advanced approach toward the problem of meaningfulness as part of his theory of method. Specifically, intentional judging- and valuing-acts in the horizon of ontology are those meaning conferring-acts that are represented as intentional methods in Husserl's transcendental theory of world-constitution. Constructing a unique being-sense for *my life* as actually real is the same "way of proceeding" that we use for conferring meanings on individual things within "the totality of real things as existent actualities." When we grasp the meaningfulness of a rational affective unity in the "external" world of sociocultural surroundings (*der Außenwelt*)—including the phenomenon of *me myself* in co-existence with others—the fundamental ontology of that unity's being-sense points reflections toward the pre-existence of pure psychology in transcendental consciousness.

It might be important to mention that in mundane ontology, the term "human being" typically denotes a pre-scientific object and its material properties, having been constituted in the conceptual space of the nature of things. However, the essence of this object in Husserl's (1965a, 180) fundamental ontology is not a mindless category of empirical taxonomy, objectified and absolutized in theoretical discourse. Rather, its *eidos* represents the way that we universally act out "the humanity of higher man" that exists with reason. This means that as objective human beings, we are subjectively being human in the world of common semblance. Inasmuch as ontology is a science of *a priori* experience, being human is a fundamental ontological experience for the pure Ego. In Husserl's (2006, 149) work, the meaningful human subject exemplifies this experience beginning from its solipsistic register.

Here is part of Husserl's (Fink, 1995) appended summary that speaks of a relationship between phenomenological psychology and transcendental philosophy within the horizon of ontology—a relationship that is played out by each of us in the world that is commonly talked about. This summary is rich in its expressions of the difference between Husserl's phenomenological attitude toward what it means to be human and the natural attitude toward an objective human nature:

> The critique of ontology and of universal philosophy in its ontological way of proceeding…[is taken as a guiding approach] by phenomenology…. [The] discovery of phenomenological psychology and therefore of transcendental philosophy first made the critique possible and showed the essential unintelligibility of the world as nature. [This resulted in a] radical alteration of the concept [of *world* as a locus of human *being* directed toward "external" things]….
>
> The powerful [so-called] instinct…for an existence that one can universally affirm [as "the ideal whole of his abilities" in the external world is first disclosed by phenomenological psychology]. Living in finitude man stands before the riddle of the world—the world is senseless [as objective nature,] all ["objective"] human endeavor is ultimately senseless, a chase after unreachable goals, "life-goals," ulti-

mately a will to life under the practical ideal of "happiness." This is senseless [except as as subjective human experience]. (p. 173)

Expressions of one's "goals" or "happiness" refer to the sense of our spirit-life as an object of affective significance—but only as that sense is correlated here and now with those contingent things and their relationships that come to hand in the external world. In order to clarify the meaning of such expressions, Husserl (1973b, §15) reflects on them within the horizon that objectivities are presented as sense *made* in the space of idealized objectivities. That is to say, as presented from the natural attitude in the transcendental register. A pre-constituted humanized world exists in transcendental subjectivity just as it is intended to *pre*-exist in order to be constituted with the semblance and idealization of infinite duration (*see* Fink 1995, 169-70). In anticipation of this transcendence, one's consciousness of something meaningful and affectively significant is fashioned to gain presence amid a world of absolute dimensions that is believed to be at hand for everyone. A constructed reality for the being-sense of an *eidos* is enclosed within its own distinctive spatiotemporal manifold of intentional experience for this same state of ontic affairness. Constructing an immanently meaningful state of affairs for an *eidos* is our intentional way of conferring meaning on an object of the mind.

The pure Ego's pre-conceptual space of the totality of all that *is*, is itself given to genetic reflection as the sense, meaning, and reality deemed likely for the eidetic structure of conscious awareness. A phenomenologist of course cannot see from the appearance of things given from the natural attitude what might have failed to gain presence as actually real. Not every potential for one's transcendental consciousness is realized with adequate evidence or on otherwise good grounds, and not every intentional form for an anticipated objectivity succeeds to fulfillment. That an intentional object *does* succeed in presenting an objectivity-as-a-whole reveals to reflections its state of ontic affairness during consciousness-formation. Under the eidetic reduction, an ontic affair-complex typically co-presents the anticipated meaning and immanent meaningfulness of a constituted objectivity with the sense of a rational affective unity here and now. In the full complexity of transcendental consciousness, a state of eidetic affairness includes ontic correlations with sense and certainty for each pre-existing element of what is now a pregiven world of human co-existence and common semblance.

Husserl (2001, 64-5) uses the term "complexity" in order to signify an "interpenetrating" of independent parts to an articulated whole structure. Each fundamental element of an object exists amid its spatiotemporal relationships of eidetic parts-to-parts and anticipated parts-to-whole, all within a unitary manifold of *I/Other* experience. Having been retained in this manifold, an original idea is then correlated with essential elements within the horizon of ontology in order for the intentional object to be subsequently realized as affectively significant and immanently meaningful. Beginning from within this horizon during consciousness-formation, both pre-existing and anticipated

one's cognitive action in the living present. A pre-conceptual composing-act on elements of pregivenness represents a turn in regard by the pure Ego in constitutive life—a turn from the partially given and only anticipated totality in solipsistic subjectivity, outward toward the conceptual space of all potential realities for one's intersubjective life-goals. With this turn of regard in pure psychology, transcendental constitution of an objective world and of one's subjective place within it could proceed to fruition.

The complete eidetic structure of conscious awareness entails all necessary correlations of objects and acts for an *eidos* to gain presence as an affective unity. Here, meaning is conferred on an *eidos* that is anticipated to be a whole thing in the world that is commonly talked about, even when that singular thing is part of a "larger" or more extensive whole. An intentional object in pre-conceptual space is thus typically grasped as absolute and infinite during life-world experiences with embodied objects of idealized dimensions. Such experiences could perhaps be described as those irreal things themselves that make up the determinable finite substrate of an objectified Nature.

As strange as it might sound, a *finite* substrate of existence is pre-scientifically conceived as naïvely "infinite" in our presuppositions of naturalized duration—or as Husserl (1983, §143) expresses it, the "determinable X" of an *eidos* yields "a countersensical finite infinity." For example, we tend to believe from the natural attitude that all rocks are hard, always have been and always will be, despite empirical evidence that rocks can indeed bend and liquify under conditions beyond human endurance. In a similar manner of ideation in fundamental ontology, we "rescue" the *eidos* of *my life* from a finite existence by acceptance of this absurdity of non-reason regarding infinite duration—and because of this passivity in empathy, *my life* becomes part of an objective Nature in its totality. (*see* Fink 1995, 173) In subsequent apperceptions of unity, we have therefore already anticipated from the horizons of epistemology and metaphysics, and correlated in the horizon of ontology, that *my life* has the immanent meaningfulness of something absolute whose being-sense goes without saying in the world that is commonly talked about.

Absent the apodictic certainty of *absoluteness* for the pregiven being-sense of something, an intentional object could become different in meaning from what was originally intended for action in the pure psychology of constitutive life. Sometimes, too, we see the absence of *absoluteness* in a logic of calculus as the intuitive presence of an essential threat or hindrance to intelligibility. Reflecting on this matter in the existential register, Ricoeur (1967, 231) suggests that we might then experience the "tragic vision" of fear when anticipating our personal "ruin" by acting with individual agency in the world of common semblance. Yet in the normal course of events, with our anticipation of knowing the meaningfulness of objective things in relationships of empathy, we confer a *true* meaning on an intentional object. Cognitive action is then directed in the transcendental register to fulfill ontic possibilities for an intentional object to become an absolute thing that is believed with certainty to be objectively real and true for everyone—including the objectification that is conceived in pre-scientific space to be *me myself*.

A cognitively modified intentional object could indeed be true in pre-scientific space—true as the result of one's unification of elements in order to be thus true as an absolute thing in the face of contingent experience. It is self-evident from the natural attitude that absolute things cannot be otherwise than what they are meant to be as correlates of certainty. I am absolutely certain in real life, for example, that in any language, time, or place, a chicken is never an apple. By fulfilling the function in constitutive life to group thematically meaningful elements, we could each "ontify," as it were, the meaning of an intentional object's eidetic *is-ness* of identity into its modality of ideation. For Husserl (1982, §3), the *eidos* of *ideation* is represented by the notion of our intuitive "eidetic seeing" (*Wesenserschauung*) a pre-existing ontic affair-complex. As a norm of practice in both regressive and genetic reflections, phenomenologists follow along with the pure Ego's eidetic *seeing* in pure subjectivity.

When meaning is conferred on an object of the mind in a form of ideation such that it cannot be otherwise than intended, said meaning is pregiven to transcendental constitutive life as apodictically certain and "individual" (*individuelle Anschauung*). Object constancy in fulfilled thought and speech indeed depends upon this intentional action of ideation in the phenomenological method proper. Here, conferred meaning on an intentional object is cast forward through protension as an ideation of true meaning that is then modified, accepted, or rejected by the performing ego in further transcending acts. Following this action, one could say, "I mean *this* and not *that*." In order to see the eidetic affairness of fundamental *I-Other* relationships in the transcendental register, reflections turn toward phases of consciousness-formation for something immanently meaningful correlated with the enduring element experienced as *me myself*. Husserl's (1973b, §44) theory of method in the horizon of ontology is intended in part to "mirror" the ontifying-acts that preserve "the meant" during the subject's experiences of immanent meaningfulness.

With our intentional acts of ontification of "the meant" into its singular ideation in the horizon of ontology, we picture an anticipated being-as-a-whole for an objectified thing of idealized dimensions in the transcendental register. During consciousness-formation of this unity, the ideation of a constituted objectivity has already come into ontic being such that its expression is believed to have meaning in the world that is commonly talked about. An intentional form of ideation in the living present serves to organize the realization of the semblance of the pictured thing's being-sense from among the seemingly endless possibilities for actualizing an ontic affair-complex. Some possibilities are fulfilled with more certainty than others, however, since some transcendental calculi enjoy more evidence for actualization of an intentional object. But even so, one's ideation of a fully composed unity now pre-exists with sense and meaning in a relationship of eidetic identity as the potential for *this eidos* in its intentional form. *This eidos* matters immanently here and now; and so, a fulfilled actual reality corresponds directly or by analogy to *this eidos* in its eidetic affairness of being-sense. The immanent meaningfulness of an intentional object endures as "the meant" in life-world experience as a result of the transcendental constitution of its intentional form of ideation.

As we stand before "the riddle of the world," each of us has a sense for any thing for a being only given a tradition of meaningfulness of intentional object that is now at hand. Oriented by this intuitive *sense* of pregivenness, we abstract in simple apperception those elements of the object's *eidos* that matter for an ontic affair-complex for *me myself* here and now. By means of the universal phenomenological method of reasoning toward parts and wholes, we then intentionally group and compose the full intentional Object in anticipation of its realization as a whole thought. Husserl (1982, §135) suggests that the genesis of a mental process of transcendence exists in this moment of pure psychology when we anticipate the fullfullment of an intentional form of ideation for something immanently meaningful. During the normal course of events, all of this pre-conceptual cognitive action occurs within the horizon of ontology in less actual time than the blink of an eye.

Yet just now in anticipation of a parts/whole structure of meaningfulness, a mental formation of cognitive action and norms of practice comes into ontic being within an eidetic affair-complex. A mental formation presents to consciousness-formation a pre-existing and limiting spatiotemporal order for all subsequent mental processes within a calculus of logic, and yields to psychological descriptions as a succession of cognitive acts in processes of judgments and valuations. The living-present profile of the subject's activities of consciousness-formation is a dynamic moment that is made coherent through the use of a descriptive language of *simultaneity* under the *epoché*. Beginning from the pure Ego's transcendental turn, genetic reflections on the objects and acts of constitutive life are both eidetic and transcendental. Consequently, the pace of the subject's constitutive life seems to slow down in rigorously focused reflections—perhaps demonstrating the so-called tachypsychia experienced as "zoning" by soldiers, athletes, and videogamers.

Under simultaneously the eidetic and transcendental reductions, reflections on the subject's accomplishments of conferred meanings in the horizon of ontology are led to reduced and bracketed elements of being-sense retained within an eidetic affair-complex. This in turn leads to the phenomenological concept of *adumbration* (*Abschattung*) during simple and higher-level apperceptions of essential elements for an intentional object. The word "adumbration" is derived from the Latin, *adumbrātus*, meaning that something first appears to us according to its immediate outline of shape and shadow. The concept of *adumbration* in Husserl's (1973a, §24) mature philosophy refers to our ability in psychic life to notice in sensory data a plurality of existents in the midst of a unity of configuration. Husserl's use of the term "adumbration" represents in part the idea that an uncorrelated object presents only a one-sided view of itself from an insular perspective within the various horizons of experience. One might say that adumbrated elements of sensory data are the "building-blocks" of consciousness-formation during a steady flow of reasoning from pre-conceptual to conceptual space. One might say, too, that the concept of *adumbration* points toward the universal phenomenological method of reasoning at the ontic origins of conscious awareness.

The concept of *adumbration* is used not only to reference correlations in genetic phases of *a priori* and contingent experience, but Husserl (1982, §4) also uses the concept in order to differentiate phenomenological psychology from empirical psychology. There is an ontic difference between phenomenological and strict empirical approaches toward their intuitive psychological matters of interest. Part of this difference turns on the distinction that empirical psychology is unable to notice by its theoretical constructions the intentional character of our ideations in pre-conceptual performances with an adumbrated object of sensory perception. Husserl (§41) explains that mental processes for acting on adumbrated objects are not themselves adumbrated objects. There are no parts to a mental process that could present a one-sided view of stimulus response to something "external." Instead, an intentional mental process is unambiguous with respect to a single essence and its being-sense within a meaningful form of ideation. In the horizon of ontology, for example, a mental process of *perception* cannot be a mental process of *knowing*.

An intentional mental process could nevertheless be an adumbrating process during the psychic order of attentive focus on an object of the mind. As the result of an adumbrating mental process of *apperception*, for instance, we could picture that our friend has brown eyes within the total configuration of her face. In this sense, an intentional mental process in pure psychology is the parallel analog of a calculus of logic in Husserl's phenomenology of reason—and just as human consciousness is always consciousness-of-something in its calculus, so too is an intentional mental process a process-of-something in its action and non-action. It is self-evident, however, that a mental process does not approximate in being-sense that *something* itself as the intended outcome of constitutive life. Empirical inquiry, Husserl argues, fails to notice our intentional action on the irreality of an adumbrated object as a psychological phenomenon of correlated *choice* and *anticipation*, rather than (say) as an epiphenomenon of involuntary behavior. There seems therefore to be no element of agency to sensory response in empirical accounts of psychic life.

There is also a difference between these two approaches for seeing a plurality of necessary elements amid an object's anticipated unity of configuration. Indeed, we ordinarily make use of the intentional function of these two sorts of intuition during both simple and higher-level apperceptions of an adumbrated object. Both sorts of intuition into the simultaneous pre-existing elements of an adumbrated object—that of an object in its plurality of appearances, and that of the core essence of the object's unity—are used for expressing the true meaning of a fully composed eidetic affair-complex in the horizon of ontology. Here, for example, is a genetic phenomenological psychological description of our typical acts of apperception with regard to the adumbrated presentational object we call a "table" in ordinary experience:

Through our physical sensations we perceive something in our field of active interest here and now. That is to say, the thing matters in terms of its dependence and distance to an intention of the pure Ego to constitute its presence in awareness. By a simple apperception of embodiment for reality construction, the spatial dimensions for what is now the intentional object are given to consciousness-formation as a solid horizontal plane resting on four supports. With this initial grasp of a potential unity-form in the horizon of ontology, we eidetically group and compose the affair-complex of *tableness* for the intentional object. We perform this action in anticipation that the original

and meaning of a "table," just as it appears in the transcendental ego's intentional form of ideation. We typically aim pre-conceptually at constituting the ideation of *table* to be self-evidently a material object in one's naïve natural world, but we generally mean the sense of *tableness* for this thing that is pictured in ideations of common semblance. If we choose, we could value and represent the ideation that this thing means an objective table universally, although we might subsequently judge in conceptual space that it does not.

In either case, the *eidos* of *tableness* is not yet fully grasped prior to our correlations of certainty for a concatenation of adumbrated elements. During the psychic order of this concatenation, an adumbration of *tableness* (such as its daily use) is an irreality in a system of apperceptions—where it is now at hand for correlation with the intentional object that is held fast in ideations of its core essence. We do not initially grasp the fulfilled intelligibility of "table" in this system, however, even if the word is said in our presence. Instead, we sieze upon the *eidos of tableness* as immanently meaningful for *this* object of apperceptive experience and not another. In higher-level apperceptions of objectivity, the pre-existing meaning of *tableness* and its retained elements are passively conferred on the universally uttered linguistic sign we call *table* in English, *Tisch* in German, or *mesa* in Spanish. This experience could have been different in pure psychology, except that the anticipated semblance of that adumbrated *eidos* was judged and valued in the horizons of epistemology, ontology, and metaphysics such that it could be grasped intuitively in conceptual space as an objectified table of idealized properties—meaning, the being-sense of "table" was already composed to be a unity of adumbrated elements.

When the pure Ego fulfills its anticipation of unity for a transcendental object, the performing ego releases its thematic grip on elements that are retained and elapse as individual things throughout our meaning conferring-acts. A constituted objectivity in the transcendental register is not the adumbrated object that was originally encountered in pre-conceptual experiences of perception. Instead, as the consequence of an intentional mental process of transcendence, we constitute the correlated being-sense of an object's core essence as the subject's *re*-cognized objectivity of immanent meaningfulness. (*see* Husserl 1973a, §24) During subsequent apperceptions of evidence for an enduring *eidos* in conceptual space, an adumbrated object is ordinarily intended to mean a phenomenal object and its correlated linguistic sign that co-exist according to cognitive modifications in ideations of unity here and now. In its configuration of unity, for example, transcended self-knowledge of this or that table is one's objectified knowledge of something particular within a generalized plurality of similar things, while the word "table" signifies the core essence of *tableness* within a symbolic order of meaning.

Still, each of us could usually think and speak of individual elements of an adumbrated object, such as color and texture, and of the eidetic structure of elements that differentiates, say, a table from a tailgate. We could construct freely and imaginatively the actual reality for any meaningful element of an intentional object at any moment during our spontaneous and theoretical reflections—but during our habitual performances in the transcendental register, we do not. We tend as a norm of practice in cognitive mental life to accept or reject a so-called countersense (*Widersinn*) for what is intended to be seen as a unity here and now. For example, a countersense to the *eidos* of *tableness* in the horizon of ontology is the adumbrated irreality of a solid horizontal plane resting on four supports. There is no reason by itself for the actual reality of the core essence of *tableness* to have meaning as a "solid horizontal plane" here and now. One's fully conceived sense of "table" as an objectified unity could also refer to a meaningful arrangement of words or numbers.

The pure Ego's construction of actual reality for the accepted countersense of an *eidos* discloses the subject's ideation of the being-sense for its core essence in the transcendental register. By means of our judgments and valuations in each contingent horizon of experience, constitutive life now proceeds genetically by grouping and composing reason-as-evidence for the meaning that was conferred on an *eidos* as the anticipated intentional object of transcendental consciousness. Our constituting-acts are thus directed in the transcendental register by one's own disclosure of meaning within the horizon of ontology for an adumbrated object of apperceptive experience—even while a grouping of elements for that object tends toward a unity of configuration here and now. According to the intentional function to confer a true meaning on an anticipated objectivity, we intend for *this* thing to gain presence in awareness as a phenomenal object that has *this* pregiven unity of sensible meaning amid a pre-existing world of objectively real things.

In the normal course of events, an intentional object is constituted in awareness as something actually real—actually real, that is, according to correlations of being-sense for an adumbrated object during the pure Ego's preconceptual experience with an enduring *eidos*. Husserl (1982, §55) explains that due to our cognitive action, an intentional object's reality is grasped in conceptual space as a meaningful unity of sense with affective significance. In the *a priori* horizon of metaphysics, where correlations of *certainty* and *absoluteness* occur, an intentional object is anticipated to become actually real with the apodictic certainty of true being by means of its transcendental modifications. As a result, the absolute quality of an object's being-sense in the world of objective things is presumed to pre-exist in Nature as self-evidently real—not as the result of one's own prior cognitions of evidence and reality, however, but because the world of absolute things simply *is* from the natural attitude. (*see* Husserl 1970, §11) In its practical use, for example, a table is intended to be absolutely self-evidently different in sense and meaning from a chair or a bench, even though the eidetic irreality of a chair or bench could be similarly apperceived as an embodied horizontal plane resting on four supports.

It is easily seen that once constructed and habituated with affective significance, the actual reality for an object of the mind is exceedingly difficult to *un*-construct. At the same time, we tend to be aware of both absolute and relative differences between intentional objects—especially if the sensible meaning of something is incorrectly or inadequately valued for its objective presence in life-world experiences. For instance, when say "table" to someone we have already intentionally modified the ontic affair-complex of *tableness* by transcending acts of valuing its adumbrated elements of sense, meaning, and intentional object to become an individual thing in its eidetic identity within every necessary horizon of experience and space of reasoning. Here, the irreal meaning of *tableness* has no actual reality in one's naïve natural world, while the absolutized and objectified word "table" already does have. We do not say, "Let's sit at the *tableness* in the corner." Instead, we passively let the linguistic sign "table" represent our conferred meaning on the unified epistemological and metaphysical elements of the *eidos* of *tableness* in their full concretion. Linguistic representations literally *re*-present elements of a transcendental thematic form of meaningfulness within an ontic state of affairs.

The Eidos *of* Theme

Husserl's (1973b, §19) notion of a thematic form of meaningfulness during consciousness-formation points reflections toward the *eidos* of *theme* in his theory of inquiry. Under the *epoché*, the *eidos* of *theme* refers to our grouping elements of an adumbrated object in relationships of parts-to-parts and parts-to-whole such that they form a unity of configuration within a construction of actual reality: "*Every actuality involves its potentialities,*" Husserl writes, "which are not empty possibilities, but rather [thematic] possibilities intentionally predelineated in respect of content." For example, the fulfilled intentional object and actual reality of the subject's awareness of a table would not be such as it is if one element of its thematic content happened to mean *liquid*. The theme of an eidetic affair-complex unifies its singular core essence with its form of ideation within the horizon of ontology; and in this way, a unity of being-sense endures as meaningfully significant throughout apperceptions of elements for what is deemed to be the same object in its eidetic identity within the structural features of transcendental consciousness.

During a steady flow of reasoning from pre-conceptual to conceptual space, thematic activity in pure and transcendental subjectivity directs the correlation of elements from every horizon of *a priori* and contingent experience. By this method of retention in pure psychology, an original substrate of experience with an *eidos* provides the intuitive eidetic form for any subsequent givenness of the intentional object in constitutive life. This universal method of consciousness-formation is the primary means by which the pure Ego's grip on an original experience of perception is retained for cognitive acts of apperception in the transcendental register. The pure Ego's construction of a thematic form of unity is intended to endure amid the objectified and idealized world that is commonly talk about—and indeed, an anticipated construction of common semblance is the genesis of our everyday intersubjectivity.

Husserl (Fink 1995, §9 note 279) allows, however, that the idea of *theme*, the essence of what is thematic and especially unthematic in constitutive life, along with the meaning and use of the term "theme" under the *epoché*, are all inadequately realized in his transcendental phenomenological philosophy. This is the case despite the self-evident irreality of the *eidos* of *theme* in the pure psychology of cognitive mental life. I would suggest that addressing the question of what is thematic during applications of the phenomenological method proper in Husserl's work goes a long way toward explaining why the development of phenomenological psychology has not been advanced in the transcendental register these many years. In order to grasp the meaning of *theme* in Husserl's methodology, just as it mirrors the phenomenological method of reasoning in its application, a brief explanatory departure from a strictly exegetic interpretation of Husserl's object-oriented reflections is perhaps called for. The question of what is or is not thematic during articulations of Husserl's methodology offers the opportunity to demonstrate his overall theory of inquiry as the method of ontology. From the psychological attitude, the method of ontology includes our ontifying-acts in pure psychology.

The *eidos* of *theme* is given to reflections in Husserl's work as two distinct but correlated modalities of "the meant" for meaningful objects and meaning conferring-acts—just as the *eidos* of *reality* is thematically represented as both irreal and actual. The *eidos* of *theme* is seen first in Husserl's (1977, 9) theory of method as the psychological theme of pure subjectivity (i.e., as presentations of the psyche's relationships to objects); and second, as *theme* shows itself in his (57f) theory of eidetic *seeing* as an intuitive representation of elements within the changing profiles of an adumbrated object (i.e., as the categorial focus of ideations in the transcendental register). If this is indeed the situation for proper reflections, then Husserl's use and meaning of the *eidos* of *theme* might be grasped as the intentional function of cognitive mental life whereby we achieve a synthesis of his theory of elements with his transcendental theory of method. This cognitive action seems to take place during the flowing movement of an intentional object from pre-conceptual to conceptual space throughout his phenomenology of reason.

One might begin to arrive at this conclusion by first examining Husserl's (1982, §§70f) theory of representation during universal experiences of pure and transcendental consciousness. In his object-oriented phenomenology of reason that references such experiences (§70), representations of an intentional object are given to reflection within the horizon of ontology as adumbrated elements of the *eidos* of *presentiation*. The term "presentiation" (*Vergegenwärtigung* = made present) signifies all at once the singular core essence of presentation, representation and *re*-presentation. With the method of *epoché* and eidetic reduction of our practices of seizing upon essences, the beingsense of the *eidos* of *presentiation* shows itself as "the primacy of free phantasy" in apperceptive experience with an adumbrated object. Here, we are free to notice—or not to notice—the essence of something that matters immanently in pre-conceptual experience. Acts of grasping the *eidos* of *presentiation* through the autonomy of our eidetic intuition in free fantasy acquire "*a position of primacy over perceptions* and do so *even in the phenomenology of perception itself*."

It makes no sense with the method of *epoché* to suppose even a metaphorical similarity between something that we notice in pre-conceptual experience and the intentional manner in which it is noticed. Although perhaps correlated in a single moment of apprehension, they are not the same matters as an identity or equivalence any more than they are the same during our experiences of *seeing* and the things that are *seen*. The color red in Husserl's theory of elements, for example, is not originally grasped as the objectively real element of color or hue that is only later apprehended in experience and represented to self and others as the color red, or *this* red, if and when we choose to notice. Under the eidetic reduction, an intentional object is typically represented as actually real by its form and content of predicating logic, linguistic signification, or grammatical structure. Said representations provide *entrées* for Husserl's (1982, §70) reflections on higher-level apperceptions of objectivity—where in correlation with the *eidos* of *presentiation*, an intentional object is originally presented in pre-conceptual space and then intentionally *re*-presented in conceptual space with all of its transcendental modifications.

Given such intentional action, the *eidos* of *presentiation* in the horizon of ontology refers by extension to the thematic form of adumbrated elements for an eidetic affair-complex that includes the particular core essence of an intentional object—no matter whether that essence might be valid elsewhere or on another occasion. Indeed, each essence that matters thematically in the horizon of ontology is self-validating in the living present as intuitively meaningful in all other horizons and regions of cognitive mental life. That is to say, we require no further reason-as-evidence for making such noticing-choices for the same element during any subsequent phase of consciousness-formation. *Presentiation* enjoys its primacy under the *epoché* as one of the first irrealities in cognitive mental life to show itself in acts of intentionality. The *eidos of presentiation* continues to show itself by our choices of *how* a retained element is to be represented throughout constitutive life.

Even so, the *eidos of presentiation* does not show itself with purely physiological responses to raw sensory data, since there is no initial element of choice there. A particular color cannot be presented pre-conceptually as *texture* to apperceptions and then *re*-presented thematically as *taste*, any more than we could choose for *sound* to be *touch*. The pure Ego's conferred meaning of *red*, for example, represents an imaginative so-called fantasy in Husserl's work, since *red* is only what we make in cognitive mental life of the physiological characteristics of optical perception. Yet the immanence of *red* is not an arbitrary sensation of optical perception in signifying expressions; instead, the core essence of *red* is represented throughout by the meaning intentionally conferred in free fantasy upon a specifically *noticed* optical perception of an adumbrated object. This situation holds for all other meaning conferring-acts on irreal elements. If we could not freely fantasize the irreality of adumbrated things, then there would be no difference in thought between red and pink within their potential ranges of perceived hue. Similarly, there would be no difference between the meanings of love and hate. In Husserl's (1982, §112) work, a fantasy is not a hallucination or hypostatization in cognitive mental life, but is instead the genesis of an actually real thing of singular being-sense. The bestowed sense of unity upon a construction of actual reality transcends an irreal grouping of elements of similar forms of meaningful content.

In the normal course of events, one's transcendental consciousness simultaneously *re*-presents two co-existing thematic forms of content during our experiences of free fantasy: a pre-existing functional relationship of intentional acts on eidetically lawful parts/whole compositions (such as perceiving-acts or conferring-acts), and those intentional objects themselves (such as love or hue). A functional relationship in free fantasy could include, for example, grasping physical properties as thematic representations of the irreality of corporeal life (*see* Husserl 1977, 151) With Husserl's (1973b, §9) sense and meaning of *mind* as the psychosubjectivity of the pure Ego in pure consciousness—and consequently as the psychological ego's cognitive action in the transcendental register—there is no mental life of physiological functions except for what we make of them in free fantasy. Our physiological functions, for instance, do not actually "speak" to us of such things as *color*, *texture*, *taste*, *hot*, or *wet*. Rather, predication of a so-called physiological language of sensation is given from the natural attitude as an absurdity of non-reason in free fantasy that discloses the meanings of particular sensory data in thematic focus.

The theory of our free fantasy of elements in Husserl's (1982, §86) phenomenology of reason stands in opposition to David Hume's 18th century empirical theories of perception—meaning, the *presentiation* of elements in a thematic form is different conceptually from perceiving "bundles" of "fused" raw sensation. In Husserl's work, *presentiation* is the pure Ego's content-free "source of all reason and non-reason" during perceptual experiences of intentional consciousness-formation. When one sees perceptual experience entirely as unintentional sensory response, an absurdity of non-reason has been passively accepted, since there is no reason to believe that perception represents mere sensation. With this pre-conceptual absurdity of non-reason, the pure Ego presents empirical evidence to apperceptions of psychological experience. One might say that the psychological ego represents the pure Ego's content-free source of all *acts* of reason and non-reason in apperceptions of empirical generalities. However, the psychological ego is not an empirical entity in this functional relationship, but is instead our irreal way of being psychological toward the *eidos* of *presentiation* in the transcendental register.

The subject's free fantasy in acts of grasping and then representing elements of an original idea to both simple and higher-level apperceptions directs regressive reflections toward the *eidos* of *perception* in the horizon of ontology. Similarly to the inclusiveness of the *eidos* of *presentiation* in the sphere of immanence, the *eidos* of *perception* includes the essence of intentional apperceptions of thematic content. As a norm of rigorous practice, phenomenologists do not presuppose what others would make of the stuff of perceptual experience during apperceptions within a regional ontology of either factual matters or empirical dimensions. Husserl (Eley 1973, 428) makes this a practice for several reasons: (1) A methodical lack of presuppositions is an important difference between phenomenological and empirical inquiry. (2) This restriction is consistent with seeing human subjectivity in all areas of constitutive life. Also, (3) it affords neutral *entrée* into the intentional acts of differentiating what the subject chooses to represent as meaningful in thought and speech.

Under the *epoché*, each naïvely implied or explicit presentation of conferred meaning *re*-presents the immanent reason and non-reason of correlated meaningfulness that is freely given in pure consciousness by the pure Ego. Beginning from this ontic origin of "the meant," the content-free source of all reason and non-reason in transcendental consciousness is presented to generative reflections as variably the transcendental ego, the psychological ego, the constituting ego, and so on. The thematic content of an ontic affair-complex is therefore transcendentally meaningful, psychologically meaningful, constitutionally meaningful, and so on. Sometimes an element is bracketed and excluded as not immanently meaningful at all. Still, whatever is represented as meaningful here and now is always thematic for action on objects in the living present. A singular core essence thus endures in its thematic representations throughout the dialectical synthesis of solipsistic and transcendental subjectivity—and then *re*-presented in mundane thought and speech as thematically transcendental, psychological, and so on. In this way, each fulfilled thematic representation under the *epoché* presents the end product of a specific intentional experience of the pure Ego.

During successive depths of "archaeological" reflections, adumbrations of the *eidos* of *presentiation* are seen in a reversed order of the pure Ego's free fantasy of elements for a unity of configuration. In regressive phenomenology, this reversed order of composition is presented for descriptions of the static thematic content of concatenated elements within an eidetic affair-complex. Each theme delineates a conferred meaning or a bestowed sense on an active idea in order for it to gain presence as an unambiguous object in conscious awareness. This reversed order of constitutive experience is then itself reversed in genetic phenomenology, and subsequently traced out within more focused phenomenological reductions of the pure Ego's variable performing egos in Husserl's "knowledge-complex"—such as the transcendental and the psychological egos. The genetic practice of seeing the immanent meaningfulness of the subject's parts/whole constitutive experience, beginning from its ontic origin according to the theme of an epistemologically bifurcated performing ego, could be carried out similarly for every *eidos* whose being-sense is represented thematically in referential thought and speech.

One way to focus on the thematic content of conscious awareness is to reflect on the subject's representations of being-sense. As a modality of the *eidos* of *presentiation*, the concept of *representation* entails simultaneously an object and an act, and a noun and a verb form. Most all of Husserl's distinctions and terms for our universal methods of consciousness-formation might be derived from this concept's application and meaning under the *epoché*. Whether the pure Ego succeeds or fails to actualize a unity of meaningfulness and intelligibility for an intentional object, multi-dimensional representations (*Repräsentieren*) of thematic content present to reflections the composition of an eidetic affair-complex for both simple and higher-level apperceptions of necessary elements. Husserl (1981, 126f) foreshadowed this theory of noematic action in a 1894 journal article, "Psychological Studies for Elementary Logic," where he writes that an eidetic representation (*Vorstellung*) "stands for" (*vorstellt*) what an affair-complex is already intended to be as a fully constituted unity. "This is another way," Husserl (p. 127) mentions, "in which one can try to give an account of the [parts/whole] characteristic traits for the distinction between independent and dependent contents."

Phenomenologists cannot notice the theme of a fully composed eidetic affair-complex until they grasp its intended sense and meaning—any more, for example, than we could understand a particular joke without its necessary punch line. A joke in its utterance is similarly and self-evidently an object and an act, a noun and a verb form. An eidetic representation of signification is seen under the *epoché* as a mathematical, logical, or linguistic sign used to reference the being-sense of something already constructed by the pure Ego. A representation of signification intentionally "points toward" a pre-existing idea that has since been modified within a distinctive spatiotemporal genetic order of constituting-acts—perhaps just as a joke is a pre-existing state of affairs that is modified in its telling in order to amuse the listener. Every representation seen in expressions of conscious awareness is thus the result of an intentional mental act within the horizon of ontology, as well as the object upon which meaning is conferred by this same act.

In a mental process of thematic representation, transcending acts in temporizing psychological processes of retention and elapse of elements serve to reduce a pregiven *eidos* of its adumbrated qualities within the horizon of ontology. A modified *eidos* is then given in subsequent apperceptions as a *re*-presentation of its core essence during the internal time-consciousness and psychic order of constitution for an anticipated unity of configuration. When an *eidos* endures thematically as the intentional object all through its initial presentation and necessary *re*-presentations, its constitution presents a unified whole structure—but precisely as pictured as a unity in the transcendental ego's form of ideation for something in the world that is commonly talked about. An intentional object thus takes its place here and now with reason and evidence as the idealized semblance of the pure Ego's being-sense for an original *eidos*. This method of consciousness-formation is indeed a preconceptual fantasy of elements within the various horizons, where it delimits ideation in pure psychology by picturing a thematic unity of adumbrated elements that is to be constituted in the conceptual space of actually real things.

Presentational objects lead reflections to an ontic relationship of correspondence between the anticipated and subsequently fulfilled being-sense of something correlated with the *eidos* of *presentiation*. Here, every ontic relationship is a self-validating correlation of elements for an anticipated unity of configuration during constitutive life. By means of our psychological processes of multiple correlating-acts of judgments and valuations within every substrate of thematic representation, ontic relationships are pre-existing and immanently present during activities of consciousness-formation in the transcendental register. The concept of *representation* in Husserl's methodology points simultaneously toward (1) the spatiotemporal order of elements among the *a priori* and contingent horizons, (2) the intentional object in eidetic compositions of potential unity, and (3) the constitutive methods in pure psychology for constructing the validity and actual reality of the subject's conscious awareness.

In this context, Husserl (1985a, 348f; 2006, 91f) seems to suggest that the cognitive mental life whereby we construct an eidetic unity of affective significance by means of our reproductive memory *re*-presents a solipsistic/transcedental synthesis of adumbrated elements. Said synthesis is necessary for a transcendental object to be experienced as something whole; and in pure psychology, a unity of configuration is indeed a teleological goal for the pure Ego. In the presentation of an intentional object as important for the advancement of phenomenological psychology, Husserl (1973b) seems to suggest as well that both (a) the norm of phenomenological reflection on an intentional object's thematic representations in his theory of consciousness, and (b) our experiences of naïve reflection on an object in awareness—where we typically "parenthesize" the thematic content of adumbrated elements as being-a-whole—entail the *same* universal method in pure psychology that we use in order to synthesize a unity out of a plurality of elements:

> [Phenomenological] inquiry into consciousness concerns *two sides...* [that] can be characterized descriptively as *belonging together inseparably.* This sort of combination...can be characterized as *synthesis*, a mode of combination exclusively peculiar to consciousness. For example, if I take the perceiving of this die as the theme for my description, I see in pure reflection that "this" die is given continuously as an objective unity in a multiform and changeable multiplicity of manners of appearing, which belong determinately to it [as adumbrated elements]. These [manners of appearing], in their temporal flow, [however,] are not an incoherent sequence of subjective processes. Rather they flow away in the unity of a synthesis, such that in them "one and the same" is intended as appearing [in conscious awareness]. (§17)

The above die could only be "this" die in Husserl's descriptions when the theme of his "pure reflection" is represented by the synthetic combination that unites the sides of the die as "one and the same." That is to say, he is describing the thematic object-content of awareness during this experience of consciouness-formation. Yet without the *three* "inseparable" themes of (1) a unified object in transcendental subjectivity, and (2) the necessry pre-existence of adumbrated elements in pure subjectivity, the die could not (3) "flow away" into a unity as the result of a transcending-act of synthesis. In order to be correlated in the horizons of epistemology and metaphysics, and in order to take their places in mundane thought and speech, Husserl has already posited an absolute difference between these three themes by means of an ontic-act of parenthesizing. This practice might well be valid for his philosophical discourse; but during Husserl's original reflections, the theme of his presentation could be seized upon at any time in free fantasy as (1) his intuition into representations of the single unified *object* of synthesis, (2) the synthesized *elements* of the intentional object, or (3) of the transcendental *method* of synthesis—which is "not an incoherent sequence of subjective processes."

Stated positively here, something "flowing away" as a unity signifies a mental process of *synthesis*. The idea of pure psychology is thus bracketed in Husserl's example of consciousness-formation as unthematic for representations of *synthesis* in his object-oriented theory of elements. The "method of ontology" presented above perhaps reflects Husserl's anti-psychologism in descriptions of the ontic givenness of an intentional object. Yet his choice of representational themes is only possible with intuition into the adumbrated elements of objects and the intentional mental acts upon those elements, all within a unity of synthesis. Just as important for applications of the phenomenological method proper, each theme of objects and acts is necessary for

Husserl's own apperceptive experience to become the actual reality that he presents in his written text. Nevertheless, the psychological theme of Husserl's method of ontology remains unwritten in his account of philosophically pure reflection—and in this instance, he never clarifies our psychological subjectivity in the transcendental register of ontic givenness.

The *eidos* of *synthesis* is independent with respect to any "multi-form" representations of thematic content in both Husserl's (1999, 319) static descriptive theory of elements and in his (Fink 1995, §11) genetic explanatory theory of method. Clearly, though, an intentional transcending *act* of synthesis is genetically dependent upon the previously posited existence of necessary elements. For example, the "flowing away" of the die's multi-form is dependent in constitutive life on its pregiven multiple sides. This only means that there are no transcendental methods, and there is no psychological theme in reflections, without representations of multiple substrates of sense and meaning during the subject's apperceptive experience. Yet according to Husserl's (1973b, §17) transcendental logic of eidetic relationships of parts-to-whole, representation of a "multiform and changeable multiplicity" is unthematic for descriptions of a synthesized unity in transcendental consciousness—*because* the multiform-matter in the horizon of ontology has already been transcended by synthesis as the thematic content of representations.

A multi-form and a unity-form are self-evidently and thematically not the same—meaning, the intentional form of ideation for one cannot be actualized as the other. A turn of thematic regard from a continuous multi-form is required in Husserl's theory of elements in order for an instance of universal *synthesis* to be represented as (say) the unity-form of "this" die. By extension, a turn of thematic regard is required in the phenomenological method of reasoning in order for a multi-form of adumbrated elements to be seen intuitively as pre-existing its unity of synthesis. Representations of synthesizing-acts in pure psychology, however, are unthematic for the objects of synthesis in Husserl's theory of elements. This, too, is self-evident. And yet, Husserl's descriptions of objects and acts as "belonging together inseparably" represent the pure Ego's intentions with respect to the *eidos* of *theme* during the construction of actual reality for a unity of function and eidetic form. In both Husserl's theory of elements and transcendental theory of method, the intentional function of "belonging together inseparably" is meaningful as the singular core essence of the *eidos* of *synthesis*. In the universal phenomenological method of consciousness-formation, the idea of synthesis *as such* is thematically an object and an act, a noun and a verb form.

There are thus different strata of themes for an *eidos* in the horizon of ontology, just as there are different strata of sense and meaning for an adumbrated object in apperceptive experience. The matter of *how* each pre-existing stratum is synthesized with others to become a unity of configuration in the transcendental register represents a psychological experience in Husserl's theory of method—that is to say, the idea of *synthesis* in Husserl's work presents a psychological theme of transcendental constitution. The question of what is proper points toward the "functional problem" of Husserl's (1982, §86) methodology: "How [are] consciousness-formations of very different and yet essentially required structures belonging to the identity of the meant [given intuitively and then conceptually determined], and how [are] these formations to be strictly described with respect to method?" For an adequate grasp of Husserl's use of terms and concepts here, we want to ask, "What is the intentional function of the synthesis of *presentiation* and *theme* in the phenomenological method of reasoning that enables us to construct and express a unity of awareness in the world that is commonly talked about?" Here is an answer:

Representations sometime point toward a multiform of elements that is never constituted as a unity-form despite its givenness to reason. For example, Husserl does not represent the ontic givenness of an intentional act that preserves the meant when describing the ontic givenness of an intentional object and its immanent meaningfulness. Yet there is another way in the pure psychology of free fantasy by which we correlate a sense of ontic givenness in the transcendental register. (*see* Husserl 1973b, §37) In the psychic order of constitution for a unity of configuration, earlier thematic representations of objects and acts are retained in reproductive memory. Such things thus preexist in the living present as pregiven adumbrated elements of thematic *re*-presentations of the pure Ego's synthesis of being-sense. When constituting an object in conscious awareness, said *re*-presentations are contingently "revisited" (iteratively) as evidence of prior validity for a state of affairs here and now. Similarly, we might grasp intuitively the presentational objects of others as actually real according to their apperceived ontic givenness—more specifically, when apperceptions in empathy agree with the pure Ego's retained adumbrations of pregiven sense and meaning. The pure Ego's transcendence of the pre-conceptual ontic givenness of being-sense into the conceptual space of actually real things is indeed the intentional function of the synthesis of *presentiation* and *theme* for the phenomenological method of reasoning.

Synthesizing the object-content of awareness is a method of fulfillment for the pure Ego in pure psychology, and is carried out by the psychological ego's grouping-acts on correlates of being-sense for a unity of configuration in the transcendental register. Husserl (1973a, §35) explains that in order for a synthesis of elements to be seen as a unity in its dialectical modifications from solipsistic to transcendental subjectivity, it is composed according to the internal time-consciousness of a single *now*. Here, each preexisting element loses its identity as a retained singularity when its temporal past and original givenness both "pass away" amid the eidetic structure of a unity-form. According to the pure Ego's logic of calculus for this "interlaced" structure, an adumbrated element could therefore pass away only as an immediate correlate of sense and meaning. Said structure of unity, Husserl (1999, 320) points out, is intended to endure into conceptual space as a so-called passive meaningfulness of objectivity. We consequently tend to accept habitually the passive meaningfulness of something deemed to be objective, not only for one's own constituted objectivities, but also for those constituted by others in the world of common semblance.

The Pure Psychology of Transcendental Consciousness

Whether an intentional object is constituted in awareness by active or passive synthesis, or a combination thereof, every pre-conceptual performance of consciousness-formation requires mental processes of intentional action in the transcendental register. Husserl (1973a, §3) seems to imply, however, that the psychological ego does not typically act to retain another adumbrated element of an *eidos* once a unity of awareness for that idea's core essence is anticipated amid its ongoing ontic affair-complex. Instead, the psychological ego traces out a pre-existing spatiotemporal order of validating apperceptions of evidence for that unity in mental processes of willing, thinking, feeling, accepting, and so on—howsoever a contingent genetic order of judgments and valuations is given to constitutive life during the dialectical synthesis of transcendental consciousness. When these various modes of action are called for by the pure Ego, the psychological ego acts within them as different themes of consciousness-formation in psychological processes of cognitive acts. Said acts belong together inseparably in conceptual space, for this is the universal phenomenological method of synthesis for a unity of conscious awareness.

In keeping with his rigorous anti-psychologism, Husserl's (1973b, §11) theory of elements is not thematic for genetic explanations of the pure psychology of synthesis—except as elements are intended-to and acted upon within an eidetic affair-complex. At the same time, however, there can be no form of ideation, intentional function, or construction of reality described under the psychological *epoché* that does not also exist as immanently meaningful "inside" an ontic affair-complex of elements for the pure Ego. Pure psychology is nevertheless free in this relationship of essences from contingent modifications of ego-life in transcendental subjectivity—even as pure psychology intuitively grounds by means of its apriority both the acts and methods by which being-sense seems to rise up and increase in significance throughout the various strata of constitutive life. And so, explanations of such things in the transcendental register as our methods of ideation, representation, or synthesis are indeed psychologically descriptive of the pre-existing actionality in pure psychology that all of us tend to enjoy intuitively. (*see* Husserl 1977, 66)

"Intuition" sometimes refers in Husserl's (1982, §3f) work to seeing the essences of singular things (*individuelle Anschauung*), now as before. Seeing pure psychology as a single experience in a steady flow of reasoning from pre-conceptual to conceptual space means to see the essence of the pure Ego's psychosubjectivity throughout the various horizons of *a priori* and contingent experience. During our everyday activities of consciousness-formation, pure psychology is partially pregiven in cognitive mental life as universal methods of constitution. Such action is intuitable by phenomenologists as judgments made and valuations concluded in representations of a unity of configuration for something in conscious awareness. Indeed, a phenomenologist's intuition of the subject's necessary judging- and valuing-acts guides regressive interpretations of psychosubjectivity in the pure consciousness of anything whatsoever. This psychosubjectivity of judgment-acts is then normatively affirming, and seen in genetic phenomenology as manifestations of the psychological ego when synthesizing an affective unity of sense, meaning, certainty, and appearance for an intentional object in the transcendental register.

With the introduction of pure psychology into the transcendental register, a variation of the phenomenological *epoché* and attitude toward the pure Ego is required in Husserl's theory of inquiry. Husserl (1970) explains this variation in his methodology and system of ego-life as mirroring the orientation within the phenomenological method proper where we experience the contingencies of transcendental subjectivity from the natural attitude:

> [Pure psychology] and transcendental philosophy are allied with each other…in virtue of the alliance of difference and identity…between the psychological ego (the human ego, that is, made worldly in the spatiotemporal world) and the transcendental ego [of objectified world-consciousness].… [I typically see myself as] living in the world, for whom the world is the totality of what…is valid as existing, [but] I am blind to the immense transcendental dimension [of this world and to the psychic being of my worldliness].… In truth, of course, I am a transcendental ego, but I am not conscious of this; being in a particular attitude, the natural attitude, I am completely given over to [objective things], completely bound by interests and tasks which are exclusively directed toward them. I can, however, carry out the transcendental reorientation [as a norm of practice]…and then I understand [by means of the transcendental epoché] the one-sided, closed, natural attitude as a particular transcendental attitude, as one of a certain habitual one-sidedness of the whole life of interest. I now have, as a new horizon of interest, the whole of constituting life…with all its correlations [in pure psychology]. (p. 58)

Following the pure Ego's reorientation from solipsistic to transcendental subjectivity (although this turn of regard might not always occur), the transcendental ego represents one's adumbrated life in the world of human co-existence and common semblance—but as seen from our "one-sided" natural attitude. The psychological ego, on the other hand, represents pure psychology transcended in that same world. In Husserl's (1970b, §58) theory of method, the spirit-life of pure psychology includes a universal theme of anticipation for conscious awareness in the transcendental register. Beginning from within the horizon of ontology, a theme of anticipation for the synthesis of an object-as-a-whole is grasped as a psychological theme of action for composing a unity of being-sense for the intentional object. When anticipating the presence of an objectivity in the world that is commonly talked about, we need no longer be directed in judgments and valuations strictly by the pregivenness of raw sensory data; and too, we need no longer be strictly bound in conceptual space by the pre-existence of our own physiological functions. After the turn in cognitive mental life from simple apprehensions in solipsistic subjectivity to higher levels of apperception in transcendental subjectivity, the psychological ego "lives" the spirit-life of pure psychology by "having 'consciousness' of the world in which [one] lives and is conscious of living." (§60)

Themes of pure psychology present for genetic reflections our intuitively given transcending acts and methods of subjective *being* and *doing*. When following psychological themes of action during judgments and valuations in the transcendental register, we tend to notice our experiences of feeling and thinking about something meaningful, both for *me myself* and for others. This notion of universal cognitive mental life is emphatically not the descriptive psychology presented in Husserl's (1977) 1925 lectures. In the spirit of renewal for psychology as a human science, Husserl in part extended in these lectures his approach to the problem of psychologism introduced in the *Logical Investigations* twelve years earlier. Husserl (2001, 85ff) addressed this issue in the *Investigation*'s second volume by separating pure logic from the pure psychology of bringing objects into pregiven logical relationships. In his 1925 lectures, Husserl meant to clarify his position on psychologistic descriptions as a matter of conceptualization when doing psychology as a scientific discipline—*not* on the issue of our psychological experiences of living knowingly and immediately in both active and passive synthesis of a unity of being-sense.

Husserl nevertheless set the course and impetus in these lectures for a phenomenological psychology of the human soul engaged in transcendental subjectivity. Here, the human soul is given to genetic reflections under the psychological *epoché* as partly our spirit of autonomy and agency when constructing actual realities in the world of co-existence and common semblance. In 1925, Husserl in effect reduced perceptual experience in pure psychology to the realm of subjective acts of spirit-life during our normative pursuit of truth and happiness. In his last years, Husserl (1973a, §71) observed once again that the normative modalization of cognitive mental life indeed takes the form of striving for certainty and consistency in life world experiences. Even when our so-called norm-consciousness refers to an original grounding in pure psychology for cognitive action that is not experienced directly (such as ethical codes and moral laws), intentional judging- and valuing-acts still point toward one's lived experience of striving for certainty and consistency in constructions of actual reality here and now. (*see* Husserl 1970, 303-4)

While reflecting on "the alliance between psychology and transcendental phenomenology," Husserl (1970, §60) described characteristics of our "soulish" pure psychology within the ontic horizon of worldly being-sense. Use of the word "soul" (*Seele*) in this context signifies "the original givenness of the psychic in the life-world," and represents the essence of all our psychological experiences of transcendental world-consciousness. Following the pure Ego's transcendental reorientation, a theme of pure psychology could include one's intersubjective experience of knowing others as transcended objects. When we objectify our spiritual ownness during this experience, Husserl (1973b, §55) explains, "I myself am the primal norm [in constitutive life of consistency and certainty] for all other men." "Now, however," Husserl (1982, §152) stresses, "this experiencing subject is...constituted in experience as something real, as *human being* or as brute [i.e., as a mere thing of impersonal life form], just as the *intersubjective communities* are constituted as communi-

during life-world experiences, the objectified human spirit is typically grasped as the impersonal "psychical reality" attributed to *everyone* as an objective thing amid the pure Ego's intersubjectively constituted "thing-world."

In Husserl's (1970, §62) mature reflections, a universal psychological theme for transcendental intersubjectivity is the irreality of an animating essence of the human soul that is inseparable from human co-existence—where now, psychological themes are lived "in straightforward life-world experience" in the transcendental register. Here, the pure subjectivity of human spirit-life is presented as a psychophysical unity of mind and body in Husserl's (§28) fundamental ontology of life-world experience. That unity is thematized as *my own* in transcendental intersubjectivity, and then objectified as a contingent array of judgments and valuations during the pursuit of one's life-goals. Furthermore, there is never a psychology of transcendental consciousness without its transcending acts directed toward realizing correlated elements of absolute truth and objective reality for one's self and for others. Only then does the essence of spirit-life in pure psychology gain presence in awareness as the embodied actual reality of comportment that we look for in empathy—and that we naïvely call "psychology" in mundane thought and speech.

But the world of embodied things is first our corporeal-life of pre-conceptual response to pure sensation, and psychology is first the mental life that begins with that response. By studying this universal development and its manifestation from solipsism to intersubjectivity, transcendental phenomenological psychology becomes a genetic phenomenology of the human soul made worldly in relationships with others. Our worldly soul is represented in Husserl's work by the psychological ego in cognitive mental life, yet Husserl's fundamental ontology of pure psychology is not a prescription for any fixed order of so-called psychological meaningfulness in one's judgments and valuations. In all cases of psychological experience, fundamental ontology takes into account each original state of human consciousness from which every intentional object and intentional act could gain presence as a unity in thought and speech. Husserl's science of essences would therefore properly include a transcendental phenomenological psychology of such unities, practiced as inquiry into the essence of the human spirit that is played out by the psychological ego in the world that is commonly talked about.

Reconstructive Phenomenology

Adumbrated elements of the *eidos* of *my life* direct regressive reflections toward the singular *I* in fundamental ontology. Here, the pure Ego of subjective experience is immanently for itself in the face of all that is *Other*. Here, too, an intentional object is correlated in solipsistic structures as the subject's self-knowledge of the pure Ego's manifestations of body and soul. Consequently in genetic reflections, the subject's naïve references to *my life* point toward the transcendental ego's ideations of common semblance for the corporeal- and spirit-life experienced by *everyone*—typically, toward an objective "human nature." Under the transcendental *epoché*, consciousness of such a world and one's place within it refers to "the 'humanization' [of] nature…as significance, imbued with spirit [*Vergeistignung*]." (Fink 1995, 169) Because of this action in pure psychology, our solipsistic subjectivity is "humanized" and transcended in the world of co-existence and common semblance.

The method of transcendental *epoché* includes a reduction of the subject's awareness of something to the phenomenologizing activity of world-constitution by which the appearance of semblance comes to presence. During this experience, the phenomenologizing ego takes "things as holding good [*Geltungsleben*] which belong to me (…among them everything that gets verified [by others] as 'existent').… [All that appears objectively 'human' is then experienced] purely as correlate [to *me myself*] in constituting life." (Fink 1995, 168) The phenomenologizing ego is the "transcendental 'onlooker'" of this same world of common semblance in Husserl's knowledge-complex, and represents in reconstructive reflections the ego-function that manifests the appearance of *me myself as ego* amid the full realization of *my life* in the transcendental register. Said appearance is typically constituted in correlation with the pregiven life-world for living knowingly as "natural" in human co-existence.

In Husserl's (Fink 1995, 169) theory of method for transcendental world-constitution, the essence of human existence that is *my own* becomes objectified and absolutized as "alien" to the pure Ego in co-existence (*Koexistenz*) with other objectified things. That is to say, the transcended existential *I* gains presence as a "coefficient" of *Otherness* during consciousness-formation of the phenomenal world. As a result of this transcendence, *my life* is correlated pre-conceptually with the bestowed sense of *I with Other* during one's intersubjective relationships. The *eidos* of *I-with-Other* represents "a tendency in human life to 'security'" among the contingencies of transcendental subjectivity. (§5) Under the transcendental *epoché*, a phenomenologist assumes the perspective of the "phenomenologizing onlooker" of the objectification of appearances for "my life as a human" during the lived experience of this same event. A transcendental phenomenologist's intuitive self-knowledge of the phenomenal world rests solely with the security of fundamental relationships within both the immanent and contingent structures of transcendental consciousness presented by the meaningful human subject.

In order for the immanent existential *I* to be disclosed as a coefficient of *Otherness* under the transcendental *epoché*, Husserl (1970, §50) makes use in free fantasy of an absurdity of non-reason in his methodology. At the genesis of reconstructive phenomenology in the horizon of ontology, Husserl presents to reflections what is universally "other" to solipsistic subjectivity in our fundamental relationships of *I* with *Other*—namely, the "alien-I" that exists in the transcendental register as a normalized "I-you-synthesis" of intersubjective experience with objectified *otherness*. This absurdity of non-reason that each of us engages during the pure Ego's transcendental reorientation is represented by the so-called alter-ego of transcendental subjectivity. In the midst of our life-span experiences with existential relationships, the phenomenon of *my life* is built up with valuing-acts upon a correlate of the apodictic *I am* and one's contingent alter-ego. The alter-ego represents a countersense in reasoning about *me myself* in pre-conceptual experiences with existential other- ... ring the dialectical synthesis of transcendental consciousness, these two apperceived formations of thematic ego-life belong together inseparably as a unity during our intersubjective relationships. As a matter of autonomy in the transcendental register, my alter-ego is my apprehension and acceptance in pure psychology of "what-is-not-me" in the phenomenal world.

A transcendental phenomenologist is a neutral observer of subjective ego life and alter-ego life in their modes of normal and alien pregivenness to self-consciousness. The method of transcendental *epoché* in effect discloses a dialectical synthesis in transcendental consciousness of the phenomenon of *my life*—a synthesis of its immanence in constitutive life and its appearance during contingent life-world experience. At the genesis of this synthesizing activity, the pure Ego is the pre-existing irreducible *I* of one's "inner" solipsistic subjectivity that is at hand *here*, even while one's intersubjective alien-I is objectively *there*, "outside" and thus "other" to the pure Ego. (*see* Husserl 1995, 176) The alien-I is therefore prone to be acted upon as an intentional object of affective significance during the normal course of events. At the fundamental level of *I* and alien-I reductions of constitutive life, Husserl's reconstructive reflections turn outward from its ontic center in order to follow along with this ongoing dialectical relationship in the transcendental register.

Phenomenological reconstructions follow the pure Ego's pregiven course of synthesis during the movement of intentional experience from preconceptual to conceptual space. Having reached (by means of the eidetic reduction in regressive reflections) the reduced fundamental relationships for the singular core essence of an *eidos*, a transcendental phenomenologist rigorously gathers and regroups in genetic reflections the necessary elements and intentional mental acts that were previously described and methodically bracketed. Reconstructions then trace out an I/alien-I synthesis precisely as the subject's solipsistic/intersubjective conflicts and contradictions are resolved (or not) for the constitution of an intentional object here and now. A complete reconstruction of the subject's presentational object under the *epoché*—typically seen as an affective unity in the world of co-existence and common semblance—begins in the horizon of ontology with the transcendental and psychological reductions, and concludes in the horizon of metaphysics for correlations of absoluteness and certainty.

Husserl's (1982, §12) phenomenological reconstructions seem to begin with genetic reflections on those already-reduced "species" (*Differenz*) of eidetically singular forms of thematic content that were composed during the subject's construction of an eidetic affair-complex. Here, purely subjective forms of thematic *I* and alien-I content are positioned in categories of correlated sense and meaning with regard to the core essence of an active idea. Each form shows itself within the horizon of ontology as an element of one's fundamental human relationships with an *eidos*, and each could be seen along the plane of immanence such that its content is self-evidently necessary in concatenations of intelligibility. These pregiven forms of individuation and difference, however, are by themselves unthematic in the transcendental register for the construction of actual reality during a dialectical synthesis of reasoning. Instead, the intended *unity* of the synthesized being-sense of these forms is anticipated and transcendentally constituted as one's self-knowledge of a phenomenological *eidos*. This experience always includes correlates of one's self-knowledge of *my life* in the world of human co-existence.

When one might say, for example, "I want to make sense of it," or "it means this to me," such self-referential expressions point toward an eidetic singular form of thematic content in one's synthesized consciousness-of-something. In reconstructive reflections, *it* signifies the intentional object that is meaningful in the transcendental register according to its I/alien-I givenness to reason here and now. *It* represents "that which" subjective regard (*Blick*) is directed in mental life for bringing to presence something actually real and objectively true. Beginning from the substrate of our fundamental transcendental relationships of *I* with *Other*, ontic categories of spatiotemporal givenness seem to rise up and out within a streaming of consciousness, much like a radiating warmth in cool air. Existing spontaneously as irreal and unspoken forms of meaningfulness within a hierarchy of strata, each form in Husserl's (1982, §124, §129) theory of elements contains a core essence that does not change during its appearances in contingent experience—for indeed, each singular core essence is now an adumbration of the so-called meant-as-meant for an intentional object in transcendental constitutive life.

Ontic singularities are first grasped in solipsistic subjectivity, but their spatiotemporal order of constitution is only seen by means of a genetic reconstruction of transcendental subjectivity. For instance, there is an eidetic singular form for the anticipated consciousness of "that red house." As I express and represent a signifying sensible meaning within this form, *it* could be variously in free fantasy *that* red house, that *red* house, or that red *house*. A region of ontic species represents a place within a hierarchy of modified sense, where the thematic content of each form for an intentional object seems to increase in its possible plurality of representations throughout a rational course of reasoning. An intentional object during this pre-conceptual experience separates thetically and nonthetically into regions of more particular ideation in our potential and grammatically permissible expressions of "the meant"—and then, a threshold of adequate being-sense seems to be met within the horizon of ontology, and a unity of configuration is synthesized out of this flux during one's intersubjective relationships. Under the *epoché* of this methodical *way*, the pure Ego's transcendence of solipsistic *sense* is revealed to reflections with each meaningful expression of unity in the conceptual space of human co-existence and common semblance.

To Husserl (1982, §2), a region of ontic species presents a horizon of delimited potential for consciousness of a rational affective unity. Consequently, each region restricts one's free fantasy during the composition of an eidetic affair-complex. The core essence of an intentional object and its regional ideation then becomes a (correlated) singular object of thematic sense and meaning in transcendental consciousness. For instance again, there are individual essences and regional ontologies that are *my own* for the ideas of *that*, *red*, and *house*. Yet each of us experiences these things similarly within the eidetic concatenation and synthesis for the intentional object of common semblance composed sensible meaning for something, as *it* becomes a unity within its plurality of expressions about material and spiritual properties. Delimited ideations that are realized in consciousness of the natural world, just as they show themselves as factual matters in naïve scientific discourse, serve to provide Husserl's (§9) descriptive phenomenology with examples of regional "categories of individua" for objectified meanings of the true nature of things.

During a genetic progression of constitutive life, species of grouped and composed elements increase in degrees of specificity of "the meant" up to its highest genus in phenomenological reconstructions—eventually, always in Husserl's (1970, §§37f) reflections, to the ontic genus that signifies self-consciousness of *my life* here and now. In this universal time and place of reasoning, the eidetic singularity (i.e., the being-sense) of self-consciousness represents "any signification whatever" in each previous species that compose the unity of one's self-knowledge of co-existence and common semblance. A typical expression of this unity is the meaningful "something of" the human world that is believed to be valid for everyone. A reconstructed complex of interlaced eidetic relationships entails (1) the subjective meant-as-meant for an intentional object, (2) the objectivities pregiven universally and contingently in *I-Other* life-world experiences, and (3) the subject's comportment in pure psychology. This complex includes as corrleates (a) the transcended sense, (b) the lived experience, and (c) one's self-knowledge of the *eidos* of *my life*.

"The Dangerous First-Person Singular"

Husserl (1982, §3, marginal note 10) admitted in 1913 that he could not yet clarify a universal phenomenological method by which an essence in pure consciousness is extended into its unified form of a presentational object in conscious awarness—since any particular essence is seen under the *epoché* within a plurality of regional ontologies consisting of contingent material and spiritual properties. In his last publications, Husserl (1970, 310) was still calling for "a *new sort of thinking*, or a peculiar *method*" that would clarify the complex conditions "of the possibility of something...that gives itself (harmoniously) in the flowing and subjectively changing manners of appearance" in the transcendental register. More than forty years before, Husserl addressed the problem of knowing the singular essence of a plurality of things in the *Logical Investigations*, the work he always considered to be the breakthrough to a radical phenomenological philosophy and psychology.

Grasping the essences of things in ontic categories of individuation during traditional concept formation is examined in the *Investigations* as the cognitive activity whereby we correlate objective knowledge with ideal relationships of formal logic. These relationships are presented in the work's first volume. The second volume consists of six studies, each of which addresses the pure subjectivity of this same experience. One of Husserl's overall purposes in this publication was to show that a synthesis of *knowing* necessarily occurs prior to the assignment of any formal logical significance to objective knowledge or to empirical observations of psychological experience. Notwithstanding Descartes's infinitely regressible representational theory of subjective knowledge (*see* Damasio 1994, 227), for the first time in modern Western philosophy Husserl described in each of his six studies the phenomenon of objective knowledge from the point of view of the one who is *knowing*—in the first person, before any third-person observer could consign psychological or metaphysical significance to its cause or origin.

With this revolutionary approach, the first volume of the *Investigations* is devoted to the study of pure logic, while the second volume describes what perhaps came to be the concept of *pure psychology* in Husserl's work. "But it is not as though the author had to apologize for it," Husserl (1975, 21) wrote later, since the acts of pure psychology were indeed meant to be separated from ideal objects of formal logic. Clarifying objective knowledge as distinct from mental life was the "essential function which [the two parts] have to perform in the context of the entire work." Yet with his early emphasis on the first-person experience of knowing the essences of things, Husserl was later faced with the question of self-reference from the natural attitude toward objective knowledge. The contingent relationship between pure consciousness of an *eidos* as an intentional object and transcendental consciousness of an objectivity, brings into question the manner of first knowing the essence of something for *me myself* within a plurality of possible appearances *for everyone*.

Part of the answer to this question of self-reference is this: Despite mundane issues of concept validity and reliability, theoretical distinctions between categories of things are not thematic for norms of cognitive mental life in the pre-scientific space of our day-to-day reasoning. From the natural attitude, there is no spontaneous ideation of parts, wholes, or their relationships during our "one-sided" life-world experiences. We tend instead to grasp the ideation and meaning of an eidetically singular form of thematic content as a unique correlate of the synthesis of living knowingly in the natural world. Because of our metaphysical correlations of spatiotemporality in the transcendental register, we think mostly in unities of configuration for particular objectivities of immediately transcended *sense*. Said objectivities are presumed to exist for everyone from one moment into the next, even as our consciousness of them endures with appropriate modifications in one's personal lifeworld. Such ongoing experience is not reflected in the discontinuous "logical" categories of referential self-knowledge of *sense-already-made* that Husserl presents for regressive phenomenology in the *Investigations*.

In Husserl's (1973b, §42) later transcendental phenomenology, versus the pure phenomenology of the *Investigations*, addressing the problem of self-consciousness includes discovering by "what intentionalities, syntheses, [and] motivations, the sense 'other ego' becomes fashioned in me." Husserl calls this the issue of "the dangerous first-person singular" during intersubjective relationships for a synthesis of *knowing*. Here, other ego-subjects are fashioned in constructions of common semblance to appear as worldly objects similar to the objectified form of one's first-person experiences with others—that is to say, as either affectively significant or not significant at all. (§43) Clearly, the experience of self-reference cannot exist but in the context of our experiences with others. When constituting "other egos" as actually real and affectively

form that we intend to realize as *not-me* during one's intersubjective relationships. Reciprocally in this calculus, the thematic form of the first-person singular *me myself* then pre-exists in its own ontic region of intersubjective being-sense for an actually real object that *is-me* in the world of human co-existence.

When signified by the first-person singular, one's self-knowledge of *my life* typically coincides in essential features with a pregiven form of ideation for the actual reality and causal characteristics of *me myself* in the natural world. This is the ideation that pictures living knowingly amid the regional ontology of one's personal lifeworld. In Husserl's (1973a, §64) mature transcendental phenomenology, spontaneous intuition into personal lifeworld experience includes the noematic structural features for something that is believed to be objectively real to *everyone*—namely, an I-You synthesis of unity in the world of human co-existence. By means of our intentional correlations with this intersubjective ethics of common semblance, the core essence of its *eidos* endures from one's fundamental *I-Other* relationships into its highest species of objectified self-knowledge of co-existence. An individual essence with its full concretions of appearances in one's personal lifeworld could then become a matter of factual reality in thought and speech during rational comportment.

Husserl (1973a, §64; 1973b, §8) seems to imply that the "generic universal" of *my life* persists as essential necessity within an intuitive (*schauende*) mental process of self-reference. In this way, the core essence of *my life* is lived knowingly as the singular "I," the element that endures for correlations with every quidditive content of self-knowledge—for indeed, the first-person singular is typically retained in the transcendental register amid its own stratum of the "fullness of self-sameness" (*Fülle des Selbst*) that *is* pure subjectivity. This stratum is the space of experience that is *my own* during consciousness-formation, and could be described in Husserl's epistemology of *sense* as a contingent "fragment" of the universal life-world. When the pure Ego seizes upon the *eidos* of *my life* as actually real and objectively true within this stratum of *knowing*, psychological processes of cognitive action are usually oriented in the horizon of metaphysics toward fulfilling "the practical ideal of 'happiness.'" In its essence, the "dangerous first-person singular" is our objectification of the apodictic *I am* in life-world experiences with others.

One argument to be made about the pure subjectivity of life-world experience, just as it was made in the *Logical Investigations* more than a century ago for a clarification of pure logic, is that descriptions of mental acts in Husserl's work are psychological, while descriptions of objects are epistemic, ontic, or metaphysical. In Husserl's (Fink 1995, §2) theory of elements, however, objectified things and their essential relationships do indeed point toward a variety cognitive action and norms of practice in pure psychology—where they could then be seen under the psychological *epoché* and reduction as instances of psychological experience with intentional objects in Husserl's theory of method. Reciprocally, by "belonging together inseparably" during a transcendental synthesis of *knowing*, those intentional acts of choice and motivation that are represented in Husserl's theory of method point toward an object of the mind that is to be clarified in his theory of elements under the transcendental *epoché* and reduction.

4.

The Theoretical Ground
of Transcendental Phenomenological Psychology

A Transcendental Logic of Objects and Acts

There is a difference in Husserl's (1970, §70) theory of consciousness between an intentional object and any act upon that object within a pre-conceptual logic of calculus. Seen in pure consciousness as the difference between essential elements and acts of cognitive mental life, this distinction persists in reflections on transcendental consciousness during the subject's presentation of life-world experience. Because of this distinction, a transcendental phenomenological "act psychology" could investigate the noematic connection between an object of the mind and its genetic method of constitution. In the *Logical Investigations*, Husserl (2001, §6f) described our reasoning in logical categories in order to clarify what such inference means when used to predicate a matter of fact for an object of self-knowledge. Later, Husserl (1973a, §2) focused on mental life during genetic progressions of consciousness-formation for that same object, particularly when cognitive action is directed toward constructing something irrefutable or self-evident by means of a calculus of logic—meaning, when one's certainty in an ideal outcome for inferences becomes apodictic during contingent experience in the transcendental register. This practice includes, for example, today's widespread use of statistical inference and predictive mathematical models in the human sciences. (pp. 393-4)

When used properly, and just as we intend, the symbolic logic of a formal calculus *will* arrive at an idealized outcome for an intentional object; yet symbolic logic has no direct basis in everyday experience. For example, we do not focus attention on any operator of association or combination when putting on our shoes. We simply want to put on our shoes so as not to be barefoot. There is no "natural" world for symbolic logic, such as there is for the irreal physics of rocks and trees—although there is indeed a pre-existing world of day-to-day experience with a transcendental logic that seems to urge or motivate us in pure psychology to make judgments in order to predicate an irrefutable state of affairs. (*see* Husserl 1973a, §1) According to a transcendental logic of calculus, it is irrefutable that if I put on my shoes I will not be barefoot. This deeper lying calculus is the essence of "formal apophantics," the Aristotelian principle of an ontic pattern of intuitive judgments within the noetic structure of a logic of forms. (Husserl 1969, §23; 1982, §147) Still, a logic of calculus does not by itself describe a pattern of psychological activity. Given as an intentional form for predicating a matter of fact, a particular calculus is an object of the mind, not the mental act involved in its use.

However, by applying the method of *Psychognosia* for eidetic *seeing*, predications of factualness yield to descriptions of both intentional objects and cognitive acts. In its phenomenological field of action, a transcendental logic and its contingent calculi are typically given to mental life "as if" or "as though" (id., §3) they are already grounded in familiarity with the world of objectified and embodied things. Acting "as if" is indeed grounded in life-world experiences, and is therefore psychologically descriptive of intentional comportment in the transcendental register. Husserl (1973a, §7) suggests that our experiences of a deeper lying logic of calculus in eidetic constructions, along with its transcendental modification in the form of the "as if," are intended to achieve apodictic certainty in one's predicative judgments. Our ability to reason inductively in conceptual space is grounded intuitively in pre-conceptual experiences of reasoning to an irrefutable or self-evident conclusion—to be more specific, a conclusion about the actual reality and truth of what already *is* in pre-conceptual space. During our ongoing cognitive development, we tend to focus on the anticipated semblance of something that has been encountered in similar experiences of judging and valuing essences and their relationships according to a transcendental logic of calculus.

Predicative judgments point toward a modification of something pre-given as pre-existing in pure consciousness. In Husserl's (1982, §§136f) regressive phenomenology, whatever shows itself in the horizon of epistemology as predicated self-knowledge of apodictic certainty could be traced back to its origins in pre-predicative regions of ontology and metaphysics. The actions that bestow sense and confer meaning on an *eidos* in the *a priori* horizons set in motion the pure Ego's genetic construction of a matter of factualness for an intentional object. Recall that something is constituted in transcendental consciousness in step-wise fashion such that a synthesized unity of the whole is dependent upon the pre-existence of its unified parts at each prior step. This psychic order of composition within an eidetic affair-complex represents a universal phenomenological method of consciousness-formation—a method that makes use of a logic of calculus for intuitive judgments and valuations in the transcendental register. The action that could be described as "psychological" follows along this same genetic sequence, as elements of an affair-complex are acted upon or passively accepted during constitutive life.

The remainder of this chapter is focused on the psychological experience of *knowing*; for when we constitute conscious awareness of something, we have thus achieved self-knowledge of an object of the mind. My aim is to present the theoretical ground for transcendental phenomenological psychology as the psychological ego's universal methods of constitution in the transcendental register—all within a field of intentional action in pure psychology. In keeping with Husserl's purpose for phenomenological psychology to represent a radical difference with traditional practices, applying our everyday methods of cognitive action as praxis in genetic phenomenology signifies an extension of his revolutionary theory of inquiry. The final chapter that follows thereafter grasps what was presented previously from this same perspective, and then carries that view into yet unexplored regions of applied transcendental phenomenological psychology. Beginning here under the psychological *epoché*, exegetic interpretations of Husserl's philosophy give over to what could be called in practice a "phenomenological-psychological imagination." Indeed, I will be pursuing the psychological ego in free fantasy according to its representations as the psychological subjectivity of the pure Ego's transcendental consciousness and self-knowledge of *my life*.

Genetic Phenomenological Psychology

Husserl does not use the term of *genetic* in an "empirical, factual, or historical sense," Farber (1940, 53) writes, "but in the sense of the intentional reference of all ideas or principles to their 'original' evidences—in the last analysis, to the direct evidence of individuals." Predicated knowledge always refers to one's *self*-knowledge of an intentional object which is achieved during a genetic sequence of constitution. When an intentional object is realized as *my* idea or *my* thoughts in this sequence, the pre-conceptual givenness of that object elapses and is no longer directly operative in conceptual space for subsequent judgments. With our so-called logic of natural induction in the transcendental register, attention in the living present is no longer thematically focused on an object of simple apprehension. Instead, attention tends to be focused on one's self-knowledge *of* that object as already truly existing here and now. One's predicated knowledge of the sense and meaning of a transcendental object could then *also* be one's own idea about something that was given originally in an "empirical, factual, or historical sense."

In genetic phenomenology, similar to Piaget's (Parsons 1958, x) genetic epistemology of developmental experience, predicated knowledge is not a psychological phenomenon, although gathering reason-as-evidence *for* one's self-knowledge could certainly be described as psychological experience. Here, expressions of self-knowledge are self-evident expressions of what one has grasped at deeper levels of now transcended simple apprehension. In Husserl's (1969, 184ff) account of genetic constitution, prior levels of pre-predicative experience are *lived* throughout the experience of predicating an object of self-knowledge in conscious awareness. During the developmental synthesis of an enduring object of the mind, immediate levels of synchronic self-knowledge imply earlier levels of diachronic comprehension. (*see* Tito 1990, 53f) Intentional acts of synthesis in psychological processes of intuitive before-and-after being-sense carry the essence of an earlier experience of simple apprehension over into our intersubjective relationships of predicating apperceptions in the transcendental register.

The phenomenological concept of *intersubjectivity* begs the question as to how the presence of universal things in solipsistic experience—such as everyday sounds and sights—could genetically become valid self-knowledge of singular sense for the pure Ego, while simultaneously valid as something actually real that is experienced as essentially the same for everyone. Generally speaking, something universal could be given in the transcendental register by a variety of particular appearances or profiles in the world of common semblance. Husserl (2001, 136) explains that when we become consciously aware of a universal object, "the primitive relation between Species and Instance emerges: it becomes possible to look over and compare a range of instances...." For example, each constituted red-colored thing in the transcendental register presents a finite instance of the range of universal *redness*. We could apprehend originally in constitutive life a particular instance of *redness* as *this*

this red in the world of all possible realities for universal *redness*. A synthesis of being-sense for *this* instance of *redness* and not another is subsequently carried over into our intersubjective relationships, where we could mutually agree that *this* red-colored thing is indeed truely red. Ironically perhaps, those who are color-blind could also come to agree in empathy that an instance of *redness* is actually real and objectively true, even while perceiving only shades of gray. Such is the influence of the *Other* during intersubjective relationships.

In applied genetic phenomenology, Husserl (1973a, §42) sets aside all but the potential for the uninterrupted presence of a durable object of the mind, along with its imaginatively modified *eidos* that is fashioned during consciousness-formation to be *my own*. This anticipated presence is represented and maintained in pre-conceptual experience by an intuitive unity of elements for that object, including such universal elements as its hyletic qualities. Consequently in constitutive life, when the pure Ego's regard is adverted toward grasping the essence of an instance of something universal during intersubjective relationships, one "attains [as a correlate] the intuitive unity of objectivity." Transcendental consciousness of *red* is indeed one's consciousness of a matter that is believed to be *objectively red*, since its intentional object is constituted to be an instance of pregiven universal *redness*. Similarly within this genetic psychic order of transcendence, awareness of *time* is awareness of *objective time*, awareness of *space* is awareness of *objective space*, and so on. Husserl (1999, 319f) concludes in his phenomenology of reason that a normative tradition of habitually making use of pregiven universals exists for both individuals and groups within our various sociocultural surroundings.

During a genetic sequence of judgments and valuations, universals and their relationships show themselves under the *epoché* as pre-existing elements that are necessary in order for one's self-knowledge of something to gain presence as actually real and objectively true. Each of us ordinarily makes use of an instance of something universal during predicative experience according to a form of ideation for an intentional object that is anticipated to be a whole thing in conscious awareness. We tend habitually to construct and use compositions of universal matters that could, for example, be partially represented in expressions of an intentional object that is "recent," "similar," or "many." Under the eidetic reduction in genetic reflections, correlates of universals are typically modified by adjectives in their practical expressions—and in this way, they signify a pregiven idealized objectivity for a singular core essence that has endured throughout all anticipated relations to truth and reality.

Upon reflection, for instance, the various hands I see day-to-day are not identical to mine. Yet they are similar enough in transcendental subjectivity to represent in constitutive life an idealized identity for the universal *eidos* of *handedness* in the world of common semblance. By analogy we could compose the actual reality for the "hands" of a squirrel or of a clock—meaning, we intentionally construct irreal compositions and ideations for an instance of universal *handedness* that exemplify the phenomenon of *hands*. Apodictic certainty in the anticipated objective similarity between the core essence of your hand and mine (and maybe a squirrel's), allows me to constitute awareness of *hands* during intersubjective relationships. Hands *as such* are finite objects in a logic of calculus that are correlated to exist *per se* during activities of clapping, waving, pointing, scratching, and so on. In this sense, the meanings of universal things in the transcendental register are only partially pregiven in pre-conceptual affair-complexes as idealizations of pre-phenomenological phenomena. A matter of partial pregivenness within a genetic logic of calculus points reflections toward a purely psychological element of *choice*.

Pre-conceptual universals do not signify the naming of something objective, since *naming* depends upon skills developed in the conceptual space of language-use. Indeed, I can conceive in language only what I have already pre-conceived as an active idea in speech. During our cognitive performances in the transcendental register, irreal universals are pictured as objectively real in pre-conceptual space—but in the pure psychology of this experience, universals are "aimed at" for their actualization during intersubjective relationships *as if* they are objectively real for everyone. In the transcendental logic of genetic constitution, an instance of something universal *re*-presents in its normative use a previous objectifying-act upon a singular core essence of an *eidos*. Consequently, an objectified *eidos* is valid for predicating a state of affairs that could be grasped as a matter of fact by everyone. An instance of predicated knowledge represents one's "personal" knowledge of something that is believed to be ideally "objective" for all of us. Predicated knowledge of a universal is a post-phenomenological phenomenon that could nevertheless pre-exist as pregiven to constitutive life by our intersubjective partners in empathy.

Husserl's mature transcendental phenomenology makes use of the eidetic and transcendental reductions in order to disclose together both the universal and "personal" elements of subjective experience for the pure Ego. At the same time, beginning with one's simple grasp of an adequately given intentional object, pure psychology provides an imaginative and intuitive path of actionality for genetic phenomenology throughout the irreal anonymity of the subject's structure of awareness. Because of this intentional action, Husserl (1977, 6) explains, the eidetic organization of fulfilled transcendental consciousness is no embodied structure in the "natural naïve world." Rather, in genetic phenomenology, the idea of transcendental consciousness "designates the complex intertwining which belongs to every concrete phase of the streaming psychic life." In its enduring totality, the pure psychology of universal mental life is an intentional "nexus of efficacy, a nexus of development, and is governed throughout by an immanent teleology [of intentional acts]." One's own psychological experience of awareness is an instance of this same universal experience of psychic life that each of us tends to enjoy.

Instances of universal composing- and grouping-acts are represented in the subject's unity of awareness by grammatical (subject-predicate-object) synthesizing "predicates of the experiential world." (Husserl 1977, 90) Post-phenomenological predicates are usually first seen during referential language-use, and have significance in both one's inner speech and in shared verbal discourse. Something could be predicated as well by its absence in speech, such as expressions that only implicate or that lack the common semblance of empathy. Still, a predicating connection in all cases fulfills the intentional func-

affairs" for a transcendental object. (p. 72) Under the psychological *epoché* and eidetic reduction, genetic patterns of predicating apperceptions point toward intentional constructions of necessary psychic nexus, or connections, during pre-conceptual performances of consciousness-formation. Simultaneously under the psychological *epoché* and transcendental reduction—starting with the pure Ego's turn outward from solipsistic subjectivity—each connection seems to "join" a partially composed grouping of elements within a total configuration of being-sense for an anticipated rational affective unity.

A pre-conceptual nexus of judging or valuing is a genetic moment of intentional connection between parts and parts-to-whole of a grouped and composed eidetic structure for an object of the mind. Each psychic connection during genetic constitution points toward and directs cognitive action to another nexus in pure psychology, and then to still more connections, generating new choices and mental formations for what is anticipated by the pure Ego to be a unified structure of intelligibility here and now. Husserl (1977, 5) writes that the pure Ego intends to achieve "the one *mental nexus universally given by internal experience* [*innere Erfahrung*]." This singular nexus "knows no separation of parts consisting of self-sufficient elements." During the transcendental subjectivity of psychic life—absent any pathological organic influence or the lack of normal maturation and development (*see* Husserl 1970, §55)—conscious awareness is indeed of a whole structure that is typically composed genetically according to a calculus for constructing a rational affective unity. The cognitive action that aims at the composition of such unity "streams on continually," and is *lived* (*erlebt*) as the psychosubjectivity of the pure Ego.

The pure Ego's psychosubjectivity is given to genetic reflections as all intentional manifestations of mental life in pure and transcendental subjectivity here and now. Psychological subjectivity is thus observed as the phenomenon of one's psychic *being* (i.e., "being psychological") within the subject's horizon for cognitive action in the phenomenological field. Here, the teleological goal of psychic life is to construct the one mental nexus of internal experience when constituting consciousness of *this* object and not another. Following the pure Ego's transcendental reorientation, our intuitive grasp of something in solipsistic subjectivity is abstracted, valued, and cast forward by a predicating-act of protension into the surrounding world (*der Außenwelt*). We do this in order for the intentional object that is *my own* to gain presence amid a construction of self-knowledge for an actually real thing of common semblance. During this psychic order of genetic constitution, one's original self-knowledge of an *eidos* is pregiven for subsequent judgments and conceptualizations in higher-level apperceptions of objectivity for its core essence. And because of these actions, a predicated object of self-knowledge is constituted in conscious awareness as a whole thing with reason and evidence. A predicated object of self-knowledge represents in conceptual space what has been composed in pre-conceptual anticipation of a unity of configuration.

Husserl (1981, 26-7) mentions in his *Britannica* article that each of us tends to enjoy a "habitual acceptance" of our preconstituted objects of self-knowledge. We do not question, for example, our self-knowledge of the "upness" of *up* when climbing a ladder. Pre-existing objects of self-knowledge are believed to be always at hand for possible future intersubjective modification and validation in personal lifeworld experiences. When the affair-complex for an object of self-knowledge is composed to include the spatiality of appearances in one's personal lifeworld, it is then at hand for the pure Ego according to the object's now-embodied coordinates of connections for the true nature of things. Under the eidetic reduction, these coordinates include the idealized and absolutized orthogonal (= 180 degrees "opposite") spatial orientations of embodiment for objectified things—such as up/down, in/out, here/there, near/far, and so on. Just as we habitually accept as pregiven the spatial dimensions of embodied things as a metaphysical orientation toward reason, so too do we habitually accept our internal time-consciousness in pure psychology as a psychic order of reasoning for *when* objects are necessarily up/down, in/out, and so on. The psychic life of the pure Ego is ordinarily conducted and experienced within a habitual psychic order of spatiotemporal dimensions.

In Husserl's (1973a, §48) transcendental theory of elements for this same experience, an object of self-knowledge in one's personal lifeworld is typically objectified and idealized during conscious-formation. (*see* Husserl 1970, §72) In order for its embodied being-sense to be fully expressed in conceptual space when oriented toward living knowingly as natural, said object depends upon our passive acceptance of so-called natural laws of causality for objectified and idealized things. Natural laws for actual reality are correlated with apodictic certainty in the horizon of metaphysics, and then grasped by apperception as necessity demands during life-span cognitive development. Due to one's habituated time-consciousness of these particular elements as instances of universal cause, Natural laws are at hand in the living present for judgments and valuations in the pure Ego's pre-conceptual calculus of logic and psychic order of constitution. With this reason-as-evidence concerning time and place, we could then say, for example, "Things always pile up when I'm feeling down," or "This chair belongs with that table over there."

Why is it, Husserl (1970, §63) asks, that the experience of *living* a genetic order of consciousness-formation is not itself seen to be a phenomenon of human imagination and achievement? Beginning (1) with our simple grasp of a potential unity within (2) the spatiality of embodied Nature, (3) a pregiven mental formation of necessary temporal connections is typically (4) capable of producing the constitution and expression in conscious awareness of (5) a sensible meaning for the objectified and idealized core essence of an intentional object. To observe this proper sequence of psychic order for the experience of self-knowledge, Husserl's (1982, §84) "archaeological" reductions must pass through the immediate and most recent transcendental layers of an object of awareness without interpretations of conferred meaning on its core essence. Husserl could not disclose a fundamental relationship of being-sense in pure subjectivity for an objectified thing other than by beginning with the eidetic reduction that reveals to reflections the enduring intelligibility of an intentional object in one's personal lifeworld. Indeed, we typically ask in reflective meditations, "What is it?" before ever wondering, "What does it mean?"

The eidetic reduction enables Husserl to perform a conceptualizing
(what is to the pure Ego) the ultimate layer of a constituted transcendental

object. Upon gaining phenomenological *entrée*, the eidetic reduction means to avoid the acceptance of any pregiven historical or cultural presuppositions for constituted appearances by first bracketing the pure Ego's transcendental re-orientation—since within the circle of transcendence, our natural attitude is already metaphysically oriented toward reason in one's sociocultural surroundings. The noetic structure of awareness for living knowingly is first presented as an intentional form of ideation for a particular *eidos* given by the now-bracketed transcendental ego. The eidetic reduction is subsequently used in order to disclose the sensible meaning of both a constructed actual reality and the necessary pre-existing irreality for that same *eidos* here and now.

By applying our everyday methods of reduction and extension as *praxis*—beginning from the subject's fundamental relationships of *I* and *Other*, and continuing outward toward the highest genus of being-sense in one's personal lifeworld—the reconstruction of a constituted object of self-knowledge could be directed by the so-called intentional gaze of the performing ego in the living present. In both Husserl's theory of elements and theory of method, this is the same bifurcated gaze of the pure Ego during every phenomenological reduction under the *epoché*. In Husserl's (1964b, 54) static descriptive phenomenology, the gaze of the pure Ego and its spatial orientations direct propadeutic reflections down and ever inward toward the cognitive correlations of the subject's existential *I* and *Other*. A phenomenologically reduced being-sense for *me myself*, along with any cognitive correlations for what is meaningfully *Other*, together represent and point toward a pre-existing psychological theme for consciousness of *my life* in the transcendental register.

During the reflective attitude of Husserl's (1973b, §33) transcendental theory of method for genetic phenomenology, the pure Ego's personal (*persön-lich*) gaze on the *eidos* of *my life* is the intentional gaze of the psychological ego that thematically orients consciousness-formation toward achieving the one mental nexus of inner experience. This gaze is focused in the living present on both what is pregiven and what is anticipated for awareness here and now. Following the pure Ego's transcendental reorientation, the gaze of the psychological ego is directed toward composing and realizing the sensible meaning of pre-existing elements and their relationships for this same nexus—all within an eidetic affair-complex of unity. From the psychological ego's point of view, an eidetic affair-complex is an irreal matter (*Sache*) for the pure Ego under the transcendental reduction. Under the psychological reduction, that complex is an immanent thing-in-itself (*Ding an sich*) for the transcendental ego's form of ideation. A partially or fully composed affair-complex pre-exists for judgments and valuations in conceptual space, where it is simultaneous with our words, beliefs, and opinions about actually real things.

Actually real things are but *mere things* when they appear as post-phenomenological phenomena in conceptual space—"mere" in the sense that their greater depths of pre-conceptual construction *ordinarily and intentionally* do not show themselves by their opaque appearances as idealized and objectified unities within a transcendentally modified personal lifeworld. We are not motivated to reflect on the irreal origins of actually real things during typical day-to-day comportment, yet each of us in our habitual judgments and valuations "returns" to the depths of our full and partial eidetic affair-complexes. In the face of life-world contingencies, as a result of the psychological ego's before-and-after gaze during the genetic order of transcendental constitution, the pure Ego reiterates elements of an affair-complex in order to orient and direct cognitive mental life toward the normative fulfillment of an original *eidos*. A complete reconstruction of a fully constituted object of self-knowledge is not possible under the eidetic and transcendental reductions without a complementary psychological reduction to the constitutive action of the psychological ego's returning to pre-existing and pregiven elements.

Husserl's (1982, §§85f) implicit genetic reflections in *Ideas I* seem to anticipate the intentional function of the psychological ego's acts of both reason and non-reason in transcendental constitutive life. During the genetic succession of a psychic order in the living present, matters of psychosubjectivity include such intentional action of the psychological ego as the turning of regard from one element or theme to another, imaginatively seizing upon essences, acts of judgments and valuations, intuitively composing an eidetic affair-complex, passive acceptance of something pregiven here and now, and so on. Under the psychological *epoché* and reduction, reflective abstractions of such pre-conceptual performances as these allow a phenomenological psychologist to infer the transcendental methods by which the intentional function of mental life to act upon objects during consciousness-formation is carried out (or not) within each potential genetic phase of transcendental subjectivity.

Beginning from the pure Ego's existential relationships in solipsistic subjectivity, the personal gaze of the psychological ego directs a streaming of cognitive action in order to achieve the subject's anticipated consciousness-of-something in one's personal lifeworld. Such action is directed both thetically and nonthetically upward and outward in contingent psychological processes according to the pure Ego's anticipation of fulfilling its constitutive goals. An intentional flow of constitution typically proceeds when elements of an intentional object are pictured in the transcendental ego's form of ideation for what is deemed to be a rational affective unity in the world that is commonly talked about. In Husserl's (1973a, §51.c) mature theory of method for genetic phenomenology, the actions of the psychological ego during this flow represents the "thematic activity" of the pure Ego whereby a succession of intentional mental acts is intended to remain uninterrupted throughout the transcendental constitution of a unified whole object.

When reasoning is ordered by a transcendental logic for a unity of parts-to-whole, discontinuous elements of an anticipated objectivity are, so to say, "bridged" by the psychological ego's action on the object-oriented contents of pure consciousness. By means of this mental formation of cognitive action, a continuous whole structure for an intentional object gains presence in the conceptual space of actually real things. In terms of constructing a unity of configuration in elemental phases of parts-to-parts and parts-to-whole, a psychological theme in its mental formation is complementary to both simple and higher-level apperceptions of an adumbrated object. Yet for the psycho-logical ego's performance of a synthetic flow of action in constituting a unified matic construction amid an interconnected streaming of mental life directed toward unity—rather than an individual element within an adumbrated multi-form of elements. Under the psychological reduction, norms and practices of cognitive mental life usually follow the intentional function to realize an unambiguous form of ideation for the singular core essence of an active idea.

Husserl (1973a, §51.c) explains that in pure psychology, the intentional function of mental life with regard to action on parts and wholes directs a genetic succession of judgments and valuations in order to construct "a unity of the two identifying activities, traversed by a single identifying activity." For example, when I blow out the birthday candles, by this intentional act on a discrete element of ideation, my party continues in its succession of further identifying acts of celebration—such as eating the cake, opening the presents, thanking my guests, and so on. Ordinary cognitive action in mental life is intentionally about fulfilling the psychological theme for a single identifying activity for *this eidos*. By fulfilling a theme of action, a signifying sensible meaning for a singular core essence is realized in conscious awareness—such as the core essence of *celebration*. Because of our cognitive action in both simple and higher-level apperceptions, the sensible meaning of a constituted objectivity gains presence in thought and speech as the actual reality of something that truly exists with reason and evidence. Here and now in one's personal lifeworld, a singular core essence with its intersubjective modifications is experienced as a concrete matter that is believed to be valid for everyone.

An experience of awareness in one's personal lifeworld entails by necessity the eidetic structures and intersubjective elements of an affair-complex for worldly self-knowledge. (*see* Fink 1995, §11 note 527) Objects of worldly self-knowledge are represented in conceptual space by the presence of mundane thought and speech. Under the transcendental *epoché*, mundane thought is presented for genetic reflections and clarifications as self-same in composed essential features with its intentional form of ideation during intersubjective relationships. Under the psychological *epoché*, a field of intentional experience in the life-world of "natural" appearances is abstracted in the living present for judgments and valuations that are contingently necessary for mundane thought and its referential speech. Mundane thought presents to one's self and others an object with the appearance of unity in the world of common semblance; and in Husserl's work, mundane thought is *any* thought of the phenomenal world other than from the phenomenological attitude. Mundane speech seems to be a universal teleological goal in the pure Ego's mental life of transcendental constitution—where in empathy, we present symbolic representations of the phenomenal world as objectively real and true. From the natural attitude, mundane speech is indeed indistinguishable from post-phenomenological language-use.

One's awareness of an objectivity in the phenomenal world tends to be, as it were, a "mirroring" of the transcendental ego's form of ideation for a genetically unified composition of adumbrated elements. Seen simultaneously under the eidetic, transcendental, and psychological reductions as a subject-predicate-object state of affairs, our expressions of actual reality present the semblance of irreal matters from the natural attitude. In phenomenological psychology, when something is believed by the subject to be actually real in one's naïve natural world, then that thing's composed affair-complex and its form of ideation include an element of self-referencing temporal orientation for an objectified existent. (*see* Husserl 1973a, §39) By implication, a mental process for grasping the spatial and temporal dimensions of objective reality during one's intersubjective relationships has its genetic origins within one's enduring solipsistic structures of self-reference toward *me* and *mine*. A constituted objectivity is actually real in mundane thought and speech precisely as I have constructed it to be with psychological processes of intentional acts and passive acceptance that are peculiarly *my own*.

Still, one's self-knowledge of a fully constituted objectivity does not gain presence in awareness as disconnected imaginings in pre-conceptual space. Instead, as a universal experience for each of us, the pure Ego grasps an object of self-knowledge in one's personal lifeworld by means of the performing ego's genetic modifications of being-sense for an enduring core essence throughout the dialectical interactions of solipsistic and transcendental subjectivity. That same core essence is then given to the psychological ego for contingent but necesary transcending acts of composing and constituting an objectified intentional object with the sense of *true being* in conceptual space. Said acts proceed in psychological processes by synthesizing the intentional object's adumbrated elements and spatiotemporal dimensions of embodiment, just as they are pregiven for the true nature of things.

Husserl (1973a, §39) noticed in his knowledge-complex of ego-life that the bifurcated "knowing ego"—seen as a self-referencing orientation within a field of intentional experience—has its own "strict localization of position" for truly existing things in one's naïve natural world. Consequently, in a genetic order of constitution, one's self-knowledge of something actually real is grasped as *my* belief, or *my* opinion, or *my* feelings, and so on. When establishing its finite "temporal position" in constitutive life, Husserl continues, the knowing ego could both imagine and seek validation for necessary elements of an intentional object that are now *my own* during consciousness-formation. Because of the knowing ego's natural attitude toward truth and reality, there is a pre-existing and self-referencing affair-complex for an embodied grouping of elements that refers to the objectifications of *me* and *mine* in mundane thought and speech. Said affair-complex is genetically composed by means of a transcendental logic of calculus for reiterations of pregiven elements.

Such genetic "steps" accompany and are anticipated with every moment of psychic life during the dialectical synthesis of transcendental consciousness. After the pure Ego's transcendental reorientation, elements of a pre-existing noetic structure in solipsistic subjectivity are carried over into our intersubjective relationships of empathy for higher-level apperceptions of an idealized semblance of objectivity. As an object's composition tends toward unity in the transcendental register, each genetic sequence within an order of consciousness-formation is intended-to by psychological processes of judging and valuing so as to constitute an object of singular sense and meaning. A transcendental logic of calculus universally includes not only elements of ob-

a calculus to its fruition. In the midst of this dynamic flow toward unity, the self-objectification of one's psychic being and spiritual ownness as a "person" usually takes place. The subject's life-span system of apperceptions for composing the unity of one's self-objectification is the primary means by which the pure Ego is in the world of objective reality. The pure Ego's intention to *live* the sense and meaning of its own constructed world of objectively real things is part of what Husserl calls the human soul.

According to Husserl's (1970, §58) directions for further studies, a reconstructive genetic psychology under the eidetic, transcendental, and psychological reductions would take into account our acts of reasoning in cognitive mental life, along with our motivation to transcend solipsistic subjectivity toward transcendental consciousness. By following this direction, "an indissoluble inner alliance obtains between psychology and transcendental phenomenology." Regarding a phenomenologist's experience with this alliance, "one can say: If I myself effect the transcendental attitude as a way of lifting myself above world-apperceptions and my human self-apperception, purely for the purpose of studying the transcendental accomplishment in and through which I 'have' the world, then I must also find this accomplishment again, later, in a psychological internal analysis—though in this case it would…be apperceived as belonging to the real soul [*als Realseelisches*]." It seems that Husserl's long called-for transcendental phenomenological psychology was intended to be practiced as an "internal analysis" of "soulish" action, where one reflects on the phenomenon of transcendental consciousness as a psychological experience in the world that is commonly talked about.

The Transcendental Reorientation:
An Affairness of Empathy

Constitutive life begins begins when adumbrated elements of an intentional object are grasped in anticipation of its unified presence here and now. The pure Ego then directs the constitution of that object from the solipsistic register to its fulfillment in transcendental consciousness by means of a contingent mental formation of intentional action and non-action on those previous elements—all this within an ongoing construction of reality for *me* and *mine* vis-à-vis the existential *Other*. Yet an intentional object in this psychic order may not be fully realized as an eidetic unity in the transcendental register, and might therefore be irrational, immature, or provisional in the conceptual space of actual reality and objective truth. Although an intentional object is meaningful within its solipsistic structures of pure subjectivity, it is nevertheless genetically incomplete and possibly ambiguous regarding evidence of its full potential for rational cognitions in life-world experiences. A fully constituted transcendental object, on the other hand, is composed such that it cannot be otherwise than intended in the world that is commonly talked about. Husserl (1982) explains this difference as a matter of "intellectually seeing" pregiven essences in the sphere of immanence:

> What we usually call evidence and intellectual sight (or intellectual seeing) is a positional, doxic and adequately presentive consciousness

which "excludes being otherwise".... The arithmetical example [of seeing a pregiven form of eidetic organization in computations] illustrates that [adequate givenness of enduring pre-existence] for us. In the example of [seeing, on the other hand, a] landscape we have, it is true, a seeing, but not an evidence [of seeing something pregiven] in the usual pregnant sense of the word, [and seeing an individual landscape is therefore strictly speaking not] an "intellectual seeing" [i.e., since the landscape provides no evidence of something pre-existing the moment of presentative consciousness].

Observing more precisely, we note two differences. In the one example [of eidetic *seeing*] it is a matter of [seeing pregiven] essences; in the other, [it is] a matter of [seeing] something individual [in the midst of a plurality of possible things]; secondly, in the eidetic example the originary givenness is adequate [for evidence of seeing something pre-existing], whereas in the example from the sphere of experience [for seeing individual things] it is inadequate [for cognition of something that "excludes being otherwise"]. (§137)

The "givenness" of a transcendental object is mediated in constitutive life by our life-span experiences with individual things within a pregiven plurality of things. Otherwise, things that matter to one in solipsistic subjectivity, such as an enduring truth or reality, are inadequately given for judgments and valuations within an indeterminate pluralism of things that matter for all. (*see* Husserl 1973a, §96.a) Part of the problem of inadequate givenness in the transcendental register, Fink (1995, §10) suggests, could be expressed this way: Although an intentional object is posited as truly existing in its solipsistic structures, and is retained for apperceptions in the horizon of metaphysics for correlations of certainty, there is no adequate reason for the pure Ego to anticipate that the object will endure throughout the contingent "external" structures of transcendental subjectivity. The problem of object constancy thus presents itself in pure psychology. In Husserl's example of intellectual seeing that is quoted above, the eidetics of a mathematical equation will never change in its givenness to reason; it either *is* or *is-not* in one's possible experiences. We can believe and be apodictically certain of the pre-existence of an equation within its formal calculus—but will this landscape still appear the same to me from another perspective, or next year, or to another person?

Persisting in the midst of change is indeed the meaning of phenomenological duration, yet an intentional object is only "holding good" as intuitable in the pure subjectivity of simple apprehension. A pre-conceptual object in solipsistic subjectivity represents one's anticipation of an actual reality in conceptual space, but it does not represent the so-called acceptedness of a transcendentally constituted object in conscious awareness. Neither do our existential relationships represent the acceptedness of one's individual identity in the diverse intersubjective world. Still, any pre-constituted object could be described with respect to its singular core essence within immanent solipsistic structures, yet outside of inter-experiential existence. A solipsistic object's pre-conceptual representations could be seen as pointing toward an irreducible pre-existing developmental relationship with the existential *Other*. While there are places for them in our cognitive repertoires, judgments based solely on such immanent, non-reversible, solipsistic conditions are passive and axiomatic—meaning, as norms of practice they are axiologically bound in reasoning to non-rational assumptions and possible misconceptions.

Under the transcendental reduction, however, reflections focus on what is bracketed as holding good for *me myself* in the world that is commonly talked about. During genetic reconstructions of the phenomenon of human consciousness, elements of intuitive individuation in pure subjectivity are returned to the personal lifeworld wherein a singular core essence is pregiven as the meant-as-meant essence of an objective actual reality. In our personal lifeworld, one might say, the transcendental ego "owns" the sense and meaning of the objectified *eidos* of *my life* in the world of human co-existence. As Husserl (1973b, §44) phrases it, the phenomenon of *me myself* in intersubjective experience represents the pre-conceptual "ownness-essence of the Objective phenomenon: 'I, as this man'. If I reduce other men to what is included in my ownness, I get bodies included therein; if I reduce myself as a man, I get…my personal ego." The personal ego represents one's transcended solipsistic subjectivity in life-world experiences with the objectified *Other*.

A dynamic human consciousness now shows itself in its intersubjective phase of genetic constitution. (*see* Husserl 1973b, §§42ff). In this fully-fledged mode of consciousness-formation, the pure Ego is in its own constructed world of human among humans. Husserl (Fink 1995, §11 note 374) stresses that "the ego can only have being [*Dasein*] in the world as something in human form that has the world, as…I-person with psychic being." Here, an intentional object that is constituted in world-consciousness is not static *in situ* according to its original solipsistic givenness, but instead yields during intersubjective experience to modifications, revisions, and maturation in one's sociocultural surroundings. Husserl's (1970, §§47ff) theory of intersubjectivity in part clarifies the pure Ego's anticipation and practices for presenting to one's self (and representing to others) what is believed to be an objective actual reality that is valid for everyone. During our ordinary experiences of transcendental intersubjectivity, the core essence of an intentional object endures amid the contingencies of one's own constructed personal lifeworld.

When an intentional object is constituted in awareness during its intersubjective phase of consciousness-formation, it is first abstracted by the pure Ego from the flux of pure consciousness, seized as *my own* in solipsistic subjectivity, and then posited as actually real in one's personal lifeworld as depicted in the transcendental ego's form of ideation. Bound by the intentional structures of this genetic field of experience, the enduring reality of *my life* is lived by the psychological ego in mental processes of seemingly continuous everyday matters of anticipation and fulfillment with the existential *Other*. A naïve representation of what is believed to be a mutually understood and universally experienced world of durable realities is potentially cognizable once the idea of an intersubjective world is grasped. Without such representations of intentionality, and without our anticipation of intersubjective fulfillment for an intentional object, Husserl's transcendental phenomenology of human consciousness would not be possible. His philosophy would remain instead within the solipsistic register of pure subjectivity. (*see* Welton 2000, 285)

Although posited and constituted to be actually real, and represented as something objective, a transcendental object is of course not literally shared in the sense that something tangible could be given from one to another. Yet neither is it merely an object of common knowledge. In Husserl's (Fink 1995, §8) mature theory of method, the subject's awareness of a transcendental object represents one's self-knowledge of the being-sense of an *eidos* that has been correlated in the horizons of epistemology, ontology, and metaphysics. We seem to share an objective actual reality in knowledge, meaning, and practice in the world for us all when each of us has made similar judgments and valuations of irreal matters during our intersubjective relationships.

One's naïve sense of human co-existence is indeed a result of the cognitive action of the psychological ego to construct a world of common semblance as the world for us all. In genetic psychology, this experience is given to reflections as the bringing-to-presence of one's personal ego. Our intersubjective communicative practices, including the normative use of grammar and syntax, are intuitively grounded in one's capacity to construct similar actual realities as others for irreal matters. No naïve science or philosophy exists except for our ability to reflect similarly upon assumptions of objective reality and universal truth. In most areas of life, rightly or wrongly, we could represent to one's self and say to others, "This is real and true for all of us."

During everyday experiences with presuppositions of mutual truth and reality, a constituted objectivity is the cognitive correlate of the psychological ego's composed elements within our intersubjective relationships of empathy (*Einfühlung*). The phenomenological concept of *empathy* is a clarification of its naïve sense in theoretical discourse—which generally refers either to one's understanding the "internal" experiences of another as objective phenomena, or as "transferring" one's subjective feelings onto something already objective. In Husserl's (1973a, §38) theory of intersubjectivity, the *eidos* of *empathy* implies the following: When the sense of something is given by another as objectively (nonthetically) *there* in rational apperceptions, it is then ordered pre-conceptually according to retentions and anticipations for something similar that is intellectually seen *here* with adequate givenness in (thetic) solipsistic subjectivity. We cannot read the minds of others, or experience the full range of historical and cultural givenness of the human condition, but we could inductively infer a sensible meaning when an alien expression or practice finds correspondence with something that is already deeply familiar. In our empathetic (polythetic, synthetic) relationships, one's thoughts are thus objectified and believed to be meaningful for everyone.

"In empathy," Husserl (1973a, §38) continues, we experience "an objective, intersubjectively common time, in which everything individual in lived experiences…is constituted" amid one's surrounding world and its immediate contents. His clarified concept of *empathy* represents neither an object nor an act, but rather a synthetic spatiotemporality for objects and acts here and

the pure Ego and its bifurcated ego-functions so as to be intellectually seen as pre-existing in the transcendental register—and because of the psychological ego's empathizing-acts, object constancy from solipsism to transcendence is maintained in conscious awareness. The living present profile of the subject's empathetic relationships represents the psychological ego's standpoint in relation to "the data of place" (*Lokaldaten*) for the synthesized "all-space" and one time of transcendental consciousness. (Husserl 1964a, 25)

The essence of an original idea is indeed the irreal one thing that co-exists for the psychological ego as both *my own* and "for everyone" during an intersubjective relationship of empathy. As part of the psychological ego's phenomenologizing action during transcendental world-constitution, an original idea in solipsistic subjectivity is cast forward by protension, and then constituted intersubjectively as a particular *eidos* that is *my own* in one's personal lifeworld—where now, that adumbrated *eidos* has the appearance of common semblance during our involvements with others. The appearance, so to say, of a "shared oneness" for an intentional object is constructed in empathy by means of our individual systems of apperceptions for gathering evidence of actual reality and absolute truth.

Husserl (1973a, §38) explains further that we seek verification of the reality of our ownness-essence as a rational affective unity, not simply by realizing qualities of one's solipsistic experiences in the transcendental register, but non-linearly by intuition into the axiological qualities of our experiences with others. In a logically reversible transitive relationship of empathy, within the all-space and one time of transcendental consciousness, we anticipate finding adequate evidence of objective reality by apperception of a pregiven mutual being-sense. Fulfillment of this anticipation shows itself when we are aware of a particular mutual experience as objectively good, bad, indifferent, and so on—sometimes as a matter of ethics or morality in higher-level apperceptions of objective truth and reality. Given as the spirit-life of pure psychology during the transcendental turn, each of us wills to see objective qualities that are held in common during a relationship of empathy. Such qualities thus pre-exist in the living present along a polar continuum of one's previous experiences with embodied spatial things. Husserl (1977, 45ff) calls this finite continuum an "intersubjective-pole" of essences and their relationships within a constructed state of empathetic affairness.

The pure Ego's intersubjective-pole is a contingent array of potential position-taking judgments necessary for the construction of objective reality in conscious awareness. Each judgment in empathy is made along this pole, and each is therefore within a finite range of pregiven "identifiable actualities" that serve to delimit activities of consciousness-formation. As a norm of practice in empathy, we intend to make similar judgments according to an intellectually seen sociocultural tradition of reality construction. Here, a range of actualities for (say) the nature of things is revisited and repeated ("reiterated") within a "universally held system of purpose." (Husserl 1977, 89) The certainty of an objective actual reality is constructed in the spirit-life of communal interactions such that *this* reality is believed to be (thetically) here for *me myself* in a relationship of empathy. What is (polythetically and synthetically) here for all of us is typically the mutually shared presupposition of embodiment in the world of common semblance. This presupposition refers to the localized center of what is now the pure Ego's intersubjective-pole within the horizon of metaphysics. With our affectively motivated spirit-life of pure psychology, we tend to experience and naïvely call this localization a "feeling of empathy."

Husserl (1980a, §45) describes a feeling of empathy as the "indirect localization" of spirit-life in the world of material things—indirect, since one's spiritual ownness is never constituted as something material. Still, the affective content of spirit-life (such as wants and needs) could reference material properties of an intentional object, including the properties of embodied co-existence. Indeed, our feelings of empathy point toward a universal spirit of co-existence and communalization during psychological experiences of reality construction. Here, I first grasp the reality of "my body" as a differentiated state of ontic individuation from my spiritual ownness in solipsistic subjectivity. For example, my intention to touch something is self-evidently not the same experience as something touching my body. In the normal course of events, I seize upon essences in the surrounding world that present the common appearance of an objective Body—i.e., an object extended materially in space within a temporal manifold of indeterminate duration. I do not know why there exists something like a Body in Nature and neither do you, yet we could both correlate on good grounds in the horizon of metaphysics that its existence goes without saying in the transcendental register.

With feelings of empathy now, the subject localizes awareness of an objective Body along an intersubjective-pole within the horizon of metaphysics according to the affective and sensual contents of previous experiences with "my body" in solipsistic subjectivity. Because of this transcendental turn in consciousness-formation, one could then "touch" objective materiality, or "smell" or "taste" it. Reciprocally, objective materiality presents "warmth," "coldness," "pain," "pleasure," and so on, within a steady flow of reasoning from pre-conceptual to conceptual space. By objectifying "my body" in the material world as an objective Body with all of its pregiven properties, I establish conditions of intellectual seeing for the essence of other embodied objects constituted by other ego-subjects, including yours. Consequently, other ego-subjects are given to reason such that they too could present and experience the sensual properties already ascribed to material things. In its fullness of expression, this state of affairs for human co-existence in the spirit of communalization represents one sense of the term, "intersubjective relationships."

A complete affairness of empathy includes a diachronic phase for the pure Ego. Here, the child first grasps the idea of intersubjective relationships, and then reiterates that idea during subsequent levels of a maturing system of apperceptions in the world of human co-existence. Our transcendental reorientation in constitutive life begins with the construction of an empathetic relationship of mutual embodiment within this same system. One of the first transcending acts in pure psychology is to localize a system for apperceiving matters of common semblance according to similar bodily sensations and affects experienced in solipsistic subjectivity. What had once been the unintentional responses when grasping the idea of the physical world) are now also intentional cognitive mental acts in affectively motivated transcendental subjectivity. During our ongoing cognitive maturation, the pure Ego's retained and revisited solipsistic sensations "give rise" to the development of a system for apperceiving an embodied world of intersubjective relationships.

While describing judgments within an ongoing system of apperceptions, Husserl (1980a, §45) advised that his theory of intersubjectivity also requires a system of "appresentations" as an adumbration of the *eidos* of *presentiation*. In this latter system, apperceived multi-forms in their embodied plurality are presented simultaneously (and often analogously) with pre-existing unity-forms of solipsistic subjectivity. The pure Ego's experience of appresentation has a two-fold meaning for genetic reflections: "On the one hand, in the case of the solipsistic subject, [this system] has its original basis in original connections of regular co-existence in such a way that the connected members and series of members in their co-presence are not just there together but refer to one another [as *I* and *Other*]. And, on the other hand, [in the case of the transcendental subject] this system develops as a system of ordered indications [of co-existence] only by means of continuous experience of… [embodied and objectified others], who are already constituted by empathy." Similar to Husserl's use of Leibnitz's term "apperception" in perceptual experience, an "appresented" matter is presented to constitutive life and then known that it is presented as pregiven. A system of appresentations is typically present at the pure Ego's transcendental turn as a source of intuitive insight or intellectual *seeing* any necessary conditions of pregivenness.

During consciousness-formation in the transcendental register, it is a peculiar characteristic of a system of appresentations that judgments and valuations must be made in order to modify the pregivenness of solipsistic spatial and temporal relations for an intentional object. Ordinarily, we are motivated in the spirit-life of pure psychology to make these cognitive position-taking adjustments along the pure Ego's intersubjective-pole in empathy. Indeed, most of us could recall the feeling of such normative adjustments of one's communal spirit when we are, so to say, trying to "get on the same page" as others in thinking about some matter—an experience we sometimes naïvely call "rapport." A similar event occurs in pre-conceptual mental life at the pure Ego's turn of regard from solipsistic to transcendental subjectivity.

A system of appresentations seems to develop similarly as does a system of apperceptions in one's ongoing cognitive development, perhaps even simultaneously and correlated in higher levels of transcendental subjectivity. Yet due to the presence of these two systems during the construction of a rational affective unity, I typically find myself in a situation where I have two essential elements presented together for cognitions in the transcendental register: (a) my bodily sensations retained from solipsistic subjectivity and (b) a correlate of the interaction between my psychic life and my corporeality during an affairness of empathy. I could nevertheless grasp with adequate givenness that others ideally have similar feelings and appearances as *me myself* within a maturing world of common semblance—*because* at the transcendental turn I grasp (as a matter of intellectual *seeing*) the essence of others as pregiven in structures of an *I-Other* (now transcended, "I-You") unity-form during appresentations of semblance along the pure Ego's intersubjective-pole.

In relationships of dependence and distance from my own corporeal existence, the essence of "other humans" does not change with the pure Ego's transcendental reorientation. Instead, because of the intentional function of cognitive mental life to construct an essential unity in the midst of a plurality of elements, I apperceive in empathy that other ego-subjects present an enduring and similar correlate of the interaction between psychic life and corporeality as I have already experienced in solipsistic structures. With this pre-existing semblance for the givenness of human co-existence—correlated in the horizon of metaphysics such that it goes without saying—I tend to notice intuitively in the transcendental register that day-to-day human comportment is directed by a feeling of empathy that is already familiar to me. During mutual constructions of objective truth and actual reality, I could then intellectually see that the comportment of others is directed in a similar or analogous way that mine is directed by this same spirit of communalization.

Not only is corporeality appresented in empathy as a mutual experience, but the spirit-life of communalization and its affective comportment are also appresented as actually real and objectively present. (*see* Husserl 1980a, §45) During the moment of internal time-consciousness and psychic order that my corporeal-life and that of others are objectified in their embodied givenness to consciousness-formation, the psychic life that is *not* my own is also objectified as the naïve notion of "other minds." In the normal course of events, objectified spirit- and corporeal-life share a "transferred co-presence" in empathy—where one grasps the idea that others are similar in thought and speech to *me myself* during life-world experiences. The objectified elements of one's self-knowledge of an empathetic relationship are then typically correlated within the horizon of metaphysics in order to constitute awareness of our absolutized ways of human *being* and *doing*.

Even so, from the transcendental ego's perspective (i.e., from the natural attitude), a pre-conceptual correlate of corporeal- and spirit-life is not thematic for constructing the actual reality for a naïve "human nature"—since in the living present, this correlate by itself is not meaningful with feelings of empathy. We do not say, for example, "Let's lift up the actually real thing that we are individually motivated in spirit-life to agree represents the objectified sense and meaning of one's corporeal-life of *handedness*." Instead, because of the psychological ego's acts of intellectual *seeing* during the pure Ego's reorientation from solipsistic to transcendental subjectivity, correlates of the *eidos* of *pure life* are pregiven as pre-existing adumbrated elements of corporeal- and spirit-life in the human world. In effect, a correlate that was once *here* solely for *me myself* in solipsistic structures (such as *handedness*) could now also be *there* for everyone in constructions of mutual sense and meaning. Empathizing-acts are intended to realize the transcendental ego's form of ideation for the common semblance of objectified things here and now—and so, we all knowingly "raise our hands" in the pre-scientific space of objectified *handedness*.

During consciousness-formation following the transcendental turn, I ⟨illegible⟩ other persons whose lives are similar in sense and meaning to my own. Ordinarily, I have no reason to think differently; and indeed, I am usually certain that others share my own experiences of objectified corporeal- and spirit-life. The co-presence of such "empathetic" reason-as-evidence typically comes to presence within the horizon of metaphysics as the presupposition of an absolute commonality for what it means to be objectively human—namely, that everyone enjoys an embodied existence of idealized spatiotemporal dimensions and naturalized affects in the world that is commonly talked about.

Still, the problem arises in psychological inquiry that representations of embodiment might not be seen as metaphysical presuppositions of objective reality that we construct during our intersubjective relationships. Husserl (1980a, §45) describes the origin of this problem as appearing when psychologists fail to bracket their own feelings of empathy. One result is that the overt behavior of another is seen to be analogous to one's own embodied comportment. This may or may not be the case, however, since this analogy does not give evidence of intellectually seeing a pattern of psychological experience that "excludes being otherwise." Consequently, naïve psychologists sometime speak instead of averages and distributions of empirical dimensions that are posited to be real and true for everyone. Such expressions within an eidetic system of apperceptions serve as common "signs" for interpretations of objectified psychic life during one's relationships of *linguistic* empathy. Here, each sign refers in theoretical discourse to an instance of a mutually agreed upon "nature" of psychological phenomena. In this traditional way of proceeding, psychologists describe psychological phenomena in agreement with the co-presented metaphysics of embodied corporeal- and spirit-life in and from the natural attitude. These descriptions typically present empirical generalities of common semblance in regional ontologies of mundane psychology.

Husserl also points out that mundane psychology could become a metatheoretical system of signs that references the co-presence of objectified corporeal- and spirit-life—but without a pre-conceptual basis in pure psychology that excludes the system being otherwise. That is to say, the system might not exist as actually real or as scientifically reliable except for the mutual action of psychologists in empathy to make it seem so. Even when the null-hypothesis is used in research strategies to give evidence of intellectually seeing objective psychological experience, construct validity for that experience is called into question because of the sophistry of this strategy. Husserl follows this point about reason-as-evidence in traditional practices with a remark that seems directed at Sigmund Freud's metapsychology within its system of signs. Here, Freud's use of the term "introjection" appears to be singled out as dependent upon a metaphysical presupposition of objectified "Corporeality" for interpretations of psychic life. In this context, Husserl (1980a) describe a relationship of linguistic empathy for seeing the embodied human psyche within a system of signs that references objectified psychological experience:

> In this way, a system of indications is formed, and there is finally an analogy between this system of signs "expressing" psychic events... and the system of signs of language for the expression of [mundane] thought, abstracting from the fact that language itself, as actually spo-

ken, also belongs to the former system [of objectified and absolutized things]. Precisely from here one could embark upon a systematic study of the "expression" of psychic life (and this has in fact already been attempted [i.e., as a critique of experimental psychology in his 1925 lectures—*see* Husserl 1977, 14f]) and elaborate, as it were, the grammar of this expression. Since here this manifold expression appresents psychic existence in [terms of objectified] Corporeality, thus there is constituted with all that an objectivity which is precisely double and unitary: the man—without—"introjection." (§45)

Despite his lack of interest in the development of psychoanalysis (*see* Mishara 1990, 29), Husserl perhaps sees Freud's use of the term "introjection" to be naïvely given within a system of signs to stand as an explanation of the metaphysical presupposition of embodied ego-life in "the outside world"—but given quite differently from Husserl's (1980a §49a) own use of the term to indicate our internal "besoulment" of the Body in empathy at the pure Ego's transcendental turn. Freud (1959a), who was a fellow student of Brentano's in Vienna, presents the concept of *introjection* as follows:

> In so far as it is auto-erotic, the ego has no need of the outside world, but...it tends to find objects there and doubtless it cannot but for a time perceive inner instinctual stimuli as painful [or pleasurable]. Under the sway of the pleasure-principle there now takes place a further development. The objects presenting themselves, in so far as they are sources of pleasure, are absorbed by the ego into itself, 'introjected' (according to an expression coined by Ferenczi); while, on the other hand, the ego thrusts forth upon the external world whatever within itself gives rise to pain [i.e., by the mechanism of projection]. (p. 78)

Freud's empirical evidence for the concept of *introjection* was gathered in empathy for what could be said about objectified and embodied responses to affectively oriented stimuli. In Husserl's work, the objective presence of *anything* is indeed grasped during such intersubjective relationships that appresent corporeal- and spirit-life as an affective unity. Yet our objectifications of psychic life, pregiven in linguistic empathy as signs of embodiment, traditionally yield to naïve inferences of natural cause in explanations of psychological phenomena. The theoretical "nature" of psychic life is then expressed, for instance, as the "mechanism of projection." Such inferences, Husserl (1977, 167) points out, require no reductions to individual pre-theoretical, or unarticulated responses in order to posit "a truth which disregards all relativity of restriction to single persons.... Everything 'merely subjective' in its various senses is thus excluded [in empathy] as disturbing the consistency of the [objectifying] theme." The psychological theme of empathy is *consistency* following the pure Ego's transcendental turn into the world of common semblance.

When examining that world, Husserl (1977, 167-8) continues, "one

could focus, not on the objectively "natural" in empathy but on the subjec tively "personal" during our striving for consistency. This orientation recognizes the pre-existence of the personal during our objectifications of mental life in the transcendental register: "Just as pre-theoretically an interest, e.g., that of curiosity, can be directed toward merely physical things and their properties, so also and even much more frequently, [it is directed] toward the personal [sphere, e.g., *my* curiosity]....[A] consistently personal interest can actually remain forever within a purely personal nexus in experience and theory, [and therefore] this nexus is itself included in the all-inclusive experiential world...." As part of Husserl's (1982, §24) underlying "principle of all principles," one's personal experience in empathy becomes a "*legitimizing source of cognition*" for psychological inquiry following the pure Ego's transcendental turn.

The Psychological Epoché

Phenomenological psychology, Husserl (1970, §71) writes, represents "an attitude which is completely strange and artificial not only to the whole of natural life but also to the psychologist of the past." This observation perhaps reflects in part the notion that a complete account of human consciousness includes both its physical and its psychological properties. Husserl (1982, §53) recognizes that the human species enjoys the corporeal kind of "consciousness connected with animated organisms"—the purely physiological consciousness that could be reduced to a neurological or metabolic substrate. But we also have the kind of consciousness where our animated organism enters the real world with autonomy and agency. During the normal course of cognitive development, the organic basis of consciousness loses its former immanence.

For example, when we experience hunger we do not perceive a metabolic event in psychic life. Instead, we typically apperceive a strong desire for something; and with maturation, we could choose how and when to act upon that desire. The psychological *epoché* cuts out from reflections the organic basis of human consciousness, just as we bracket in pre-conceptual experience the countersense of our own thoughts as something physical. In this sense, the psychological *epoché* reveals human spirit-life as the transcendence of mere corporeality in the world that is commonly talked about—and in this sense as well, transcendental phenomenological psychology is psychology with a soul.

References to the psychological *epoché* signify a method of reflecting on the psychosubjectivity of another, just as we could inspect a range of motivation and comportment without reference to bodily functions—for indeed, it is absurd to suppose that physical bodies engage in such acts of volition. Husserl's (1982, §53) application of the psychological *epoché* and its reflective attitude is focused instead on the cognitive mental life that could be described as intentional action on elements of consciousness-formation. The psychosubjectivity of conscious awareness is given to genetic reflections in Husserl's (Fink 1995, 164) theory of method by the psychological ego. As an epistemological bifurcation of the pure Ego in Husserl's theoretical "knowledge-complex," the psychological ego is the performing ego of transcendental psychosubjectivity. Representations of the psychological ego in Husserl's system of ego-life point toward pure psychology made worldly by transcending acts in the subject's psychic life of world-consciousness. Under the psychological *epoché*, the psychological ego is the way that humans are being psychological with reason and fantasy in the world that is commonly talked about.

The phenomenological *epoché* itself implies in its practice that a radical matter or state has been in existence for *my life*, and could endure in its pre-existence into awareness; but here and now during reflections on its givenness, the matter is typically no longer such as it was. This is not to say that the original matter will necessarily never again come to presence during consciousness-formation. Neither does it mean that a pre-existing matter does not present itself for reflections on the intentional modifications of its irreal pregivenness. For example, when applying the intuitive eidetic method of *Psychognosia*, the idea of a particular tree could be seen to exist in pre-conceptual experience simultaneously and severally under the *epoché* as an evergreen conifer as well as an *arbor vitae*. Yet when we speak of the latter in conceptual space, we mean an instance of the former. Absent the reflective method of *Psychognosia*, one could not freely imagine under the *epoché* that expressions of an "evergreen conifer" or of an "*arbor vitae*" refer intuitively to the same core essence of an *eidos* in the subject's prior experience. Rather, a phenomenologist would perforce have recourse to one's own knowledge of trees.

Husserl's (1982, §79) praxis under the *epoché* is intended to arrest the powerful urge for deductive inferences of self-observation during interpretations of phenomenological data. With the elimination of one's tendencies for inferences of actual reality and objective truth from our own life-world experiences, Husserl's application of the *epoché* is indeed an absurdity of non-reason for phenomenologists. This means that Husserl does not presuppose a naïve state of affairs in his data, as one would do from the natural attitude—that is to say, as one would reason in a calculus of logic intending to realize the true nature of things in mundane thought and speech. Instead, by presenting to reflections the countersense to one's naïve acceptance of actual reality for an intentional object (i.e., the countersense of an eidetic form of that object's pre-existing irreal essence) the phenomenological *epoché* signifies in its use that something intentionally happened to an original idea—and that it happened during a finite succession in cognitive mental life from its genesis as adumbrated stuff in hyletic perception to its representations as an object of self-knowledge. The psychological *epoché* is thus meant to obviate our tendency to infer the sense and meaning of a course of psychic life from one's own habitual thinking about the so-called nature of psychological phenomena.

From a phenomenological psychologist's point of view, a genetic reconstruction of conscious awarenes is not complete without considerations of intentional composing- and grouping-acts in the spirit-life of pure psychology. Husserl (1980a, §30) calls this action the "psychological ego-idea" that is given under the *epoché* as "modes of comportment" of the pure Ego. Modes of comportment are experienced immediately as what we do or are *inclined* to do as the consequence of one's own judgments and valuations. Although such things could usually be recollected or reconstructed, spontaneous modes of

we do consistently for physical events and overt behavior. Instead, they typically remain in the living present as the irreal "soulish" urge, feeling, or desire to carry out the intentional function in mental life to act upon objects of affective significance. In this way, psychic life is thematically and teleologically *about* something during our universal and personal modes of comportment. The psychological *epoché* reveals to reflections the intentional gaze of the psychological ego that directs such normative performances.

The pure Ego's psychosubjectivity in the transcendental register is given to reflections as the cognitive action whereby pure consciousness of an *eidos* is transcended in order for an idea to gain presence in the kind of conscious awareness we experience as self-apperception—meaning, when we are knowingly conscious of something. Sometimes psychosubjectivity occurs as well when an *eidos* is *not* fully constituted in awareness. Once its original encounter is transcended and habituated, there typically comes a time when we no longer act upon our earliest experiences with an *eidos*. In this normal course of events, a previous experience is thus "neutralized" in the transcendental ego's intentional form of ideation, and is therefore excluded from further cognitive action—such as relearning to add each time we are engaged in counting. (*see* Husserl 1982, §113) In this case, the calculus for knowing how to add *there* is retained in eidetic memory and pregiven amid the interlaced spatiality of psychic life when we intend to count *here*. The contingency of active and passive psychosubjectivity is experienced as normal praxis.

Husserl (1973a, 27) noticed under the *epoché*, however, that preconceptual errors certainly do occur, along with their correlated errors of apperception and reality construction in conceptual space. For example, one might act upon what is believed to be a pregiven actual reality, when only the essence of something pre-exists as a retained ideation *there* that has not been previously constituted *here*. This kind of error sometimes occurs in the transcendental register when the psychological ego acts upon a retained irreal "anticipative picturing" of some previously fantasized matter—rather than on an adumbrated element that could find evidence of common semblance here and now. In this case, we might say that someone is engaged in "wishful thinking" or "confabulation." Errors in judgments also occur when a predicated matter is the mistaken reproductive memory of something actually real.

Welton (2000, 271f) raises some questions about the fallibility of memory to provide adequate evidence of an intentional object in conscious awareness Under the psychological *epoché*, memory *as such* is a pre-conceptual matter of ideation and reconstruction, rather than a naïvely conceived organic function of indeterminate origins. Still, when one remembers something, given to reflections as a remembering-act in pure psychology, what precisely *is* the object that is acted upon? What is a phenomenological psychologist to bracket here and now as an extra-psychic element in one's memory of something long past? During the internal time-consciousness of the living present, recollections of prior irrealities often take precedence in judgments over immediate perception in the psychic order of retention and anticipation. Whatever is then carried forward as pregiven is not an element of an adumbrated object *there*, but is instead the "impression" of an apperceptive event we intend to experience *here*. During this same phase, we typically correlate the feeling or affect of an "involuntary memory" of something.

Still, in all cases of experience under the psychological *epoché*, it does not matter for consciousness-formation if one's recollections are ever apperceived as more than a vague impression of something, when that impression itself is presented for action in the transcendental ego's intentional form of ideation. Whether a long-past ideation has ever been constituted by the psychological ego, or ever will be, its retention within an eidetic affair-complex serves to provide adequate evidence of its anticipation for fulfillment here and now. Indeed, whatever the pure Ego anticipates to be fulfilled as actually real in thought and speech typically shows itself as the "privileged" intentional object of cognitive action in the living present. Welton (2000, 278) seems to verify in his own studies that the psychological ego is affectively motivated in transcendental constitutive life to make active or passive judgments on something retained in memory; and it does not matter, he suggests, whether that *something* in its intentional form gains presence either through pensive rumination that seeks adequate evidence of its presence or as the involuntary memory of something: "It may require an act of recollection to recall what I had for breakfast this morning but no such act when I walk into a room that I have not inhabited for a month and automatically flip on the light switch."

Fallible or not, one's memory is an essential element in the sphere of immanence for the all-inclusive structure of transcendental consciousness. Husserl intends for his theoretical knowledge-complex to include each bifurcation of the pure Ego for this structure by applying various intuitive modes of the *epoché*. For example, the transcendental *epoché* discloses the givenness of the transcendental ego's natural attitude toward an intentional object of self-knowledge, while the psychological *epoché* discloses the givenness of the psychological ego's normative attitude toward intentional action. More precisely, a cognitive act by the psychological ego points toward the "how of givenness" for the transcendental ego's object of ideation. The method of *epoché* involves in its fullness all possible givenness of the pure Ego in the rich flux of pure consciousness. As a methodologically restricted portion of the method of *epoché*, the psychological *epoché* allows genetic reflections to focus on the pure Ego's psychosubjectivity as the dynamic action of intentional experience exclusive of any clarifications of extra-psychic things in Husserl's theory of elements—such as an object of self-knowledge, or what I had for breakfast.

According to Husserl's (1970, §72) studies in the transcendental register, the psychological *epoché* is applied in order to abstract a field of intentional action for reflections on the pure psychology of mental life during the dialectical synthesis of solipsistic and transcendental subjectivity. Pure psychology is then usually set aside as unthematic for descriptions of constituted phenomena in Husserl's (1973b, §11) object-oriented theory of elements. Reflections under the psychological *epoché*, however, could focus in genetic phenomenology on Husserl's theory of method for seeing our intuitive acts of pure psychology during one's transcendental world-constitution—meaning, for seeing the cognitive action of the subject's constitutive life in the "world for us all." In Husserl's (a psychic givity) object-oriented phenomenology, considered elements of an adumbrated object are not thematic for descriptions of intentional acts. Yet from the perspective of the psychological ego within its field of action, the pure psychology of mental life is revealed under its own *epoché* as a temporal sequence of intentional acts and passive acceptance directed toward objects of the mind. These are the same objects for which necessary elements are being contingently grouped and composed by our judgments and valuations in the world that is commonly talked about.

The pure Ego's psychosubjectivity toward an object of the mind is indeed the subject's experience of pure consciousness that is represented in the transcendental register by the psychological ego under the psychological *epoché*. Transcending-acts of the psychological ego follow the pure Ego's mental formation for acting upon the object-oriented elements pictured in the transcendental ego's form of ideation. Here, acts of grouping and composing by the psychological ego are intended to actualize (as affective unities) the constituted objectivities in transcendental consciousness that are subsequently clarified in Husserl's phenomenology of reason and theory of elements. Under the psychological *epoché*, fulfilled action in pure psychology is implied to exist by one's expressions of sensible meaning for normative modalities of realized presentational objects—since the normative modality of *anything* self-evidently requires acts of judging and valuing.

For example, when referring in thought and speech to an intentional object, the subject might present signifying expressions of a "recent event," "similar emotions," "many things," and so on. In all cases and contexts, an idealized "recent" signifies *objectively recent* under the psychological *epoché*—not recent only in this instance, and not recent only for *me myself*. Significations of something objective imply previous objectifying-acts by the psychological ego. On the other hand, the significance of "event" could be anything that we imaginatively choose to represent as constructed sense and meaning for the *eidos* of *event*. Therefore, one's intuitive grasp and self-knowledge of a "recent event" requires further grouping-acts of reason-as-evidence in the transcendental register in order for that object to gain presence as a fully composed unity of synthesized *a priori* and contingent experience.

Phenomenological descriptions of a deep grammatical structure, given in Husserl's (Bachelard 1968, 16f) so-called logic of language and in Husserl's (1994, 20-51) "logic of signs," are intended to clarify his theory of elements rather than his transcendental theory of method. Yet Husserl (1994, 21) noticed even in his non-phenomenological studies that there is a strong component of interaction within a system of signs between language-use and the psychological—namely, our intentional speech-acts of *referring* to something pre-existing. Under the psychological *epoché*, it does not matter (i.e., it is unthematic) to the psychological ego what objective language if any is used in order to refer to the pregiven core essence of an *eidos*. Witness our signifying expressions of metonymy, where the word "crown" refers to the monarchy, and where a sigh could reference any number of affective states. One's use of linguistic significations clearly refers to a pre-existing and retained *sense* of something within a calculus of logic for signifying expressions. Said calculus is itself a pregiven object-oriented element for the psychological ego in the background actionality of the phenomenological field.

Under the psychological *epoché*, linguistic objects are not by themselves thematic for the pure psychology of speech, any more than objects of formal logic are themselves thematic for the psychological experience of reasoning. Like objective knowledge, language *as such* has no mental life of its own. In Husserl's (1973a, §50.b; 1982, §§10f) work, the coming-into-being of a deep structure of grammar is the consequence of our intentional use of signs and preferred syntax for asserting or confirming the presence of something within a pregiven category of objectified sensible meaning. And so, cognitive acts of apprehension and habituation during language-use, along with one's normative speech-acts during judgments and valuations in linguistic categories and syntactical arrangements, are all part of our expressions of mental life that could be described as psychological in genetic phenomenology.

Yet by beginning regressive reflections as he does with the eidetic reduction, Husserl must set aside for reconstructive reflections the fulfilled transcendental level of constitutive life that was first encountered upon *entrée* into the circle of transcendence. The eidetic reduction brackets not only the horizon of metaphysics, but also the stratum of transcendental consciousness where apperceptions of language-use present themselves as sociocultural artifacts of empathetic relationships. One's lived experience of signifying expressions does not then show itself directly in regressions to the existential register of pure subjectivity. In genetic psychology, however, the lived experience of signifying expressions is seen under the psychological *epoché* when the pure Ego structures the being-sense of an *eidos* such that transcended self-knowledge of its core essence could be represented in linguistic empathy as already existing with reason and evidence. Linguistic representations in conceptual space refer to the psychological ego's intentional acts upon preexisting being-sense during the production of mundane thought and speech.

In this light, Mohanty (1989, 155) stresses that it is not a proper application of the phenomenological *epoché* to submit signifying expressions of self-knowledge solely to deconstructive practices of linguistic analysis. Despite its appeal for interpretations of presented sense and meaning, uncovering contradictions and conflicts within an objective textual/subtextual form does not necessarily reveal what we intend with our intersubjective communicative practices of linguistic empathy. Absent the method of *epoché* in the transcendental register, conclusions from regressive reflections on linguistic representations and their implied speech-acts would not then mirror the pure Ego's subjective sense of the a-historical and a-cultural *eidos*. Instead, such conclusions would tend to present that *eidos* as already modified in the mundane thought of a particular theorist. Without putting a naïve theoretical concept or conclusion in clarifying parentheses, one would speak in linguistic empathy, for example, of "Derrida's deconstruction" or "Rorty's deconstruction."

It might be a difficult notion to grasp from the natural attitude, but when making use of a mutually understood language in linguistic empathy, any formal discourse, even among phenomenologists, is mundane discourse in the world of common semblance. Under the psychological *epoché*, using a mutually understood signifying expression of mundane sense is a universal way of communicating in both everyday experience and in scientific exchange. For reasons of conforming to linguistic empathy, expressions of "Husserl's phenomenology" or "Sartre's phenomenological method" (versus "Husserl's philosophy" or "Sartre's methodology") are typically used in naïve theoretical discourse. A rigorous phenomenologist nevertheless sees under the *epoché* that elements of mundane speech are intentionally composed according to eidetic relationships of apodictic certainty and being-sense for an object of self-knowledge. Mohanty (1989, 155) proposes that this construction could itself be abstracted from the universal phenomenological method of consciousness-formation as a "path to be traversed" throughout the composed objects and grouped elements of transcendental consciousness. It seems evident that a similar practice of abstraction under the psychological *epoché* could be used to appropriate Husserl's theory of inquiry for the discipline of psychology.

A path of consciousness-formation could indeed be abstracted and traversed as a streaming of cognitive mental life throughout a field of intentional action. A fully constituted objectivity in this field, including its linguistic expression, is originally given from the onesided natural attitude in its straightforward (*geradeau*) mode of *seeing* in one's personal lifeworld. This same transcendental-subjective level of awareness first shows itself under the psychological *epoché* by its constituted appearance of embodied spatiotemporal dimensions of empirical concretions. One's fulfilled transcendental consciousness of an object in this field presents a unity of configuration for the necessary elements and act-relationships of one's self-knowledge of something here and now. Our judgments and valuations directed in the living present of volitional action strive to maintain this unity throughout the sedimented depths of both *a priori* and contingent experience—and by means of this action, a parallel "psychological" horizon of cognitions encompasses the region of pure consciousness where mental life is seen to be the the subject's self-generated rational comportment. By implication, one could see under the psychological *epoché* what is *not* rational comportment among the various horizons.

Husserl (1982, §124) illustrates a parallel horizon of actionality in pure psychology by the example of rationally seizing upon the essence of *white*. We say, "this is white," but we mean also that we have already *thought* this is white. The thing of which we speak could indeed be something that could be recognized by everyone as the color white; yet by predicating that something *is* white, the psychological ego "co-presents" a "mental stratum" for the *eidos* of *whiteness* along with the intentional object of which one thinks and speaks. Recall that the pure Ego's predication of a matter of factualness represents a pre-existing injunction in pure psychology—namely, an injunction to constitute something actually real and objectively true according to a transcendental logic of calculus and one's tradition of reality construction.

Under the psychological *epoché*, the apperceived stuff of *whiteness* in Husserl's example of predicative experience is bracketed as an element of the intentional object during consciousness-formation. Any presented active or passive judgment upon such an object of the mind—seen in its calculus of adumbration, retention, protention, and unification—represents the pure psychology of mental life in the transcendental register. With every predication of the pure Ego, and with every reduction in pure and transcendental consciousness, non-psychic elements are bracketed under the psychological *epoché* and thus stand out in relief for Husserl's object-oriented reflections. In order to "attain its total horizon," Husserl (1970, §71) explains, the psychological *epoché* is in practice "a 'phenomenology of the phenomenological reduction.'" When a reconstruction of the subject's concious awareness of something proceeds through a psychology of transcendental subjectivity, the phenomenological method of reduction *itself* is revealed as fundamental human experience.

Fink (1970, 85-7) wrote in the 1930s that advancements in phenomenological studies could begin with the idea that the phenomenon of conscious awareness is an intentional state of affairs—where in the transcendental register, the meaning of Husserl's maxim "to the things themselves" is in practice the maxim "to the affairs themselves." Under the psychological *epoché*, the affair-complex for an *eidos* is constructed during consciousness-formation by cognitive acts of pregiven pure psychology so as to meet the contingencies of transcendental subjectivity. In the flow of reasoning to achieve this goal, each seized-upon eidetic affair matters immanently and thematically for the pure Ego's psychosubjectivity. It perhaps bears repeating under the psychological *epoché* that the affair itself of the pure Ego's psychosubjectivity is lived in the transcendental register as one's experience of constituting objectivities for *me myself* as well as "for everyone" in the world that is commonly talked about.

The Practical Performance of Psychosubjectivity

Husserl (1982, §§76f) introduced our universal methods of constitution as rational norms of practice in *Ideas I*. Along with his (Husserl 1970, §§71ff) later *discors de la méthode* for the phenomenological method proper, Husserl consistently rejects the formalisms of logic and grammar as proper representations of an intentional composition of elements for an eidetic affair-complex. The subject's eidetic compositions in the transcendental register, whether presented as matters of fact or as intuitive evidence of truth and reality, pre-exist any naïve reflections on the inferred logic and grammar for those same affairs. Husserl (1982, §9) claims that when something is grasped in the pre-existence of any matter whatsoever, applications of the science of geometry best exhibit the practical performance of composing and constructing an eidetic affair-complex that encompasses both pure and transcendental consciousness. Under the psychological *epoché*, intentional composing- and constructing-acts represent the practical performance of the pure Ego's psychosubjectivity toward the anticipated realization of an affair itself.

The practical performance of psychosubjectivity could be described under the psychological *epoché* according to an order of action seen during exemplary cases of consciousness-formation. A singular core essence endures amid this immanent order of internal time-consciousness as the pure Ego's presumptive *thingness* (i.e., its categorial *being*) for apperceptions of its idealized dimensions in the transcendental register. This peculiar action of the human spirit is directed in anticipation of realizing the essence of an idea's *thinghood* itself, as the pure ego's life-world. Any such core of affairs sustains a spatiotemporal form of a core essence in its eidetic affair-complex of conscious awareness—but precisely as that complex is composed within a psychic order of constitution that begins in the solipsistic register.

During this psychic order, the psychological ego's normative gaze is not initially focused on any historically given objectified content in the subject's sociocultural surroundings. Instead, the psychological ego's judging- and valuing-acts are first directed toward pre-existing and anticipated elements of an adumbrated object here and now. This state of affairs is not so different from an applied geometry of the ideal shapes of things, where attention is focused on elements of length or degrees in order to realize the anticipated dimensions of a square or a circle. Our typical norm of practice for constructing an eidetic affair-complex in the transcendental register could indeed be seen as a pre-conceptual applied geometry in pure psychology. (*see* Husserl 1970, §9.b) Under the psychological *epoché* in genetic phenomenology, applied geometry is the universal *way* of constitutive life when the pure Ego is oriented in reason and fantasy toward the world that is commonly talked about.

Beginning in his early writings, Husserl (1994, 486-7) seems to suggest that just as the appearances of geometrical shapes are not solely apprehended in forms of ideal categories, the psychological ego's gaze is not solely upon pregiven ideal objectivities during consciousness-formation,. "But one could nevertheless take it for granted," Husserl writes, that ideal concepts are "carried over to approximations" when we intentionally *apply* ideal shapes in order to grasp the appearances of things as unities of configuration. (p. 497) Seen as a transcendental method of constitution during the normal course of events, grasping the appearance of things as categorial unities for consciousness of idealized approximations is a rational norm of practice.

Later on, Husserl (1970, §9.b) remarked that an applied geometry of reality construction—from *a priori* irreality to contingent actuality—is given to genetic reflections as a "general method of knowing the real." Seen under the *epoché* as a universal practice of reasoning, our method of "knowing the real" actualizes "the certainty, binding us all, of one and the same world...[and] runs uninterrupted through all changes of subjective interpretation [of reality]." For example, none of us could seize upon elements of something actually real when those elements exist outside the solipsistic potential that is *my own* for consciousness of idealized spatial dimensions. The idea of a shape bound by four angles, for instance, must have already been grasped in order to understand references to a town square. Yet at the same time, apprehension of something actually real is delimited by our internal time-consciousness of idealized temporal relations in the world of common semblance. In all cases, however, there is no self-knowledge of the real, and no evidence of reality in constituted objectivities, outside of our own "knowing the real" that is the consequence of the cognitive action taken upon an object's apperceived *thingness*. Under the psychological *epoché*, everything other than the pure Ego's bestowed sense and conferred meanings for spatiotemporal *thingness* is literally *non*-sense and meaning-*less* during ordinary worldly experience.

"Understanding the real" and "knowing the real" are experientially the same in one's personal lifeworld. The eidetic strata of understanding and knowing, Husserl (1970, §9.b) writes, are "concretely one thing" in the natural attitude. We typically come to understand the so-called nature of things by inductive inferences of pregiven sense and meaning when knowing the real in the natural world—that is to say, through our cognitions in empathy of an enduring actual reality for mutual objects and their relationships. Although we cannot rationally conceive of something like Nature or the Mind of God as the same as one's own experiences of reality construction, the immanence in pure consciousness of such holistic *thingness* is not necessarily a theological or a supernatural principle in the world that is commonly talked about. (*see* Husserl 1982, §51) Presuppositions about things outside the potential for ordinary experience point toward the pure Ego's metaphysical bounds for constructing the reality of a pregiven matter that contains correlations of *certainty* and *absoluteness*. As we strive to realize the quality of *absoluteness* in thought and speech, the psychological ego's cognitive action is directed toward grouping the at-hand elements that are necessary parts for a whole structure. And when our thoughts are simultaneously directed toward *certainty* for this structure, the pure Ego's "mind's eye" for seeing such delimitations might be called "imagination" in ordinary experience. It might also be called "faith."

As a matter of anticipaton in the normal course of events, what was constructed to be actually real but a moment ago has already elapsed during the swiftness of thought in the living present. Yet Husserl (Fink 1995, 177) stresses that the living present "is not a point in time" that represents the conclusion or the goal of the pure Ego's spatiotemporal configuration of conscious awareness. Rather, in an applied geometry of consciousness-formation, the living present "is something existent" (*Seiendes*) that each of us experiences "in relative normalcy" as one's center of volitions. The living present is indeed experienced as an immanent urge, drive, or motivation for self-knowledge of the real here and now. Under the psychological *epoché*, this immanence of spirit-life is also seen to direct a unique modality of universal comportment in the transcendental register—which is, namely, phenomenologizing the appearance of a rational affective unity for constituted objectivities and constructed realities in the world of common semblance.

Husserl (1970, 353ff) is explicit in his treatise on "the origin of geometry" that an applied geometry of "knowing the real" best exemplifies his sense of inquiry into a pre-existing topological field of pure and transcendental consciousness. One's practical performance for knowing the real is "available to us through tradition (we have learned it, and so have our teachers).... We know of its handed-down, earlier forms…but with every form the reference to an earlier one is repeated…. We understand its persisting manner of being…as a continuous synthesis in which all acquisitions [within that tradition] maintain their validity." (p. 355) As an example of the pure Ego's comprehension of pre-existence when knowing the real, Husserl (1973a, §29) points out that we learn in developmental experience that the reality of *one* thing cannot be known unless that thing exists within a plurality of similar real things. For instance, this table is not "really" a table unless there are such things existing that we have learned to look for and to call "tables." Similarly, the pl___ ___ ___ of ___ ___ ___ ___ ___ ___ ___ ___ ___ ___ ___ ___ ciousness of a unity-form because it is constituted in the pregiven world of other real existents. In this way, *my life* is experienced in empathy as an objectified rational affective unity in the world of human co-existence.

Recall that constituted objectivities are typically seen in empathy as embodied spatial unities that are analogous with idealized dimensions of here/there, up/down, and so on. A transcendental phenomenologist, Husserl (1973a, 68) explains, notices that an eidetic stratum of embodied unities *re*presents "a [constructed] *field* of spatial things…[that co-presents] along with it, the entire layer of investigations which have reference to the constitution…of things in all of its levels." Put another way, during reflections on the givenness of an intentional object here and now, normative expressions of one's self-knowledge of embodied dimensions co-present the immanence of the pure Ego's comprehension of an object's pre-existence. For example, if I refer to something "over there," I also refer to my pre-existing comprehension of certain data of *place* along the plane of immanence. Similarly, if my choice of words is tensed or conditional during significations of an intentional object, I show my pre-existing comprehension of internal time-consciousness for necessary elements during a psychic order of constitution.

In propadeutic "archaeological" reflections, a transcendental object is seen to be constructed of elements from various sedimented layers of sensible meaning. Each element of regional sedimentation is consequently seen within a self-referencing affair-complex for an original *eidos* that is siezed as *my own*—even as each layer presents a discrete adumbrated spatiotemporal species of eidetic singularity for that same *eidos*. A unity of configuration for this pre-conceptual state of affairs is anticipated in its composition and aimed at during consciousness-formation, while the complex *as a whole* is intended to be constituted as actually real in the transcendental register. This topology of conscious awareness provides a methodological "trajectory" for Husserl's (1982, §§10f) genetic inquiry into the transcendental constitution of an object of the mind. Here, genetic reflections begin under the *epoché* with a phenomenologist's own grasp of pregiven spatial strata of pre-existing irreal things. These strata are presented to reflections in categories of anticipated *being* and *doing* precisely as they reference the singular core essence of an original *eidos*. Under the psychological *epoché*, all such strata are in the living present of the pure Ego's psychosubjectivity here and now.

Under the psychological *epoché* and eidetic reduction, elements of *my life* pre-exist in the midst of all senses as regional adumbrations of the *thinghood* that is seize upon as *my own*. These elements are then correlated as the unity-form *me myself* by means of higher-level apperceptions of its *eidos* within a tradition of reality construction. In Husserl's (Fink 1995, 177) mature theory of method, a constructed reality for the *eidos* of *my life* represents the way we intend to *be* in "essential coincidence" with a sociocultural tradition for what it means to be ideally human. For instance, some foods are eaten by hand while others might properly require the use of utensils. A typical norm of reality construction is to synthesize a "formation of particular fields of sense, [along with] their combined action." This action is directed toward something meaningful within a system of appresentations of reality. (Husserl 1973a, 68) Following our chosen norms of practice, the reality of something is such as it is in empathy, not because of any exterior natural cause, but because *this* is the intended actual reality for a sensible meaning that arises from the mutual cognitive activity of individuals within a common space of reality construction.

Focused simultaneously in the living present on both the pure Ego's logic of calculus and on the transcendental ego's form of ideation for something in the world that is commonly talked about, the psychological ego directs its cognitive action toward fulfillment of conscious awareness in one's personal lifeworld. Here, a tradition of reality construction is analogous in empathy to pre-existing methods of action and passive acceptance in pure psychology. For example, in our sociocultural traditions for composing an eidetic affair-complex, a beginning is always experienced before an end, yet a predicate might be experienced either before or after the presence of a subject and its object. Matters of apodicticity and contingency within a psychic order of constitution are seen by the psychological ego with adequate givenness in a mental formation that repeats a tradition's elements of thought and speech.

A succession of psychological processes within a single mental process of action—such as grouping and composing elements within a process of *knowing*—streams throughout constitutive life in order to fulfill the form of ideation for an *eidos* here and now. Intentional acts in cognitive mental life flow from pre-conceptual to conceptual space in a nonrandom sequence of construction during each genetic phase of transcendental constitution. Accordingly, and because of this sequence, a mental formation of cognitive action traces out a psychic order of transcendence that aims to realize a fully composed eidetic affair-complex as a rational affective unity. A fulfilled mental process that follows a pre-existing order of constitution for something actually real is a teleological goal of the pure Ego in the transcendental register.

An eidetic construction of awareness therefore shows itself under the psychological *epoché* and transcendental reduction by its connections for parts and wholes in the final composed layer of a presentational object—that is to say, by its necessary *is*-relations in concatenations of unity. Husserl (1964c, 14; 1970, §41) explains that when used properly, the transcendental reduction discloses the species levels of eidetic identity along with the acts of psychosubjectivity that were seen and bracketed in reductions to the pure Ego's existential relationships. Even so, the full complexity of psychosubjectivity is only revealed by a psychological reduction of the field of action wherein the various pre-conceptual strata are transcended for the synthesis of a unity-form. In the midst of this complexity that aims toward unity, Husserl (1970, §71) noticed that the practical performance of psychosubjectivity shows itself under the psychological *epoché* "in various steps." For indeed, any application of the universal phenomenological method of consciousness-formation can "reveal its sense, its inner, necessary requirements, and its scope only in steps."

An Applied Geometry of "Knowing the Real"

Before any phenomenological reduction or genetic reconstruction could take place, an object of the mind is given to reflection by the transcendental ego's straightforward gaze on something that matters in the world of human co-

existence. This means that pure Ego has intentionally constructed and constituted its objects of self-knowledge to be unities of sensible meaning, and that
said unities now have the appearance of common semblance within a mutually embodied surrounding of idealized dimensions. Each of us engages in this
phenomenologizing comportment in order for an intentional object to be
constituted such that it could be recognized by everyone as actually real and
objectively true. The universal phenomenological method of this day-to-day
experience in pure psychology is analogous with practices of an applied geometry of reality construction. Under the psychological *epoché*, an applied geometry of "knowing the real" could be seen as a "phenomenology of the
phenomenological reduction" in Husserl's tradition of inquiry—that is to say,
as a reduction of the pure Ego's methods by which an intentional object is
brought to presence in eidetic structures of transcendental consciousness.

The spatiality of the final species layer of a fully constituted object of
subjective self-knowledge, just as it first presents itself for reflections on the
subject's conscious awareness of something here and now, could be depicted
as follows under the psychological *epoché*:

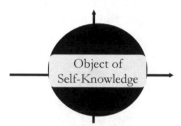

Figure 4.1. Under the Ψ *Epoché*

Figure 4.1. depicts what a phenomenological psychologist could first
see upon reflection of a predicated object of self-knowledge. In its presentation by the meaningful human subject, the object has already been made *my
own* by the transcendental ego of another. By adopting the intuitive eidetic
method of *Psychognosia* as praxis for observations and descriptions of objects
and acts, a constituted objectivity is seen from the phenomenological attitude
to exist in transcendental consciousness as the meant-as-meant representation
of an original *eidos*. Here, beginning temporally from its fundamental solipsistic relationships of *I* and *Other*, a grouped and composed transcendental object is presented to others as an embodied existent of idealized dimensions.

Under the psychological *epoché*, the subject lives the sense and meaning of an anticipated rational affective unity of these same spatiotemporal dimensions during the experience of transcendental constitution. To bring this
experience to fruition, the phenomenologized appearance of common semblance for an intentional object is constructed and constituted as actually real,
even as its irreal sphere of immanence "passes away" in representations of actual reality and absolute truth. The sedimented inner structure of a predicated
object of self-knowledge is therefore initially opaque for phenomenological
observations and descriptions. Consequently, there are no intentional acts of
the psychological ego to be seen.

206

In Husserl's (Fink 1995, 165) account of transcendental phenomenology, a fully constituted object of self-knowledge presents the subject's apodictic belief-certainty and being-sense of an *eidos*—but given from the natural attitude as a post-phenomenological representation of predicated truth and constructed reality. Each discrete element of an intentional object's multiform composition has already been transcended and *re*-presented within a unified whole structure. When an intentional object is given by the phenomenologizing ego with the appearance of a fully composed unity, it could be described as the idealized semblance and intentional approximation of a seamless "monad." A monad's appearance in conceptual space, Husserl (1977, 5) observes, reveals "no separation of parts consisting of self-sufficient elements." For indeed, the pure Ego has already found adequate evidence of an objectivity's phenomenologized unity of composition and actionality as *this* whole object of *nous* and not another. One could then say, "I have made up my mind."

As part of the pure Ego's volitional experiences of agency in the living present, a fulfilled object of self-knowledge cannot be other than intended in its unified and objectified form of appearance—even when that object in awareness gives evidence of an illusion or deliberate lie. Husserl (1981, 126f) explains in his "psychological studies for elementary logic" that monad-like objects point toward our "relational thinking" in pre-conceptual experience. Relational thinking could be seen as a mode of psychosubjectivity for seizing upon essences of parts and wholes during constitutive life; but given by its mundane appearance in the transcendental register, a monad does not show its relationships of parts and wholes within its synthesis of objects and acts. This condition presents the problem of meontics in Husserl's theory of method—in this case, where a symbolic order of signifying expressions does not itself represents any subjective experience of ontic origin.

Yet despite its seamless appearance in the natural attitude, a monad-like object is nevertheless a transcendental object. It is thus at hand for noticing the object's pre-existing spatial coordinates of embodiment and pregiven categories of signification. These data have been iterated within the *a priori* horizons and then *re*-presented as correlates of sense, meaning, and certainty during the subject's contingent experiences. Under the psychological *epoché*, the pure Ego's fully constituted opaque monad for an intentional object and its core essence presents to reflections a psychological theme of *aboutness* for the pure Ego's eidetic affair-complex. A constituted object of self-knowledge is intentionally *about* its subjective inner life of transcendental consciousness.

The psychological *epoché* is applied initially and in part to uncover our experiences of knowing the real during phases of pure and transcendental subjectivity. When the subject is aware of something that was constituted in structures of actual reality with reason and evidence, a phenomenologist could see under the *epoché* that a fully-composed monad-like object exists in transcendental consciousness as a "synthetical unity" of two different formations of irreality here and now: the irreality of its spatial coordinates and categories of signification, and the irreality of its bestowed sense and conferred meaning. Embodied coordinates and categories of signifying expressions are extra psychic things that are retained (developmentally) and given to reflection as pre-phenomenological elements in constitutive life; where typically, they are passively accepted for consciousness-formation in the world that is commonly talked about. Although both the sense and meaning of a presentational object are extra-psychic as well, they are elements of the pure Ego's contingent affair-complex that does not exist in the transcendental register without our intentional judging- and valuing-acts in cognitive mental life.

Universal things such as space and time pre-exist the living present of a constituted monad, and would ordinarily be present in mundane thought and speech whether expressed explicitly or implied as necessary for any given case. When universals are pregiven as a-historical matters in the life-world, they are apperceived in relational thinking as nonthetic objects that are believed to pre-exist in the world of common semblance. An idealized reality for an anticipated object of self-knowledge is similarly valued "for everyone" and pregiven in one's personal lifeworld as a presupposition about the so-called true nature of a monad-like objectified phenomenon. Correlated by the psychological ego in the horizon of metaphysics, this presupposition finds evidence of its pre-existence during intersubjective relationships of empathy. In this way, a monad-like transcendental object is constituted with the apodictic certainty of *absoluteness*, and then represented to one's self and to others as the analogous semblance of an ideal objectivity. Under the psychological *epoché*, the appearance of a monad-like object in referential expressions provides *entrée* into the circle of transcendence for inquiry into the pure Ego's constitutive activities and methods of reality construction here and now.

Husserl (1964c, 8) seems to imply that there are thematic differences within a psychic order of reality construction between (1) the *a priori* irrealities of universal things, (2) the contingent irrealities of eidetic structure, and (3) the actual reality of a constituted unity in conscious awareness. Under the psychological *epoché*, a phenomenologist could indeed see the subject's idealized elements of spatiotemporal relationships, naïve concepts, and linguistic categories that are valid for everyone during relationships of empathy—such as the embodied association between the diameter and circumference of a circle, that the front of something solid also has a back, or that an adjective is meant at least implicitly to modify a noun. Yet the *composition* of an eidetic affair-complex for a monad-like object is not a similarly idealized presupposition in empathy. Contingent grouping activities and idealizing-acts depend upon the cognitive action of the psychological ego in pre-conceptual performances that are peculiarly *my own*. Even so, this action is already completed and has passed away for a fully constituted object in conceptual space; and therefore, such performances cannot be seen directly when cognitive mental life is metaphysically oriented toward certainty in the natural attitude.

It follows that a phenomenologist cannot directly evaluate from signifying expressions of an embodied monad-like object any irreality of psychosubjectivity. Under the psychological *epoché*, it is an error to presume that cognitive mental life shows itself solely from our natural attitude toward the sheer appearance of things. It also follows that our psychological experiences are not lived as straightforward unities of probable configuration or as embodied distributions in the transcendental register. Husserl (1964c, 8-9) warns that "the whole meaning and reality" of human psychic life "rests exclusively" with the cognitive action of intentional experience during mental processes of consciousness-formation. In all events of ordinary thought and speech, our pre-conceptual performances of psychosubjectivity construct and constitute a world of co-existence that matters affectively to the pure Ego in the conceptual space of everyday life—wherein "I conceive" what is actually real and objectively true for *me myself* as well as "for everyone." Here, in the midst of this spatiotemporal flow toward unity, an intentional object gains presence in conscious awareness as the consequence of the psyche's operations of *nous* that encompass a multitude of contingent judging- and valuing-acts in accordance with one's sociocultural tradition of reality construction.

As a matter of autonomy throughout the complex (pure and transcendental, solipsistic and intersubjective, pre-conceptual and conceptual) flow of reasoning about parts and wholes, the pure Ego seems to tell Husserl (1964c, 11-15) that *I am* "the sole source…capable of judgment" of *me myself* against all *Other* in the world that is commonly talked about. *I am* the apodictic existent that predicates the phenomenon of *my life* in the world of co-existence and common semblance. In this light, a phenomenologist under the psychological *epoché* intends to "pursue the steady flux" of the pure Ego's psychosubjectivity "toward being and life" itself in the transcendental register. Evidence of the subject's cognitive mental life during this pursuit is "derived without alteration" from the source of our experiences in empathy—which is, namely, the transcendental ego's predication that *I am human*. A phenomenologist could then anticipate seeing the so-called two-sidedness of an objectivity in transcendental subjectivity: the side of its constitutive life, and the side of its constructed appearance in one's personal lifeworld. By means of this eidetic *seeing*, "a new kind and an endless sphere of being" presents itself with the identification of the transcendental ego as *my own* way of being in the world.

This is now the transcendental register of pure subjectivity that presents to reflections both the subject's universal and personal experiences of consciousness-formation—where the first-person "I" is immediately immersed in the pure Ego's constructed realities. One's first-person experience of conscious awareness is given partly by the temporality of a presentational object: the temporality of its necessary pre-existing irreality, and the temporality of its constructed actual realty. In the beginning, Husserl (1964c, 16-17) notices, a transcendental phenomenologist could anticipate seeing "the structures of phenomenological temporality." Elements of internal time-consciousness, including any contingent "before-and-after" psychic order of action in the living present, exist in the transcendental register when the subject is aware of something actually real in one's personal lifeworld. It is always the case, however, that pursuing the flow of transcendental constitution with the method of *epoché* means that a phenomenologist suspends one's own self-knowledge of *me myself* when evaluating the first-person experiences of another.

Beginning from the child's first apperception of elements that matter thematically for the *eidos* of *my life*—typically, in relation to its existential Other, the subject's consciousness-of-something comes "alive" during life span activities directed toward such elements and their modifications. A phenome nological psychologist is intent on observing this irreal structure of living temporality as it shows itself here and now in the pure Ego's performing ego-life. When applying Husserl's (Fink 1995, §6) transcendental theory of method, a genetic phenomenologist attempts to observe and describe the structure of constitutive life as an ongoing and continuous (i.e., correlated stratum-by-stratum) operation of *nous*, rather than to deconstruct an order of discrete elements within a fully constituted object of self-knowledge. The sphere of immanence for a unified affair-complex cannot yet be seen, though, since an intentional object is initially given to reflections in its straightforward linear embodied form of orthogonal spatial orientation for a monad-like transcendental object. Still, in its sphere of immanence, the affair-complex for that object is not itself a theoretical monad in pure subjectivity.

An eidetic affair-complex is not symmetrical with equal parts and uniform moments until its elements are transcended and given in conceptual space by its unified, objectified, and idealized seamless appearance of embodied opaque concretion. It follows that pre-conceptual activity in the solipsistic register has then already passed away as the immediate locus of intentional experience. Yet during this psychic order of retention and elapse in the pure Ego's internal time-consciousness, each asymmetrical concatenation of elements within an affair-complex is seen under the psychological *epoché* to be *asymptotic*—rather than "naturally" and "ideally" linear within the embodied orthogonal dimensions of one's fully conceived conscious awareness. In an applied geometry of "knowing the real," something constructed to be asymptotic varies as it approaches a pregiven value or condition. In order for an intentional object to be correlated with evidence of objectivity and common semblance in the horizon of metaphysics—that is to say, in order to be certain of such relational things—a concatenation of elements asymptotically tends non-linearly toward realizing a pregiven idealized concept or category of sensible meaning in one's sociocultural surroundings. During our everyday experiences in empathy, such idealizations are thus presumed on good grounds to be pre-existing and at hand for *everyone* here and now.

In a typical mental formation of cognitive action, each connection of judging- and valuing-act within and between asymmetrical concatenations is a temporal coordinate of asymptotic construction for a fully composed eidetic affair-complex—even while the affair-complex itself tends toward realizing a whole structure of ideal spatial orientation. Each interlaced cognitive connection "binds," as it were, this asymptotic flow toward unity, and could be seen under the psychological *epoché* to be a temporal coordinate for a streaming of multiple psychological processes of cognitive action within their intentional mental processes. Such action is directed in the living present iteratively back and forth between the two-sided parts/whole composition of a rational affective unity; that is to say, between the side of its constitution and the side of its anticipated constituted phenomenologized appearance.

The pure Ego's psychic order of intentional action adjusts the spatio-temporality of this back-and-forth streaming throughout the concatenated elements of an intentional object. Said order typically follows one's habitual logic of calculus for composing an affair-complex for the core essence of an original *eidos*. This non-linear trajectory of constitution and reality construction takes place within a contingent field of judgments and valuations—specifically, within an asymptotic array of cognitive action for the normative fulfillment of one's self-knowledge of something here and now. "It was Husserl's genius," Mohanty (1989, 12-13) observed, that he "brought to the forefront the method of *epoché*" as scientific praxis, where he himself is "aiming asymptotically" at clarifying our pre-reflective practices to be consciously aware of something. Rigorous application of the psychological *epoché* in effect mirrors our everyday mental life in the world that is commonly talked about.

The Eidetic Reduction in Pure Psychology

The psychological *epoché* is used to disclose the immanence of pure psychology during the constitution of any phenomenon whatsoever. By means of this *epoché* and its application, the extra-physical character of human consciousness is seen throughout each delimiting horizon of epistemology, ontology, and metaphysics. Cognitive acts on elements of consciousness-formation within these horizons follow a transcendental logic of calculus in order to compose a unity of configuration for an object of the mind. A typical form of calculus in this field of actionality is to iterate the core essence of an *eidos* throughout both *a priori* and contingent experiences for correlations of sense, meaning, appearance, and certainty. A simultaneous calculus of reasoning for correlated evidence of actual reality is used for "knowing the real" here and now—all within a temporal spread from pre-conceptual to conceptual space.

Husserl, (1982, §124) noticed in his object-oriented reflections that correlating-acts in pure psychology are "expressible by means of 'significations.'" Said significations *re*-present and refer to the being-sense of an intentional object within a region of ontology for something constructed to be actually real. When the pure Ego is spontaneously "busied" in the living present with pre-conceptual performances of consciousness-formation, the quidditive content of constitutive life gains presence in the phenomenological field as one's self-generated correlate of an intentional state of affairs for an enduring *eidos*. The ultimate expression of that same object-oriented content is a fully correlated unity of being-sense. "Anything that is," Husserl (1970, §48) writes, "whatever its meaning and to whatever region [of intelligibility] it belongs…is an index of a subjective system of correlations."

If a phenomenologist is to grasp the idea of human consciousness as a complex affair of eidetic composition and intentional constitution, then an intuitve approach for seeing its underlying plane of immanence for systematic correlations must be developed. Indeed, it might be argued that all forms of correlation in rigorous methodologies, including statistical correlations and expressions of correspondence in logical constructions, demand an underlying "factor" of pre-existing sense and meaning for any validating evidence of nonrandom association. Husserl's (1982, xx) reduction to the "'eidetic' universality" of intentional experience with an object of self-knowledge provides such an approach for phenomenological descriptions and genetic explanation of the correlated act-object structure of fulfilled conscious awareness.

When adopting the method of *Psychognosia* for eidetic *seeing*, each phenomenological reduction reveals a state of affairs for the correlation of an act and an object under the *epoché*—an act of reflection and the object of that reflection. (*see* Husserl 1964a, 96ff) As an act of reflection in Husserl's (1964c, 30) methodology, the eidetic reduction "neutralizes the appearance" that is given by the transcendental ego's ideation of something from the one-sided naïve natural attitude. As an object of reflection, predicated self-knowledge is seen under the eidetic reduction to be the subject's sense of an *eidos* now in the world of human co-existence and common semblance. Inasmuch as such expressions represent a transcendence of indeterminate *sense* from reduced levels of constitutive life, the eidetic reduction reveals to reflections the givenness of bestowed sense for a phenomenological *eidos* here and now.

By means of an applied geometry that mirrors *a priori* methods of pure psychology, Husserl's eidetic reduction of the subject's performances of consciousness-formation when knowing the real could be depicted as follows under the psychological *epoché* of the pure Ego's transcendence of *sense* in one's personal lifeworld:

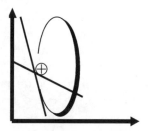

Figure 4.2. The Eidetic Reduction

As seen in Figure 4.2., Husserl's eidetic reduction could be thought of as a 90-degree rotation of a monad-like object of self-knowledge on its orthogonal axes of idealized spatial orientation for its embodied presentation to one's self and to others. For regressive practices of applied phenomenology, the eidetic reduction *de*-centers the straightforward point of view of the transcendental ego's natural attitude toward the objectified sense of an intentional object. Evaluations and descriptions of the immanent structure of necessary elements and potential mental formations could now begin. From the phenomenological attitude, an idealized and absolutized intentional object is no longer opaque for reflections on the pre-conceptual bestowed sense and conferred meaning of an *eidos*—even when that active idea is presented in agreement with one's sociocultural surroundings. Also, an embodied, monad-like, fully constituted objectivity in one's personal lifeworld no longer masks from phenomenological observations any correlating-acts in psychic life that have already modified its composition during operations of *nous*.

Under the psychological *epoché* and eidetic reduction, an object of self-knowledge is seen to be elliptical within asymptotic lines of noematic structure—rather than ideally symmetrical within its only anticipated orthogonal axes of spatial orientation for an embodied monad-like object. Here, the

212

intentional object is not yet fully correlated in the (now bracketed) horizon of metaphysics. Here too, lines of asymptotic structure show themselves as concatenations of bestowed sense and conferred meaning, along with any other element necessary for the object's constitution in the transcendental register. Asymptotic concatenations of elements are composed by the psychological ego by means of various transcending-acts of valuing and judging at points of connection within a mental formation for an eidetic affair-complex. One such nexus is represented in Figure 4.2. by the sign of a simple additive, $\oplus$. This means, for example, that what is contingently two and three things together in a calculus of logic signifies *also* a unity of five things that is believed to be valid for everyone in its calculus for the structure as a whole.

When the psychological ego groups essential elements according to the pure Ego's logic of calculus for composing a unity of configuration, an intentional object tends toward idealized spatiotemporal dimensions in anticipation of its realization. The construction of an asymmetrical asymptotic eidetic affair-complex, along with its contingent mental formation of temporal connections, is intended in part to align, as it were, the sense of our pre-existing beliefs *here* to pregiven dimensions of actual reality and absolute truth *there*. The pure Ego does this in order to predicate similar meanings to *me myself* and to others during polythetic relationships of empathy.

Applications of the eidetic reduction represent in pure psychology what Husserl (1982, §109) calls our universal "neutrality modification" in the phenomenological method proper. Husserl explains that this method of preconceptual reasoning during consciousness formation has no "fixed terminology," either in scientific discourse or in ordinary language. Yet when the neutrality modification is followed as praxis in applied phenomenology, the eidetic reduction does not cancel out any constituted object or constructed reality that shows itself in mundane thought and speech. In effect, the eidetic reduction under the *epoché* fixes for reflections a static spatiality of pre-existing correlations for the pure Ego's eidetic affair-complex here and now.

The neutrality modification, Husserl (1982, §109) continues, is the "counterpart of all producing" in constitutive life. According to the pure Ego's everyday internal time-consciousness, something previously constituted is typically retained in memory and passively accepted, but we do not usually *re*-constitute self-knowledge of an enduring *eidos* each time that its active idea is correlated during consciousness-formation—although we might seem to "change our minds" as the pure Ego's regard is adverted in the living present.to another theme or adumbrated category of self-knowledge for that same *eidos*. Similarly, a phenomenologist abstains from producing something to be actually real that has its genesis in either the constitutive life of another or in the phenomenologist's own transcendental subjectivity. With applications of the eidetic reduction, the production of a phenomenologist's self-knowledge of a presentational object is thus neutralized for reflections and evaluations of *sense* given by the meaningful human subject here and now.

Each of us could experience the neutrality modification in pure psychology as a norm of cognitive mental life for constituting one's awareness of *thinking*. For example, we might wonder in pre-scientific reflections, "what do

I mean here," or "what do I want to say now?" Regarding a particular *eidos* in pre-conceptual experience, we seem to ask in the most general sense, "what do I want to *do* with it?" In Husserl's methodology, a phenomenologist imaginatively reflects on the sense of the pure Ego's neutrality modification here and now as itself an affair to be observed and evaluated. Used as the means of eidetic reduction under the *epoché*, a phenomenologist's own neutrality modification of reflective thinking is intended to disclose a necessary irreality of human reasoning—namely, a concatenation of correlated elements of sense and meaning within a composed eidetic affair-complex. As an example of the irreality that shows itself under the eidetic reduction of an object of self-knowledge, recall the previous presentation of an eidetic concatenation within the horizon of epistemology. Thetic and nonthetic categories of *sense* are intentionally grouped around the core pure sense of *I* and *Other*—all with respect to the meaningfulness of the intentional object, *my shoe*.

$$((I=[[\text{myself}]\oplus[\{\text{here}\}\oplus\{\text{is=have/own mine}\}]])$$
$$\oplus(Other=[[\text{shoe}]\oplus[\{\text{there}\}\oplus\{\text{is=foot-cover}\}]])).$$

Within its affair-complex of parts and wholes, a concatenation of ontic singularity (such as "my shoe") is seen under the eidetic reduction to be an asymptotic line of correlations for one's consciousness-of-something here and now. During the internal time-consciousness of this state of affairs, each grouping-act of the psychological ego represents the pure Ego's turn in regard from one element or theme to another in its thetic and non-thetic here/there givenness within the horizon of space—even as the concatenation-as-a-whole approaches idealized embodied dimensions for the meant-as-meant structure of an intentional object. Throughout its genetic construction, a composition of elements in eidetic concatenations represents what is intended and anticipated in the living present to come to presence as something concrete in transcendental consciousness. Here, fulfilled actual reality for an objectivity is such as it is because of the psychological ego's transcending-acts of grouping and composing adumbrated elements of an enduring *eidos*. With typical maturation and cognitive development, such activities are in agreement with a pre-given tradition of reality construction in one's sociocultural surroundings.

When the neutrality modification in pure psychology is applied as the practice of eidetic reduction, a phenomenologist reflects under the psychological *epoché* on the being-sense of what already matters thematically for the appearance of a constituted objectivity in pre-scientific space. In this methodical way of proceeding, the psychological ego's mental formation of intentional action on an eidetic singularity is disclosed. For example, in our naïve reflections we could think about something that is sensible and meaningful to *me myself*, and most likely to everyone else as well. At the same time we could usually think about *how* something has come to be sensible and meaningful, or at least how we notice that something matters to one's self and to others. For this reason—literally, this reason-as-evidence for the presence of distinctive pre-existing strata of sense and meaning—every phenomenological reduction under the *epoché* requires a phenomenologist's reflective thinking on the pure Ego's activities of consciousness-formation.

On the other hand, the subject's *own* expressions of reflective thinking reveal under the eidetic reduction the pure Ego's anticipation for a fully composed unity "as a '*neutralized*' believing, deeming likely, or the like." (Husserl 1982, §109) All through the sedimented layers of sense and meaning for things that matter thematically in constitutive life, the irreality of deeming an *eidos* likely as a unity exists in anticipation of its actualization within an eidetic affair-complex. In reductions to the pure Ego's existential relationships and then outward genetically—throughout all the adumbrations of elements and throughout the delimiting horizons of intelligibility (epistemology), meaningfulness (ontology), and presuppositions of certainty (metaphysics)—all else but what could be abstracted as the pure Ego's neutralized believing and its intentional correlates is bracketed under the eidetic reduction.

In its neutrality, Husserl (1964c, 12-13) stresses, the eidetic reduction changes nothing about a fully constituted object of self-knowledge and its necessary connections of intentional mental acts. Rather, the eidetic reduction reduces what pre-exists an intentional object's appearance in one's personal lifeworld to its "essence in consciousness, in which I live as my own self...the so-called intentionality [of my life just as *I am*]." Under the psychological *epoché* and eidetic reduction, there is a singular identity for an intentional object in one's personal lifeworld because the same intentionality pre-exists for that object in all correlations of irreality and actuality during every phase of constitutive experience. Indeed, there is a singular identity to the intentionality that is *my own* during the continuity of constitutive life. "This identity," Husserl (p. 17) observes, "is an immanent and descriptive trait of...intentional experience and of its phases [throughout both pure and transcendental subjectivity]."

One aim of the eidetic reduction under the psychological *epoché* is to see what *can* appear as expressions of self-knowledge by means of one's cognitive action. Here, the object-content of reflections includes presentations and (at least partial) *re*-presentations of the invariant core essence of a phenomenological *eidos*. Each core essence thus serves as an underlying basis of the pure Ego's correlates of reason during an intentional object's manifestations and modifications in the transcendental register. Here, a core essence is seen under the eidetic reduction to be a constant singularity during its givenness to contingent correlations of sense, meaning, and certainty. A reduction of conscious awareness to the eidetic organization and transcendental logical extensions of the essence of an original idea is meant by Husserl (1982, §16) to be a critique of universal human reason. Husserl intends for the eidetic reduction to represent the practice of a phenomenological "theory of knowledge."

This is truly a revolutionary approach toward explanations of our experiences of conscious awareness, and Husserl intends to be similarly revolutionary in his phenomenological methodology. When Husserl uses the term "universal human reason," for example, he does not mean to imply any modalization of behavior or comportment. Instead, the term refers to our day-to-day way of thinking spontaneously. This way during consciousness-formation is intentionally directed toward achieving some goal of sensible meaning in normative thought and speech—where we could know intuitively that we are indeed thinking about something that matters to one's self and to others.

Likewise, Husserl does not mean that transcendental subjectivity is in any sense an average mode of consciousness in which the majority of humans is engaged at any one moment. Rather, with the method of *epoché* and eidetic reduction, our natural attitude represents *the* distinctive modal conduct of ordinary and spontaneous thought. Factual matters in science and philosophy that presuppose that there *is* a pre-existing truth to be found on the average are constructed and constituted within the modal conduct of our natural attitude during relationships of empathy. Such matters pertaining to psychic life are thus formed without grasping how an irreal average of *anything* could be present as a consequence of our strivings to achieve normality and typicality in the world of idealized approximations. Under the psychological *epoché* and eidetic reduction, the average comportment of humans is not a random variable of psychic life; but instead, it is an intentionally constructed and complex way of *being* and *doing* in one's naïve natural world.

In object-oriented reflections under the transcendental *epoché*, Husserl sets aside any implied calculus for living knowingly as "natural," such as our naïve expressions of the nature of things. He thereby presents to reflections what remains of human comportment absent the transcendental ego's calculus for a naturalistic abstraction. What remains, Husserl (1982, §§33-55) notices, is the irreal "anonymous" *residuum* of pure consciousness that is already and always at hand for everyone—meaning, what is experienced by each of us as sentient beings. Under a parallel psychological *epoché*, universal essences of sentient comportment pre-exist as potentials for action in pure psychology. Even when oriented from the natural attitude, where normative comportment is not in thematic focus, said potentials are nevertheless at hand for intentional acts on essential elements of eidetic concatenations. Such matters would of course include the contingent concatenations that exist "on the average" in conceptual space according to presupposed manifestations of truth and consistency in the world that is commonly talked about.

Under the transcendental *epoché*, pure consciousness is seen to be the a-historical non-physiological consciousness experienced as as the immediate awareness of sentient *being*. Under the eidetic reduction, pure consciousness is also represented as pre-existing achievements of human reasoning found in historical and cultural records of inter-generational thought and speech. Yet under psychological *epoché* and eidetic reduction, only constructed actualities in our modal conduct of living naturally vary historically and culturally amid the diachronic/synchronic synthesis of transcendental consciousness. Husserl (1970, 349-51) explains that one's knowing-acts of reasoning unify by synthesis our subjectively constructed actualities with the pregiven irrealities of what is historical and cultural in one's personal lifeworld—such as the irrealities signified by expressions of objective truth. Here, something naïvely grasped as historically or culturally ideal is made actually real according to a tradition of reality construction in one's sociocultural surroundings. In its totality, then, pure human consciousness under the eidetic reduction is also transcendental consciousness, since the necessary irrealities of constitutive life are transcended during everyday rational thinking and sentient comportment.

Under the psychological *epoché* and eidetic reduction, the pure Ego's synthesis of transcendental consciousness typically includes elements of anticipated objectified and embodied things in the natural world. During a steady flow of reasoning toward unity in the transcendental register, synthesizing-acts of objectification and embodiment point toward necessary cognitive correlations for the identity of intentionality bestowed upon an object of the mind here and now. Throughout the living-present contingencies of transcendental constitution—all through the personal alterity of differences and changes in expressions of pure consciousness—an identity of intentionality endures thematically in pre-conceptual representations of the meant-as-meant essence of being-sense for an intentional object. However, the subject's synthesizing-acts of transcendence for constructing being-sense are revealed only by Husserl's (1973b, §8) transcendental reduction of the pure Ego's consciousness-formation and its eidetic structure. Under the psychological *epoché*, the transcendental reduction also discloses a pre-conceptual field of correlated personal, intersubjective, and inter-generational cognitive action.

Regressive phenomenology in Husserl's tradition is a descriptive inquiry into the identity of intentionality for an object of self-knowledge. Here, the *epoché* is applied in order to follow the reversed gaze of the pure Ego into the pre-existing depths of constitutive life. All else is imaginatively set aside in reflections under the eidetic reduction but what the pure Ego deems likely for constituting the presence and actual reality of an intentional object. Having reached the existential relationships of *I* and *Other* for the core essence of a presentational object, genetic reflections then turn outward, retracing constitutive experience back toward one's personal lifeworld in the conceptual space of actual reality and objective truth. Consciousness-formation under the psychological *epoché* begins in pure psychology with our fundamental relationships in solipsistic subjectivity toward a phenomenological *eidos*, and typically continues throughout a life-span system of apperceptions in the world of human co-existence and common semblance. Said system is experienced much like one's reproductive memory of time and place for persons, events, and relationships. Eventually, an identity of intentionality is retraced to the eidetic stratum where an objectivity is first presented to reflections as an opaque monad-like post-phenomenological phenomenon of embodied dimensions.

Husserl's (1982, §128) regressive practices lead reflections back to elements that are intended-to in pure consciousness, but they do not directly evaluate the acts of modification and extension that are necessary to be conscious of an actually real object. Neither does the human spirit of autonomy and agency necessarily show itself in regressive phenomenological psychology as the motivating force (*dynamis*) for constructing a rational affective unity during intersubjective relationships. In Husserl's (Fink 1995, §§6f) reconstructive genetic phenomenology, on the other hand, the pure Ego is already functioning as the transcendental ego in the world of common semblance. And by grouping and composing elements of an anticipated state of affairs for a unity of awareness, the psychological ego is already fulfilling its transcending acts during life-span experiences with others. A reconstructive phenomenology in

Husserl's tradition is therefore not precisely a descriptive evaluation of human consciousness, yet neither is it merely an explanation of the sense and meaning of mundane thought and speech. Instead, a phenomenological reconstruction is a clarification of the subject's transcended objects and transcending acts of constitutive life—but only as that living temporality pre-exists as pregiven to consciousness-formation. Such pregivenness is seen within a regressive examination beginning with one's fundamental human relationships.

From deep within the horizon of ontology, at the existential center of the eidetic reduction in pure consciousness, the pure Ego "tells" the phenomenological onlooker that from now on *I am* the transcendental ego of the meaningful subject's contingent experiences of conscious awareness. In the pure psychological field of intentional action, *I am* the psychological subjectivity of human spirit-life in the transcendental register. Following this turn of regard in the phenomenological method proper, genetic reflections are focused under the psychological *epoché* on the cognitive synthesis of elements and on our transcending methods of constitution. All this is seen under a transcendental reduction to the necessary irrealities of the subject's self-knowledge of something here and now—even while that *something* is constructed in empathy to be actually real in the world that is commonly talked about.

The Transcendental Reduction in the Field of Actionality

A reconstruction of one's transcendental consciousness of something starts in Husserl's (Fink 1995, §37) theory of inquiry from the pure Ego's fundamental relationships of *I* and *Other* in pure subjectivity. Reconstructions then trace out the genetic course of constitution for what is (due to regressive reflections) a fixed eidetic affair-complex here and now. In this way, a step-wise clarification of the subject's conscious awareness is articulated as the documentation of a "transcendental dialectic" of "phenomenologizing itself" throughout the tensions, conflicts, and resolutions between solipsistic and transcendental subjectivity. Under the psychological *epoché*, the subject's contingent transcending- and phenomenologizing-acts are carried out by the psychological ego in cognitive mental life during one's intersubjective relationships of empathy. Said action typically continues on toward the constitution of an intentional object in one's personal lifeworld.

Genetic reflections on this dialectic in the living present, along with its normative extensions of *sense* during the pure Ego's experiences of world-constitution, make use of Husserl's mature transcendental reduction. Here, the psychological *epoché* and transcendental reduction disclose together the background field of action for constitution of an object of common semblance in the world of human co-existence. By means of this reduction, the subject's cognitive action could be seen in its dynamic mode of personal-lifeworld construction; and because of this action, an object of the mind is fashioned to have the appearance of objective truth and actual reality—both to one's self and "to everyone" in the world that is commonly talked about.

By means of an applied geometry of *a priori* pure psychology, a transcendental reduction of conscious awareness could be depicted as follows under the psychological *epoché* when the subject presents referential expressions of knowing the real:

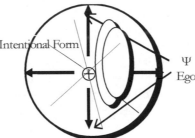

Figure 4.3. The Transcendental Reduction

With the transcendental reduction in applied phenomenology, psychological reflections could be rotated in pure consciousness a full 180 degrees "opposite," as it were, to the anticipated semblance of actual reality for an object in awareness. Each of us usually constitutes the presence of a unified transcendental consciousness-of-something, since that *something* is intentionally composed and constructed within a state of affairs that aims to maintain the *a priori* unity of pure consciousness in the transcendental register. A unity of sensible meaning and actual reality for *this* table, for example, is constituted within the noetic structures of all potential tables that could be encountered in one's personal lifeworld; and similarly, the unity of *my life* is constituted as a phenomenon within the structures of all potential human co-existence in the world for us all. In Figure 4.3., the transcendental reduction under the psychological *epoché* represents an eidetic depiction of the pure Ego's intentional construction of any state of affairs whatsoever for an object of the mind that gains presence in conscious awareness.

Our everyday experience of constitutive life is exemplified in Figure 4.3. as the psychological ego's action on elements for composing an eidetic affair-complex of worldly self-knowledge. Here, the psychological ego is grouping elements of sense and meaning for an intentional object according to the transcendental ego's form of ideation for the singular core essence of an original *eidos*. Intentional grouping- and composing-acts within the unity of pure and transcendental consciousness are represented together under the psychological *epoché* and transcendental reduction as the background actionality of pure psychology. The transcendental constitution of the presence and appearance of a post-phenomenological phenomenon universally proceeds by means of the pure Ego's psychic order and internal time-consciousness of this field of intentional action and non-action.

Although an affair-complex is indeed spatially static under the transcendental reduction for clarifications of objects in Husserl's theory of elements, the psychological ego is nevertheless engaged in the dynamic temporal action of cognitive mental life on those same objects and their elements according to Husserl's transcendental theory of method. In order to fulfill the intentional function of mental life to act upon objects, the psychological ego's gaze in simple and higher-level apperceptions is directed in the living present toward an anticipated "manifold-unitary continua and synthesis" of the intended composition for a fully constituted transcendental object. (Husserl, 1982, §86) A composition of unity is imagined and anticipated in the pure Ego's eidetic affair-complex, and then presented for actualization of its idealized semblance by the transcendental ego's intentional form of ideation for something in one's personal lifeworld. Under the transcendental reduction, there is a pure psychological background of actionality in every phase or stage of transcendental subjectivity—and in every system of ego-life, as well.

After the pure Ego's transcendental turn in the phenomenological method proper, the noetic structure of an affair-complex is modified from spatiotemporal conditions of solipsistic subjectivity in order to construct the irreal "one time" of intersubjective relationships. In anticipation of this event, the psychological ego gathers both *a priori* and contingent evidence for the dialectical synthesis of a transcendental unity of apperception for this structure. As a memorial function during a steady flow of intentional action throughout the "manifold-unitary continua and synthesis" for a fully constituted object of the mind, the multiple gaze of the psychological ego "scans" for temporal points of connections within and between eidetic concatenations. Retained in eidetic memory and cast forward by protension, such connections represent one's intuitive judgments and valuations regarding necessary elements of an adumbrated object—necessary, that is, so that the entire structure of connections tends asymptotically toward the one mental nexus that fulfills the pure Ego's intention for a unity of configuration. A fulfilled structure of conscious awareness presents to reflections a correlate of the transcendental ego's intentional form of ideation for transcended objects and the psychological ego's mental formation of transcending acts.

The transcendental ego's form of ideation is given to reflections as a categorial identity for retained elements of an adumbrated object here and now. This form extends throughout consciousness-formation as a singularity in the living present for judgments and valuations regarding an original *eidos* in the transcendental register. Under the psychological *epoché,* said form thus represents a theme of *aboutness* for the composition of elements beginning with the pure Ego's existential relationships with the core essence of an *eidos.* In Husserl's (1982, §86) theory of elements, a form of ideation contains the elements for "all of the basic kinds of possible consciousness and variations" of an intentional object in order for one to experience the being-sense of something whole. Yet prior to an object's constituted presence, a form of ideation is "presumptive" in pure consciousness—meaning, transcendental consciousness of *this* singularity is only deemed likely among the contingencies of reality construction. The psychological ego's mental formation of cognitive action, however, is meant to actualize what is deemed likely and presumptive within its form of ideation. Pictured in Figure 4.3., the psychological ego is even now following its mental formation for constructing the spatiotemporal dimensions for an eidetic singularity by acts of embodiment.

Husserl (1982, §86) suggests that the gaze of the psychological ego is directed toward grasping pre-existing and pregiven "particularities" when grouping essential elements within a form of ideation. Each element of parts, wholes, and their relationships is grasped "from the 'teleological' point of view of their function, making possible a 'synthetical unity' [of awareness]." Seen in Figure 4.3. as the laminated composition of species layers of adumbrated "particularities," a presumptive object of self-knowledge is being modified in its composition to meet the contingencies of constitutive life in the transcendental register. In this depiction, pre-conceptual elements of an intentional object are being grouped to coincide in essential features with the transcendental ego's form of ideation for something actually real in the world of common semblance. Under the psychological *epoché* and transcendental reduction, necessary modifications of an intentional object occur as a consequence of the psychological ego's transcending acts of world-constitution in co-existence with other ego-subjects. Said modifications conclude at temporal coordinates of connections ("⊕") within asymptotic lines of structure for a unified eidetic affair-complex of conscious awareness here and now.

The structure of an affair-complex contains unique correlates from both the *a priori* and contingent horizons of constitutive life. Each correlate is an element of being-sense for the core essence of an *eidos*, and each elapses or is retained by means of multiple simultaneous psychological processes of judgments and valuations. In the living present of cognitive action, these processes follows a mental formation for a unity of activity in order to realize the pure Ego's internal time-consciousness of an anticipated whole structure. Transcending acts of structuration and actualization occur within the temporal sequence and psychic order of a mental formation—howsoever an adumbrated *eidos* is modified here and now in order to "fit", for instance, any pregiven spatial dimensions of embodiment or presuppositions of apodictic certainty from developmental experience. A succession of psychological processes represents a genetic sequence of action for synthesizing an essential identity for an intentional object within a single mental process of thematic content. Here, an object tends toward an idealized appearance of common semblance when the psychological ego's transcending-acts of apperception follow one's tradition of reality construction during relationships of empathy.

There is but a single mental process in pure psychology that streams throughout each thematic phase of transcendental subjectivity for the core essence of an *eidos*—*because* that core essence presents an ontic singularity of intelligibility and meaningfulness during consciousness-formation. Under the transcendental reduction, any expression of being-sense in conceptual space points toward a pre-existing mental process of thematic pre-conceptual action. A mental process thus serves intuitively to ground contingent psychological processes for that same expression. For example, when the core essence of an *eidos* is deemed likely for actualization, a mental process of *judging* is represented by an experience of *judgment* about that *eidos* in one's personal life-world. Reciprocally (i.e., according to a transcendental logic of calculus), for instance, each act in a psychological process of noticing the core essence of an adumbrated object is a choosing-act for or against that element being retained within a mental process of *choice*. Similarly in a mental process of *valuation*, each act in a genetic psychological process for valuing an *eidos* in the world of human co-existence represents a valuation made of that idea during a relationship of empathy—and so on within the full complexity of "interlaced" cognitive mental life in the phenomenological field of active and passive actionality.

The subject's expressions of intelligibility direct reflections toward a field of intentional action and non-action in pure psychology. Under the psychological *epoché* and transcendental reduction of this field, an object is seen (in Figure 4.3. for example) to be asymmetrical in its intentional fitting to pregiven orthogonal coordinates of actual reality pictured in the transcendental ego's form of ideation. Here, a lack of isomorphism (= one-to-one correspondence, or symmetry of form) in adumbrated elements is typically present, since we cannot know everything about something in immediate awareness—even if sometimes it might seem that we do. This lack of complete information requires grouping more reason-as-evidence for the synthesized unity of an object when asymptotic lines of composition tend toward idealized categories of sensible meaning. Without further grouping-acts by the psychological ego, an affair-complex for a transcendental object is only deemed likely in pure subjectivity; or else, it fails to gain presence as a fully constituted objectivity precisely as intended and anticipated by the pure Ego. In this latter case, we might have the sense or feeling of something existing in thought, but we say that we can't quite "put our finger on it." *It* is "just on the tip of my tongue." The necessity for constructing further reason-as-evidence is usually intended to by the pure Ego's reorientation from solipsistic subjectivity to transcendental subjectivity during intersubjective relationships of empathy.

Recall that when a constituted objectivity is believed in empathy to be valid for everyone as for one's self, an intersubjective affair-complex includes the knowing ego as a self-referencing element that is retained with the sense of *my* idea or as *my own* thoughts about something objective. We therefore have no need to know everything in the Galilean worldview of approximations in order for an object to be grasped as one's self-knowledge of something here and now. Under the psychological *epoché* and transcendental reduction, the knowing ego functions in reason and fantasy—whether rational or not—as the "constituting ego" for conscious awareness and self-knowledge of actually real things during world-constitution. When applying Husserl's (Fink 1995, §11) transcendental reduction in object-oriented reflections, the knowing-constituting ego takes its asymmetrical place amid each asymptotic concatenation as the "absolute temporal position" for thematically grouping retained elements of an intentional object. A phenomenological *eidos* is thus *my idea* within its worldly horizon. In the previous concatenation of elements for the *eidos* of *my shoe*, the knowing ego is represented by the term, "myself."

By its "strict localization" for the psychological ego's grouping activities, the knowing-constituting ego "indexes" the coming-into-being of a constructed actual reality that is believed to be valid for everyone. That is to say, the experience that is *my own* serves to direct attentive focus during activities of consciousness-formation in the transcendental register. The strict localization of the knowing-constituting ego in an eidetic affair-complex is experienced as the objectified and absolutized sense of one's own thoughts. We ordinarily experience our thoughts as something already objective during intersubjective relationships; and so, we do not spontaneously reflect on their subjective origins. Husserl (Fink 1995, 164) noticed, however, that in all horizons of transcendental constitutive life, a pre-existing core essence is itself "centered" as the pre-conceptual object of predication deemed likely amid its eidetic affair-complex and form of ideation—not the knowing-constituting ego as a self-referencing element in each concatenation that orients constitutive life to one's personal lifeworld. Neither is the alien-I of transcendental consciousness that represents the objectified pure Ego "I-in-the-world" the center focus of an intersubjective affair-complex.

Under the psychological *epoché* and transcendental reduction, the subject's consciousness of *my life* is therefore rarely if ever symmetrical in terms of the fulfillment of one's anticipations with others. We might indeed come to believe that we know what we want in life; but as a matter of fact and practical experience, we tend to comprehend only an idealized "what" that does *not quite* seem to gain presence as the same thing that was originally pictured pre-conceptually. The knowing ego, comprehending and believing with certainty what it means for *me myself* to be human with feelings of empathy, is the subjective origin of one's asymmetrical personal lifeworld—where in actual reality, we can only *approximate* dimensions of anticipated outcomes.

In Husserl's system of ego-life under the transcendental reduction, the knowing-constituting ego is already immersed in contingent experience, and already anticipating its predicated objects to gain presence in one's naïve natural world. Yet since the pure Ego is immanently for itself in pure subjectivity, the knowing ego cannot constitute self-consciousness of the apodictic *I am* according to a tradition of reality construction. That is to say, such surrounding traditions are oriented in empathy toward the objectified *otherness* of "everyone." I cannot say with certain knowledge of contingencies, for example, that my appearance to others always mirrors what I see as *me myself*. In Husserl's (Fink 1995, §§11f) transcendental theory of method, the phenomenologizing ego therefore stands outside of the knowing ego's indexing of elements; and from this perspective, synthesizes the appearance of *me in my world* as a monad-like transcendental unity during intersubjective relationships of empathy. The psychological ego's phenomenologizing-acts are thus purely subjective transcending acts of synthesis in the world of common semblance.

Husserl (Fink 1995) seems to suggest that one's personal lifeworld is a transcendental object of self-referential world-constitution—while on the other hand, the action in pure psychology of phenomenologizing the presence and appearance of *me in my world* as a seamless monad presents to reflections a transcendental method of consciousness-formation:

> In the *dualism* of transcendental life (i.e., transcendentally constituting life and phenomenologizing life!) lies the basis for the problematic of transcendental self-reference—and not...in the *monism* of psychic being. [It is] precisely because the subjective performance of phenomenologizing is *different* from the transcendental performance of <world-> constitution...that the *problem*, the *question* of the transcendental "being" of phenomenologizing exists [in the appearance of worldliness versus its motive and method of constitution]. (§4)

Husserl's emphasis on the dualism of transcendental consciousness—that of the appearance of its object and that of its method of constitution—provokes three questions for applied phenomenology under the transcendental reduction: (1) How is a phenomenologist to see constitutive life under the psychological *epoché*, while suspending one's own world-constituting experience of intellectual seeing? (2) By what practice that is not problematic for setting aside one's naïve intuition about objects and acts, does a phenomenologist follow in order to see such things in the judgments and valuations of another? (3) What is to keep genetic reflections in the transcendental register focused on the subject's psychic life during activities of world-constitution? Here is what seems to be Husserl's answer to these and similar questions: As a norm of practice for genetic reflections on the lived experience of transcendental subjectivity, a phenomenologist could assume the perspective of the phenomenologizing ego in the world that is commonly talked about; for indeed, the phenomenologizing ego represents the pure Ego's functioning in spirit and reason as its own "onlooker" of *my life as a whole*. (*see* Fink 1995, §10)

In Husserl's "knowledge-complex" of ego-functions, the phenomenologizing ego (like the transcendental ego) is an epistemological bifurcation of the pure Ego following its transcendental reorientation. Adopting the perspective of the phenomenologizing ego in reflections therefore represents the phenomenological attitude toward world-constitution as a subjective experience of *knowing*. By applying this perspective in the transcendental register—as strange as it sounds as an absurdity of non-reason—a phenomenologist intends to set aside the metaphysical presupposition of one's own existence in the world of common semblance. Husserl (Fink 1995, §11) explains that the phenomenologizing ego gives by synthesis the sheer appearance of *absolute* reality to our constituted objectivities, including the appearance of *me myself* as the absolute unity of what the pure Ego is deemed *to be* in the human world. Each of us thereby "makes ordinary" our intentional experiences of transcendental subjectivity within the horizon of one's own natural attitude.

Continuing with this explanation and its impact on Husserl's methodology, the transcendental reduction brackets any presented or implied logic of induction that leads to a naturalistic abstraction for an object of self-knowledge. As a countersense to our natural attitude in Husserl's (Fink 1995, §11) mature reflections, the phenomenologizing ego (*unlike* the transcendental ego) does not enjoy a naïve "human attitude" in constitutive life. Instead, the phenomenologizing ego looks at the *eidos* of *my life*, and seems to wonder as a "retro-inquiry" (*Rückfrage*) in pure psychology if its core essence has the appearance (*Erscheinung*) of *me myself* during one's intersubjective relationships. When the sheer appearance of *my life* is deemed likely in the transcendental ego's form of ideation for a seamless monad, then transcending acts of the psychological ego construct according to this form a unity of *me myself* in life-world experiences. By means of the psychological ego's transcending- and phenomenologizing-acts in the horizon of metaphysics, the phenomenon of *my life* is synthesized to be the objectified and absolutized experience of one's own being-in-the-world. We consequently live our lives knowingly with sense and meaning, secure with others in co-existence and common semblance.

When the subject predicates or implies to know something with certainty by means of this universal method of consciousness-formation, a phenomenologist could then see one's fully-fledged awareness of a presentational object. Predicated *knowing* is how the psychological ego "makes ordinary" the lived experience of *me myself* in one's personal lifeworld, and is thus how the transcendental circle and dialectic of constitutive life is closed within the horizon of metaphysics. The pure Ego's transcendental subjectivity appears in the manifest world as one's knowing comportment—which necessarily includes the pure Ego's correlated spirit-life of agency and motivation in pure psychology *for* that comportment. As depicted in Figure 4.3., the psychological ego is therefore experienced anonymously in one's thematic focus on a transcendental object, and also stands with the phenomenologizing ego outside of the knowing ego's natural world of actual reality and objective truth.

The Psychological Reduction

In Husserl's work, the psychic life of conscious awareness entails a field of affirmation and denial of *a priori* and contingent elements. Here, the psychological redution is used to disclose the cognitive acts of the psychological ego amid a flow of reasoning from pre-conceptual to conceptual space. The psychological ego in Husserl's (1982, §37) egology acts as the pure Ego's "mind's eye" of intellectual seeing when seizing upon essences and groups of elements necessary for consciousness-formation. Such intentional action occurs within a built-up system of apperceptions throughout a dialectical synthesis of solipsism and intersubjectivity. During the life-span development of this system, the psychological ego engages mental processes of noematic construction within bounds of one's maturing natural attitude. We therefore intuitively come to see, and consistently aim to maintain, an ongoing mental formation that structures *my life* to be a rational affective unity in thought and speech.

Cognitive action in the transcendental register is directed in psychological processes according to a genetic psychic order of constitution. Said order follows the pure Ego's logic of calculus for composing both *a priori* and contingent elements of anticipated being-sense for an affair-complex. The internal time-consciousness of this order encompasses simultaneously—both diachronically over time and synchronically at any particular time—all salient regions of immanence and transcendence here and now. The primitive notion of universal psychic life in Husserl's (1982, §86) theory of consciousness includes our pre-conceptual experiences of a pregiven unity of corporeal- and spirit-life. Cognitive action directed toward these hyletic elements in various strata of *knowing* represents the "psychological function" ("*psychische Funktion*") of apperceptive experience in Stumpf's phenomenology of the human world.

When we speak naïvely of psychological experience, we usually mean an objectified unity that is lived during expressions of synthesized corporeal- and spirit-life. As necessity demands in the living present for awareness of any such unity, the pure Ego directs mental formations consisting of multiple psychological processes of contingent transcending act toward every preconceived adumbration of *body* and *soul*. This self-referencing action serves to compose an eidetic affair-complex for self-knowledge of objectified psychic being-in-the-world. By extension and generalization of this experience, a streaming of cognitive action is seen under the psychological *epoché* in all redu-ced strata of apperceptions and appresentations for the contents of conscious awareness here and now—howsoever said form is deemed likely for the unity of one's ownness-essence during ongoing life-span experiences.

In Husserl's (1973a, §3) mature reflections on psychic life, perhaps in deference to his rigorous anti-psychologism, the psychological reduction is only applied for clarifications of intentional acts upon an "item of cognition." Under the psychological *epoché*, such "items" are pregiven as pre-existing ele-ments of noematic construction for an object of the mind. Seeing the mental activity of pure consciousness during acts of cognition in the transcendental register represents Husserl's (1970, §§69f) clarification and modification of Brentano's act psychology of human intentionality. This radicalization of Brentano's phenomenognosis is practiced in genetic phenomenology as a psy-chological reduction of constitutive experience and reality construction for the object-content of awareness—but only when said content is self-evidently present in propadeutic regressive reflections on the subject's consciousness-formation. The psychological reduction presents a theme of *aboutness* for such action in the transcendental register, where genetic reflections are focused on a succession of cognitive acts upon (and passive acceptance of) essential ele-ments of an intentional object in the world that is commonly talked about.

The psychological reduction under its own *epoché* could be depicted as follows within an applied geometry of *a priori* pure psychology when the pure Ego is "being psychological" in the transcendental register:

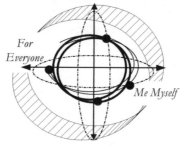

Figure 4.4. The Ψ Reduction

One of the first things the psychological reduction could reveal to re-flections is an adumbrating mental process for scanning elements of a pre-sumptive rational affective unity. This process indeed represents the ongoing activities of consciousness-formation amid a background of pure psychology. Given in the living present by the direct gaze of the psychological ego, Figure 4.4. shows an abstracted mental formation of transcending acts within the subject's personal lifeworld of intersubjective relationships. Such mental for-mations include a series of dynamic psychological processes for fitting a com-position of elements to idealized spatial coordinates of embodiment. Retained elements in this psychic order are pictured in the transcendental ego's form of ideation in anticipation of a unity of configuration in the world of common semblance. In this way, the psychological reduction also reveals the field of action for the pure Ego's transcendental method of world-constitution. For a complete depiction of transcendental consciousness, the psychological reduction could be imaginatively superimposed upon the eidetic and transcendental reductions under the psychological *epoché*.

The pure psychological field of action is represented in Figure 4.4. by an idealized one-dimensional internal/external manifold of intentional experience. A complex state of diachronic/synchronic psychic life in this field consists of thetic and nonthetic acts of retention and elapse of elements. Each act is directed in its affair-complex by a psychic order of constitution according to the internal time-consciousness of a transcendental logic of calculus. A contingent calculus in its region of cognitive action and passive acceptance is then used to compose a unity of configuration in the transcendental register.

During the ordinary lived experience of transcendental subjectivity, a psychic order of action and non-action is directed simultaneously in constitutive life toward *me myself* and toward whatever is intended to be self-evidently real "for everyone." Recall that the one-dimensionality of a mental process represents our presuppositions of "oneness" for spatiotemporality in the world of common semblance. (*see* Husserl 2001, 16) It might therefore be useful to think of the delimiting horizon of the psychological reduction as exhibiting the topological features of a single-surface Möbius strip in the space of applied geometry (*see*, e.g., Rucker 1977, 53); or as Husserl (1973a, §42c.) expresses it, "the form of space which is ordered with time." Psychic life in the transcendental register is bound by the contingencies of *here* and *now*.

The psychological reduction brackets for genetic reflections any implied or explicit instance of cognitive mental life during subjective performances of consciousness-formation. Here, the subject's cognitive activity is interpreted in the transcendental register as the pure Ego's psychosubjectivity in one's personal lifeworld. The psychological reduction thus presents to reflections the intentional function of cognitive mental life to act in spirit and reason upon pregiven and anticipated elements of an intentional object. When fulfilling this function, the psychological ego's action on elements initiates and maintains all necessary eidetic relationships within a psychic order of constitution. For example, the legs of a table are self evidently different than for the legs of a horse, whereas we say that a rose by any other name would smell as sweet. One's psychic order of ideation and constitution follows a transcendental logic of calculus for each object of the mind, and is typically experienced as habitual judgments and valuations of objective truth and actual reality.

A mental formation with its logic of calculus directs a streaming of psychological processes for grouping elements of an eidetic affair-complex at spatiotemporal connections of bestowed sense and conferred meaning. With maturation and ordinary cognitive development, each connection becomes consistent with elements of one's sociocultural tradition of reality construction. Grouping- and composing-acts are carried out by the psychological ego according to the transcendental ego's form of ideation for "knowing the real," that is to say, for grasping both the irreality and actuality of things in the world for us all—including our subjectively structured objectivities and their mutually conceived associations in empathy. Reality construction is a pre-eminent psychological theme and norm of practice for constituting a unity of awareness in transcendental consciousness. Said unity is lived by the psychological ego during first-person (singular and plural) relationships with others.

One could see in Figure 4.4. a pre-conceptual fitting of parts-to-parts and parts-to-whole at points of connection ("●") within asymmetrical concatenations of essential elements for a transcendental object. Each nonlinear concatenation intentionally tends asymptotically toward anticipated orthogonal and therefore idealized dimensions of embodied thought and speech. A temporal connection amid a psychological process is typically within and between lines of eidetic structure for an anticipated rational affective unity in transcendental consciousness. During this action, a teleological goal of each psychological process is to constitute conscious awareness of a fully composed intentional object in the transcendental register—where now, this object could be represented in one's personal lifeworld as valid for everyone and simultaneously valid for *me myself*. "The psychological reduction," Husserl (1970, §70) points out, "has to reduce at once the consciousness of the individual thing and also [of the thing's] world-horizon." The horizon of each world of things—"each thing that we experience, that we have to do with in any way…including ourselves when we reflect upon ourselves"—limits the potential sense and meaning of the contents of awareness here and now.

The psychological reduction also reveals the psychological ego's gaze within a mental formation of intentional action. Here, transcending-acts in their psychic order served to temporize both pre-conceptual and conceptual space into a delimited synthetic spatiotemporal unity in the transcendental register. This is the same experience of internal time-consciousness that orders the constitution of an actually real object here and now. In the living present of this experience (that exists for judgments and valuations "in relative normalcy" for everyone), the psychological ego phenomenologizes an object of the mind to appear to one's self and to others as an idealized unity of common semblance. Under the psychological *epoché* and reduction, the psychological ego thus represents the psychosubjectivity of phenomenologizing action in one's empathetic relationships. During typical phenomenologizing comportment, we seem to wonder, for example, "Is this really what I mean to say?" or, "Is this right and normal?" The psychological ego then acts with affirmation or denial within a logic of calculus on any such motive as an element of the pure Ego's affair-complex for a unity of being-sense.

In ordinary mental processes of constitution, the gaze of the psychological ego is initially directed toward the irreal correlates of *a priori* experience that are retained in eidetic memory of common semblance—rather than toward any potential actual reality in one's personal lifeworld. The psychological ego's "retro-inquiry" of phenomenologizing iteration includes returning to the pure Ego's most fundamental level of existential relationships. Elements of an affair-complex that are described as static things in regressive reflections are seen in genetic reflections to be iterated by the psychological ego in order for the appearance of an intentional object to be constituted as a unity here and now. Also, further reason-as-evidence for whatever pre-exists in solipsistic subjectivity might still need to be gathered and grouped by the psychological ego in the transcendental register—although subsequent validating evidence of essential sense and meaning might not always be achieved amid the asymptotic structures of awareness. The existence and explanation for such necessity, failure, success, and error in constitutive life does not show itself within a purely descriptive phenomenological psychology.

Under the psychological *epoché*, Husserl (1970, §71) notices, all humans "become pure souls, ego-subjects of self- and world-apperceptions." A genetic phenomenological psychology of "pure souls" is therefore practiced as inquiry into the spontaneous and autonomous human spirit in pure psychology—the spirit that is peculiarly *my own* during life-world experiences with others. In Husserl's theory of inquiry, a universal pure psychology pre-exists in one's interpretations of mental life, and of any psychological phenomenon whatsoever during applications of the phenomenological method proper. Indeed, Husserl stresses that an intuitive psychological *epoché* of mental life applies "in advance to every possible experience of others" in the "mental stratum" of the world-horizon that delimits human co-existence. With this so-called psychological modification of the method of *epoché*, a phenomenological psychologist focuses reflections under the psychological reduction on the ir-real cognitive action within the presented world-horizon of another.

The psychological *epoché* is first applied, however, to the (mostly empirical) objects of self-knowledge about psychological experience that we naïvely bring into an investigation of human consciousness. Under the *epoché*, such objects are extra-psychic post-phenomenological phenomena. With this rigorous practice of applied phenomenology, a phenomenological psychologist abstains from preconceptions of necessity for each contingent psychological experience seen under the psychological reduction. Any such necessity must show itself in reflections with ontic and epistemic evidence in the cognitive mental life of the meaningful human subject—just as elements of an intentional object must show themselves with similar evidence in object-oriented phenomenology. Expressions of Husserl's phenomenological attitude specifically and strongly emphasize that a phenomenolgist is not to presuppose any experience of consciousness-formation presented by another. In this light, there is no proper phenomenological psychologcal attitude that has not been first submitted to the psychological *epoché*, where a psychologist suspends for inquiry any potential self-apperceptions of the same psychic life as the subject in reflective focus. (*see* Husserl 1980a, p. 411)

Seen as typically present under the psychological *epoché* and reduction, each of us experiences the objects of the knowing-constituting ego and the acts of the phenomenologizing-psychological ego during ordinary activities of consciousness-formation. A phenomenologist must then bracket these things as one's own when reflecting on the cognitive mental life and psychological experiences of another in the world of common semblance. Husserl (1970, §71) explains that the necessity for a phenomenological psychologist's "self-bracketing" is a question of rigorous application of the *epoché*—specifically, it is a matter of *what* is seen as "the reduced phenomenon of internal psychology," either that experienced by the meaningful human subject or that experienced by the psychologist. Perhaps when a psychologist has rigorously assumed in free fantasy the perspective of the phenomenologizing onlooker of transcendental consciousness, one has learned and experienced the phenomenological attitude toward human mental life, both universal and personal.

In summary, the psychological reduction is applied in order to see *all at once* the pure and transcendental consciousness of an intentional object here and now. During the flow of this experience from pre-conceptual to conceptual space, the psychological ego's gaze is directed toward forming temporal connections for noematic structures of awareness within a mental process of constitution. In this process, each connection is an instance of cognitive action or non-action amid an identifying order for *this eidos* and not another. As a result of this order, a constituted object "looks right and normal" to the transcendental ego because it is intended by the pure Ego and composed to appear that way by the psychological ego's phenomenologizing-acts in empathy. A psychological process in this field consists of cognitive acts of judging and valuing at points of connections for the retention, elapse, and protension of necessary elements during the constitution of an intentional object and its constructed actual reality. All through one's activities of consciousness-formation, the core essence of an *eidos* is pregiven in the living present as the meant-as-meant "picture" in the transcendental ego's form of ideation for "aiming" toward something in the world of human co-existence and common semblance. The scanning gaze of the psychological ego presents to reflections a succession of psychological processes that follow the internal time-consciousness and psychic order of action for this same state of affairs.

The psychological reduction reveals as well the rich patterns of mental life during the ongoing development and employment of a system of apperceptions for the production of mundane thought and speech. A phenomenological psychologist, however, is not intent on one's own production of such things during genetic reflections. It is enough from the phenomenological attitude in meditative solitude to grasp that the pure Ego of another has already intentionally constituted its own objectivities by its own intentional acts. When an intentional object is given by the phenomenologizing ego to the pure Ego as adequate in appearance for its presence in the subject's personal lifeworld, only then is it self-evident to a transcendental phenomenologist that an object of the mind has acquired the apodictic reason-as-evidence that is necessary for it to become actually real in conscious awareness. By assuming the perspective of the phenomenologizing onlooker during the constitutive performances of another, the actualized appearance and noematic structure of a phenomenon could gain presence in a phenomenologist's rigorously neutralized transcendental consciousness as well. This clarifying event of evidence leading to understanding is a goal of applied transcendental phenomenology.

Husserl (1982, §§137f) sometimes uses the term "apodictic" in the context of *evidence* partly to signify a degree or state of certainty for what is self-evident about an intentional object during consciousness-formation. When a transcendental phenomenologist assumes the perspective of the phenomenologizing onlooker in genetic reflections—and thereby leaves behind the Cartesian way of methodically reflecting on the naïve *ego cogito*—then a phenomenologist's own ego-functions for determining self-evidence with apodictic certainty are suspended for observations of the mental life of another. Otherwise, the voice of the transcendental ego in its telling of "I am being human in thought and speech," and the voice of the psychological ego in its telling of "I am the psychosubjectivity of this same experience," would be denied for reflections on the irrealities of *my life* presented by the meaningful human subject. A phenomenologist could not then properly evaluate what is made actually real and apodictically certain with reason and evidence during the constitutive performance of the pure Ego.

Under the psychological reduction, a phenomenological psychologist interprets the subject's intentional acts and norms of practice in order to explain one's methods of consciousness-formation—typically, during one's constitution of a rational affective unity. Or else, how the subject might have indeed failed to constitute awareness of something with affective significance according to reason and evidence. Anything in imagination that is *not* constituted to have an actually real presence in the one's naïve natural world is unthematic for either empirical observations or for "natural" inductive inferences of objectivity. Yet in Husserl's tradition, the pure consciousnesses of any intentional object or act whatsoever is a matter of inquiry for applied transcendental phenomenology. Anything that appears in reductions with the method of *epoché* already pre-exists for interpretations and explanations within a potential synthesis of unity that *is* transcendental consciousness. By implication, the psychological reduction could disclose what is *not* acted upon by the psychological ego during the constitutive indexing of elements by the knowing ego. For example, the pure Ego might not call for cognitive action in conceptual space on a retained correlate for *me myself* that signifies an adumbration of the *eidos* of *fear* in pre-conceptual experience.

After the transcendental turn in the phenomenological method proper, explanations of constitutive life under the psychological reduction are partly in terms of how one's cognitive action functions in spirit and reason so that a singular core essence of an *eidos* is simultaneously valid for *me myself* and for everyone in one's personal lifeworld. In Husserl's (Fink 1995, 165) theory of world-consciousness, one's personal lifeworld represents a thematic "identity of acceptedness" for the pure Ego during all of its modes of performance in pure and transcendental subjectivity. The subject's representations of a personal lifeworld point toward the pure Ego's grasp of an embodied world of human co-existence and common semblance. Said world is typically seized upon as an object of the mind during consciousness-formation, and then experienced in empathy as a fragment of the universal life-world of objectified and absolutized Nature. The pure psychological field of action for consciousness of a personal lifeworld exists as intended for *me myself* in pure subjectivity, but apperceived as experienced by everyone during communal interactions.

Given to reflections under the psychological *epoché* as living knowingly with others, and correlated in the horizon of metaphysics as absolute and apodictic being in the world, the core essence of the life-world does not itself change during contingent experience. Instead, one's *personal lifeworld* changes in its duration as the consequence in pure psychology of our individual "chase after…'life-goals,' ultimately a will to life." (Fink 1995, 173) The psychological reduction reveals this will of the psyche and this spirit-life of the pure Ego, all within the enduring and changing profiles of transcendental consciousness.

Cognitive Development in the Transcendental Register

In Husserl's (1980a, p. 413) work, a phenomenologist's natural attitude is set aside by means of the *epoché* and its series of reductions in favor of a revolutionary non-empirical human-scientific theory of inquiry. This rigorous self-*epoché*, however, does not eliminate the pure psychology of choice and motivation during reflective abstractions that make up the praxis of applied phenomenology. While prescribing inductive inferences of universal elements of human consciousness, Husserl (1982, §33) warned phenomenological philosophers—even as they bracketed the subject's psychological experiences as unthematic for object-oriented reflections—not to forget that phenomenological clarifications do not, and cannot, proceed to fruition without the phenomenologist's own cognitive mental life of free fantasy and imagination. Just as with our ordinary pre-conceptual experiences of everyday reasoning, Husserl's methodic practices rely upon one's enduring spirit-life of autonomy and agency during applications of the phenomenological method proper.

And yet, since the subject of such application indeed exists "within the world of men and brutes," Husserl (1973b, §61) writes, a phenomenologist "encounters the familiar natural-scientific problems of psychophysical, physiological, and psychological genesis" regarding ways of being human—including the psychological experience of cognitive mental life and its developmental origins. The spirit-life of each person endures in pure psychology and begins with our will to life, but the mental life that could be described as "psychological" in naïve accounts begins only later. The cognitive mental life of transcendental subjectivity originates with the genesis of a world-horizon for the potential achievement of one's life-goals and their transcendental methods of fulfillment. In this light, Husserl suggests that the development and growth of cognitive mental life is "the course [in] which every child must build up his idea of the world [within a life-span field of objects and acts]."

Our first intentional acts in this course of development include seizing upon the *eidos* of *world* as the determinable substrate and psychological theme of pure life. We then judge, value, retain, and cast forward elements of existential relationships relating to *my life* that are experienced in this same world of pure *being* and *doing*. Prior to those transcending acts that could be naïvely described as psychological, a child grasps the idea of a horizon in pure consciousness for pre-existing worldly things that are *not* determined by one's animate organism. Husserl (1973b, §61) noticed that when we live knowingly in the transcendental register, some pre-existing things at the genesis of constitutive life are thus already "Other" to one's solipsistic corporeal "live-bodily (purely 'biological')" experience of *me myself*. Throughout the duration of cognitive development, some pre-existing things are therefore judged to be *not my own* during life-world experiences of objective truth and actual reality.

During the normal course of events for the experience of conscious awareness, each of us follows the pure Ego's internal time-consciousness of a before-and-after state of affairs with respect to one's original grasping the idea of being-in-the-world. Intuitive norms of practice are thus already established in the living present for retention and elapse of essential elements of an intentional object—*prior* to the turn from solipsistic subjectivity to our intersubjective relationships of empathy. Just as important, we have already experienced the human spirit of anticipation in pure subjectivity for the fulfillment of one's life-goals in the pre-scientific space of everyday life. And so, beginning from our most fundamental relationships in time and space, and reaching out toward the most immediate levels of intentional experience, our potentials in cognitive mental life are realized in the midst of one's own constructed world-horizon of transcendental consciousness.

The construction of an ongoing world-horizon is indeed the genetic origin in pure psychology of the child's psychic development. During a typical course of development, cognitive mental life continues to mature from its existential origins when an apperceptive system is built up within the delimited bounds of the natural world. In this way, an intuitive logic of calculus for judging- and valuing-acts is pregiven for the phenomenon of *my life* in the world of co-existence and common semblance. Under the psychological *epoché* and reduction, genetic reconstructions of cognitive mental life could begin at the genesis of one's intuitive grasp of the universal life-world. Here, intuition of the life-world as our day-to-day spatiotemporality and essential ground for *being* and *doing* is the beginning of our reasoning about the world that is commonly talked about, along with one's personal place within that same world.

The pure Ego continues this course of development in its personal lifeworld during the dialectical synthesis of the solipsistic *eidos* of *I-and-Other* and the intersubjective *eidos* of *I-with-Other*—all within a built-up system of transcending apperceptions. (*see* Husserl 1970, §58) In this same system for the constitution of one's self-consciousness in empathy, we judge and value the idea of *me myself* in relation to the alter-ego and to other ego-subjects. Normal maturation in cognitive mental life endures throughout one's life-span experiences of transcendental subjectivity by synthesizing-acts directed toward an anticipated unity-form of retained correlates of such elements. Every instance and experience of this action of *being* is intended to exist as *my own* within a plurality of possible expressions of objectified being-in-the-world.

Simultaneously over the diachronic time of personal relationships, and sometimes within a very limited synchronic time of spontaneous thought, our synthesizing activities in cognitive mental life are intended to compose a unity of self-objectification in the world of common semblance. When seen under the psychological *epoché*, the pure Ego is willed into its being-in-the-world here and now, not by synaptic arrangements or neurological organizations, but by the cognitive mental life whereby we co-exist with others during life-world experience. This universal state of affairs characterizes the essential difference between our "mindless" consciousness relative to the human organism, and our sentient consciousness relative to the human soul.

Applied Transcendental Phenomenological Psychology

An Overview

The psychological in human affairs cannot reasonably be separated from the mental life necessary for conscious awareness, for otherwise we are no more than organic vessels of electrical and chemical interactions that provoke involuntary patterns of behavior—a notion that is surely contradicted by our experiences of willing, thinking, and feeling. Yet when the phenomenon of conscious awareness is seen to be caused by cognitive action intentionally directed toward "external" things by one's "internal" psychic conditions, three areas of inquiry could encompass the field of applied transcendental phenomenological psychology: (1) in regressive phenomenology, operations of *nous* on elements of pure consciousness according to immanent relationships of *I* and *Other*; (2) in genetic phenomenology, the dialectical association between solipsistic and transcendental subjectivity; and (3) the acts of the psychological ego that constitute the subject's awareness of things in the world of human co-existence and common semblance. Each area is composed of deeper lying strata of the synthesized unity of transcendental consciousness. Throughout the phenomenological field of objects and acts, both actual reality and presuppositions of the nature of things are constructed as directed by the will of the psyche within a background of pure psychology.

References to *Psychognosia* in psychological studies signify a way of eidetic *seeing* in ordinary experience and theoretical reflections, where we "aim at" ideas and their relationships by means of one's own mental processes—or as Cairns (1940, 5) paraphrases Locke, "'the perception of our own minds within us.'" This ordinary and universal method has been applied as a technique for inquiry into the most basic kinds of human experience as far back as Aristotle's dialectical approach in the third century BCE, and has continued to be used under other names into the 21st century—including Freud's technique of psychoanalysis. (*see* Smith 1920, 21-2) *Psychognosia* is indeed the intuitive ground of non-empirical thinking when using the phenomenological *epoché* for interpretations of conscious awareness to be a rational affective unity of objects and acts. Intentional acts on objects are lived in the pure psychology of this unity, and point toward the core essence of an *eidos* in its mental formation of internal time-consciousness and psychic order of constitution.

Essences and elements of both pure and transcendental subjectivity are clarified in Husserl's theory of elements as objects of *nous* in eidetic affair-complexes, while intentional acts are found in his theory of method within volitional processes of noematic action. Said action is carried out by means of a genetic succession of cognitions according to a transcendental logic of calculus—all this in order for one to be knowingly conscious of something in the world that is commonly talked about. When documenting the subjective expression of this universal performance, transcendental phenomenological psychologists investigate the psychosubjectivity of the pure Ego that predicates the existence, sense, and meaning of presentational objects.

The pure Ego's psychosubjectivity is represented by the psychological ego in Husserl's system of ego-life—which is itself presented as a system of interactions between adumbrations of our experiences of pure subjectivity. Under the psychological *epoché* and reduction, the psychological ego is seen to be the way that the subject is "being psychological" during life-world experiences here and now; that is to say, when the pure Ego engages its spirit-life of autonomy and agency for intentional action in the world for us all. Constitutive performances are traced out within a genetic reconstructive phenomenology according to the psychological ego's acts upon (and passive acceptance of) elements of ideation for an object deemed likely for its presence in awareness. As a delimitation of this nonrandom event, a field of intentional action provides a horizon of potential cognitions during activities of consciousness-formation. These mostly judging- and valuing-acts bring an object of the mind to presence in correspondence with the transcendental ego's form of ideation for something actually real and objectively true. Interpretations of the psychological ego present eidetic evidence of the subject's psychic life amid a flow of reaoning from pre-conceptual to conceptual space.

In Husserl's so-called egology, the phenomenologizing ego is the self-conscious mode of the pure Ego when realizing the appearance of an intentional object in the world of common semblance. By assuming in reflections the perspective of the phenomenologizing onlooker, the practice of Husserl's transcendental phenomenology emulates this universal method for seeing the human world as indeed a world for us all. In this sense, applied transcendental phenomenology adopts the essence of naïve theoretical reflection as scientific praxis. In this sense, as well, each clarified unity of essences is the same post-phenomenological phenomenon given from the natural attitude in conceptual space—only now, it has been modified by *epoché* to reveal the pure Ego's subjective experience with the core essence of an *eidos* in pre-conceptual and pre-linguistic performances. During our everyday activities of consciousness-formation, the psychological ego carries out its phenomenologizing-acts in order for the semblance of an irreal object to appear as actually real "for everyone." Consequently, the same psychological phenomenon in both naïve and phenomenological reflections points toward an intentional object that has been acted upon by the psychological ego in cognitive mental life.

With our everyday reasoning toward self-knowledge of an intentional object, things that are determinable but unknown in direct experience tend to be axiologically grounded and closely approximated by embodied constructions of idealized dimensions. This method of *knowing* when used by naïve psychologists typically leads to notions of psychological experience in regions of empirical generalizations. When "psychological facts" are then predicated in such regions to be objectively true, they point toward a pre-existing irreality that is necessary for psychological phenomena to gain presence as actually real in mundane thought and speech. The teleological goal of this injunction is to grasp an irreality of psychic life as an instance of the human spirit of autonomy and agency during our strivings for truth and consistency. Any such irreality is seen under the *epoché* as an element of pure psychology, that is seized upon as a norm of practice in the transcendental register—and indeed, this norm represents the intuitive praxis of naïve human-scientific psychology. Adopting a phenomenological psychological attitude in Husserl's tradition means to articulate this norm knowingly within a rigorous methodology.

Mundane notions of psychological phenomena typically and habitually come to presence in the transcendental register as presentational object made up of correlates of embodied and objectified mental life. For example (Anderson 1990, 20f), there is the predication that "neural representations" of information in one's brain cause permanent memories in one's mind. Under the psychological *epoché*, the indirect asymptotic cause of the existence of any phenomenon in naïve psychological discourse (such as "neural representations") is the similar constitutive experiences of psychologists who intend for an *eidos* to gain presence in its idealized and objectified form of appearance for everyone. In order to be expressed as a matter of fact within a region of empirical generalizations, this form is fulfilled in linguistic empathy by means of a system of signs referring to objectified mental life. The *eidos* for the empirical factualness of "neural representations" is itself represented in theoretical reflections as "the neural basis of cognition." (pp. 18ff)

And yet, there is no compelling evidence that either representations or cognitions are themselves *caused* by neural activity—although as the genesis of this injunction for constructing a matter of factualness, there is certainly a correlation in metaphysics between the physical and the spiritual. But with little concern for the *why* or the *how* of this correlation during interpretations of empirical data, we tend to rely upon a presupposition of the nature of things during relationships of empathy for predicating the actual reality of a conclusion of facts. In empathy, we see only extensions of an objectified Body in pre-conceptual space; and despite all good scientific warnings, "correlation equals causation" when oriented in reason from within the horizon of metaphysics. However, any constituted objectivity in its embodied form of factualness could then be known and understood as objective knowledge by everyone from the natural attitude. Sometimes objectified knowledge of a phenomenon is given in empathy for many generations to come.

In Husserl's tradition of inquiry, the cognitive action that results in the subject's awareness of any belief, opinion, or object of self-knowledge is a matter of study for applied transcendental phenomenological psychology. Every such resulting state of affairs is seen in reflections to be an intellectual achievement of intentional experience in psychic life, and each such matter is therefore a teleological goal of the universal method of consciousness-formation that is fulfilled by means of cognitions. The phenomenon of conscious awareness is meant to be viewed under the psychological *epoché* as a *logos* of the psyche in the transcendental register, yet the psyche in pure psychology directs cognitive mental life in operations of *nous* that includes in depths of reflection more than solely the intentional acts upon objects in the transcendental ego's thematic regard. The psychological experience of mental life also includes our peculiar human spirit, where each of us intends to construct actual realities and to know objectively real things as consistently true. The self-evident manifestation of this spirit-life of the species is part of what Husserl refers to as the human soul.

Naïve psychological concepts pertaining to the mental lives of humans are seen in Husserl's methodology to be the objects (not the subjects) of inquiry in the transcendental register. Within the act-object structure of this register, the psyche and its motivating spirit in pure psychology provide the effective cause for any such concepts having gained presence in mundane thought and speech. The psyche made present in the material world is the human mind in theoretical reflections on the intellectuality of the species, but the mind is also universally grasped as the very soul (*Seele*) of humanity during subjective expressions of body and spirit. The psyche cannot therefore be described or explained in transcendental phenomenological psychology as either corporeal- or spirit-life independent of one another. With Husserl's (1982, §36) modifications of strict Cartesianism, both regions of the human soul first exist together within an undifferentiated solipsistic state of pure potential that is represented by the *eidos* of *nous*. The essence of *mind* is a substrate of this *eidos* in pre-conceptual experience, where a particular state of mind is only later transcended and constituted to be a different region of the soul.

The pure Ego wants to grasp both regions of body and spirit as subjective self-knowledge of the world of human co-existence, along with one's objectified place in that same world. We habitually think about these regions together and separately, rationally and non-rationally, and will our thoughts in pure psychology toward the direction of one or the other as each comes to matter during constitutive life. Only when the psyche so wills a difference during consciousness-formation, and directs cognitive mental life toward realizing one or the other region of the soul, does a so-called psychic event show itself in transcendental phenomenological psychology. Only then is there any psychological connection in pure subjectivity between the undifferentiated psyche and any existent that is not one's inherent corporeal body and autonomous spirit in the world that is commonly talked about. Even so, having one's awareness of something as other than an undifferentiated state of solipsistic irreality in the transcendental register requires the pure Ego to make actual reality exist in thoughts of a constituted objectivity. Said action typically includes thinking within the bounds delimited by something like God, such as an absolute and infinite Nature or the Law, as well as comprehending one's own physical body as an object in the space of all natural things.

Each of us is always surrounded by (and already actively within) the space of natural things when our thoughts are oriented toward objective phenomena. Consequently, we tend to think spontaneously about a natural world and its empirical manifestations of actual reality. (Husserl 1982, §28) This day-to-day comportment presents a personal horizon of objects and acts that delineates Nature in its totality—a totality that is naïvely grasped within the horizon of metaphysics as an enclosed manifold of cause and effect. Thus delimited, we busy ourselves psychologically with willing and thinking about things that matter in *my life*, both objective and potential. Sometimes we choose to theorize about our surrounding world so as to know something about the true nature of things—given under the *epoché* as correlating the noetic structure of a transcendental unity of apperception within the horizon of epistemology. And when we do so choose to reflect on these things, we could assume a theorizing attitude as an intuitive point of view. In the pure psychology of this attitude we intend and are motivated affectively to investigate something, inspect something, count something, conceptualize something, compare something, distinguish something, collect something, suppose something, infer something, and so on, and on. In our theorizing attitude, the natural world seems infinite in its capacity to motivate our acts of imagination and interest in the actual reality of one's own constituted objectivities.

Likewise from our theorizing attitude, we could grasp a correlation of intentional acts and emotional states oriented toward such affairs as liking something, shunning something, being glad about something, hoping for something, fearing something, reaching a decision about something, and so on. Indeed, it seems that whenever we intend to be aware of anything whatsoever there is an affective element of motivating spirit-life present with that intention. In our theorizing attitude, we could engage in these acts of pure psychology separately and together—all within subjective psychological processes of cognitive connections in and between elements of an intentional object. In order to achieve self-knowledge and conscious awareness of an elemental state of affairs, psychological processes stream throughout various regions of pregiven life-world experience for correlations of sense, meaning, and certainty—no matter where our theorizing attitude might intentionally lead. In the life-world horizon that entails all contingencies for living knowingly in the world of natural things, intentional acts of a universal theorizing attitude vary historically and culturally for individuals and groups.

When I adopt a theorizing attitude toward my surrounding world, Husserl (1982, §28) notices, I am conscious of the world "as immediately present" for willing, thinking, and feeling. Each of these characteristics of human intentionality represents a subjective psychological theme for a universal mental process in the world that is commonly talked about. Psychological themes for living naturally and adopting a personal point of view toward one's surrounding world, Husserl continues, "are embraced by the one Cartesian expression, *cogito*" (= *Latin*, for "I think"). In transcendental phenomenological psychology, the Cartesian *cogito* represents the psyche's "fundamental form of 'active' ['*aktuellen*'] living" in cognitive mental life from the natural attitude—no matter what one wills and thinks, and no matter what personal point of view one takes toward the surrounding world. Husserl (1973b, §8) claims that Descartes "names" as the *cogito* our attitude toward the things that are *mine* in the Objective world. Under the psychological *epoché*, the Cartesian *cogito* represents our capacity in pure psychology for knowing universal life-world experiences, along with our capacity for knowing something reflectively and theoretically about one's *own* worldly experiences.

Yet for the psyche in pure consciousness there are other *cogito* than the Cartesian *cogito* of life-world experience, and there are other worlds of common semblance in the transcendental register than the world of naturally lawful objects. To make this point Husserl (1982, §28) gives the example of thinking about numbers: It is self-evident that numbers do not exist for perceptions of their objective physical presence. Instead, we confer meaning and bestow sense on the idea of numbers to be a matter that is discernible by means of various intellectual stimuli. As the idea is retained and cast forward through protension, the transcended *eidos* of *numbers* is not (usually) anticipated to appear magically or as *sui generis* in conceptual space. Rather, a numerical matter is grasped pre-conceptually as the affair-complex for an objectively lawful sequential organization and relationship of actually real things in the Objective world. When we write "4," for example, we signify that something already has a position within a sequential organization (i.e., the category "between" three and five). But first we need to construct a pre-existing group of relations within an affair-complex in order for the significance of "4" to be seen in its eidetically lawful position during consciousness-formation.

The intentional function in spirit and reason for signifying "4" begins by adopting the so-called mathematical attitude within a pre-conceptual space of anticipated objectivities—more specifically, amid an empathetic relationship for the mutual construction of actually real numerical things as objects of common semblance. During this intersubjective endeavor of constitutive life, we seize upon the essence of numbers according to handed down traditions for grasping numerical categories as matters of fact. From the mathematical attitude, the psyche is busied with the actual reality of the world of mathematics—but only insofar as one has already grasped a horizon of lawful mathematical acts upon lawful mathematical objects, and only insofar as one has an affective interest in numbers and not (say) colors, shapes, or language.

Each world of numbers, colors, shapes or language has its own immanent *cogito*, busy within its own horizon of objects and acts. As long as the pure Ego wills to think about objective things of common semblance we continue living in the natural attitude of the *cogito*. The natural attitude orients our presuppositions of a pregiven and continuous horizon of idealized objects and lawful relationships. From the natural attitude, we look intuitively for pregiven things and naïvely expect to see them in every world in which the psyche is busied. Oriented by this perspective, one's intuition is directed within a tradition of reality construction toward the apodictic certainty and reason-as-evidence pregiven for an intentional object during our intersubjective relationships—where tensions and conflicts between solipsistic and transcendental subjectivity are resolved in communal interactions. These methods of reasoning are undisturbed by our non-intuitive theorizing during social relations, where things are learned as mere facts—"mere," since they are not directly experienced by an immanent *cogito*, and not built up starting from the solipsistic register. Mere facts could nevertheless reference such impersonal matters as institutions, laws, and *de facto* rules in one's sociocultural surroundings.

In all horizons of experience and every space of reasoning, the subjective essence of the *cogito*, Husserl (1970, §62) points out, is the pure Ego, *I*. Phenomenologically, *I* am the identity of the one who thinks. Under the psychological *epoché*, "I think" represents the first-person life of the psyche that has its expressions of actual reality in the natural world as objectified psychological experience. The subject's expression of this same life-world experience presents the so-called psychological *cogito* to reflections on cognitive mental life in the transcendental region. "I think" under the psychological reduction means, "I simultaneously think here and not there" amid the spatiality of consciousness-formation. At any moment in the pre-conceptual flux of all potential worlds of objects and acts, the pure Ego is positioned to be "awake" in mental life (thetically) *here* in this world. The transcendental ego and its form of ideation is thus intentionally not *there* in a similarly pre-existing world that is now (nonthetically) *not-here* in the spatiotemporality of pure psychology. In the next moment of the living present, ego-life and psychological experience could flow into another world, and then into another, always in anticipation of grasping a world's pregiven objects and acts—and all within a streaming (polythetic) mental process of willing, thinking, or feeling.

When seen under the psychological *epoché* and reduction, the subject's life-span performance of consciousness-formation typically include in pure psychology four correlated phyla of cognitive mental life: (1) the child's grasping of the human world as a horizon of potentials for actualizing the *eidos* of *my life* here and now, (2) the genetic development of an apperceptive system for judgments and valuations within the delimiting horizons of epistemology, ontology, and metaphysics, (3) intentional experience with appresented analogous objects and constructed actual realities of common semblance, and (4) empathetic relationships of co-existence in one's personal lifeworld. Each phylum is represented by its particular norm of practice for transcending acts or passive acceptance in the midst of a complex field of cognitions. Here, psychological processes interrelate and habitually repeat the acts on objects that come to hand for consciousness-formation within and between each phylum. During the living-present flow from solipsism to intersubjectivity, throughout the unity of pure and transcendental consciousness, the simultaneous totality of these phyla of action comprises the proper domain of inquiry for applied transcendental phenomenological psychology.

The Psychological Experience of Rational Thought

The initiating act of a mental process of *thinking*—what Husserl (1969, §3) calls "the sense-constituting mental process"—is to change the position of pre-conceptual experience in order to grasp the essence of another world's pregivenness. (*see* Husserl 1982, §35) A pre-existing "situatedness" of spatiotemporal *place* is indeed the ground (*Boden*) of our ordinary intuition during constitutve life. One such intiating act, for example, is to move consciousness-formation from the physical thing-world to the world of functions and relationships. The subject's positioning of intuition within a flux of potentials for rational thought occurs during a genetic sequence in time for a succession of psychological processes of action and non-action. Each process in this psychic order consists of cognitive acts upon, or passive acceptance of, essential elements of a phenomenological *eidos*. By means of these intentional acts, a world's pregivenness is intellectually seen by the pure Ego, and is thus intuitable for constitutive activities by the performing ego. By these acts as well, the *cogito* of living knowingly in various possible worlds is positioned *here* within a particular mental formation and psychic order of presumptive self-knowledge. Consequently, the subject's experience of "I think" is delimited by a spatial horizon of objects upon which some action is directed in *this* world and not another. For instance, we do not rationally look for the chemical compound of the number four. Neither do we commonly speak of a bowl of weather.

A mental process of *constitution* likewise streams within and between worlds of objects and acts, precisely as it is willed to be streamed by the psyche in cognitive mental life. Here, multiple psychological processes simultaneously flow in contingent mental formations toward realizing appresented elements of both this-world and not-this-world for the pure Ego and its existential *Other*. According to our discerning judgments and valuations, *this* element is not *that* element in rational concatenations. The position of ego-life toward the objects of not-this-world is given to reflections as the pure psychological mode of non-action, where the psyche is knowingly not busy *there* in the living present. Anything that could be *there* is now nonthetically "other" to the pure Ego's thetic active and passive busiedness in pre-conceptual performances. The Cartesian *cogito*, seen under the psychological *epoché* as the psyche's living out ego-life naïvely in the transcendental register, is transformed in higher-level apperceptions of objectivity into an embodied spatiotemporal *cogito* of naïve self-knowledge in *this* world. It is then transformed into another *cogito* in another world, and so on—all within a complex polythetic mental process of constitution for an objectivity in conscious awareness.

Each position in ego-life, Husserl (1982, §114) observes, is a doxic position in rational thought. This means that the pure Ego has reason to believe that it is positioned here-and-now as a sequence in time and space within *this* pregiven horizon of worldly experience and not another. An intuitive ("protodoxic") belief in the spatiotemporal "positionality" of rational thought allows each of us to posit the enduring existence of objects and arts in each world; and so, we have enduring beliefs and opinions about those same pre-existing things that could be experienced as objectified self-knowledge here and now. Yet even when the pure Ego does not rationally posit the enduring existence of something, one could still have the basis for beliefs, opinions, and subsequent self-knowledge of that same thing. For example, I have no experience with actually real Martians. As a correlate of rational thought, however, I could have an opinion about their existence and self-knowledge of what I believe to be true about Martians, since in either case I am thinking about the same intentional object—namely, something in the "world" of Martians. An intuitive basis for self-knowledge is pregiven, rationally or not, as a consistent psychological theme of *aboutness* in cognitive mental life.

During ordinary experiences of thinking, Husserl (1973, §36; 1977, 22; 1982, §114) suggests, constituted things are adumbrations of a pre-existing state of affairs, where each such state has a correlated irreal counterpart of *aboutness* to its anticipated actual reality. *Aboutness* is the affective psychological theme of an intentional object—meaning, psychological experience is motivated in pure psychology to be about *this* thing and not another. *This* thing matters immanently, and therefore it matters intuitively and thematically as well. Recall that an adumbration is first given to consciousness-formation as the simple shape and shadow of raw sensory data. As we repeat (by means of an iterating psychological process) this primitive relationship of parts to whole within a system of apperceptions, each element of sense and countersense for an intentional object "shadows" constitutive life as a potential for actualization. When we reason in the mode of "as if," the shadow of *aboutness* is then also a potential for doxic positing. For example, do you suppose that Martians call themselves "Martians?" Whether Martians truly exist, thinking about them *as if* they are actually real is the cognitive action here and now.

The potential for positing something as actually real is disclosed by the pure Ego's neutrality modification in pure psychology. To repeat, Husserl's (1982, §109) concept of *the neutrality modification* has no fixed terminology in scientific discourse or in ordinary language. Words do not yet exist to describe the content of a concatenation of elements before the quidditive "it-thing" is deemed likely for constitutive life. As the counterpart of all production in pre-conceptual experience, one's neutrality modification represents an eidetic necessity in the living present for disclosing to the knowing ego the idea of what is (or is not) to be posited as actually real. Under the psychological *epoché* and eidetic reduction, the neutrality modification is played out in cognitive mental life by rejecting or accepting a pre-existing element or its shadow when structuring the affair-complex for an intentional object. Husserl (§§106-7) explains this universal activity in the tradition of Brentano's work as the psychological ego's intentional acts of "denial" and "affirmation" within a cognitive "retro-related modification" of consciousness-formation. Because of this action, the pure Ego becomes rationally positioned for judging and valuing elements of *this* intentional object and not another during a steady flow of reasoning from pre-conceptual to conceptual space.

Recall that the pure Ego's neutrality modification is the rationale and theoretical basis of Husserl's eidetic reduction. By means of this reduction, the *eidos* of an intentional object is disclosed to both regressive and genetic reflections. Here, under the eidetic reduction, the subject seems to wonder, for example, "What am I talking about?" or, "What do I truly believe?" When the neutrality modification is applied as a method of reflection on the construction of an ongoing affair-complex, each parallel rejected or accepted countersense of a presentational object is seen to be thematically *about* the same matter in psychological consciousness of a potential unity. Therefore, both (a) the correlates of an actually real thing, and (b) its thematic shadow of *aboutness* that is experienced during acts of denial and affirmation of essential elements, disclose together the active phenomenological *eidos* here and now. In the doxic part of a constituted rational affective unity, the singular core essence of an *eidos* is lived as one's opinion, belief, and consequent self-knowledge of something actually real; while in its shadow part, a singular core essence is lived as the "mere thought" about the same *eidos* in its irreal pregivenness: "Oh, I'm just thinking about Martians." (*see* Husserl 1982, §109)

During pre-conceptual activities of consciousness-formation, at the origins of the subject's doxic positing, the psychological ego typically acts on the side of the rational construction of an anticipated constituted objectivity and its actual reality. One way to begin this intentional action, for example, is to wonder what Martians would call themselves. An initial constitutive and actualizing act in pure psychology could also include doubting, remembering, wishing, and so on. Any action meant to deem an actual reality likely for an intentional object, in effect, "moves" one's rational thoughts away from its position of neutrality between the doxic positing part and its indeterminate irreal counterpart. (see Husserl 1982, §114) By such action, an enduring separation of psychological processes of judging- and valuing-acts within a streaming mental process of *thinking* is established during the ordinary psychic life of consciousness-formation. On one side of this separation stands the rational production of conscious awareness and actual reality in the world that is commonly talked about; while on the other side, our solipsistic thoughts stand in passive acceptance of that same production. Enacting this separation represents the genesis of rational thought in transcendental constitutive life.

Every rational consciousness is either an actual or potential "positing consciousness," Husserl (1982, §117) writes. "The earlier concept of 'actual positing,' [i.e., positing an actuality,] and along with it that of positionality, undergo therefore a corresponding extension" in reflections on constitutive life. In the living present of constitutive life, the subject's positing-acts and correlated positioning-acts of world-consciousness have the "unique primacy" in eidetic law and transcendental logic of initiating the production of actual reality. Simultaneous multiple psychological processes stream throughout all regions of pure and transcendental subjectivity in order to realize whatever was affirmed or rejected as the pure Ego's meant-as-meant being-sense for an intentional object. Anything that is self-evidently real in pure subjectivity has the potential for actual reality in transcendental subjectivity. One could think, for example, "I certainly do believe that an apple in each hand gives me two apples. This is self-evident. If I had two more hands, I could have two more apples. This is self-evident, too. Naturally, it's not possible to have four hands, but it's likely that I could put two apples in each hand to have four."

The above example points toward a mental process of rational thinking that is directed to fulfill one's self-knowledge of a matter that rises to the level of sensible meaning. During this flow of reasoning from pre-conceptual to conceptual space, the core essence of the irreality of apples-in-hand is preserved in free fantasy for action throughout the living present of constitutive life. At the same time, its intentional object is posited as presumptively real in pure subjectivity, and transcended in psychological processes toward constituting awareness of having-four-apples in the natural world. Certain that I could have two apples in hand, my doxic positing moves on to the potential of having four. The embodiment of the *eidos* of *apple* is then merely thought of in its shadow of *aboutness*—even while this adumbration is retained in memory as an eidetic necessity within an affair-complex for having apples in hand here and now. Any remaining potential for having four hands in life-world experience "passes away" (elapses) in pure psychology during the construction of actual reality for this positing consciousness.

Various intentional acts of positionality for rational thought have just occurred in this example of everyday positing consciousness. The mental process represented here was initiated in part by the pure Ego's "unique primacy" of intuition into one's corporeal-life of *handedness* amid an embodied natural world. Simultaneous psychological processes of acting upon the elements of hands, apples, and numerical categories within their particular worlds of pre-existing objects and acts serve to compose the affair-complex for the concatenation of having two hands and four apples. The irreality of the unified sense of this concatenation is valued as true and judged as likely in its logic of calculus, and then posited as actually real from the perspective of one's natural attitude during a relationship of empathy—where humans do not usually possess four hands within a tradition of reality construction.

Husserl (1982, §122) remarks that "a new eidetic modification now occurs" when positing an actual reality during intersubjective relationships of empathy. "The pure Ego can withdraw wholly from the positing [of something uniquely *mine* in solipsistic subjectivity, whereby]…it releases the positional correlate from its 'grip,' 'adverting to another theme' [in transcendental subjectivity]." Absent this release, one might fail to constitute the world of human co-existence as a world of common semblance; and in this event, I might come to disagree with you about some essential matter. Yet whether we are in agreement or in opposition regarding the true nature of things, psychological processes of positionality and positing produce an eidetic modification of an intentional object in the transcendental register. Sometimes these modifications occur rationally during intersubjective relationships by our intentional acts of passively letting something *be* just as it already *is*.

Rational thought in the transcendental register is an experience of the ego-*cogito* in Husserl's (1982, §122) system of ego-life, and points reflections toward the subject's consciousness of the posited and constituted full intentional Object—what Husserl calls the "being in the midst of all senses." Here, the intentionality of ego-life is centered in pure psychology as the "actionality mode" of the pure Ego's psychosubjectivity for the "articulated synthesis" of one's personal comportment in transcendental subjectivity. During the subject's ordinary activities of consciousness-formation, said comportment is directed toward an objectified *eidos* in worldly experience—but directed such that each rational act in cognitive mental life preserves an *eidos* within "a whole stream of mental processes" that is peculiarly *my own*. This action is indeed experienced in one's personal lifeworld "as the unity of one consciousness" for a constituted objectivity. A unity of consciousness is thus a teleological goal of the psychological ego within a flux of possibilities for the coming-into-being of a transcendental object of simple certainty and consistent presence. Manifestations of the essence of this mode of comportment are what we naïvely tend to see as rational conduct with appropriate affect when one is "being psychological" in the world that is commonly talked about.

The Affective Unity of Conscious Awareness

Naïvely judged by a multiplicity of personal and cultural norms, and depicted in mundane discourse as objectified overt behavior, non-rational human comportment is a presentational object in traditional theories of "abnormal" psychology. (*see* Nevid, Rathus, and Green 1994, 2-8) Husserl (1982, §84) suggests, however, that each example of the subject's overt behavior points reflections toward the "all-inclusive phenomenological structures" of pure consciousness that come under the comprehensive name of "intentionality."

244

An all-inclusive structure of intentional experience is the "general theme" of Husserl's (§82) object-oriented phenomenology, where eidetic structures are described in his theory of elements and evaluated in his phenomenology of reason. Yet in Husserl's (§63) theory of method, when the full intentional Object comes to presence in the midst of all senses, a structure of consciousness also includes a field of action for universal and contingent experiences of intentional comportment—rational or non-rational, individual and in groups.

When applying the method of *Psychognosia* for reflections on the subject's comportment, the thematic grip of ego-life is seen to be both object-oriented and act-oriented in the pre-conceptual flux of pure consciousness. A phenomenologist could then interpret representations of the knowing ego, the perceiving ego, the intersubjective ego, and so on, during an intentional flow of reasoning toward awareness of an object of the mind. Every bifurcation of ego-life has the same constitutive theme in its grip during this flow, since each performing ego is focused on the same meant-as-meant essence of an *eidos* within the various strata of consciousness-formation.

At every phase of consciousness-formation, however, the psychological experience of ego-life is properly evaluated in its field of action under the psychological *epoché*—not in Husserl's parallel object-oriented reflections, and not within a regional ontology of mundane psychology. But even so, without their intuitive presence throughout his work, the methods and practices of pure psychology could not provide the norms for Husserl's reconstructive genetic phenomenology. Likewise, the turn from solipsism to intersubjectivity would perhaps not occur in Husserl's transcendental idealism.

When the ego-*cogito* is busy with an anticipated full intentional Object, a field of psychological experience could be described in Husserl's (1982, §122) theory of method beginning with the pure Ego's "adverting to another theme" of world-consciousness. Seizing upon a new or different world of objects and acts is also the genesis of a transcendental phenomenological psychology of rational comportment. Husserl (§84) stresses that "ego-advertence, this being-busied-with-the-correlate object actionally, this being-directed-to-it (or also away from it and yet with the regard upon it) is not to be found in every mental process." Some mental processes of sensory response are non-intentional with regard to an immediate object of the mind.; and therefore, they represent only a "potential field of perception" in pure psychology. Since a potential *as such* is not a presentational object, non-intentional responses do not find their way into the methodology of object-oriented phenomenology as a norm practice for reductions and clarifications. Yet each of us could usually notice such responses in our own comportment and in the comportment of others.

There could occur with non-intentional sensory responses (such as a spontaneous laugh or shudder) what Husserl (1982, §84) calls an affective "stirring" in pure psychology. With such stirring, feelings, or "drives" as the genesis of a mental process, intentional acts of the psychological ego are aroused and carried out at "different distances" from the pure Ego's intentions for noticing something that matters in constitutive life. More generally, affective elements of an original matter and its perceived shadow of thematic *aboutness* are motivated to be retained or to elapse during the ongoing composition of an affair-complex. For example, when the pure Ego intends to experience the *eidos* of *sorrow*, the psychological ego is aroused to enact the the reality of the phenomenon of sorrow. This action could include "revisiting" an element of non-intentional affective response to physical sensation, such as seeing a baby's crying as thematic for a sorrowful response. By reiterating this original experience, the pure Ego could then live that element affectively (one "undergoes suffering") that is already correlated in transcendental subjectivity as an adumbrated part of the objectivity called "sorrow."

Or else, one's affective stirring elapses in its shadow of thematic *aboutness*, even as a mental process flows on to another theme and to another *cogito* during the constitutive life of an intentional object. As our thoughts move on within a flow of reasoning during the normal course of consciousness-formation, and the necessary elements of (say) being sorrowful pass away as contingency demands, the psychological ego is aroused in the living present to realize the presence of a new theme of elements, and then another. However, when elements of sorrowfulness are retained during the movement of an object of the mind from pre-conceptual to conceptual space, a unity of awareness could include the apprehended analogous affect of sorrow within a system of intuitive apperceptions. One's evoked affect of sorrow would then "feel" similar to a pregiven physical sensation. This situation seems to hold for each experience of psychic life, and is thus part of the all-inclusive structure of intentionality for a unity of consciousness in the midst of all senses. "With respect to their own essence," Husserl (1982, §84) writes, our experiences of affective stirrings "are likewise already 'consciousness of something.' As a consequence…[we have] accepted this cogitatio [of ego-advertance to an affect] as a particular modality of…[universal] intentionality."

During both rational and non-rational comportment, the psychological ego performs specifically aroused acts in order to realize an affective unity in conscious awareness. As the pure Ego's psychosubjectivity in the transcendental register, the psychological ego represents the *cogito* of extra-physical consciousness in one's naïve natural world. Specifically, the psychological *cogito* lives knowingly and affectively during life-world experiences within bounds of a mental process of intentional action. From the phenomenological psychological perspective in Husserl's tradition, living a succession of multiple transcending acts amid an intentional mental process is one way that we humans are being psychological in the world that is commonly talked about. The subject's experience of an affect during this process points toward an underlying theme for the pure Ego during consciousness-formation—namely, an immanent psychological theme of *aboutness* and its correlated affect that remains a consistent direction of action toward an object in the midst of all senses.

At the genesis of rational comportment, the psychological ego begins a sequence of cognitive action so that what is apperceived as essential necessity might be gathered in eidetic concatenations according to an affective orientation of awareness. This orientation is experienced as one's personal point of view amid an idealized and objectified surrounding of common semblance. In the conceptual space of our mutual constructions of objective reality and absolute truth—where things are already *mine* and *theirs*—this affect is *mine*: "This is what I truly feel,"or else "I really don't care." Elements of an intentional object are static and pregiven in the spatiotemporality of a mental process during personal lifeworld experience, and pre-existing objects of the natural world are at a relative stasis for judgments in the living present. Here, the living present exists not only as the pure Ego's center of volition, but also as the psychological ego's standpoint in relation to "the data of place" (*Lokaldaten*) for the synthesized all-space and one-time of conscious awareness. (*see* Husserl 1964a, 25) The living present thus provides the psychological ego's spatiotemporal and affective orientation for transcending acts.

The psychological ego represents the psyche in the world of transcendental objects and naturalized affects, but it does not therefore represent our natural attitude toward such irreal things. Instead, that role in ego-life is fulfilled by the transcendental ego under the transcendental *epoché*. The primary role of the psychological ego in transcendental phenomenological psychology is to act upon object-oriented elements of affective significance with normative judging- and valuing-acts within a pregiven psychic order of constitution. This action fulfills the cognitive function for an intentional object to be constituted here and now according to the transcendental ego's form of ideation for spatial unities and the pure Ego's internal time-consciousness of temporal duration. Under the psychological *epoché* and reduction, the appearances of what would be mere phases of space and time from the natural attitude point toward an anticipated unity of those same phases in pre-empirical, pre-conceptual, and pre-linguistic performances of consciousness-formation. An intentional form of ideation for this same unity, embodied and correlated with certainty in the horizon of metaphysics, pictures for the psychological ego only the content of each posited phase of idealized linear time and rectilinear space that matters within an apperceptive system of awareness.

Affectively motivated psychological process within a life-span system of transcending apperceptions effectively cause the presence of our natural attitude to be grasped as one's day-to-day awareness of objective reality. For example, we typically become aware that a chicken and a duck are both birds *by nature*, since both have hyletic feather-stuff given to apperception as an element of an embodied bird-object—leaving aside here any element of the feather-stuff of penguins. Processes of cognitive action group the essential elements of an object in the natural world, but only as that object is pictured in the transcendental ego's form of ideation here and now. A form of ideation for the full intentional Object pre-exists in order for an eidetically lawful concatenation of elements to be constructed within an affair-complex of anticipated actual reality. Subsequent psychological processes synthesize and objectify the elements of an affair-complex so as to constitute one's transcendental consciousness of a "unity within all senses." By means of this intentional function—throughout all transcending acts of retention and elapse of elements during relationships of empathy—whatever is depicted as intended in the "pre-empirical flow of time" remains static and constant ("held fast") within the psychological ego's contingent mental formation. (*see* Gurwitsch 1964, 161-62; Husserl 1964a, 165-67)

When empirical evidence for an object of the mind is anticipated and then apperceived, the intentional object's phenomenologized appearance exhibits a uniform content in the natural world—meaning, essential elements of consciousness-formation have been ordered by the psychological ego to be a unity of embodied concretions within the horizon of Nature in its totality. During pre-conceptual experiences of transcendental subjectivity, there is, as it were, a continual "thickening" of the empirical givenness of something in one's naïve natural world. Because of the intentional function to objectify raw sensory stuff of hyletic perceptions, higher-level apperceptions are of necessary groups of essential elements within an eidetically lawful composition for a unified whole structure. Said structure is typically constructed from the natural attitude to be empirically concrete and thus opaque. By disclosing its elements as they are ordered by the psychological ego, the method of *epoché* and eidetic reduction seem to spread out for genetic reflections the givenness of empirical reality for an *eidos*. Empirical evidence of reality shows itself in an affair-complex, for example, by the following partial concatenation of bracketed elements for one's conscious awareness of the *eidos* called "chicken":

$$((\text{bird}=[\text{feathers}]\oplus[\text{claws}]\oplus[\text{beak}]\oplus[\ldots])$$
$$\oplus(\text{doesn't fly}=[\text{not-duck}]\oplus([\text{not-goose}]\oplus[\ldots])).$$

While a concatenation of affirmed and denied elements is not usually symmetrical or open-ended, psychological processes affect its orderly and coherent continuation during a mental life of perceiving, remembering, constructing, and so on. For instance, in accordance with the transcendental logic of eidetic associations, I cannot become aware of the experience of sorrow unless and until there is reason for the psychological ego to act upon an element of the *eidos* of *sorrow*. Sorrow endures as my psychological theme only as long as there is reason to be so aroused in eidetic concatenations. As each intentional act is called for by the pure Ego, for so long as my psychological theme is about sorrow, at least one act of the psychological ego will be a sorrow-act within a psychological process of judgments and valuations. More fundamentally, the *eidos* of *sorrow* is in my thematic grip as an affective orientation throughout constitutive life as long as a posited reality is intended to be lived sorrowfully; and my lived experience of suffering sorrow will continue for as long as sorrow endures as the core essence of an eidetic affair-complex.

In Husserl's (1982, §35) *Ideas I*, mental processes are sometimes characterized as undifferentiated actionality in pure psychology. Given from his (§84) object-oriented phenomenology of reason, both the action and non-action of mental life are collectively referred to as *cogitationes*—meaning in Husserl's tradition, the human intentionality directed toward objects by means of cognitions. The psychosubjectivity of this experience is interpreted as the psychological ego, which is the ego-subject of psychic life that carries out a theme of eidetic necessity in processes of affectively motivated cognitive action. In Husserl's (1973b, §44) theory of transcendental constitution, the psychological ego discloses by its acts of arousal "'my animate organism' and 'my psyche', or myself as a psychophysical unity—in the latter, my personal ego, who operates in this animate organism and, 'by means of' it…is affected by this world." When we live our acts of arousal with the object of that arousal, together as a psychophysical unity here and now, the experience of pure psychology gains presence in the transcendental register as an affective union of body and soul. The psychological ego presents to reflections our personal way that this union is expressed to one's self and to others.

During the normal course of psychosubjectivity for said union, our thetic inner life of pure and transcendental subjectivity is directed toward the external nonthetic space of objectified Nature. Husserl (1982, §62) noticed that in the conceptual space of natural things, the human soul of affective experience is embodied and correlated to mean "my being-as-ego" in the world of co-existence and common semblance. At greater depths of consciousness-formation, elements of this life-span state of affairs represent the existentiality of the pure Ego, *I*, in fundamental relationships to its *Other*. Bound by these limits of thetic givenness, everything that is believed to exist with meaning and posited as factually real within the horizons of ontology and epistemology, or as absolutely true and certain within the horizon of metaphysics, could be embodied by acts of the psychological ego in nonthetic space as well.

Embodied in Nature by multiple and simultaneous psychological processes, the appearance and being-sense of an actually real object approximate pregiven idealized dimensions of color, shape, distance, and so on. By this ordinary method of consciousness-formation, we constitute what is believed to be typical in one's personal lifeworld, including what is believed to be a typical affective orientation toward others. Husserl (1970, §9.b) distinguishes the constitution of typicality as occurring within the "Galilian" worldview of approximations—where typical things are seen in one's naïve natural world not only as approximations of ideal dimensions in the transcendental register, but also as intuitive approximations of an object's original givenness during the course of intellectual and affective development.

Typical things of transcendental subjectivity are objectified things of embodied dimensions within pre-conceptual and pre-linguistic categories of differentiated *thingness*. We tend to experience these categories and their correlates as implicates of natural cause when constituting one's self-knowledge of the nature of things. During the ongoing development of a system of rational apperceptions—including our most sophisticated apperceptions in scientific methodologies—categories of objectified things are grasped by the psychological ego as eidetic forms of approximation. For example, a chicken and a wren are both similar and different within the approximating form of "bird" that further differentiates them from (say) the *thingness* of "dog." At the conceptual level of similarity and difference in the world that is commonly talked about, embodied objects are similar to one another in that each is experienced within the horizon of metaphysics as something that is present and endures by natural cause; yet each is different in one's awareness of its epistemic sense and ontic meaning of individual pre-conceptual *thingness*.

Every core essence of an embodied object has its own pre-conceptual mental formation of internal time-consciousness and psychological theme of *aboutness* within the *a priori* and contingent horizons—including the objectification of one's physical self (*Ichlieb*). From the genesis of the psychic life, and continuing throughout the constitution of an affective unity, there is thus an epistemic and ontic similarity of dimensions between the physical form and organic functions of one's body and all embodied things correlated in the horizon of metaphysics. (Husserl 1980a, §§63f) There is also a similarity between a pre-linguistic construction of elements for an intentional object and one's utterance of that object's *thingness* in linguistic empathy. It is precisely this *likeness* of sense, meaning, and certainty in pre-conceptual and conceptual space that gives evidence of psychological processes of thematic unifying-acts amid an "interlaced" structure of intentional experience. Unifying-acts are mostly grouping-acts for composing concatenations of essential elements within an eidetic affair-complex. (*see* Husserl 1982, §49)

Still, Husserl (1982, §35 note 79) admitted in 1913 that he could not clarify completely the idea of a psychological process of such "actional" (*aktuelle*) connections within the mental sphere of pure consciousness, especially since concatenations also include a modality of "non-actionality" (*Inaktualität*) or passivity during intersubjective relationships. While reflecting on the pure psychology of this experience, Husserl (§85) nevertheless described an affectively motivated succession of cognitive processes within a continuous streaming of mental activity—all directed toward constituting an object of the mind. By means of this action in the transcendental register, the psychological ego synthesizes one's human spirit and intentionally embodied worldly existence as a unity of awareness during life-world experiences with others. In Husserl's theory of inquiry, an affective synthesis of body and soul represents "the peculiar Object of psychology" in the world of human co-existence and common semblance. Enacting this synthesis in thought and speech represents the essence of psychic life in transcendental phenomenological psychology.

The Intentional Function of Intersubjectivity

Among the "simultaneously coaffecting substrates" of pure and transcendental consciousness, a state of similarity-and-difference for an *eidos* is "co-given originaliter" for apperceptions of elements deemed necessary by the pure Ego to constitute *this* objectivity and not another. (Husserl 1973a, §33) When preconstituted in pure subjectivity and retained in eidetic memory, forms of similarity-and-difference are at hand for contingent modification of an intentional object in the transcendental register. Said forms are thus intellectually seen in the living present with adequate givenness during intersubjective relationships, where they are seized upon in empathy as correlates of actual reality and objective truth. With our acts of simple and higher-level apperceptions, the core essence of an intentional object is typically recognized within these forms in conceptual space; and by this constitutive method, a singular core essence is passively accepted as pre-existing within a pregiven form of idealized objective reality for an original *eidos*. In this way, an objectified thing is present in conscious awareness according to its unique "spatial position" of sense and meaning relative to similarities and differences with other previously objectified things. (§43.b)

Psychological processes of cognitive action and non-action fulfill the intentional function for constructing a relationship of similarity-and-difference for the core essence of an *eidos* in the world for us all. Due to this intersubjective orientation toward common semblance, natural things are constituted as objectified things that are analogous in shape, color, distance, and so on within their taxonomies of factual matters. During the psychic order that makes use of this function for positing judgments and valuations, each objectified thing has its own spatial position within pre-existing categories of sense and meaning: "This thing is a bird." Each objective thing also exhibits its own embodied categorial identity for what is preconstituted and now passively accepted: "This bird is a chicken." Similarly, "I am a human. Humans behave according to their true nature." When the psyche wills to constitute an intentional object to be objectively real, the pure Ego usually makes an analogy of sense and meaning with other objective things. Correlated in the horizon of metaphysics for apodictic certainty, an analogy is constructed for an intentional object within pregiven categories of objects in one's sociocultural surroundings. Analogies are thus typically present in awareness as metaphysical presuppositions regarding the true nature of things.

Constructing the complex spatial position of a full intentional Object during intersubjective relationships begins with a concern for the existential otherness of that object's elements—rather than with concern for the pure Ego's sense of solipsistic *place* for an object in the transcendental register. Following *entrée* into an empathetic relationship (by means of the transcendental *epoché*), an intentional object is seen to exist with sense and meaning relative to its similarity and difference with a pregiven idealized object. For instance, a chicken is seen to be more similar to a duck in size and shape than to a wren. A single chicken is more similar to a single wren than to a flock of ducks. The spatial position of objectified things implies the pre-existence of correlating-acts within and between concatenations of necessary forms of similarity-and-difference—meaning, a multi-form and a unity-form are presented together for judgments of common semblance within a system of apperceptions. Each pre-conceptual correlation of these elements is the result of a cognitive act of retrogression (*Rückgang*), where the psychological ego returns in eidetic memory to the essence of its original ontic psychological theme and epistemic form of ideation in order to hold constant whatever is intended and posited to be self-evidently real "for everyone." (*see* Husserl 1973a, §5)

Husserl (Eley 1973, 416-19) sometimes uses the term "analogy" in the context of reality construction in order to signify the pure Ego's predication of the same categorial being-sense of an *eidos*, both during one's intersubjective relationships and during one's pre-predicative experiences with the core essence of that same idea. In the pure Ego's appresentational system, an analogy refers to a "perennial" "semblance of semblance" that directs the positing of a transcendental unity of apperception in one's naïve natural world. A difference in the solipsistic sense of a particular thing for me only is thus transcended during our relationships of empathy so as to gain presence as the similarity of appearances typically given to everyone—which is, namely, the appearance of unity for the correlate "*I* with *Other*." Building upon this correlate in linguistic empathy, for example, one's belief in the similarity of appearances for pregiven things shows itself in mundane philosophy and science as the intuitive basis of analogies between causality and the symbolic representations of a factual nature. (*see* Husserl 1982, §52)

Still, one's self-knowledge of objectified things cannot exist in empathy without a transcendental method of analogy pregiven in pure psychology; and indeed, the psychological ego engages such a method as a norm of practice amid a life-span system of intersubjective apperceptions. The comparability and identity of objectified things are in this system as contingent matters in one's habitual thought and speech (and in our "normative" sciences of ethics, grammar, and logic as well), for we must *choose* to make these connections of objectified sense and meaning. Yet neither can one's ordinary self-knowledge of objective things exist outside a horizon of potential for an analogy that provides apodictic certainty of common semblance. Quite creatively, our natural attitude itself provides a horizon of being-sense when we choose to make analogies between the objectified nature of things. In an analogy of similarities within the horizon of our natural attitude, one could say with certainty, for example, "I worked like a dog today," or "*S* is *p* and *q*."

During our intersubjective experiences of daily life, the fulfilled being-sense for any particular analogy is a correlate of how pregiven things are (diachronically) similar in empathy, even while simultaneously different "in this case" of (synchronic) sense and meaning. Husserl (1970, §62 note 4) remarked that it is particularly difficult from the natural attitude for us to grasp the beginnings in pure psychology of a method of analogy for recognizing pregiven categories of objectified things. How could I possibly know, for instance, how a dog "works" as a matter of human work ethic? An analogy clearly represents the construction and use of an absurdity of non-reason during apperceptions of common semblance. Most especially perhaps, it is difficult for us to grasp the presence of other ego-subjects as intentional modifications by analogy of one's corporeal- or spirit-life in pre-conceptual space; since in ordinary life-world experience, we tend to see other humans as living existents of an undifferentiated body and soul.

Even so, the psychological theme of being-human-with-others could be given "originaliter" as contingent forms of similarity-and-difference for adumbrated elements of the *eidos* of *being human*. Being human would not then be siezed upon as a species of undifferentiated things in solipsistic structures, and would not be passively experienced solely as an objectified (I-You or I-Other) unity-form of common semblance. Instead, with our free fantasy directed toward self-knowledge of human co-existence, each of us could grasp both general and particular similarities and differences between ego-subjects as eidetic forms of differentiated objectified features and characteristic conduct. (*see* Husserl 1980a, §§13f) It follows that these forms could also be used to construct the phenomenologized appearance of *me myself* in empathy. By extension of this everyday correlative method of consciousness-formation, we could grasp the apperances of others as similar but different during their "personal" expressions of embodied intersubjectivity. Any individualizing-act of this sort in transcendental subjectivity points toward the universal lived experience of constructing an affair of idealized similarity-and-difference for *this* objective thing and not another in the world for us all.

An original form of apperception for analogous unities is repeated during the formation of a life-span state of affairs for the intersubjective correlate "*I* with *Other*." And indeed, the genesis of *any* intersubjective relationship in the world for us all—including retrogressions to elements of solipsistic subjectivity in one's personal lifeworld—is this same lived experience of apperception. A proper region of inquiry for transcendental phenomenological psychology is therefore the living-present psychosubjectivity of "personal" corporeal- and spirit-life that is seen in its similarities and differences during intersubjective relationships. Examples of such comportment for constructing idealized approximations "for everyone" are revealed in naïve psychological theories of "personality." (*see* Hall and Lindzey 1978, 477-8)

During ordinary consciousness-formation, the intentional methods and habitual practices of pure psychology are experienced intersubjectively as one's cognitive mental life of action and non-action with others—an experienced especially seen when we judge and value conditions of similarity-and-difference for a matter of mutual *sense*. The psychological ego is typically in its modality of non-action when the pure Ego intends *not* to modify in empathy what is pregiven as the preconstituted appearance of a phenomenological *eidos*. But when the psychological ego enacts what Husserl (Fink 1995, §11) calls the phenomenologizing ego's "retro-inquiry" (*Rückfrage*) as a transcendental modification of the appearance of something preconstituted, other cognitive acts then proceed to gather and group reason-as-evidence for one's apodictic belief and self-evident truth about an *eidos* here and now. Something is constructed in this manner to be objectively true, both for *me myself* and for everyone in the world of common semblance.

To be sure, if this subsequent action fails or if an original idea is forgotten, further retrogressive cognitive acts by the psychological ego are no longer aroused in the world of common semblance—even as the singular core essence for another *eidos* is thematically seized upon within a mental process of constitution. It is surely the case, as well, that an *eidos* could be constituted during intersubjective relationships as true for me but not for you. In the normal course of events, however, each of us constructs an enduring actual reality for the objectification of my-life-with-their-life in analogous forms of similarity-and-difference with one's ownness-essence and the apperceived and appresented lives of others. Building up this eidetic structure of unity for an object of common semblance is the lived experience and intentional function of the psychological phenomenon of intersubjectivity.

The Phenomenological "Person"

One's sprit-life of imagination and intuition is not analogous with any representation of objectified psychological phenomena, although manifestations of the human spirit could be experienced by each of us and described as "psychological" in mundane theoretical discourse. From the phenomenological attitude (versus naïve presuppositions of natural cause), one's spirit-life is an element of *motivation* within a logic of calculus that is necessary for us to be consciously aware of something here and now. (*see* Husserl 1982, §47) In this light, transcendental phenomenological psychology is not simply a regressive examination that describes mental acts as static things in pure psychology. Instead, transcendental phenomenological psychology means to clarify the human spirit and psychic life present when one is conscious of something in the world that is commonly talked about—and in particular, to explain the dynamics of mental life that is motivated by our "soulish" spirit in the world of co-existence and common semblance. Husserl (1977, 99) admits, however, that his study of the human spirit and psychic life lack "a most broad concept of 'person,' which is indispensable [for phenomenological psychology]."

Perhaps the most general sense of the phenomenological "person" is given by Husserl (1973b, §45) as a transcendental dialectic of the conflicts, tensions, and contradictions found in the ego-life of the meaningful human subject. Here, in his "Fifth Cartesian Meditation," Husserl reduced from our intersubjective relationships of empathy the essence of intentional experience in the transcendental register that is "peculiarly my own." When the transcendental *epoché* is applied rigorously in reflections on the subject's apperceived unity of human co-existence, the exterior manifestations of one's animate organism and physiological consciousness are bracketed as dependencies of the pregiven natural world—the world of metaphysical embodiment and common semblance that goes without saying as objectively real and concretely present. Whatever is then left outside of this bracketed calculus for a naturalistic abstraction is one's "spiritual ownness" in transcendental consciousness. One's spiritual ownness is typically experienced in agreement with a (socially mediated) pre-existing manifold of embodied dimensions; and within these dimensions, the phenomenological "person" is revealed as "my personal ego" in human co-existence. Husserl (1977, 168) strongly suggests that the so-called nature of "people" is never a proper theme for phenomenological examinations of the psychic life of persons.

With each phenomenological reduction, psychological reflections are directed to the motivating spirit-life of consciousness-formation in pure psychology—but only as our spirit of autonomy and agency is played out during the immediate experience of cognitive mental life that is *my own* here and now. A psychological theme of cognitive action points toward the pure Ego's intentions to live the ownness-essence and psychic being of the personal ego that is affected by the external world and one's objectified place within it. This intention is ordinarily fulfilled during experiences of empathy, where the pure Ego's internal time-consciousness of *me-in-my-world* is constantly present as the transcendental ego's temporalized past, present, and anticipated future in the world of human co-existence. When the *eidos* of *my life* is similarly reduced to its ownness-essence with feelings of empathy, the objectification of *my life as a person* is reconstructed and given to consciousness-formation as one's "memories [of] my successive-temporal life." (Fink 1995, 169) A sense of being a "person" is thus bestowed upon the unity and subsequent objectification of one's ownness-essence within a "revisted" experience of intersubjectivity. The sense and meaning of being a "person" is immanent in transcendental consciousness "similar to the way that something [exists] in memory."

Just as with something retained in memory, we are neither immediately nor spontaneously aware of the subjective origins of a "person." Something pregiven in the past of the internal time-consciousness of *my life*, or that is anticipated in its future, exists but partially for action in the living present as alien to solipsistic subjectivity—meaning, the pregivenness of one's ownness-essence is prone to be objectified as an intersubjective "person" during apperceptions of contingent worldly experiences. Here, the transcendental ego cannot directly grasp the *never-been* or *not-yet* elements of the intentional object *my life*, although we could anticipate such things as actually real and act in pure psychology *as if* they are objectively true. A fully-fledged transcendental object includes both its adequate givenness in empathy, as well as its inadequately pregiven and anticipated elements retained in eidetic memories of solipsistic subjectivity. In effect, our memories of a pattern of eidetic associations anticipate the construction of a rational affective when we seize upon the *eidos* of *my life as a person*. We tend to reproduce from memory only what has already been anticipated to be actually real and objectively true, even when these things have perhaps never been previously constituted to be so.

Husserl (1964a, 94-6) suggests that one's memory of what is salient for consciousness-formation represents an "intuitive capacity" of intentional experience for the personal ego. Our reproductive memory intuitively establishes a "null-point" (*Null-Oder*) in cognitive mental life between retained elements that are at variable distances from the pure Ego's regard here and now—such as the solipsism of my ownness-essence versus my intersubjectivity in the world that is commonly talked about. The living present of transcendental subjectivity is "always and essentially the edge-point [*Randpunkt*] of an interval in time," where the recent past and an immediate anticipation are "closest" to the pure Ego's "personal" intentions during the internal time of constitutive life. Beginning from a temporal null-point in pure psychology, a cognitive balance of (pregiven) "before" and (anticipated) "after" is maintained as the horizon for a chain of intervals that make up a psychic order of constitution for an intentional object. By means of this order, the psychological ego establishes "the external point of the actual now" in conscious awareness. The "actual now" also represents the objectively real time of *my life as a person*, and is thus at hand for judgements when one's ownness-essence is positioned amid this same pre-existing nonlinear sequence of temporal intervals.

The psychological ego acts to retain this state of affairs in eidetic memory as an ongoing pattern for knowing something actually real in one's personal lifeworld. By will of the psyche in constitutive life, the psychological ego is only thematically aware of the internal time of intentional acts that directs the pattern's fulfillment. The pure Ego's apprehension of non-linear before-and-after internal time is an arousal to order in eidetically lawful succession not only the psychological ego's transcending acts, but also by those acts the necessary psychic order of ego-life for each bifurcated performing ego. (see Husserl 1964a, 164) The actual posited clock- or historical-time of

255

any object phenomenon represents an intentionally embodied time of temporal duration, such as comprehending the actually real growth of an apple from its seed. One's self-knowledge of this particular relationship is asymptotically adjusted in transcendental consciousness in order to "fit" idealized dimensions appresented with one's personal experiences with the pregiven typicality of before-and-after relationships. As a result of this pregivenness, we then seem to know intuitively that the seed is planted in order to grow the fruit.

Yet during the pre-conceptual to conceptual flow of reasoning in the correlated one-time of the living present, an apple and its seed co-exist within an irreal "all-space" (*All-Raumes*) of transcendental consciousness. The parallel times of the apple and its seed pre-exist together amid the flux of potentials for each to gain presence in awareness separately as contingencies demand. Temporal intervals of contingent experience are typically grasped all at once as the simultaneous synchronic/diachronic one-time of an actual apple and its irreal seed—or vice versa as each is ordered spatially for sense and meaning within its eidetic affair-complex. Similarly, each *cogito* in its world of objects and acts has its own pre-existence and ownness-essence with that world retained in eidetic memory. Consciousness of *my life as a person* is constituted within the internal time and enclosed space of one's personal interests in *this* world that is held in thematic grip by the transcendental ego's form of ideation here and now. We can never express from the natural attitude (or grasp in ordinary transcendental consciousness) the totality of being a person at the "the external point of the actual now." We experience but a fragment of that anticipated totality in empathy, even as we intentionally and consistently direct our thoughts toward that singularity during life-world experience.

Whenever the subject's life-world experience is delimited by this same ordering of space and time, other *cogitos* and bifurcated egos within the pure Ego's "knowledge complex" are not thematically aware of the psychological ego's acts that asymptotically transcend subjective spatiotemporality. It follows, then, that our enduring psychological experience of being a "person" in transcendental subjectivity does not exist as actually real in one's day-to-day thematic grip—although we might indeed grasp our so-called personhood as an objectified phenomenon of embodied dimensions in one's sociocultural surroundings. Husserl (Fink 1995, 180) stresses that an enduring experience of *my life as a person* is nevertheless a necessary irreality in the transcendental register for constructing the oneness of conscious awareness in both his theory of elements and transcendental theory of method. Psychological processes for ordering the internal-time and all-space of one's memories and anticipations exist as necessary irrealities of personal experience during intersubjective relationships of empathy.

A synthesis of time and space is a theme of constitutive life that is followed throughout a genetic succession of eidetically lawful acts upon an object of the mind. And so, when the pure Ego's prescription for ordering the spatiotemporal *oneness* of conscious awareness is fulfilled in the transcendental register, a presentational object is intentionally about *this eidos* here and now. Clearly, transcending acts during consciousness-formation do not exist outside the psychological ego's horizon for memory and anticipation of retained elements. "By memories," Husserl (Fink 1995, 169) explains, "my successive-temporal life is constituted in modes of past, present, [and] future." Naïve expressions of *my life* point toward these constructive modes and their unity, and signify one's personal existence in life-span duration. The experience of *my life* is then typically measured in empathy along a polar continuum consisting of seconds, hours, years, decades, epochs, and so on, in one's intentionally embodied naïve natural world. The unique correlate of a unitary, homogeneous, objective time of *my life as a person* represents the pure Ego's *place* within the synthesized historical and actual time of a naturalized abstraction for a world of common semblance.

"Of course," Husserl (Fink 1995, 172) points out, the ego-life of a person does not exist in "individual isolation" in a world that is constituted solely along an intersubjective-pole of pregiven identifiable actualities—such as embodied clock-time or a history of personal relationships. Rather, each person also "struggles" for an idealized existence in the spatialized and temporalized surrounding of an absolutized Nature and its contingent world of objectified things. In Husserl's (p. 171) mature reflections, one's naïve natural world is constructed so as to pre-exist as a unity of co-existence and common semblance for intuitive (non-linear) activities of consciousness-formation. In order to perform its transcending acts, the psychological ego first situates the pregivenness of that world's retained elements along an idealized continuum of each person's "normal satisfaction of their endeavors, of their [so-called] 'needs,' in the personal horizon of their whole life."

Bound by the pure Ego's personal horizon of worldly wants and needs, the transcendental ego enters a relationship of empathy as the meaningful subject of one's natural attitude. During the normal course of events, when we join with our intersubjective partners in empathy we do so neither out of defense from pain or hope for pleasure, nor to infer the "inner life" of another. Instead, we typically act with feelings of empathy in order to answer the call of our human spirit of truth-seeking in one's personal lifeworld. When we then experience something that is believed to be genuinely true for all of us in empathy, whatever is intersubjectively here for *me myself* includes the truth of one's "personal" experience within the all-space of objective things. One's own naïve history of living knowingly in that space is constructed to be actually real here and now, even as *my life* gains presence as an affective unity that could be valued as true during the one-time of the living present. Reciprocally, the alter ego-life of intersubjective partnerships of persons and groups could be similarly valued for apperceptions of analogous semblance or essential differences in the world that is commonly talked about.

From the natural attitude, one's experience of being a person includes a regard for others also living naturally. And yet, Husserl (Fink 1995, 171) remarks, one's "normal satisfaction" from this perspective is "relative, temporary, with a finitude that never stands firm." One's belief in an objectively true nature of personal relationships points toward the pure Ego's objectifications of an idealized and absolutized Nature that can only be aimed at asymptotically in the transcendental ego's form of ideation. An idealized "nature" of human co-existence is eidetically depicted as something typical for everyone, but not experienced concretely as actually real during personal interactions. Consequently, we correlate in empathy the *eidos* of *my life* with ideations of an absolute Nature in order to apperceive life-world experiences that seem to be at hand for everyone. This event represents the lived experience of one's natural attitude toward other ego-subjects within the horizon of metaphysics. Here, we tend to believe with certainty the nature of meaningful categories of persons within an idealized world of objectified co-existence. The communal, historical, and cultural givenness of the correlates of objectified co-existence point toward the domain of inquiry in Husserl's science of essences for the discipline of phenomenological anthropology. (*see* Husserl 1981, 315-323)

The co-existence of *persons* is lived by means of the pure Ego's life-span synthesis of one's experiences with the objectified existence of others. The phenomenon of patriotism is an example of the realization of this synthesis; where in empathy, we express the unity of a "collective personality." (see Stein 2000, 133f) On the other hand, the normal form of co-existence with the otherness of *people* during life-world experience traces out the intentionally constructed "historical environing" that affirms the "sort of thing in which [a person] can fulfill his needs or which lets him hope for a unity for his life in satisfactory [objectified] form." (Fink 1995, 172) Everyday references to one's people, as well as expressions of "people" in the sense of "everyone," signify an objectified group of ego-subjects (actual or imagined) with whom we are engaged with on-going feelings of empathy. Such references point toward our presuppositions about "the social character of the world of common experience"—the world of objects and acts that is seen as an eidetic composition of intersubjective "community." (*see* Gurwitsch 1972, 124f) Said composition is correlated in the horizon of metaphysics to become the idealized normal form of spatiotemporal environing for the naïve nature of the *socius*—from the Latin, meaning having something in common. Insight into the human world of common spatiotemporal environing represents the domain of inquiry for phenomenological sociology.

In Husserl's (Fink 1995, 172) transcendental theory of method, we stand in "normal hope" of fulfilling one's "needs" when constructing the actual reality for *my life as a person*. Expressions of one's needs during this intersubjective performance refer to the valuation of a satisfactory form for the *eidos* of *my life* within an affairness of empathy. As a typical norm of practice for the psychological ego, from the beginnings of our cognitive development and continuing throughout our communal interactions, there is but a single idealized normal form of actual reality for an object of the mind—namely, an affective unity in thought and speech. *My life as a person* is one such unity that is valued and judged in the living present of ordinary experience. More specifically, the psychological ego composes a unity of personal existence by means its acts that transcend all at once the inadequate "alien" and the "normal" pregivenness of adumbrations of *my life*. These life-span elements co-exist for apperceptions with things that are seen within the intersubjective "generative context" of one's social, cultural, and political surroundings. (see Fink 1995, 171-2) When correlated in the horizon of metaphysics, the normal form of personal existence includes the alien (nonthetic) pregivenness of both other persons and groups of persons in temporal duration. Consequently, the mutually constructed inter-generational existence of the *Other* goes without saying as infinite and historical in the pure Ego's (thetic) personal horizon.

Because of the psychological ego's retention of elements that are pre-given *there* throughout the generations for "everyone"—and that are then passively accepted and grasped in empathy as *my own* here and now—a person's individual needs are typically fulfilled in the transcendental register during our ongoing intersubjective parterships with groups of objectified "friends," "family," or "nation." (Fink 1995, 171-2) Our consistent strivings to fulfill one's needs during these relationships presents a life-span horizon of so-called empathetic endeavors with the objectified *Other*. Absent the psychological ego's *telos* of an affective unity within this horizon, a singular correlate of sense, meaning, semblance, and actual reality for one's ownness-essence could become ambiguous during apperceptions of similarities and differences for *my life as a person*. Although recurring and habitual transformations and transitions between objects take place during one's intersubjective relationships, there is only one universal form of apperception for any synthesized affective unity in the pure Ego's personal horizon. The meaning and intelligibility of this form is exemplified in thought and speech as a norm of objective truth.

A presupposition of objective truth is correlated in the horizon of metaphysics and naïvely experienced as something absolute—since this is all that I *can* determine about the *eidos* of *truth* with reason and evidence from the natural attitude. The validity of a norm of objective truth consequently goes without saying for intuitions and anticipations during constitutive life. Although anticipations could fail or be forgotten in transcendental subjectivity, the psychological ego usually constructs an idealized form of absolute reality and objective truth for an intentional object during a relationship of empathy. Husserl's (1973b, §61) "psychological" concept of *empathy* in the pure Ego's personal horizon is correlated in the horizon of ontology as a substrate of intersubjective *being* and *doing*; and so, clearly, the concept does not refer only to a social activity for a group of persons or to our spirit of communalization. Empathetic experience also represents our individual actions that are intended to establish a cognitively balanced idealized temporal connection of *truth* between an intuitive grasp of *me myself* and the enduring *eidos* of *my life as a person*.

It seems clear as well that the concept of *empathy* is not to be understood in Husserl's work entirely as "the experience of the other" (*Fremderfahrung*). Rather, a relationship of empathy is an intentionally constructed state of affairs for the pure Ego in the transcendental register. In order to clarify the normal form of empathetic affairness, Husserl (1973b, §42f) makes the distinction that one's habitual comportment toward other persons is subsumed under his theory of "intropathy." (*see also* Steinbock 1995, 63f) This means that with our apperceptions of an objectified person or community of persons as being *Other* to one's ownness-essence, there exists in empathy the possibility for the transcendental ego's bias toward objective truth as a privileging attitude regarding elements of normality and abnormality. From within one's personal horizon, for example, we might say intropathically, "I feel the same as you about this. Don't we all? Only someone lacking in normal feelings or good judgment would fail to do so."

In empathy, Husserl (1980a, §50) writes, "a person is precisely a person who represents, feels, evaluates, strives, and acts and who, in every such personal act, stands in relation to something, to objects in his surrounding world." During our intersubjective experiences with the surrounding world, connections of temporal intervals of spatial categories are constructed by the psychological ego for both individual persons as intentional objects, and for objectified groups of persons—and it is here that *my life as a person* is constructed to be a rational affective unity. In the normal course of events, this unity has already been correlated in the horizon of metaphysics such that its idealized form is intellectually seen by the transcendental ego to exist as valid for everyone in empathy. An empathetic relationship of intersubjective partnerships thus includes a cognitively balanced experience and idealized reality for *me myself* as a synthesized unity in the world of human co-existence. The pure Ego seems to seek constant experiential proof of validity for this unity during our strivings for consistency. As the surrounding world of common semblance changes with our maturing and developing intersubjective partnerships, we usually change *as persons* intropathically in order to maintain an intuitive sense of validity for *me myself* according to a norm of objective truth.

The subject's personal lifeworld includes pre-conceptual correlates of sense and meaning for individual persons, groups of persons, and generations of persons in one's sociocultural surroundings. These and other thematically "personal" elements in the transcendental register are carried forward through protension as elements of the affective unity of *my life* in conceptual space—the space of reasoning wherein "I conceive" of *me myself* during life-world experiences. The personal ego thus assumes a place (here and now) within a relationship of ("alien") difference and ("normal") similarity to others in the world of co-existence and common semblance. (*see* Husserl 1973b, §29) When delimited during consciousness-formation by the pure Ego's personal horizon for what is seized upon as *my own*, we tend to think and speak of the unity of *me myself* as a "person" in the world that is commonly talked about.

According to Husserl's (Fink 1995, 169-70) transcendental theory of world-constitution, the pure Ego intends to have the normal form of a personal lifeworld in conscious awareness; and so, a teleological goal of the psychological ego is to compose the semblance of *me myself* to be an affective unity of actual reality and objective truth during the subject's experiences of co-existence. The first act of the psychological ego toward this goal is to adumbrate the pregiven universal life-world of its elements of ideation for a delimited affairness of empathy within the pure Ego's personal horizon. Husserl (p. 171) explains that these transcending acts "aim after a universal accord [between ego-subjects] through correction" of the "open-ended environing" that is pregiven as the world for us all. Seen under the *epoché* as a typical norm of practice, retained elements of the life-world are intersubjectively "appropriated…practically and then also theoretically, and that [sense of co-existence is] again then put to practical use" for synthesizing *my life as a person* within the pure Ego's now-communalized eidetic affair-complex.

Generative Phenomenology and Psychology

A norm of objective truth in one's personal lifeworld is at hand for future judgments within the pure Ego's system of transcending apperceptions. Here, a norm of objective truth is experienced as an "abiding property" of one's habitual comportment toward typicality and consistency in the world of human co-existence. (*see* Husserl 1973b, §32) Because of the psychic order and internal time-consciousness of this system, eidetic antecedents pertaining to historical or cultural co-existence have already gained presence in the subject's surroundings as objectified communal affairs. These matters usually exist as real *prior* to the constitutive life that begins with the child's original grasping the idea of a sociocultural world—meaning, before the pure Ego's personal horizon is built up with normal maturation during life-world experiences of common semblance. It follows that those things pregiven in historical and cultural records as matters of fact or norms of practice are not directly experienced in simple apprehension of an original idea. Instead, they are correlated and "revisited" as pre-existing factical matters of objective truth and absolute reality, and then expressed as orienting metaphysical presuppositions during intersubjective relationships of empathy. Representations of culture and society point toward our communalized way of living in objectified co-existence.

Stein (2000, 129-31) noticed that naïve references to "community" (*Gemeinschaft*) and its conjugates signify a union of individuals here and now; yet they also signify a "mechanical" structure of association (*Gesellschaft*) that has an enduring historical character from one generation to the next. Both forms of expression are adumbrations of the *eidos* of *sociation* (*Vergesellschaftung*). At the genesis and throughout a diachronic system of apperceptions of this *eidos*, our changing and maturing sociocultural world is experienced as the pure Ego's transcendence of the open-ended life-world. (*see* Gurwitsch 1964, 382-5) Described in this context by Schutz (1970, 79), one's sociocultural environing presents a horizon of common semblance that is "preorganized" during life-world experiences with others. Since a sociocultural envioning is partly the result of pre-existing inter-generational achievements, it is similar but different for each of us in the world that is commonly talked about. During the normal course of events, we experience historical representations of culture and society as synchronic "fragments" of the universal life-world in one's immediate surroundings of co-existence and common semblance.

A strict (thus naïve) realist might protest that there is no such inter-generational reality replicated in cognitive correlations of community; and certainly, there is no sense to a purely subjective psychology where reality is *not* constructed and constituted *here*, solely within my own thoughts. Still, one could perhaps make the case for a "generative" phenomenological psychology that takes into account the pre-existing normative structures of the subject's sociocultural surrounding—specifically, when those structures are pregiven in the pure Ego's personal horizon. Applications of the phenomenological method of reasoning in this field might indeed represent the essence of inquiry we call "social psychology," where persons in groups are seen to conform to predelineated standards of comportment during communal interactions.

However, a universal inter-generational method of consciousness-formation for persons in groups cannot be inferred from an anthropological description of the pure Ego, *I*—given as "I-man" in the duration of objectified human co-existence. (*see* Farber 1968, 120ff) Neither can the psychic life of persons be inferred from historical manifestations of the *socius* without accepting as evidence the metaphysical presupposition of an invariant human nature played out in predictable distributions of group behavior. Furthermore, in Husserl's (Steinbock 1995, 3ff) account of generative phenomenology, our grasp of things in one's sociocultural surroundings is not always originally given by perceptions of raw sensory data. The psychic order of inter-generational constitutive life is thus ambiguous and called into question for expressions of ego-life; and more fundamentally, for the turn from solipsism to intersubjectivity. Even so, I want to argue against the notion that the psychosubjectivity of the pure Ego must play no part in generative phenomenology.

As actual time passes in one's personal lifeworld, and our reproductive memory of past experience fades, an original grouping of elements is eventually no longer thetically *here* in constitutive life—and never will be again in the same intentional form and with the same transcendental modifications as it once enjoyed as the pure Ego's adumbrated object of simple perception. Husserl (1964a, §32) remarked that the temporal points of connections for elements in our reproductive memory undergo a "sinking back into the past" within the field of a "unitary, homogenous, Objective time." During apperceptions of objective reality, what we tend to remember about a previously objectified matter is not then the appearance of the stuff that was first grasped pre-conceptually in a mental process of perception. Instead, we retain in our compositions of an enduring eidetic affair-complex the "memorial appearance" (i.e., the "remembered immanent primary content") of an objectified phenomenological *eidos*. (§37) The memorial appearance of an objectified *eidos* could be given by the verbal logic of historical and cultural narratives during intersubjective relationships of community. (*see* Steinbock 1995, 213-19)

When the primary content of an objectified *eidos* is nonthetically *there* during intersubjective relationships—in a narration of what is believed to be factually real and objectively true for an embodied group of persons in which we count ourselves as members—it could be pregiven in thetic "primordial constitution" (*Ur-konstitution*) here for judgments about *me myself*. It could then be retained in eidetic memory as an element of consciousness-formation that is at hand in the living present of a communal affair-complex. (*see* Steinbock 1995, 155) In effect, one's eidetic memory retains and carries over into our communal interactions a pattern of objective truth for a state of affairs in the pure Ego's personal horizon. It seems to Ricoeur (1967, 135-6) that much of "Husserl's originality lies in this methodical progression from solipsism to community." Under the psychological *epoché*, one could see a progression in psychological consciousness of a unity from mental processes of simple apprehension of an intentional object in solipsistic subjectivity, to normative structures of intentional acts upon that object during intersubjective relationships of community. This movement points toward the presence of higher-level apperceptions of objective reality in the transcendental register.

As a norm of practice, the pure Ego predicates its empathetic endeavors of communalization to be objectively real for everyone. Adumbrations of the *eidos* of *sociation* in communal narratives are then seized upon by the psychological ego as elements of common semblance here and now. Guided by the transcendental ego's ideations of objective reality, adumbrated elements of *sociation* that are deemed to be necessary for consciousness-formation are grouped and composed as the primary content of intersubjective experience within a communal affair-complex. When oriented in the living present toward typicality in the naïve Galilean worldview, as well as by our everyday feelings of empathy, matters in narratives that prescribe communal interactions are preconstituted as approximations of pre-existing injunctions for every person's normative action or non-action—but preconstituted such that with necessary correlations and contingent modifications in the pure Ego's personal horizon, such matters gain presence as factually real and objectively true for *me myself*. In the normal course of events for a maturing worldview, each of us is intersubjectively partnered with actual or imagined groups of persons in the world that is commonly talked about. During one's preconceptual experiences in this world, some of our intersubjective partnerships pre-exist as pregiven by means of inter-generational narratives of communal interaction. Husserl (Steinbock 1995, 220ff) calls this intersubjective affairness of irreal community one's "normatively significant" homeworld (*Heimwelt*).

In typical homeworld comportment, the verbal logic of narratives in vocational, family, cultural, or national histories stands for what is said to exist in empathy here and now. These inter-generational matters are correlated in the horizon of metaphysics, and point toward a pregiven injunction for one's passive "habitual acquisition" of objective truth. Under the psychological *epoché*, what is said to exist for all of us in one's normatively significant homeworld implies a tradition of reality construction for what goes without saying in communal interactions. Interpreting Ricoeur's (1984) terminology for this state of affairs, the grammatical parts-to-whole eidetic structure of a narrative's "saying" what is "paradigmatically" (= objectively) real and true refers to a transcendental logic of "syntagmatic" (= denotative) objects and acts within a communal affair-complex. The inter-generational "language of description" that is given by co-workers, family, friends, or nation generates the "liminal structure" (= finite boundaries) of the norms for an objectified community of persons here and now. (*see also* Steinbock 1995, 268-70)

Any such verbal logic, however, is bracketed in regressive reflections by the eidetic reduction as culture-bound and metaphysically prejudiced, and can only be seen as a calculus for consciousness-formation with the radical skepticism of the transcendental reduction. One could then see in genetic reflections that a matter of diachronic communal life in historical narratives, along with its synchronic mode of reality construction, is grasped by the pure Ego within a system of appresentations of objectivity in the transcendental register. Here, a "language of description" pictures the semblance of what is intended to be actualized as objectively real, even as the transcendental ego's form of ideation pictures an analogous actuality as objectively true. In this system for constructing the being-sense of common semblance—fulfilling now a prescription for judgments and valuations on elements that are simultaneously *here* and *there*—the psychological ego performs acts of validation for an expressible and signifying union of the paradigmatic and syntagmatic orders of a narrative's story. A unity of meaningfulness for the full intentional Object is thus achieved in the horizon of ontology for what is anticipated to be real and true for a communalized eidetic affair-complex. (*see* Eley 1973, 416-19)

In Ricoeur's (1984, 52f) analysis, the "emplotment" of an intergenerational narrative traces out a "conceptual network" of action for "doing something." The kind of action signified in historical narratives implies practical goals and motives for the agents involved with the event being narrated. Yet under the psychological *epoché*, "doing something" is also a psychological theme of *aboutness* for the psychological ego when grasping the transcendental ego's form of ideation for elements given in historical narratives. Recall that a particular act of the psychological ego in Husserl's (Fink 1995, 170) theory of method is to adumbrate the pregiven life-world of the transcendental ego's elements of ideation. Retained elements are then intersubjectively "appropriated…practically and then also theoretically, and that [sense of co-existence is] again then put to practical use." The pure Ego perhaps does no less during our communal relationships than to put inter-generational narratives to practical use in one's normatively significant homeworld.

As a universal method of consciousness-formation, it is the pure Ego that grasps the emplotment and action-terms for "doing something" in one's normatively significant homeworld. A mental formation in this affair could indeed contain a calculus for grasping an inter-generational narrative in the transcendental register as an injunction for action here and now—such as taking a particular stance toward political or ideological matters, or perhaps as appropriating certain religious sentiments. When correlated in the horizon of metaphysics for what goes without saying, normative rules and practices would thus pre-exist the psychological ego's act of advertence to another form of ideation for doing *something else* during a relationship of empathy. In the psychological field of action for this matter, transcendental logical rules for conferring meanings and bestowing sense on our intersubjective relationships could be pregiven for a mental formation by a narrative's language of description for communal interactions. In terms of dependence and distance in the living present for this psychic order of transcending acts, we typically picture the *what* of doing something before grasping (if ever) its *how*.

Leaving aside the influence of our sociocultural narratives, Husserl's concept of *homeworld* perhaps represents a more general synthesized union of the normal/alien pregivenness of things when constructing the rational affective unity of *me myself* in one's personal lifeworld. (*see* Steinbock 1995, 178f) Passive structures of intersubjective experience gain presence when the psychological ego's mental formation of transcending acts is directed toward a pre-existing parts/whole unity of "likeness" in the living-present profile of the natural world—a world we naïvely experience as a manifold of continuous anticipation and fulfillment of generalities and approximations. (Husserl 1973a, §81) In the pure psychology of this affair, we "aim" at constituting in awareness *something like* what already exists pre-conceptually as a unity of configuration. With the psychological ego's passive acceptance of a pregiven element of normalized similarity-and-difference for what is "self-same in general" (§93.a), we could represent to one's self with reason and evidence, and express to others with feelings of empathy, "this is real and true for all of us."

Each of us could say in one's personal lifeworld, just as it was said before in expressions of objective truth during our intersubjective partnerships, "this is supposed to happen all the time" or "this is not the right thing to do." We could then anticipate the presence of the same rational affective unity according to its descriptions and logic of calculus precisely as pregiven in one's life-span communal interactions. Constrained by such passive horizons within a tradition of reality construction, an intentional object could become an idealized exemplar of what one believes intuitively to be a lawful objective reality; saying, "that's just the way it is." During our homeworld experiences of consciousness-formation, a communal affair-complex is presupposed for judgments and valuations as "a past temporal dimension in order for sense to be constituted in the present! Eventually this 'Ur-konstitution' peculiar to a genetic phenomenology will be ensconced within a 'Stamm-konstitution' peculiar to a generative phenomenology." (Steinbock 1995, 155)

There is a radical expression that Husserl (Steinbock 1995, 194) uses, *Stamm* (= literally, the stem or trunk of a collective unity), which refers to the feeling and its motivation to construct a communal affair-complex. During this ordinary experience with persons and groups, adumbrated elements of the *eidos* of *sociation* are composed during our empathetic relationships just as they are pregiven for apperceptions in one's sociocultural surroundings. In *Stamm*-constitution, an idealized sense and meaning for an intentional object is bound within the naturalized law-like horizons of such intersubjective polar events as births and deaths, beginnings and endings, and limitations and delimitations. With *Stamm*-constitution, we intend to make a world of signifying and expressible meaning for each of us, where we think of "us" in idealized terms of one's family, one's country, one's profession, and so on. During our mutual *Stamm*-constitution of things that endure throughout the generations, we all become communal "home-comrades" (*Heimgenosse*) in transcendental consciousness of the world that is commonly talked about. (*see* pp. 222f)

When we extend our intuitions of the past within a fundamental ontology of communal interactions, when we each think similarly about what is actually real and objectively true for all of us in empathy, we could then construct the normatively significant homeworld of *my life as a person*. We do this in pure psychology with the same intentional methods and motivations as when we exercise our intuition into pre-existing ideations and mental formations for any intentional object whatsoever. This universal method of transcendental constitution is in stark contrast to either the naïve notion of a timeless human nature or to mundane theories of mindless responses to neurological stimuli. When spontaneously focused in the living present on its mental formation and psychological theme of *aboutness*, the psychological ego tends to be passively indifferent to the origins of any mutually grasped elements of *Stamm*-constitution. *Stamm*-constitution of one's consciousness of communal interactions is nevertheless part of our everyday intersubjectivity.

Enworlded Consciousness

From the beginnings of the child's psychic development we are motivated in pure psychology to *do something* during every waking moment. Indeed, our thoughts never seem to be at complete rest in mental life. A universal urge or desire of the human spirit for intellectual activity is played out day-to-day in the transcendental register amid a flow of reasoning from pre-conceptual to conceptual space—and in this way, we are being psychological in the world that is commonly talked about. During this activity, Husserl (Fink 1995, §§11ff) writes, the psychological ego "enworlds" the transcendental ego as the pure Ego's intersubjective "world-constituting agent." "Phenomenologizing then also presents itself as psychological." (Marginal note 384) In the normal course of events, intentional enworlding (*Verweltlichung*) progresses according to the phenomenologizing action that constitutes awareness of common semblance in each world of objects and acts where the pure Ego is busied, both in general and in "this case" of particular sense and meaning. This is how the psychological ego actualizes what is deemed to be genuinely true and factually real from the natural attitude. As the phenomenologizing actor in constitutive life, however, the psychological ego has its own normative (not natural) attitude toward such irreal things as common semblance.

The psychological ego lives in relationships with irreal and actual things by fulfilling its mental formation of consciousness-formation with valuing- and judging-acts upon both one's ownness-essence and the essences of intentional objects. As a norm of practice following the pure Ego's transcendental reorientation, the psychological ego continues its intentional acts in cognitive mental life by constructing contingent first-person affairs for the elemental "self" of the transcendental ego's naïve experience of *me myself*. Here, the pure psychology of our spirit-life pre-exists in body and soul at the developmental origins of transcendental subjectivity, and endures throughout each phase of world-constitution as one's own experiences of universal psychic being. During the constitution in consciousness of *my life as a person*, pure psychology and its psychological ego-life co-exist in both normal and alien associations precisely as the psyche wills to grasp the phenomenon of *my life* from the natural attitude. (see Husserl 1977, 97f)

Our natural attitude presents no horizon for the psychological ego that would entail potentials for acting in a world of existential nothingness—since, clearly, consciousness of *nothingness* is experienced as "consciousness-of" a transcendental object. Things that matter thematically in the transcendental register pre-exist in the transcendental ego's form of ideation as anticipated outcomes of constitutive life. Anything expressed from the natural attitude, including the semblance of one's life-goals, needs, and personal worldview, gains presence in awareness by the psychological ego's transcending acts. When presented from the natural attitude, all fantasies in imagination could be fulfilled as constituted objectivities in one's personal lifeworld. All metaphysical presuppositions are composed to be part of the pure Ego's being-sense for an *eidos* in the world that is commonly talked about. And all reality in a naturalized structure of consciousness exists as both irreal and ac-

266

tual during the lived experience of being an embodied person within the intersubjective world of objectified and absolutized things. Yet the unity of this eidetic structure is only *contingently* present in transcendental consciousness.

During the transcendental constitutive life of a worldly unity-form, the psychological ego is bound by the "limited horizon" of the transcendental ego's form of ideation here and now—for otherwise, "the normal course of events" for the subject's awareness of similarities and differences in each world of objects and acts does not occur. But when the normal course of events does indeed occur in psychic life, consciousness-formation cannot be other than intended in order for the apodictic *I am* to be grasped as truly existing in unified relationships with the pure Ego's existential *Other*. In Husserl's (1970, 399-400) transcendental theory of method, this field of action defines "the scope of self objectification...[which is] the truly absolute horizon [for all that could exist from the natural attitude due to one's cognitive action]."

Grasping the rational affective unity of *me myself* in this manner of being objectively human represents a norm of adequately given self-knowledge of *my life* in the transcendental register. More generally, this norm is grasped in cognitive mental life as a psychic order of anticipated unity for correlations and constructed relationships of real and irreal things in *this* world and not another. This same norm of action is then typically *re*-cognized in the horizon of metaphysics during one's intersubjective relationships—where now, it is repeated in apperceptions of what is (doxically) supposed to be objective and true for the comportment of others. When this norm is used for constructing a matter of similarity-and-difference for objects and acts in the world of common semblance, it is the genesis in spirit-life of what we choose to represent as self-knowledge in mundane thought and speech. One could consequently think and say, for instance, "this is the real and true nature of things."

Husserl (1973a, §86) implies that a presupposition of objective truth could arise in the horizon of metaphysics solely as an affective correlate of the pure Ego's consciousness of a pre-existing unity. "It has the feeling of truth," one might say. Typically, though, rational comportment toward objective truth is pregiven as a norm in the psychological ego's mental formation with anticipation of fulfillment in the transcendental register "precisely because, before all experience [of judgments and valuations, such norms] prescribe rules for its later course." "On the other hand," Husserl (§43.c) warns, "the relations of likeness and similarity are completely indifferent to such disconnectedness not actually joined together [by a norm of truth-seeking]"—meaning, we are not motivated to apprehend "just any formation [of similarity and difference when seeking the truth of worldly matters, but rather we have] an interest in formations which claim to be the precipitate of cognitions." (§3)

For example, the psychological ego has no motivation to grasp as a rational affective unity whether a chicken is in truth similar to a duck or different from a wren, when a mental formation in the living present is intended to fulfill the form of ideation for the *eidos* of *tableness* in the world of common semblance. The cognitive mental life of the psychological ego begins in the transcendental register within a mental formation of similarities and differences for *this eidos* in *this* world and not another. Said *eidos* is an original idea of immanent meaningfulness that is thematically intended-to and intentionally acted upon during psychological experience here and now.

Mental formations in the transcendental register prescribe rules of cognitions in psychological processes of transcending acts and passive acceptance. Anticipated outcomes of the psychological ego's judging- and valuing-acts in these formations are typically grasped in conceptual space as genuine and correct because they follow normative rules of an intellectually seen (and thus pregiven) tradition of reality construction for each encounterd world of objects and acts. Here, psychological processes stream throughout a genetic succession of intentional action that correlates the worldly elements of what is presupposed and posited by the pure Ego to be genuinely true in one's socio-cultural surroundings—but true only when normative rules are followed for rational comportment. Otherwise, one's spirit-life in the mental sphere of pure consciousness is free to vary all things possible and impossible in their richest forms of imagination and fantasy. Husserl (1973a, §47) characterizes the "work of cognition" in the transcendental register as the subject's "creative spontaneity" during the production of conscious awareness. For the psychological ego, cognitive methods exist during this production as living-present norms for apprehending something that is anticipated to be known thematically as "the object simply and solely, valid 'in and for itself.'" (§28)

The subject's ordinary awareness of human co-existence is indeed consciousness of an irreal/actual unity "in and for itself." When we express or imply that the human world (*Umwelt*) is objectively real and absolutely true, intersubjective elements have already been composed to be a thematic unity in one's personal lifeworld. Said composition includes the pure Ego's grasp of the presence of other ego-subjects as solipsistic "alien" pregivenness—i.e., as the correlate of past and anticipated co-existence. The pregivenness of such otherness is usually retained as an enduring stratum of elements in rational concatenations, and then co-presented with the alter ego-life of the phenomenon of *my life as a person*. Because of our streaming psychological processes for grasping such immanent facticity, each person could enact with reason and evidence a similar but different succession of psychological connections for a unity of self-consciousness. All of this cognitive action occurs within a complex (polythetic, synchronic/diachronic) system of transcending apperceptions directed toward the *eidos* of *my-life-with-their-life*.

A system of transcending apperceptions is used to build up a series of "interlaced" connections for a unity of world-consciousness—in particular, a series of correlates resulting from judging and valuing similarities and differences for an *eidos* in categories of thematic content. Here, cognitive action is part of a mental process of consciousness-formation; where by means of this "interlacing" construction, an intentional object asymptotically tends toward idealized dimensions in the world that is commonly talked about. Here, too, cognitive action follows a psychic order of retention, elapse, anticipation, and protension of elements for an adumbrated object of the mind. A typical norm of psychic life is to construct a rational affective unity out of this complexity. For example, a mental process of world-consciousness begins by seizing upon the adumbrated stuff of one's ownness-essence as a worldly object of anticipated self-knowledge. Correlated elements in thematic categories of being-sense for said object are then pictured in the transcendental ego's form of ideation in order to construct the actual reality of *me myself*. This state of affairs seems to imply that not all potentials for the *eidos* of *my life* are constituted as actually real and objectively true in rational concatenations. Some things perhaps remain in the living present, unfulfilled in one's imagination and fantasy.

Streaming back and forth between apperceptions of spirit-life and corporeal-life, the iterative order of what goes without saying in the world for us all synthesizes the semblance of absolute commonality for embodied co-existence within the horizon of metaphysics. This psychic order is governed by the pure Ego's internal time-consciousness of a normative sequence of action during a genetic succession of spatial unities that make up the total configuration of awareness. Seeing the certainty of something *here* indeed depends upon grasping the *eidos* of that thing as already *there* for judgments and valuations—even when both strata are synthesized as a unity that is naïvely seen "everywhere." For instance, there must already be retained elements of *up* and *down* if I am to grasp an embodied experience of arising or descending. Similarly, a metaphysical orientation of unity for the human world is typically experienced in pure psychology prior to the transcendental ego's arriving at a phase in constitutive life calling for apperceptions of contingent differences for *me myself*. Contingent differences in empirical generalities of spatiotemporality become self-evident during apperceptions of *me myself* as an embodied existent in the midst of one's personal lifeworld of other embodied existents.

Within bounds of reason and fantasy, human imagination seems limitless in its expressions of an embodied nature of things. Our day-to-day psychic being of such spirit-life includes the motivation to grasp one's naïve natural world as the embodied correlate of intersubjective experience during relationships of empathy. In both Husserl's (1973a §38) theory of elements and in his (Husserl 1973b, §13) transcendental theory of method, intersubjectivity includes that genetic phase of transcendental subjectivity where we construct the actual reality for something that could be grasped by everyone from the natural attitude as objectively real and true. In the normal course of this action, a presupposed absolute Nature, and an apprehended nature of things, are appresented and apperceived together in empathy as a matter of fact in the world that is commonly talked about. Each element of this matter of factualness—that of an absolute Nature and that of the nature of things—is already correlated within the *a priori* horizons so as to be predicated as analogous with all other matters of truth and reality during life-world experiences.

For example, I could discern from representations of the world of common semblance given in a roadmap whether to turn right or left within its depicted "factual" dimensions of embodiment. It goes without saying for everyone that we do not turn in or out of the flat plane of the map in order to go in our intended directions. Yet whether I become lost in this empathetic endeavor is determined by my skill in reading the map and its accuracy for fulfilling my intentions. Both elements of skill and accuracy, however, exist outside the metaphysical bounds of the nature of things seen in the map. Such elements are presupposed to exist with one's normative use of the map—although sometimes without good grounds for believing so. In the natural attitude, there is no guarantee of fulfillment when something is appresented as the factual semblance of objective reality and absolute truth. When grasped in empathy such that it goes without saying in one's naïve natural world, each "fact" of self-knowledge is only a (subjective) portion of the same objectified world that is believed to exist as real and true for all of us. "This world is," Husserl (1973a, §38) writes, "the life-world…of mutual understanding, our earth," from which intersubjective experience itself springs forth.

We all turn individually in a similar orienting direction when making judgments and valuations that aim to achieve a mutually experienced world of objects and acts. Here, expressions of the life-world represent our metaphysical *sense* of human co-existence when aiming toward such mutuality. Husserl's (1970, §41) transcendental reduction is partly used to disclose the subject's grasp of an embodied and absolutized world of concrete reality that arises from this intuitive ground (*Boden*) of transcendental subjectivity. A reduction to the essential elements and intrinsic acts during pre-conceptual life-world experiences also provides Husserl's (§42) *entrée* for reflections on world-constitution as universal human comportment. The concept of *world* is seen in the transcendental register, not as a naïve cosmology but as a constructed irreality of time and place—specifically, as a stratum of pre-existing objects and acts correlated in the horizon of metaphysics. From the phenomenological attitude, each worldly stratum is contingently necessary in order for an enworlded object to be experienced as actually real and objectively true with apodictic certainty. At the same time, our performances of world-constitution point reflections toward the psychological theme for a mental process of phenomenologizing action during the pure Ego's intersubjective relationships. Pre-conceptual performances of world-constitution indeed represent "the special kind of 'simultaneity'" of the transcendental ego's form of ideation and the transcending acts of the psychological ego. (*see* Fink 1995, §9)

The simultaneity of contingent objects and acts in conscious awareness reveals to genetic reflections a grouping of categorial forms of thematic content in the living-present profile of consciousness-formation. Typically included in this profile are the spatiotemporal relationships of elements for *me myself* as an object of the mind in one's personal lifeworld. Acting on retained elements of solipsistic and intersubjective pregivenness, the psychological ego synthesizes the semblance and appearance of an intentional object to be a unity of configuration during day-to-day experiences of actual reality and objective truth. Correlated in the horizon of metaphysics for what goes without saying, our self-knowledge of a constituted object-as-a-whole is spontaneously enworlded in the transcendental register as something apodictically certain with evidence of natural cause—*because* the being-sense of Nature in its totality is already composed to pre-exist in the transcendental ego's intentional form of ideation within the world of transcended objects, and *simultaneously* in the psychological ego's mental formation of necessary transcending acts.

"The antithetic distinctions of the transcendental theory of elements and the transcendental theory of method," Husserl's (Fink 1995, §11) writes, "disappears [during world-constitution] in the final [polythetic] synthesis of absolute knowing." Indeed, the simultaneity of phenomenologizing acts and phenomenologized objects points toward both the *what* and the *how* of cognitions in the world of common semblance. (§4) Because of this simultaneity in the living present, the psychological ego is limited in its actions by the transcendental ego's form of ideation for *what* is to be grasped as the object-content of cognitions. Sometimes the appearances of things that are pictured in ideations of common semblance are acted upon by the psychological ego *as if* they already exist as real for apperceptions. During our typical experiences of awareness, the psychological ego fulfills a contingent order of judgments and valuations that is intended to meet one's anticipations in a personal life-world for living knowingly as "natural"—the *how* of cognitions. Within this order, the *eidos* of *my life* is grasped according to the pure Ego's pre-conceptual perspective on elements of pregivenness for *me myself* during life-world experiences. In this way, activities of world-constitution are intentionally fulfilled as one's transcendental consciousness of a unity of configuration for *me-in-my-world*. This state of affairs is experienced as *my own* way of being in the world.

In Husserl's (1982, §§35-6) phenomenology of reason, a field of cognitive action is seen as all judging- and valuing-acts directed at objects by the psychological ego (or *not* directed by exclusion or advertence) in order for one to be conscious of something here and now. A horizon of both active (*aktiv*) and passive (*passiv*) actionality thus pre-exits in the living present for potential transcending acts when constructing the actual reality of one's personal lifeworld. If the appearance of the pure Ego's personal lifeworld is to be held constant during phenomenologizing activities, then cognitive acts cannot exceed the bounds of this horizon for rational comportment. For example, despite any creative urge to do so, I cannot rationally judge and value my life as a *flower* in representations of actual reality. Beginning from the most fundamental substrates of solipsistic subjectivity, and held fast in relationships of *I* and *Other*, the essence of one's personal lifeworld is grasped in psychological consciousness as an affective unity of *being* and *doing* during ongoing life-span experiences. The genetic origin of one's personal lifeworld is retained in eidetic memory as one's own "fragment" of the universal life-world.

The subject's personal lifeworld is represented in empathy as the remembered past and anticipated future of *my life as a person* in co-existence with the existential *Other*. Here, adumbrations of the universal life-world provide a horizon for psychological consciousness of a unity during experiences of a mutually distributed (sociocultural) grasp of an objectified world. Delimited thus by its field of action within a spatially and temporally embodied community of similar souls, the psychological ego constructs the actual reality for objectified things in the conceptual space of an intuitively pregiven and adequately seen personal lifeworld. Under the psychological *epoché* and reduction, one's personal lifeworld is is seen to be constructed according to the psychological ego's point of view in the living present on precisely what is believed with certainty to be a mutual grasp of actual reality and objective truth. This point of view orients the *telos* of the psyche during our day-to-day intersubjectivity, and directs genetic reflections toward the psychic being and lived experience of transcendental subjectivity in its full complexity.

For instance, when we first grasp the idea of intersubjective relationships within a maturing system of apperceptions, we then constitutes psychological consciousness of a union of body and soul as something universally human that is at-hand for cognitions. Retained elements of this experience are grouped and composed such that one's personal lifeworld of similarity and difference gains presence with affective significance as contingency demands. And so, an object in the subject's personal lifeworld is subsequently phenomenologized to have the appearance of common semblance within the synthesized unity of one's lived experiences in the world of human co-existence. An exemplary expression of phenomenologizing action is of reflecting on the appearance of *my life* as a rational affective unity throughout the development of a life-span system of apperceptions. Said experience is often expressed and naïvely represented as "introspection." This same mode of comportment is described in Husserl's (1973a, §89) theory of method as spontaneous acts of intuitively "seeing ideas" of common semblance for *me myself* within an intersubjective plurality of self-sameness ascribed to "everyone."

The epistemological evidence for Husserl's concept of a personal lifeworld is found in his transcendental theory of elements, not in his transcendental theory of method. One's personal lifeworld contains elements of sense, meaning, and certainty that are distinctly *my own* in the transcendental register. As a locus of cognitive action, one's personal lifeworld represents the synthesis of any number of deeper lying things in pre-conceptual experiences that are apprehended as a unity in conscious awareness. It must be said, however, that sometimes we fail in this accomplishment to construct the rational affective unity of *my life* here and now. But even so, the lived experience of one's personal lifeworld is typically seen in similar sense to the shirt that one chooses to put on. This particular shirt could be one of any number of other shirts during the a-historical and universal experience of putting on a shirt; but for me, this is *my* shirt that I am putting on here and now. Yet at the same time, each of us usually learns during the course of maturation that there is a practical way to put on and to wear a shirt, and we tend to notice when anybody including one's self does not make use of this mutual norm of practice.

In all cases of normative comportment, our a-historical experiences with elemental sense and meaning make up a "proper theme of philosophy" in Husserl's (Fink 1995, §2) transcendental idealism and science of essences. Husserl's theory of world-consciousness thus includes our universal methods of constitution that make up the psychosubjectivity of a-historical *being* and *doing*. The subject's ever-present world of such universal things is indeed represented by the notion of a personal lifeworld, which is the purely subjective space of contingent experience where we strive for truth and consistency with others here and now. The subject's awareness of human co-existence during life-world experience points reflections toward all the potential things that could gain presence in thought and speech as a consequence of the pure Ego's phenomenlogizing activity to "humanize" the appearance of its constituted objectivities in conceptual space—and in particular, toward the psychological ego's humanizing-acts on elements in the transcendental ego's form of ideation for *me myself* in the world that is commonly talked about.

272

Final Reflections on Transcendental Phenomenological Psychology

The meaningful subject of transcendental psychosubjectivity is the psychological *cogito* that knowingly acts in the intersubjective world of objectified human co-existence—or sometimes, when the subject does *not* transcend the solipsistic register of consciousness-formation because of some organic or developmental influence, or might indeed fail in one's intention to construct a matter of rational affairness, or perhaps chooses to be non-rational with others. Still, in all such contingencies of spirit-life, expressions of the psychological *cogito* refer to our experiences of knowing extra-physical things in the world that is commonly talked about. Under the psychological *epoché*, cognitive action during this experience is represented by the psychological ego, just as it appears in ego-life with other ego-subjects in the transcendental register.

Husserl's (1982, §36) psychological reduction under its own *epoché* focuses genetic reflections on the intentional actions of the psychological ego in processes that are "unconditionally" directed toward realizing compositions of retained elements during each phase of transcendental subjectivity. When guided by this norm of practice, admumbrated elements of universal *being* and *doing* are composed according to the pure Ego's psychic order of internal time-consciousness for an anticipated unity-form in conscious awareness. By means of this orientation in contingent mental formations, psychological phenomena are situated within the full range of potential cognitive mental life from solipsistic subjectivity to the highest genus of pure psychology—which is, the lived experience of psychic being in one's personal lifeworld.

The complex state of affairs that Husserl (1982, §34) calls the "Heraclitean" flux of pure human consciousness generally matters similarly but differently for phenomenological philosophy and phenomenological psychology. What matters most for philosophers are clarifications of the essential elements of this complexity, while what matters most for psychologists are the methods by which said elements are made present to consciousness by our intentional acts in cognitive mental life. (*see* Mohanty 1989, 102) It follows from methodological necessity that Husserl's phenomenological psychology of affective inner experience is grounded in practices of his theory of method, rather than his theory of elements. (*see* Fink 1995, §2 note 11)

Thus grounded by the pure Ego's methods of *being* and *doing*, the subject's experiences of cognitive mental life point reflections toward the primitive concept of *actionality* in pure psychology. During the normal course of events, this concept is seen as a succession of transcending acts on elements of an intentional object. Objects by themselves are neutral regarding any action taken upon them during consciousness-formation, including any observation of their presence, for they have no mental lives of their own. Applied transcendental phenomenological psychology nevertheless remains directed toward the theme of pure phenomenology—which is, namely, "the essence of consciousness" here and now. This theme is articulated in Husserl's tradition of inquiry as the intentional coming-to-presence of a composed unity of being sense out of pre-existing noumenal elements. Every such unity is an object of the mind in transcendental phenomenological psychology.

The discipline of psychology is often interpreted in Husserl's work and characterized in mundane discourse as "positive science." (*see* Bachelard 1968, 195) And indeed, phenomenological psychology mostly addresses issues of everyday psychological experience instead of its pathologies or anomalies, where psychic life typically aims toward the practical ideal of "happiness." Yet this issue perhaps confuses Husserl's (1973b, §13) comparisons between "positive psychology" as an objective "science of nature," versus his later perspective toward phenomenological psychology as a science of "*all transcendental cognition*…. [That is to say, as] a science that forms the *extremest contrast to sciences in the hitherto accepted sense*, positive…." Positive psychology addresses objectified matters of practical life rather than general principles of living, but without including their subjective origins of autonomy and agency that we experience as the immanence of "pure psychic life." (Fink 1995, §3 n.33)

For example, Husserl (1965a, 74) noticed that matters of practical life typically show themselves in reflections as the ways that we normatively regulate our active powers when intending to know something factual within "a doctrinal content that is constantly growing and branching out in new directions." Husserl (2001, 16-17) also noticed that during this regulating activity in psychic life, every positive science "represents a set of external arrangements, which, just as they arose out of the knowledge-acts of many [past] individuals, can again pass over into just such acts of countless individuals, in a readily understandable manner." Husserl's remarks about this fact-gathering practice that intuitively grounds our methods of doctrinal exactness in positive science seem to imply a mutual regulation of inter-generational knowing-acts during intersubjective relationships of empathy—which is clearly the *same* experience of pure psychology that we all tend to enjoy in the normal course of events.

Pure psychology is similarly experienced in empathy when we construct theories of practical life that are guided by existential interpretations that are situated ("proximally and for the most part") in the historical world; and similarly when reasoning is guided by meta-concepts of an objectified and naturalized "unconscious" in culture and society. Yet Husserl's science of essences—those essences realized by our knowing-acts both individually and over generations—is meant by Husserl (2001, 22) to resemble a radical "science of science" (*Wissenschaftslehre*) in Bolzano's sense of rigorous theory construction and concept formation. Here, irreal objects pertaining to practical life, culture, or society become actually real only when they are acted upon in cognitive mental life to make them be so in conscious awareness. During reflections on the subject's normative patterns of thought and speech, naïvely presented "facts" are seen to be idealized matters of factualiness in Husserl's tradition of inquiry. In any event, Gurwitsch (1966, 445) insists, the essence of phenomenological psychology as a positive science of doctrinal exactness "has never existed and cannot exist." (*see also* Husserl 1970, §72) The psychic life of humans is not so precise as the workings of machines and molecules.

When using the intuitive method of *Psychognosia* as praxis for observations and descriptions, applications of pure phenomenology clarify essences that tend asymptotically toward finite idealized limits of sensible meaning. At the same time, the pure psychological methods of those activities tend toward realizing rational affective unities in thought and speech. These two fields of experience represent the *eidos* of *the phenomenological method proper* in Husserl's methodology. The essence of *Psychognosia* is thus a practice of non-empirical thinking that reveals under the *epoché* only finite horizons of intentional experience in pure consciousness. Our transcendental experience of understanding leading to self-knowledge of pre-existing irreality is indeed played out within these *a priori* and contingent horizons during consciousness-formation. If this were not the case, then Husserl's methodology in the transcendental register would remain theoretically grounded in a metaphysics of *understanding* and its historical givenness, rather than arising from intentional acts of idealization in the a-historical Galilean worldview. Transcendental phenomenological psychology finds its intuitive ground amid the human potential for finite experiences of cognitive mental life in the world that is commonly talked about— including its full complexity of typicality and approximations.

In order to begin reflections on the *I-Other* experiences of the meaningful human subject, a phenomenologist assumes the pure Ego's perspective toward an intentional object during reductions to one's existential center of awareness. With Husserl's "archaeological" phenomenology, there is no cognitive action to be seen *here* in reflections, since the pure Ego is not being psychological by acting on objects directed toward the actual *now* during a genetic course of constitution—meaning, the sphere of immanence for the original givenness of such action is being reduced to its origins. More precisely, the *telos* of the psyche for intentional acts and passive acceptance has already been fulfilled in reduced levels of consciousness-formation, just as an ancient artifact has already fulfilled its function during events long past. In addition to the enduring *eidos*, all that could be seen directly in regressive reflections under the *epoché* and eidetic reduction are the elements of a presentational object, themes of constitutive life, and universal acts of *nous* that permeate pure consciousness (such as willing, thinking, or feeling). Any descriptions of psychic life beyond these methodological limits must rely upon a metaphysics of the existential or empirical "nature" of psychological phenomena.

However, due to the transcendental turn in Husserl's methodology, psychological reflections focus on the dynamic field of cognitive action during the genetic constitution of an object *here* and *now*. The in-place noematic structure from regressive reflections provides a topology for reconstructions of the subject's constitutive life in the transcendental register. This register also includes any living-present pregivenness to reason and intellectual *seeing* that is retained in eidetic memory as contingency demands. During reflections on the movement of ego-life from solipsistic subjectivity to transcendental intersubjectivity, a phenomenologist's insight now adopts the perspective of the phenomenologizing onlooker of the pure Ego's *telos* of world-consciousness. (see Fink 1995, §§2ff) In this way, a transcendental phenomenologist follows the phenomenologizing ego's character of being a neutral observer of the first-person "*I*" of both immediate (subjective) and mediate (intersubjective) experience. When an object is constituted with the appearance of objective truth and actual reality in the pre-scientific space of post-phenomenological phenomena, the phenomenologizing actor is seen to be the psychological ego in both immediate and mediate psychic life. Each of us is being similarly psychological when we grasp a world of embodied things with feelings of empathy, along with our place as a person within that same world.

Under the psychological *epoché*, a turn of regard toward the intersubjective phase of constitution is given as the pure Ego's advertence to the transcendental register of pure human consciousness. An act of advertence in constitutive life from the pure Ego's thematic grip on a singular core essence in solipsistic subjectivity, to that same essence in its transcendental modifications, represents a stage of the way from phenomenological psychology into clarifications of concepts in Husserl's transcendental idealism. This stage uncovers an enduring *eidos* in its regional ontology of empirical generalities; and simultaneously, its idealized dimensions of common semblance, both for individual persons and for communities of persons throughout the generations.

The field of action for the pure Ego's day-to-day psychosubjectivity entails three "interpenetrating" phyla of intentional experience that provide the means to fulfill the *logos* of the psyche in the transcendental register: (1) the child's original grasping the idea of the world as a range of possibilities for being human among humans, (2) the genetic development of a life-span system of apperceptions in pure psychology, and (3) the coming-into-being of a rational affective unity of objectivities and actual realities in one's personal lifeworld. Each phylum is necessary in the living present for the subject's ordinary transcendental consciousness, and each is represented by its particular norms of practice and its affectively motivated transcending acts. Unifying psychological processes typically interrelate and habitually repeat the acts upon objects within each phylum for the duration of constitutive life.

Just as the primitive concepts of point and line are radical in Euclid's geometry, so too are the phenomenological concepts clarified in Husserl's philosophy of transcendental idealism radical for eidetic inquiry into human psychic life. Phenomenological primitives and their interconnected structures of objects, acts, affects, and motivations are explained in Husserl's theory of elements and transcendental theory of method—where such things are given to reflection as typically present in order for an object of the mind to be constituted as a unity of configuration in conscious awareness. Each of us could spontaneously enlist our psychological processes in cognitive mental life for transcending the primitive notions of sentient *being* and *doing* that are expressed in Husserl's theory of pure consciousness. Transcending the irrealities of pure consciousness is part of what it means to be fully human.

To review: A flow of reasoning from pre-conceptual to conceptual space includes intentional mental processes of choosing, remembering, feeling, and so on. Each mental process gives rise to multiple simultaneous psychological processes of cognitive action that abstract, group, and compose essential elements of an intentional object. Elements are ordered by the psychological ego within an eidetic affair-complex according to a logic of calculus for correlating an ongoing unity of sense, meaning, and certainty among the *a priori* and contingent horizons. Unique correlates of being-sense are then pictured in the transcendental ego's form of ideation for an anticipated affective unity in the world of common semblance. Cognitive action of the psychological ego—including its phenomenologizing-acts in empathy—fulfill said anticipation as a synthesis of elements that is intended to approximate pre-existing ideal dimensions in one's sociocultural surroundings. Rigorous phenomenologists are neutral observers of this activity that is peculiar to our transcendental consciousness-of-something, where that *something* is constructed to have the appearance of actual reality in the world that is commonly talked about. From the transcendental phenomenological attitude, being conscious of something actually real is also part of what it means to be fully human.

By following Husserl's humanisitc perspective toward consciousness-formation, phenomenologists attempt to see eidetic affair-complexes that are intuitively grounded in pure consciousness—but only as such complexes show themselves as intentionally constructed in *this* instance of experience that is peculiarly *my own*. The elemental composition of an object of the mind in the solipsistic register might not always be modified and realized in the transcendental register; but when it *is*, retained elements that are deemed likely by the pure Ego for constituting the presence of something objectively true are made actually real during intersubjective relationships of empathy.

Although there is the assumption in Husserl's tradition that not every element of an eidetic affair-complex will show itself during any single moment of reflection, the psychological ego is nevertheless seen under the psychological *epoché* and reduction to be acting upon essential elements in order for an intentional object to be constituted as actually real and objectively true—both for one's self and for our intersubjective partners in empathy. In the midst of this field of actionality, the psychological ego presents itself in genetic reflections as one's personal ego when following with anticipation the psychological theme of the pure Ego's life-goals here and now, Husserl (1973b, §38) noticed that the psychological ego is not so restricted to rational comportment in life-world experience as is the concept of *mind* in his theories of pure consciousness: "This is already shown by memory of our childhood." There is thus a place in Husserl's transcendental theory of method for psychological descriptions of intropathic "normality" and "abnormality" as forms of individualized comportment during communal interactions. (see Husserl 1973a, §§93f)

Still, as we strive for consistency in our lives with others, humans typically choose to be normal and rational as habitual practices of the pure Ego's modalities of intentionality. Any disclosed active or passive cognitive performance for constituting what is believed to be normal and rational could therefore be interpreted as the meaningful subject's transcended pure psychology in the world that is commonly talked about. Transcending pure psychology, too, is part of what it means to be fully human. In the pre-scientific space of everyday *being* and *doing*, a priority in psychological experience is to enact our spirit-life of seeking the truth and "nature" of actual reality during intersubjective relationships of co-existence and common semblance. Seen in Husserl's science of essences as fundamental human experience, we do all of this, and more, by intentionally enworlding the essence of a durable reality for *my life as a person*. Perhaps only when fulfilling this priority of spirit-life do we commonly think and speak of such things as *my life*, and of what it means for each of us to be fully human with one another.

Bibliography

Allison, H. E. 1983. *Kant's Transcendental Idealism: An Interpretation and Defense.* New Haven, CT: Yale University Press.

Anderson, J. R. 1990. *Cognitive Psychology and its Implications.* New York: W.H. Freeman.

Bachelard, S. 1968. *A Study of Husserl's Formal and Transcendental Logic,* trans. L. Embree. Evanston, IL: Northwestern University Press. (Original work published 1957)

Barnes, H. E. 1969. *An Existentialist Ethics.* New York: Alfred A. Knopf. (Original work published 1967)

Bernet, R., I. Kern, and E. Marbach 1993. *An Introduction to Husserlian Phenomenology.* Evanston, IL: Northwestern University Press.

Blackburn, S. 1994. *The Oxford Dictionary of Philosophy.* Oxford: Oxford University Press.

Boehm, R. 1970. "Husserl's Concept of the 'Absolute.'" In *The Phenomenology of Husserl: Selected Critical Readings,* ed. R. O. Elveton, 174-203. Chicago: Quadrangle Books.

Bolzano, B. 1972. *Theory of Science,* ed. and trans. R. George. Berkeley: University of California Press. (Original work published 1837)

Brentano, F. 1995. *Descriptive Psychology,* trans. B. Müller. London: Routledge. (Origninal work published 1982)

Brough, J. B. 1981. "The Phenomenology of Internal Time-consciousness." In *Husserl: Shorter Works,* by E. Husserl, 271-6. Notre Dame, IN: University of Notre Dame Press.

Bruzina, R. 1995. Translator's introduction to *Sixth Cartesian Meditation: The Idea of a Transcendental Theory of Method, with Textual Notations by Edmund Husserl,* by E. Fink, vii-xcii. Bloomington: Indiana University Press.

Burge, T. 1996. "Individualism and Psychology." In *Readings in Language and Mind,* ed. H. Geirsson and M. Losonsky, 374-400. Cambridge, MA: Blackwell.

Cairns, D. 1940. "An Approach to Phenomenology." In *Philosophical Essays in Memory of Edmund Husserl,* ed. M. Farber, 3-18. Cambridge, MA: Harvard University Press.

———. 1976. *Conversations with Husserl and Fink,* ed. R.M. Zaner. The Hague: Kluwer.

Carr, D. 1970. Translator's introduction to *The Crisis of European Sciences and Transcendental Phenomenology,* by E. Husserl, xv-xliii. Evanston, IL: Northwestern University Press.

Churchland, P. S. 1990. *Neurophilosophy: Toward a Unified Science of the Mind-brain.* Cambridge, MA: MIT Press. (Original work published 1986)

Copleston, F. 1985. *A History of Philosophy.* New York: Doubleday.

Damasio, A. R. 1994. *Descartes' Error: Emotion, Reason, and the Human Brain.* New York: G.P. Putnam's Sons.

de Boer, T. 1978. *The Development of Husserl's Thought*, trans. T. Plantinga. The Hague: Nijhoff. (Original work published 1966)

Deleuze, G. 1994. *Difference and Repetition*, trans. P. Patton. London: The Athlone Press. (Original work published 1969)

Dilthey, W. 1977. *Descriptive Psychology and Historical Understanding*, trans. R. M. Zaner and K. L. Heiges. The Hague: Nijhoff. (Original work published 1924)

Edie, J. M. 1964. Introduction to *The primacy of perception: And Other Essays on Phenomenological Psychology, the Philosophy of Art, History and Politics*, by M. Merleau-Ponty, xii-xix. Evanston, IL: Northwestern University Press.

Eley, L. 1973. "Afterword: Phenomenology and Philosophy of Language." In *Experience and Judgment: Investigations in a Genealogy of Logic*, by E. Husserl, trans. K. Ameriks, 399-429. Evanston, IL: Northwestern University Press.

Embree, L. 1993. Foreword to *An Introduction to Husserlian Phenomenology*, by R. Bernet, I. Kern and E. Marbach, ix-x. Evanston, IL: Northwestern University Press.

Farber, M. 1940. "The Ideal of a Presuppositionless Philosophy." In *Philosophical Essays in Memory of Edmund Husserl*, ed. M. Farber, 44-64. Cambridge, MA: Harvard University Press.

——. 1963. "First Philosophy and the Problem of the World," *Philosophy and Phenomenological Research*, Vol. 23, No. 3, 315-34.

——. 1968. *The Foundation of Phenomenology: Edmund Husserl and the Quest for a Rigorous Science of Philosophy*. Albany: State University of New York Press. (Original work published 1943)

Fink, E. 1970. "The Phenomenological Philosophy of Edmund Husserl and Contemporary Criticism, Preface by Edmund Husserl." In *The Phenomenology of Edmund Husserl: Selected Critical Readings*, ed. and trans. R. O. Elveton, 73-147. Chicago: Quadrangle Books.

——. 1995. *Sixth Cartesian Meditation: The Idea of a Transcendental Theory of Method, with Textual Notations by Edmund Husserl*, trans. R. Bruzina. Bloomington: Indiana University Press. (Original work published 1988)

Foucault, M. 1977. *Discipline and Punish: The Birth of the Prison*, trans. A. Sheriden. London: Allen Lane. (Original work published 1975)

——. 1999. "About the Beginnings of the Hermeneutics of the Self." In *Religion and Culture*, by M. Foucault, ed. J. R. Carrette, 158-181. New York: Routledge. (Original work published 1993)

Freud, S. 1959a. "Instincts and their Vicissitudes." In *Collected Papers*, Volume 4, by S. Freud, trans. C.M. Baines, 60-83. New York: Basic Books. (Original work published 1915)

——. 1959b. "The Unconscious." In *Collected Papers*, Volume 4, by S. Freud, trans. C.M. Baines, 98-136. New York: Basic Books. (Original work published 1915)

Gadamer, H. G. 1989. *Truth and Method*, trans. J. Weinsheimer and D.G. Marshall. New York: Crossroad. (Original work published 1965)

Gay, P. 1988. *Freud: A Life for OurTtime*. New York: W.W. Norton.

Gazzaniga, M.S. 1992. *Nature's Mind: The Biological Roots of Thinking, Emotions, Sexuality, Language, and Intelligence*. New York: BasicBooks.

Giere, R. N. 1996. "Visual Models and Scientific Judgment." In *Picturing Knowledge: Historical and Philosophical Problems Concerning the Use of Art in Science*, ed. B. S. Baigrie, 269-302. Toronto: University of Toronto Press.

Golomb, J. 1976. "Psychology from the Phenomenological Standpoint of Husserl," *Philosophy and Phenomenological Research*, Vol. 36, No. 4, 451-471.

Grayling, A.C. 1995. "Modern Philosophy II: The Empiricists." In *Philosophy: A Guide Through the Subject*, ed. A. C. Grayling, 484-544. Oxford: Oxford University Press.

Gurwitsch, A. 1964. *The Field of Consciousness*. Pittsburgh, PA: Duquesne University Press.

——. 1966. *Studies in Phenomenology and Psychology*. Evanston, IL: Northwestern University Press.

——. 1974. *Phenomenology and the Theory of Science*, ed. L. Embree. Evanston, IL: Northwestern University Press.

Hall, C.S. and G. Lindzey 1978. *Theories of Personality*, 3rd ed. New York: John Wiley & Sons.

Heidegger, M. 1962. *Being and Time*, ed. J. Macquarri and E. Robinson. San Francisco: HarperCollins. (Original work published 1927)

——. 1982. *The Basic Problems of Phenomenology*, rev. ed., trans. A. Hofstadter. Bloomington: Indiana University Press. (Original work published 1975)

——. 1997. *Phenomenological Interpretations of Kant's Critique of Pure Reason*, trans. P. Emad and K. Maly. Bloomington: Indiana University Press. (Original work published 1977)

Held, K. 1998. *Begrüßungsansprache bei der INTAS-Tagung in St. Petersburg am 3.6.1998*. (*Welcoming Speech to the INTAS Conference in St. Petersburg on March 6, 1998*.) Retrieved March 15, 2002 from Shizuoka University Web Site: http://www.hsss.shizuoka.ac.jp/ Shakai/ningen/hamauzu/russia/begreess.html

Hempel, C.G. 1965. *Aspects of Scientific Explanation: And Other Essays in the Philosophy of Science*. New York: The Free Press.

Henrich, D. 2003. *Between Kant and Hegel: Lectures on German Idealism*, ed. D.S. Pacini. Cambridge, MA: Harvard University Press.

Hocking, W. E. 1940. "A System of Metaphysics." In *Philosophical Essays in Memory of Edmund Husserl*, ed. M. Farber, 251-261. Cambridge, MA: Harvard University Press.

Husserl, E. 1956. "Persönliche Aufzeichnungen" (Personal Notes), ed. W. Biemel, quoted in "The Development of Husserl's Thought" by J. Mohanty in *The Cambridge Companion to Husserl*, ed. B. Smith and D. Smith, 45-77. Cambridge: Cambridge University Press, 1995.

Biblography

———. 1964a. *The Phenomenology of Internal Time-Consciousness*, ed. M. Heidegger, trans. J. S. Churchill. Bloomington: Indiana University Press. (Original work Published 1928)

———. 1964b. *The Idea of Phenomenology*, ed. and trans. W. P. Alston and G. Nakhnikian. The Hague: Nijhoff. (Original work published 1950)

———. 1964c. *The Paris Lectures*, ed. S. Strasser, trans. P. Koestenbaum. The Hague: Nijhoff. (Original work published 1950 as *Cartesian Meditationen und Pariser Vortrage.*)

———. 1965a. *Phenomenology and the Crisis of Philosophy: Philosophy as a Rigorous Science & Philosophy and the Crisis of European Man*, trans. Q. Lauer. New York: Harper & Row. (Original works published 1911 and 1935)

———. 1965b. *Erste Philosophie (1923/24): Erster Teil: Kritische Ideengeschichte (First Philosophy (1923/24): First Part: The Critical History of Ideas)*, ed. R. Boehm, Husserliana Volume 7. Dordrecht: Kluwer.

———. 1969. *Formal and Transcendental Logic*, ed. P. Janssen, trans. D. Cairns. The Hague: Nijhoff. (Original work published 1929)

———. 1970. *The Crisis of European Sciences and Transcendental Phenomenology: An Introduction to Phenomenological Philosophy*, ed. W. Biemel and D. Carr, trans. D. Carr. Evanston, IL: Northwestern University Press. (Original work published 1954)

———. 1973a. *Experience and Judgment: Investigations in a Genealogy of Logic*, ed. L. Landgrebe, trans. J. S. Churchill and K. Ameriks. Evanston, IL: Northwestern University Press. (Original work published 1948)

———. 1973b. *Cartesian Meditations: An Introduction to Phenomenology*, ed. S. Strasser, trans. D. Cairns. The Hague: Nijhoff. (Original work published in French 1931, first German edition 1950)

———. 1975. *Introduction to the Logical Investigations: A Draft of a Preface to the Logical Investigations (1913)*, ed. E. Fink, trans. P. J. Bossert and C. H. Peters. The Hague: Nijhoff.

———. 1977. *Phenomenological Psychology: Lectures, Summer Semester, 1925*, ed. W. Biemel, trans. J. Scanlon. The Hague: Nijhoff. (Original work published 1962)

———. 1980a. *Ideas Pertaining to a Pure Phenomenology and to a Phenomenological Philosophy, Second Book: Studies in the Phenomenology of Constitution*, ed. M. Biemel, trans. R. Rojcewicz and A. Schuwer. Dordrecht: Kluwer. (Original work published 1952)

———. 1980b. *Ideas Pertaining to a Pure Phenomenology and to a Phenomenological Philosophy, Third Book: Phenomenology and the Foundation of the Sciences*, ed. M. Biemel, trans. T. Klein and W. Pohl. Dordrecht: Kluwer. (Original work published 1953)

———. 1981. *Husserl: Shorter Works*, ed. P. McCormick and F. A. Elliston. Notre Dame, IN: University of Notre Dame Press.

———. 1982. *Ideas Pertaining to a Pure Phenomenology and to a Phenomenological Philosophy, First Book: General Introduction to a Pure Phenomenology*, ed. K. Schuhmann, trans. F. Kersten. Dordrecht: Kluwer. (Original work published 1913)

——. 1994. *Early Writings in the Philosophy of Logic and Mathematics*, trans.
D. Willard. Dordrecht: Kluwer. (Original work published 1980)

——. 1997. "The Amsterdam Lectures." In *Psychological and Transcendental
Phenomenology and the Confrontation with Heidegger (1927-1931)*, ed.
and trans. T. Sheehan and R. E. Palmer, 213-239. Dordrecht:
Kluwer.

——. 1999. *Analyses Concerning Passive and Active Synthesis: Lectures on
Transcendental Logic*, trans. A. J. Steinbock, excerpted in *The
Essential Husserl: Basic Writings in Transcendental Phenomenology*, ed.
D. Welton, 316-21. Bloomington: Indiana University Press.

——. 2001. *The Shorter Logical Investigations*, ed. D. Moran, trans. J. N.
Findlay. London: Routledge. (Original work published 1913 as
the second German edition of *Logische Untersuchungen*)

——. 2003. *Philosophy of Arithmetic: Psychological and Logical Investigations*, trans.
D. Willard. Dordrecht: Klewer (Original work published 1891)

——. 2006. *The Basic Problems of Phenomenology: From the Lecture, Winter Semester
1910-1911*, ed. I. Kern, trans. I. Farin and J.G. Hart. Dordrecht:
Springer (Original work published 1973)

Kagen, J., and J. Segal. 1992. *Psychology: An Introduction*, 7th ed. New York:
Harcourt Brace Jovanovich.

Kant, I. 1965. *Critique of Pure Reason*, unabridged ed., trans. N. K. Smith.
New York: St. Martin's Press. (Original work published 1787)

Kirkpatrick, R., and F. Williams. 1957. Translators' introduction to *The
Transcendence of the Ego: An Existentialist Theory of Consciousness*, by
J.-P. Sartre, 11-27. New York: The Noonday Press.

Kisiel, T. 1996. "The Genesis of Being and Time." In *Phenomenology,
Interpretation, and Community*, ed. L. Langsdorf, S. H. Watson, and
E. M. Bower, 29-50. Albany: State University of New York Press.

Klein, J. 1940. "Phenomenology and the History of Science." In
Philosophical Essays in Memory of Edmund Husserl, ed. M.
Farber, 143-163. Cambridge, MA: Harvard University Press.

Kockelmans, J. J. 1973. "Theoretical Problems in Phenomenological
Psychology." In *Phenomenology and the Social Sciences*, ed. M.
Natanson, 225-280. Evanston, IL: Northwestern University
Press.

Kuhn, H. 1940. "The Phenomenological Concept of 'Horizon.'" In
Philosophical Essays in Memory of Edmund Husserl, ed. M. Farber,
106-123. Cambridge, MA: Harvard University Press.

Lauer, Q. 1965. *Introduction to Phenomenology and the Crisis of Philosophy*,
1-68. New York: Harper & Row.

Lycan, W. G. 1990. "Introduction to Part V." In *Mind and Cognition: A
Reader*, ed. W. G. Lycan, 277-81. Oxford: Basil Blackwell.

Malmquist, C. P. 1994. "The Theoretical Status of Depressions in
Childhood." In *Clinical Faces of Childhood*, ed. E. J. Anthony and D.
C. Gilpin, 173-204. Northvale, NJ: Jason Aronson. (Original
work published 1976 as *Three Clinical Faces of Childhood*.)

Bibliography

Matas, J. 2002. *Philosophy: Provisional Course Notes*. Retrieved November 30, 2002 from DeSales University Web Site: http://www4.allencol.edu/~jm02/ON-PHILOSOPHY.html

McCormick, P. 1981. "Husserl on Philosophy as a Rigorous Science." In *Husserl: Shorter Works*, by E. Husserl, 161-5. Notre Dame, IN: University of Notre Dame Press.

Merleau-Ponty, M. 1964. *The Primacy of Perception: And other Essays on Phenomenological Psychology, the Philosophy of Art, History and Politics*, ed. and trans. J. M. Edie. Evanston, IL: Northwestern University Press. (Original works published 1947 to 1961)

———. 1968. *The Visible and the Invisible: Followed by Working Notes*, ed. C. Lefort, trans. A. Lingis. Evanston, IL: Northwestern University Press. (Original work published 1964)

Miller, J. 1993. *The Passion of Michel Foucault*. New York: Simon & Schuster.

Misch, G. 1930. *Lebensphilosophie und Phänomenologie. (The Philosophy of Life and Phenomenology)* Berlin: B. G. Teubner.

Mischara, A. 1990. "Husserl and Freud: Time, Memory and the Unconscious." *Husserl Studies* 7: 29-55.

Mohanty, J. N. 1989. *Transcendental Phenomenology: An Analytic Account*. Oxford: Basil Blackwell.

———. 1995. "The Development of Husserl's Thought." In *The Cambridge Companion to Husserl*, ed. B. Smith and D. W. Smith, 45-77. Cambridge: Cambridge University Press.

Moran, D. 2000. *Introduction to Phenomenology*. London: Routledge.

Moustakas, C. 1994. *Phenomenological Research Methods*. Thousand Oaks, CA: Sage.

Mulligan, K. 1995. "Perception." In *The Cambridge Guide to Husserl*, ed. B. Smith and D.W. Smith, 168-238. Cambridge: Cambridge University Press.

Nakhnikian, G. 1964. Introduction to *The Idea of Phenomenology*, by E. Husserl, ix-xxii. The Hague: Nijhoff.

Natanson, M. 1973. *Edmund Husserl: Philosopher of Infinite Tasks*. Evanston, IL: Northwestern University Press.

———. 1988. "'The Strangeness In the Strangeness': Phenomenology and the Mundane." In *Edmund Husserl and the Phenomenological Tradition: Essays in Phenomenology*, ed. R. Sokolowski, 183-95. Washington, DC: The Catholic University of America Press.

Nevid, J.S., S. A. Rathus, and B. Greene. 1994. *Abnormal Psychology in a Changing World*, 2nd ed. Englewood Cliffs, NJ: Prentice-Hall.

Ornstein, R. 1986. *The Psychology of Consciousness*, 2nd rev. ed. London: Penguin Books.

Palmer, R. E. 1997. "An Introduction to the Amsterdam Lectures." In *Psychological and Transcendental Phenomenology and the Confrontation with Heidegger (1927-1931)*, ed. T. Sheehan and R. E. Palmer, 119-212. Dordrecht: Kluwer.

Bibliography

Parsons, A. 1958. "Translators' Introduction: A Guide to Psychologists." In *The Growth of Logical Thinking from Childhood to Adolescence*, by B. Inhelder and J. Piaget, vii-xx. New York: Basic Books.

Patočka, J. 1996. *Heretical Essays in the Philosophy of History*, ed. J. Dodd, trans. E. Kohák. Chicago: Open Court. (Original work published 1990)

Piaget, J. 1954. *The Construction of Reality in the Child*, trans. M. Cook. New York: Basic Books.

———. 1976. *Judgment and Reasoning in the Child*, trans. M. Warden. Totowa, NJ: Littlefield, Adams. (Original work published 1928)

Ricoeur, P. 1967. *Husserl: An Analysis of his Phenomenology*, trans. E. G. Ballard and L. E. Embree. Evanston, IL: Northwestern University Press.

———. 1969. *The Symbolism of Evil*, trans. E. Buchanan. Boston: Beacon Press. (Original work published 1967)

———. 1984. *Time and Narrative: Volume 1*, trans. K. McLaughlin and D. Pellauer. Chicago: The University of Chicago Press. (Original work published 1983)

Rollinger, R.D. 2004. "Brentano and Husserl," in *The Cambridge Companion to Brentano*, ed. D. Jacqette, 255-76. Cambridge: Cambridge University Press.

Royce, J. R. 1987. "Theoretical Psychology." In *Concise Encyclopedia of Psychology*, ed. R. J. Corsini, 1118-19. New York: John Wiley & Sons.

Rucker, R. v. B. 1977. *Geometry, Relativity, and the Fourth Dimension*. New York: Dover Publications.

Sahakian, W. S. 1968. *History of Philosophy*. New York: Harper & Row.

Sainsbury, M. 1995. "Philosophical Logic." In *Philosophy: A Guide Through the Subject*, ed. A. C. Grayling, 61-122. Oxford: Oxford University Press.

Sartre, J.-P. 1957. *Transcendence of the Ego: An Existentialist Theory of Consciousness*, trans. R. Kirkpatrick and F. Williams. New York: The Noonday Press. (Original work published 1936-37)

———. 1976. *The Emotions: Outline of a Theory*, trans. B. Frechtman. New York: Philosophical Library. (Original work published 1948)

———. 1994. *Being and Nothingness*, trans. H. E. Barnes. New York: Gramercy Books. (Original work published 1943, with additional material published 1953)

Schürmann, R. 1990. *Heidegger on Being and Acting: From Principles to Anarchy*, trans. C. M. Gros and R. Schürmann. Bloomington: Indiana University Press. (Original work published 1982)

Schutz, A. 1970. *On Phenomenology and Social Relations*, ed. H. R. Wagner. Chicago: The University of Chicago Press.

Scruton, R. 1982. *Kant*. Oxford: Oxford University Press.

Smith, B. 1995. "Common Sense." In *The Cambridge Companion to Husserl*, ed. B. Smith and D.W. Smith, 394-437. Cambridge: Cambridge University Press.

Bibliography

Smith, B. and D. W. Smith. 1995. Introduction to *The Cambridge Companion to Husserl*, ed. B. Smith and D. W. Smith, 1-44. Cambridge: Cambridge University Press.

Smith, E.J. 1920. *The Technique of Psychoanalysis.* New York: Nervous and Mental Disease Publishing Company.

Spiegelberg, H. 1981. "On the Misfortunes of Edmund Husserl's *Encyclopaedia Britannica* Article 'Phenomenology.'" In *Husserl: Shorter Works*, by E. Husserl, 18-20. Notre Dame, IN: University of Notre Dame Press.

Stein, E. 1986. *Life in a Jewish Family: Her Unfinished Autobiographical Account*, ed. L. Gelber and R. Leuven, trans. J. Koeppel. Washington, DC: ICS Publications.

———. 1989. *On the Problem of Empathy*, trans. W. Stein. Washington, DC: ICS Publications. (Original work published 1917)

———. 2000. *Philosophy of Psychology and the Humanities*, ed. M. Sawicki, trans. M. C. Baseheart and M. Sawicki. Washington, DC: ICS Publications. (Original work published 1922)

Steinbock, A. J. 1995. *Home and Beyond: Generative Phenomenology after Husserl.* Evanston, IL: Northwestern University Press.

———. 1996. "Homeworld/Alienworld: Toward a Generative Phenomenology of Intersubjectivity." In *Phenomenology, Interpretation and Community*, ed. L. Langsdorf and S. H. Watson, 65-81. Albany: State University of New York Press.

Tito, J. M. 1990. *Logic in the Husserlian Context.* Evanston, IL: Northwestern University Press.

van den Berg. J. H. 1975. *The Changing Nature of Man. Introduction to a Historical Psychology*, trans. H.F. Croes. New York: Dell. (Original work published 1956 as *Metabletica, of Leer der Veranderingen*)

Van de Pitte, M. 1981. Introduction to "Author's Preface to the English edition of Ideas." In *Husserl: Shorter Works*, by E. Husserl, 36-42. Notre Dame, IN: Notre Dame University Press.

Van Doren, C. 1991. *A History of Knowledge: The Pivotal Events, People, and Achievements of World History.* New York: Ballantine Books.

Welch, E. P. 1941. *The Philosophy of Edmund Husserl: The Origin and Development of His Phenomenology.* New York: Columbia University Press.

Welton, D. 2000. *The Other Husserl: The Horizons of Transcendental Phenomenology.* Bloomington: Indiana University Press.

Weyl, H. 1940. "The Ghost of Modality." In *Philosophical Essays in Memory of Edmund Husserl*, ed. M. Farber, 278-303. Cambridge, MA: Harvard University Press.

Wild, J. 1940. "Husserl's Critique of Psychologism." In *Philosophical Essays in Memory of Edmund Husserl*, ed. M. Farber, 19-43. Cambridge, MA: Harvard University Press.

Index

1925 lectures on psychology, 13-15,
19, 23, 43, 68, 108, 109, 111, 116,
122, 165, 193
abnormality, 55, 244, 259, 277
absolute, 27, 44, 61, 71, 73, 74, 82,
88, 96, 97, 125, 131, 147-9, 153,
160, 166, 188, 192, 206, 213, 222,
224, 231, 237, 247, 258, 259, 261,
267, 269, 270
absurdity, 63, 148, 157, 167, 195, 224,
252
act psychology, 9, 23, 45, 59, 67, 68,
98, 173, 226
actual now, 255, 256, 275
actual reality, *vii, viii, x, xii*, 2, 3, 6, 7,
21, 23, 27, 28, 30-5, 41, 44, 49, 52,
53, 62, 63, 70, 73, 75, 78, 83-6, 93,
95, 100-2, 104, 108, 116, 121, 125,
129, 135-7, 140, 143, 146, 149, 152,
153, 154, 156, 159-62, 165, 166,
168, 171, 172, 174-6, 180, 182, 184-
7, 191, 195, 196, 202, 204, 206, 207,
211, 213, 214, 217-19, 222, 223,
225, 227, 228, 230, 232, 234, 236-9,
241-5, 247, 250, 253, 258-60, 269,
271, 275-7
adumbration, 149-56, 158-64, 169,
181-3, 188, 191, 195-7, 200, 202-4,
213-15, 220-2, 225, 226, 235, 252,
253, 258, 260-5, 278, 269, 271
affair-complex, 102-4, 121, 125, 129,
130, 134-6, 138, 139, 141, 145, 147,
149-51, 153, 154, 156-8, 163, 168,
169, 174, 177, 178, 180-3, 197, 201-
3, 205, 207, 208, 210, 213-15, 218-
23, 225, 227-30, 234, 239, 243, 244,
246-8, 250, 251, 256, 260, 262-5,
269, 276, 277
affect, 3, 95, 130, 135, 171, 178, 189,
191, 196, 244, 246, 247, 276
affective inner experience, 94
affective orientation, 246
affective unity, 37, 41, 47, 53, 99, 101,
123, 127, 135, 138, 144, 164, 169,
178, 181, 188, 190, 193, 203-6, 210,

225, 226, 228, 231, 234, 242, 244,
246, 250, 255, 257-60, 264, 265,
267, 268, 271, 272, 276
agency, 35, 36, 39-42, 67, 70, 71, 98,
106, 126, 129, 131, 135, 141, 144,
148, 151, 165, 194, 207, 217, 225,
232, 235, 254, 274
a-historical, *vii, xi, xii*, 32, 46, 69, 72,
109, 111, 132, 199, 208, 216, 272,
275
alien-I, 167-8, 223
all-space, 188, 247, 256, 257
alter-ego, 167, 168, 233
Amsterdam lectures, the, 111-17
analogy, 57, 58, 131, 149, 176, 192,
203, 251, 252, 254
analogous, *ix*, 54, 73, 86, 131, 190-2,
204, 206, 208, 246, 251-3, 257, 263
analytical psychology, 43, 69
analytic philosophy, 60
anthropic principle, 56
anthropological, 26, 51, 71, 262
anticipation, 3, 37, 41, 51, 78, 120,
123, 125, 126, 133-6, 139, 147, 148,
150-2, 164, 181, 184-8, 196, 197,
201, 213, 215, 220, 223, 226, 233,
240, 255, 256, 259, 264, 267, 268,
276, 277
anti-psychologism, 61, 127, 160, 163,
197, 226
antithetic, 270
apodicticity, 65-7, 70, 72, 74, 75, 82,
94-8, 115, 124, 125, 133, 145, 149,
153, 167, 172, 174, 176, 179, 185,
205, 206, 208, 209, 221, 223, 230,
231, 239, 251-3, 267, 270
apophantics, 173
apperception, 7, 21, 37, 51, 52, 67,
68, 73, 82, 84, 90, 100, 108, 121-5,
127-33, 137, 138, 148, 150-9, 161,
163-5, 175, 178, 179, 181-5, 187-90,
192, 196, 199, 201, 204, 209, 217-
26, 229, 233, 237, 240-2, 246-53,
255, 257, 259, 261, 262, 265, 267-9,
271, 272, 276

applied phenomenology, *vi*, *vii*, 14, 29, 77-9, 88, 89, 99, 107, 212, 213, 219,224, 229, 232

applied geometry, 82, 202, 204-6, 210, 218, 226

appresentation, 190-3, 225, 240, 241, 252, 253, 256, 269

approximation, 202, 207, 216, 222, 223, 249, 253, 263, 264, 275

Aquinas, T., 57

Aristotle, *viii*, 18, 57, 61, 90, 118, 234

arousal, 245, 248, 255

as if, 72, 101, 173, 174, 242, 255, 271

asymmetrical, 210, 213, 222, 223, 228

asymptotic, 210-14, 220-2, 228, 236, 255-7, 268, 274

authenticity, *xv*, 45, 48, 49, 53, 62, 115

autism, 2

autonomy, 35, 36, 39, 70, 99, 106, 128, 132, 134, 155, 165, 168, 194, 209, 217, 229, 232, 234, 237, 254, 174

average, 192, 216

axiological, 121, 124, 185, 188, 235

before-and-after, 71, 100, 137, 140, 175, 209, 232, 255, 256

behavior, 14, 21, 26, 42, 50, 51, 55, 151, 192, 196, 215, 234, 244, 262

being psychological, 25, 26, 157, 178, 194, 226, 234, 244, 246, 266

being-in-the-world, 22, 42, 44, 46, 49-51, 53, 97, 98, 142, 209, 224, 225, 231-3, 271

being-sense, 31, 32, 39, 75, 85, 126, 141-4, 146-56, 158, 159, 162-5, 168-70, 172, 175, 178-80, 183, 187, 188, 199, 200, 207, 211, 214, 217, 220, 221, 225, 228, 243, 249, 251, 252, 263, 266, 269, 270, 273, 276

Bell, W., 81

Berkeley, G., 79

bestowed sense, 33, 51, 102, 104, 120-2, 127, 127, 139, 158, 167, 202, 207, 212, 227

bifurcation, 12, 39, 95, 98, 104, 116, 138, 180, 183, 187, 194, 197, 209, 224, 255, 256

Blackburn, S., 143

Boden, 38, 40, 240, 270

Bolzano, F., 58, 60, 274

Book I (*Ideas I*), 17-19, 24, 82, 86, 92, 96, 98, 107, 118, 122, 181, 201, 248

Book II (*Ideas II*), 24, 82, 90-4, 97, 98, 105

Book III (*Ideas III*), 82, 90

bracketing, 8, 18, 20, 37, 52, 68, 78-80, 84, 92, 94, 102, 107-9, 111, 112, 122, 145, 150, 158, 160, 168, 180, 186, 192, 194, 196, 199, 200, 205, 224, 227, 229, 232, 248, 254, 263

brain, 33, 69, 101, 128, 236

Brentano, F., *viii*, 24, 32, 57-60, 62, 67, 68, 72, 92, 98, 114, 193, 226, 242

Brough, J.B., 84

Bruzina, R., 46

Cairns, D., 107, 234

calculus of logic, 62-5, 126, 150, 151, 173, 179, 195, 198, 212, 213, 264

Cartesian *cogito*, 238, 241

Cartesian Meditations, 68, 117

Cartesianism, 49, 59, 230 237, 238

Cassirer, E., 67, 117

Churchland, P. S., 26

circle of transcendence, 4, 5, 18, 94, 124, 180, 199, 208, 224

co-existence, *vii*, *xiii*, 24, 42, 43, 86, 94, 99, 101, 124, 142, 146, 169, 170, 172, 186-91, 204, 206, 209, 212, 217-19, 221, 224, 229-31, 233, 234, 237, 240, 244, 249, 250, 252, 254, 256-8, 260-2, 264, 266, 268-73, 277

cogitationes, 67, 68

cognitive development, 3, 20, 33, 43, 69, 96, 129, 174, 177-9, 190, 194, 227, 232, 258

cognitive mental life, *vii-ix*, *xvi*, 11, 13, 14, 16, 19, 20, 22, 26, 33, 34, 36, 38, 40, 41, 53, 54, 77, 80, 83, 86, 94, 98, 101, 103, 104, 122, 126, 130-7, 142, 145, 152, 154-6, 159, 163-6, 171, 173, 181, 182, 184, 191, 194, 195, 200, 205, 208, 209, 213, 218, 219, 222, 227, 229, 231-42, 244, 253-5,

266-8, 273, 275, 276

common essence, 100, 140, 141

common semblance, 42-4, 51, 53, 93, 95, 96, 101, 103, 124, 128-30, 132-4, 136, 142-8, 152, 154, 162, 164-72, 175-8, 182, 187-9, 191-3, 196, 199, 202, 203, 206, 208-10, 212, 217, 218, 221-4, 227-31, 233-5, 239, 244, 246, 249-54, 257, 260, 261, 263, 266, 267, 269, 271, 272, 277

common sense, 10, 64

communal, *xiii*, 1, 9, 35, 36, 43, 47, 72, 80, 101, 107, 129, 131, 188-91, 231, 239, 258, 259, 261-6, 269

community, 41, 106, 109, 258, 259, 261-3, 271

complexity, 30, 75, 94, 123, 126, 147, 170, 205, 221, 268, 271, 273, 275

composing-acts, 37, 148, 177, 195, 201, 219, 227

concatenation, 99, 103, 104, 158, 168, 169, 205, 210, 212, 214, 216, 220, 223, 228, 241-3, 246-8, 250, 251, 260, 268, 269

conceptual space, 38-40, 51, 54, 65, 66, 70, 79, 84, 85, 99, 100, 103, 116, 120-5, 131, 132, 136, 139, 142, 145, 146, 148, 150, 152-7, 159, 162-4, 168, 169, 171, 174, 175, 177-85, 192, 196, 199, 201, 205, 207, 208, 210, 211, 217, 228, 230, 231, 235, 239, 242, 243, 246, 250, 266, 268, 271, 272, 276

conferred meaning, 33, 51, 97, 104, 120, 121, 133, 143, 144, 149, 150, 156-8, 179, 202, 207, 212, 227

Conrad-Martius, H., 81

consciousness-formation, *vii, x, ix, xiii- xvi*, 4, 13, 20, 29, 32-4, 36, 38, 39, 44, 52, 55, 59, 67, 71, 75-7, 80, 82-7, 95, 97, 99-102, 115, 116, 120, 123, 124, 130, 132, 138-43, 146, 147, 149-54, 158-63, 167, 169, 172-2, 176, 177, 179-81, 183, 186, 188-91, 194-7, 200, 201, 203-5, 207-9, 211-15, 217, 218, 220-3, 225-7, 229-31, 234, 235, 237, 240-2, 244-6, 249,

250, 253-5, 258, 261-8, 270, 273-5

consciousness-of, 115, 135, 266

consistency, *xi*, 165, 193-5, 216, 225, 235, 236, 241, 244, 256, 257, 259-61, 272, 277

constituting-acts, 40, 153, 159

constitution, 27, 28, 31, 33, 34, 37, 39, 40, 42, 43, 46, 52, 54, 55, 67, 68, 71, 77, 80, 83, 84, 86, 87, 90, 92-4, 99, 100, 108, 124, 126, 133, 134, 137, 138, 142, 145, 148, 158, 161-3, 169, 173-5, 177, 179, 181, 182, 188, 201-6, 209-12, 217-28, 230, 231, 233, 234, 239-41, 247-9, 253, 255, 262, 265, 266, 270, 271, 275

Continental School, *xvi*, 41, 74, 76, 77, 89

contingent, 10, 12, 14, 15, 17, 24, 27-9, 33, 34, 36, 39, 54, 59, 62, 65-7, 74, 75, 78, 83-5, 88, 89, 95, 98, 102, 103, 107, 111, 115, 116, 118, 121, 124-7, 130, 133, 138-40, 142, 147, 149, 153, 154, 159, 163, 166, 168-73, 181, 183-5, 188, 200, 202, 207-11, 213, 216, 218, 220, 221, 223, 225, 228, 241, 246, 247, 250, 252, 255, 263, 266, 267, 271, 273, 276

Copernican turn, 78, 93

co-presence, 100, 190-2

core essence, 137-9, 143, 145, 151-5, 158, 159, 161, 163, 168, 169, 172, 176-9, 181-3, 185, 186, 195, 198, 199, 201, 203, 207, 210, 211, 215, 217, 219-22, 224, 230, 231, 234, 235, 242, 243, 248-53, 276

corporeal-life, 35, 36, 41, 94, 96, 97, 99-101, 132, 140, 141, 166, 191-3, 225, 237, 243, 252, 253, 269

correlation, *viii*, 14, 21, 23, 24, 29, 32, 40, 49, 52, 53, 70, 76, 82, 85-7, 89, 91-103, 108, 118, 122, 124, 125, 127, 129-35, 138, 140-57, 159, 160, 162, 164, 166-8, 170-2, 176, 179, 180, 185, 187, 189-91, 220, 221, 225, 228, 231, 236, 238, 240-5, 252, 263, 264, 267-70, 276

countersense, 153, 167, 194, 195, 224,

241, 242

Crisis of European Sciences, The, 97, 119

cultural, 20, 47, 48, 50, 52, 71, 72, 77, 97, 109, 131, 179, 187, 216, 238, 244, 258, 261-3

Daubert, J., 118

day-to-day (*Umwelt*), *xii*, *xiii*, 11, 13, 18, 19, 40, 53, 59, 63-5, 68, 97, 107, 124, 130, 135, 139, 171, 173, 176, 180, 188, 191, 206, 215, 233, 237, 247, 256, 266, 269-71, 276

deconstruction, 199, 209

deduction, 13, 17, 21, 52, 131, 195

deeming, 52, 134, 147, 154, 181, 215, 217, 220-2, 224, 226, 235, 242, 250, 263, 266, 277

deep structure, *xi-xiv*, 7, 37, 198

Deleuze, F., 47

dependence, 10, 45, 54, 62, 76, 79, 80, 84, 87, 104, 110, 129, 138, 145, 149, 151, 158, 161, 174, 177, 179, 190, 192, 254, 264

Descartes, R., *viii*, 32, 41, 56, 65-8, 70, 73, 74, 94, 100, 170, 238

descriptive phenomenology, 8, 9, 14, 24, 28, 169, 180, 218, 229

descriptive psychology, 13, 15, 17, 19-21, 23, 58, 59, 68, 92, 122, 165

determinable X, 137, 148

diachronic, *x*, 175, 189, 225, 233, 252, 261, 263

diachronic/synchronic synthesis, 216, 227

dialectic, 43, 47-51, 53, 133, 136, 138, 158, 162, 163, 167, 168, 183, 197, 218, 220, 224, 233, 234, 254

diegetic, *ix*

difference-and-identity, 164

Dilthey, W., *viii*, 21, 32, 45, 46, 68, 69, 71, 72, 91, 96, 109-12

"Dilthey-Husserl Correspondence," 91

doxa, 122

duration, 96, 125, 131, 132, 138, 140, 147, 148, 189, 231, 232, 246, 255, 257, 258, 276

dynamis, 135, 217

ego advertence, 55, 176, 213, 244-6,

264, 271, 275

ego-*cogito*, 244, 245

ego-life, 23, 37, 38, 40, 42, 43, 53, 78, 92, 94, 97, 98, 107, 116, 134, 141, 164, 167, 193, 194, 209, 220, 223, 34, 240, 241, 244, 245, 247, 254, 255, 257, 262, 266, 268, 273, 275

egology, 94, 225, 235

ego-pole, 52

ego-subjects, 38, 39, 41, 106, 189, 191, 229, 233, 248, 252, 258, 260, 261, 268, 273

eidetic memory, 85, 87, 127, 196, 220, 228, 250, 251, 262, 271, 275

eidetic ontology, 18, 20, 21, 24, 31-3, 104

eidetic reduction, 124, 126, 129, 132, 133, 139, 147, 156, 168, 176, 177, 179, 180, 199, 204, 211-18, 242, 248, 263, 275

eidetic science, *xii*, *xiii*, 6, 18, 60, 61, 101, 120, 274

eidetic *seeing*, *xii*, *xv*, 76, 115, 116, 149, 155, 173, 185, 209, 211, 234

eidetic singularity, 18, 168, 169, 203, 214, 220

eidetic structure, 7, 13, 40, 75, 77-9, 82, 85-7, 95, 102, 104, 120-4, 140, 147, 148, 152, 178, 182, 208, 228, 244, 250, 253, 263, 267, 276

eidos, *xii*, 7, 18, 22, 26, 32, 36-8, 41, 44, 49, 53, 75, 78, 85, 86, 89, 95, 97, 100-3, 107, 108, 114, 115, 120-2, 124, 127, 129, 130, 133, 134, 137, 138, 143, 147-50, 152, 153, 156, 158, 159, 161, 162, 168, 172, 174, 176, 177, 180-2, 187, 188, 196, 198, 199, 201, 203-6, 210-15, 219-22, 224, 230, 231, 234-7, 240, 242, 244, 245, 248-51, 253, 256, 262, 267, 268, 275, 276

elapse, 138-40, 152, 159, 175, 203, 210, 221, 227, 230, 232, 243, 245-7, 268, 275

elements, *vii*, *viii*, 12, 21, 27, 32, 33, 35, 37-9, 41, 42, 47, 53, 57, 59, 63, 71, 73, 76, 78-80, 82, 85-9, 91, 92,

95-7, 99, 101-4, 108, 111, 123-5,
127, 129-32, 134, 137-41, 143-5,
147-63, 166, 168, 169, 173, 174, 176-
8, 180-4, 186, 187, 190, 191, 194,
196-222, 225-32, 234, 235, 238, 240-
50, 252, 255, 256, 259, 260, 262-6,
268-71, 273, 275-7
elliptical, 57, 212
embodiment, 50-3, 55, 91, 128-34,
140-2, 148, 151, 153, 154, 166, 173,
177, 179, 183, 188-93, 200, 206-8,
210, 212, 214, 217, 220, 221, 226,
228, 231, 235, 236, 241, 243, 247-
51, 253-7, 262, 267, 269-71, 276
Embree, L., 51
emotions, 48, 58, 198, 238
empathetic endeavors, 259, 263, 270
empathy, 3, 96, 101, 103, 118, 123,
135, 148, 176, 177, 182, 187-91,
193, 203-5, 208-10, 213, 216, 218,
221-3, 228, 230, 231, 233, 236, 244,
247, 250-61, 265, 269-71, 274-7
empirical, *xi, xii*, 1-4, 11-13, 15-21, 26,
30, 32, 42, 43, 58, 59, 65, 67, 69, 70,
72, 73, 75, 76, 83, 88, 90, 92, 106,
108-11, 122, 129, 131, 146, 151, 157,
170, 175, 192, 193, 200, 229, 231,
235-7, 248, 269, 275, 276
Encyclopaedia Britannica article, the
("Phenomenology"), 26, 27, 83, 113,
116, 178
entelecheia, 135
entrée, 4, 10, 14, 19, 68, 93, 94, 101,
102, 108, 116, 122, 124, 133, 136,
137, 143, 145, 157, 179, 199, 208,
220
enworlding, 166, 266, 277
epistēmē, 122
epiphenomenon, 151
epistemology, *vi-viii*, 6, 10, 11, 12, 15,
16, 20, 21, 29-32, 38, 39, 45, 46,
50-2, 58, 60, 61, 64, 71, 74, 75, 78,
80, 82, 87, 90, 91, 93, 94, 97, 98,
100, 103, 106, 116, 120-9, 131,
133-5, 139-41, 148, 152, 154, 158,
159, 165, 172, 174, 175, 180, 187,
194, 211, 214, 215, 224, 229, 237,

240, 249-251, 272
error, 1, 5, 16, 23, 32, 43, 66, 69, 79,
88, 89, 120, 124, 131, 196, 208, 229
essence, *vii-ix, xii, xiii, xv*, 6, 7, 11-16,
18-22, 24, 26, 28, 30-3, 37, 42, 43,
45, 47, 70-8, 81-5, 88, 91, 94-7, 99,
100, 102, 105, 106, 109-12, 114-16,
120-3, 125, 127, 130, 133-46, 149,
151-63, 165-73, 175-7, 179, 181-6,
188-90, 195, 196, 198-201, 203,
207, 210, 211, 215-17, 219-22, 224-
6, 230, 231, 234, 235, 239, 240, 242-
6, 248-51, 253-6, 258, 259, 261,
264, 266, 270-4, 276, 277
ethics, 1, 44, 56, 91 96, 105, 165, 172,
188, 252
Euclid, 276
Euclidean, 90
exclusion, 52, 54, 63 74, 78, 79, 88,
107, 108, 119, 158, 184, 185, 192
193 196, 271
exemplary, *vii, viii*, 21, 33, 69, 71, 96,
110, 111, 121, 201, 236, 265, 272
exemplification, 84-6, 109, 121, 130,
146, 176, 204, 219, 259
existential, *xiv*, 7, 28, 42-4, 51-4, 79,
103, 105, 112, 119, 124, 130, 138,
167, 180, 181, 184-6, 199, 205, 209,
215, 217, 220, 228, 232, 233, 241,
249, 251, 266, 271, 274, 275
existential anthropology, 45
existential ontology, 48-50
Experience and Judgment, 119
expressible constructs, 104
extra-physical, 101, 114-16, 121, 140,
211, 246, 273
extra-psychic, 17, 21, 26, 134, 196,
197, 207, 229,
fact, 2-4, 10, 18, 20, 24, 27, 31, 40, 44,
46, 47, 50, 61-6, 69, 78, 79, 106,
109-11, 114, 192, 235, 236, 239
factual, 2-5, 7, 19, 21, 29, 31, 41, 51,
61-3, 65, 66, 69, 72, 79, 82, 106,
131, 157, 170, 172-5, 200, 216, 236,
249-51, 253, 262, 263, 266, 269,
270, 274
facticity, 48, 49, 53, 85, 261, 268

fallibility of memory, 196

fantasy, 19, 145, 156, 159, 194, 202, 269

Farber, M., 12, 47, 107, 175

Fechner, G.T., 21, 56

feelings, *xiii*, 7, 23, 33, 49, 76, 100, 105, 115, 121, 124, 130, 135, 163, 164, 179, 183, 187, 190, 195, 196, 222, 234, 238, 240, 245, 246, 248, 259, 260, 265, 267, 275, 276

feelings of empathy, 188, 189, 191, 192, 223, 254, 257, 258, 263, 265, 275

feigning, 101

Ferenczi, S., 193

field of actionality, 39, 41, 134, 173, 174, 197, 200, 218, 221, 227, 231, 240, 244, 245, 267, 271, 276

"Fifth Cartesian Meditation," 254

finite, 21, 45, 48, 85, 102, 140-2, 148, 175, 176, 183, 188, 195, 263, 264, 274, 275

Fink, E., *xiv*, 41, 107, 116, 146, 185, 201

"First Philosophy," lecture on, 107

first-person, 42, 77, 170-2, 209, 228, 239, 266, 275,

flow, 39, 40, 47, 79, 99, 125, 127, 130, 132, 136, 137, 150, 154, 155, 160, 161, 163, 170, 181, 183, 189, 201, 205, 209, 210, 217, 220, 225, 227, 230, 235, 240-3, 245-7, 256, 266, 271, 276

flux, 25, 85, 116, 121, 129, 139, 169, 186, 197, 209, 239, 240, 245, 256, 273

for everyone, *ix*, 11, 26, 27, 30, 39, 40, 53, 63, 95, 124, 132, 134, 140, 147, 153, 170, 171, 175-7, 182, 186-8, 191, 201, 203, 208-10, 216, 222, 227, 228, 231, 235, 236, 251, 253, 257, 260, 263, 267, 269, 277

form of ideation, 37, 42, 52 54, 130, 132, 144, 149-52, 154, 159, 161, 205, 235, 239, 247, 251, 256, 257, 263, 264, 266, 267, 269-72, 276

Formal and Transcendental Logic, 117

formal ontology, 10, 118

Foucault, M., 5, 47, 51

free fantasy, 155-8, 160, 162, 167, 169, 174, 229, 232, 243, 252

free variation, 30, 39

Frege, G., 60

Freud, S., *xi*, 21, 87, 192, 193, 234

full intentional Object, 134, 150, 244, 245, 247, 264

fullness of self-sameness, 172

fully human, 215, 276, 277

functional problem, 161

fundamental ontology, *vi*, 7, 9, 10, 19, 20, 43-5, 75, 112, 120, 124, 134, 144, 146, 148, 166, 172, 265

Gadamer, H-G., *xiv*, 107

Galilean worldview, 44, 222, 263, 275

Galileo, 44

Galton, F., 21

gaze, 180, 181, 196, 201, 202, 205, 217, 219, 220, 226, 228, 230

Gemeinschaft, 261

generative phenomenology, 47, 261, 262, 265

genetic phenomenology, 9, 14, 20, 21, 23, 24, 39, 42, 62, 68, 82, 92, 99, 102, 121, 133, 134, 149-51, 158, 163, 166, 174-7, 179-81, 184, 197, 202, 209, 217, 226, 229, 234, 245, 265

genetic psychology, 184, 187, 199, 221

geometry, *xi*, 6, 18, 60, 82, 140, 144, 201, 276

"German Meditations," 117

Gesellschaft, 261

Gestalt, *ix*, 50, 59

givenness, 36, 37, 41, 47, 71, 85, 88, 102, 125, 126, 130, 133, 137, 138, 140, 142, 160, 162, 165, 168, 169, 175, 184-7, 190, 191, 195, 197, 204, 212, 214, 215, 217, 247-50, 255, 258, 275

God, 139, 202, 203, 237

goes without saying, 18, 51-3, 72, 91, 91-7, 124, 131, 136, 148, 180, 191, 254, 258, 259, 263, 264, 269, 270

Good, the, 91

good grounds, 15, 90-4, 147, 121, 269

Göttingen Circle, the, 81, 92, 93

Graz, the School of, 72

Greek *epoché*, 74, 107

groups, 7, 39, 80, 107, 109, 129, 176, 213, 225, 238, 244, 248, 257-63

grouping-acts, 8, 177, 195, 198, 214, 222, 250

group-theoretical, 103

Gurwitsch, A., *ix*, 9, 107, 274

habitual, 2, 19, 20, 33, 38, 71, 80, 87, 99, 103, 125, 129, 131, 152, 162, 164, 176, 178, 180, 204, 210, 214, 227, 236, 237, 240, 252, 253, 259-61, 263, 276, 277

habituated, 53, 153, 179, 196

halo of indeterminateness, 86, 121

happiness, 147, 156, 172, 274

Hegel, F., *viii*, 1, 4, 5, 41, 50, 76, 78

Heidegger, M., *xiii-xvi*, 5, 9, 10, 41, 45, 46, 48-51, 77, 104, 105 112, 113, 117-19

Held, K., *xiii, xiv*

Heraclitean flux, 273

here and now, *x*, 15, 21, 24, 29-31, 44, 46, 52, 54, 70, 72, 74-80, 83-5, 87, 89, 94-8, 100, 115, 121- 6, 129, 134, 137, 139, 141, 144, 145, 147-9, 151-3, 158, 159, 162, 165, 168-70, 172, 175, 178, 180-2, 184, 187, 191, 195-7, 200, 202-8, 210-14, 217, 218, 220- 2, 225-7, 230, 233, 235, 240-3, 247, 249, 253-7, 263, 264, 267, 268, 271-3, 275, 277

Hering, E., 113

Hilbert, D., 66

historicism, 48, 60, 69, 91

historical, 1, 20, 24, 26, 45-8, 50, 55, 65, 71, 72, 77, 78, 102, 108-10, 112, 131, 132, 175, 179, 187, 208, 216, 238, 255, 257, 258, 261-4, 274, 275

holding good, 166, 185, 186

homeworld, *xiii*, 263-5

horizons, 22, 23, 29, 35, 39, 40, 43, 44, 51-3, 72, 77, 82, 90, 91, 94, 95, 97-9, 101, 102, 108, 110, 118, 120-

28, 131, 133-5, 138-40, 142-61, 163-5, 167-9, 172, 174, 178, 179, 185, 187-9, 191, 199, 200, 203, 207, 208, 210, 211, 214, 215, 217, 218, 221, 222, 224, 225, 227-9, 231-3, 235-41, 244, 247, 249, 251, 252, 255-61, 263-7, 269-71, 275, 276

human among humans, *xvi*, 186, 276

human condition, *vii, ix, xiii*, 9, 10, 25, 42, 106, 187, 274

human nature, 130, 143, 146, 166, 191, 262, 265

human science, *vi, viii ix, xi, xii, xiv*, 2, 5, 9-11, 13, 25, 33, 60, 62, 66-70, 77, 82, 87, 90, 91, 105-11, 116-18, 128, 165, 173, 232

human spirit, 1, 35, 36, 39, 67, 71, 78, 91, 96, 105-7, 112, 131, 132, 165, 166, 189, 201, 217, 229, 233, 235, 236, 250, 253, 254, 257

human world (*Umwelt*), *vii, xiii*, 29, 47, 97, 98, 146, 147, 170, 172, 187, 224, 225, 235, 240, 258, 267-9, 272

humanistic psychology, *v*, 277

Hume, D., *viii*, 19, 92, 157

hyle, 82

hyletic, 176, 195, 196, 225, 247, 248

hypostasis, 136, 156

I am, 167, 172, 209, 215, 218, 254, 267

I and *Other*, 103, 104, 130, 139, 141, 142, 180, 190, 206, 214, 217, 218, 234, 271

I-in-the-world, 223

I-Other, 147, 149, 170, 172, 190, 252, 275

I-person, 186

I with *Other*, 167, 169, 251, 253

I-You synthesis, 167, 172, 190, 252

Idea of Phenomenology, The, 76

ideal, 15, 19, 41, 42, 61, 63-7, 82, 106, 126, 147, 170, 173, 202, 210, 216, 249, 274, 276

ideal lawfulness, 61

idealization, 41, 53, 64-6, 73, 78, 93, 94, 102, 103, 112, 124, 126, 128, 141, 147-9, 154, 159, 173, 176, 177,

179, 180, 183, 191, 201-3, 205-8, 210, 212-14, 216, 220-3, 226-8, 235, 236, 246, 247, 250-3, 256-60, 265, 268, 274-6

idealizing-acts, 208

Ideas, The (Ideen), 17, 81, 90-2, 98, 105

ideation, 13, 37, 38, 45, 52, 54, 67, 71, 149, 151-3, 155, 159, 161, 163, 166, 170, 171, 176, 181, 182, 191, 197, 220, 227, 230, 235, 257, 260, 264, 265, 269, 271, 272

imagination, *x*, 4, 26, 27, 30, 34, 40, 56, 69, 137-9, 174, 179, 203, 231, 232, 238, 253, 266, 268, 269, 275

immanence, 1, 38, 39, 71, 73, 82-5, 87-90, 94, 96, 98, 102, 119, 123, 127, 137, 139, 140, 143, 147-50, 152, 155-9, 163, 166-8, 177, 180, 184, 185, 194, 197, 201-6, 210-12, 215, 223-5, 237, 239, 241, 246, 254, 262, 268, 275

inauthenticity, 45, 48, 49, 62

indeterminable, 27, 42, 44

indeterminate, 6, 185, 189, 242

induction, 3, 4, 45, 72, 107, 143, 175, 224

inductive, 2, 3, 13, 14, 17, 22, 27, 54, 63, 131, 139, 174, 187, 195, 232

infinity, 24, 34, 43, 57, 64, 85, 96, 99, 111, 125, 148, 170, 237, 238, 258

Ingarden, R., 81

injunction, 63, 66, 95, 122, 125, 200, 235, 236, 263, 264

insight, *xiii, xiv*, 13, 28, 32, 36, 40 46, 113, 115, 190, 258, 275

instrumentalism, 32, 76, 136, 137

intellectual sight (*seeing*), 184, 185, 187, 189-91, 224, 225, 260, 275

intelligibility, *ix*, 6, 101, 121-3, 127-9, 131-42, 144, 148, 152, 158, 168, 178, 179, 211, 215, 221, 222, 259

intentional function, 40, 127, 130, 136, 141, 151, 153, 155, 161-3, 181, 182, 196, 219, 227, 239, 247, 248, 251, 253

intentional object, *ix*, 6, 11, 21, 26, 28, 29, 34, 35, 37, 38, 40, 41, 44,

47, 51, 53, 55, 67, 68, 71, 75, 77, 78, 83-7, 90, 94, 95, 98, 99, 101, 102, 104, 108, 110, 116, 120-30, 132-9, 143-5, 147-60, 162-4, 166, 168-79, 181, 183-90, 195-8, 200, 204, 207, 209-15, 217-21, 226-31, 233, 235, 238, 239, 241-8, 250, 251, 255, 259, 260, 262, 264-6, 270, 273, 275-7

intentional structure, *xiv*, 39, 74, 84, 92, 118, 138, 177, 186, 214, 220

intentionality, *x*, 1, 35, 38, 50, 54, 57, 58, 70-2, 80 82-5, 89, 98, 100, 112, 117, 129, 133, 156, 157, 163, 186, 215, 217, 220, 226, 238, 244, 246, 277

inter-generational, 46, 47, 216, 217, 258, 261-4, 274

intersubjective experience, 42, 53, 142, 165, 167, 186, 222, 252, 260, 263, 264, 269, 270

intersubjectivity, 13, 35, 48, 52, 154, 166, 175, 186, 187, 190, 223, 225, 240, 245, 250, 253, 255, 262, 265, 270, 271, 275

intersubjective-pole, 188-90, 257

Introjection, 192, 193

intropathy, 259, 260, 277

introspection, 6, 272

intuition, *vii- x, xii, xiii, xvi*, 2, 3, 8, 11-13, 17-21, 23-9, 32, 38-40, 44-6, 50, 52-4, 62-4, 71, 72, 74, 76, 82-8, 93, 94, 96, 99, 102, 106, 110-16, 126, 127, 130, 132, 125-7, 139, 140, 142-4, 148, 149, 151, 152, 154-6, 160-3, 167, 171, 172, 174-8, 181, 185-8, 190, 195, 197, 198, 201, 206, 211, 215, 224, 255, 256, 259, 260, 265, 267, 270-2, 274, 275, 277

involuntary memory, 196, 197

irreality, 14-23, 27, 28, 30, 31, 33-9, 41, 42, 49, 52-4, 68, 70, 73-9, 82-6, 88, 92, 93, 95, 99, 100, 102, 104, 107, 112, 116, 117, 121, 123, 124, 137-40, 145, 151-7, 165, 169, 173, 176, 177, 180-2, 187, 188, 195, 202, 203, 206-9, 214-16, 218, 220, 228, 29, 231, 235, 237, 241-3, 253, 256,

263, 266-8, 270, 272, 274-6
is-ness, 18, 24, 31, 120, 121, 127, 149
isomorphism, 222
It, 139, 169
iteration, 21, 53, 137-9, 145, 162, 180, 207, 211, 228, 269
judging-acts, 33, 36, 54, 86, 129, 146, 163, 165, 183, 201, 207, 209, 210, 233, 235, 243, 247, 266, 268, 271
judgment, *vi*, *viii*, *ix*, 2-4, 8, 11, 13, 14, 16, 18, 23, 27-9, 32, 34, 44, 48, 51, 58, 60, 62, 63, 65, 67, 74, 77, 79, 83, 86, 89, 91, 94-6, 99-101, 106-9, 119, 125, 129, 134, 138, 139, 150, 153, 159, 163, 165, 166, 173-6, 178-82, 185, 187, 188, 190, 195-7, 199, 200, 209, 210, 220, 221, 224, 227-9, 240, 241, 248, 240, 251, 259, 263, 265, 270, 271
Kaizo article, the ("Renewal: Its Problem and Method"), 106, 107
Kagen, J. and Segal, J., 55
Kant, I., *viii*, *xvi*, 1, 4, 5, 15, 19, 32, 41, 56, 60, 67, 74, 76, 77, 88, 89, 92, 97, 121, 131, 132
Kaufmann, F., 81
Kirkpatrick, R. and Williams, F., 49
Kierkegaard, S., 105
Kisiel, T., 45
knowing, 54, 77, 120, 122, 123, 126, 128, 151, 171, 172, 174, 205, 225
knowing-acts, 216, 274
knowing-constituting ego, 222, 223, 229
knowing the real, 202-7, 210-12, 219, 227
knowledge-complex, 10, 12, 98, 133, 158, 167, 183, 194, 197, 224, 256
Kockelmans, J. J., 43
Königsberger, L., 57
Koyrè, A., 81
Kronecker, L., 56
Kuhn, H., 22
Kummer, E., 56
Lambert, J. H., 1, 2, 4, 5
Landgrebe, L., 107
language, *vi*, *xiii-xv*, 6, 11, 50, 54, 69,

85, 127 136, 144, 149, 150, 157, 177, 182, 192, 198, 199, 205, 213, 227, 239, 242, 263, 264
Lauer, Q., *xvi*
Law, the, 237
lawful, 131, 156, 238, 239, 247, 248, 255, 256, 265
law-like, 30, 111, 265
laws of nature, *ix*, 71
leading clues, *xi*, *xiv*, *xvi*, 47
Leibnitz, G. W., 56, 107, 190
life-goals, 36, 147, 148, 166, 172, 231-3, 266, 277
life-span, *vii*, 20, 96, 142, 167, 179, 183, 185, 217, 225, 226, 232, 233, 240, 247, 249, 252, 253, 257-61, 265, 271, 272, 276
life-world (*Lebenswelt*), *xiii*, 29, 34-6, 38, 40, 43-7, 53, 94, 95, 97, 98, 116, 141, 148, 153, 165-8, 170-4, 181, 182, 184, 186, 191, 195, 208, 224, 229, 231-3, 235, 238, 239, 250, 252, 256-8, 260, 261, 264, 269-72, 277
likeness, 41, 249, 264, 267
linear, 210, 247
linear perspective, 131
linguistic, 54, 73, 152, 154, 156, 159, 198-200, 208
linguistic empathy, 101, 103, 192, 193, 199, 236, 250, 252
Lipps, T., 118
lived experience, 15, 16, 20, 21, 28, 36, 47, 68, 72, 84, 91, 104, 111, 130, 138, 141-3, 165, 167, 170, 187, 193, 199, 227, 230, 246, 248, 253, 258, 267, 271-3
living present, 30, 34, 38, 39, 47, 51-4, 67, 70, 72, 78, 79, 83, 85, 87, 95, 100, 103, 121, 125, 127, 130, 134, 136-42, 145, 147, 149, 150, 156, 157, 162, 175, 179-81, 188, 191, 197, 200, 203-5, 207-11, 214, 217, 220, 221, 225, 226, 228, 230, 233, 240-3, 246, 247, 250, 255-8, 261-5, 267, 269, 271, 276
Locke, J., 69, 110, 234
logic of calculus, 62-7, 70, 71, 74, 79,

86, 89, 101, 103, 104, 130, 134, 138, 144, 145, 148, 162, 173, 174, 177, 183, 200, 205, 210, 211, 213, 221, 225, 227, 228, 234, 254, 265, 276
logic of signs, 198
logic of forms, 61, 62, 173
Logical Investigations, 15, 16, 30, 61, 62, 65-7, 73, 75, 76, 81, 82, 90, 92, 118, 122, 132, 165, 170-3
logos, 33-6, 236, 276
Lycan, W.G., 54
Mach, E., 113
Malmquist, C.P., 3
Marcuse, H., 107
Masaryk, T., 56, 57
Matas, J., *xvi*
mathematics, *xii*, *xiii*, 6, 9, 18, 26, 57, 58, 60, 66, 85, 90, 108, 113, 121, 129, 145, 158, 173, 185, 239
mathesis, 106, 107
matter of fact, 2, 5, 18, 19, 31, 41, 44, 62, 63, 71, 72, 78, 96, 122, 125, 173, 177, 223, 236, 269
maturation, 129, 135, 178, 186, 189, 194, 214, 233, 261, 272
McCormick, P., 69
me-in-my-world, 142, 254, 271
me myself, 40, 44, 53, 94, 95, 116, 122, 134, 142, 146, 148-50, 165, 167, 171, 172, 180, 186, 188, 191, 192, 198, 201, 204, 209, 213, 214, 223-5, 227, 228, 231-3, 251-3, 257, 259, 260, 262-4, 267, 269-72
meaningful, *ix*, *xiii*, 3-6, 10, 12, 13, 15, 19, 20, 23, 30, 37, 43, 53, 55, 80, 82, 121, 123, 125, 127, 130, 132, 135, 137, 140, 143, 144, 146-64, 166-70, 180, 184, 187, 191, 231, 154, 257, 258, 264, 268, 272, 273, 275, 277
meaning-*less*, 202
means to be human, *viii*, *xi*, 7, 9, 45, 80, 105, 106, 146
meant, the, 120, 143, 145, 149, 155, 157, 162, 170
meant-as-meant, 186, 206, 214, 217, 230
Meinong, A., 72, 73

memorial appearance, 262
memory, *viii*, 53, 85-7, 100, 127, 196, 197, 213, 220, 228, 243, 254-6, 262, 277
mental formation, 52, 96, 109, 126, 139, 150, 178, 179, 181, 184, 198, 205, 210, 212-14, 220, 221, 225-8, 234, 238, 240, 241, 247, 250, 264-8, 270, 273
mental process, 1, 23, 32, 33, 41, 52-4, 61, 65, 82, 83, 94, 115, 116, 127, 138, 150, 151, 160, 163, 172, 182, 186, 205, 208, 210, 221, 225-8, 230, 234, 238, 241-6, 248, 253, 262, 263, 268, 270, 271, 276
meontics, 116, 208
Merleau-Ponty, M., 45, 50, 51, 119
metaphysical historicism, 71, 72
metaphysical naturalism, 131
metaphysics, *viii*, *xiii*, 11, 18, 27, 28, 40-4, 46, 47, 49-52, 60, 70, 72, 76, 82, 90-8, 108, 110-12, 121, 124-6, 128, 129, 131-3, 135, 136, 140, 143, 144, 148, 152, 154, 159, 160, 168, 170-2, 174, 179, 180, 185, 187 9, 191-3, 199, 203, 208, 210-12, 215, 224, 231, 236, 240, 247, 249, 251, 254, 257-64, 266, 267, 269, 270, 273, 275
metapsychology, 87, 192
metatheoretical, *xi*, 11, 13, 25, 33, 126
method, *vii-xv*, 14, 17, 18, 20, 28, 32, 37, 40, 46, 47, 56, 58, 59, 69, 72, 76, 81, 99, 102, 109, 120, 146, 158, 159, 161, 163, 164, 174, 180, 201, 205, 208, 212, 218, 231, 232, 239, 245, 253, 265, 268, 273, 274
method of *epoché*, 37, 74, 83, 87, 100, 101, 133, 144, 155, 195, 197, 199, 209, 210, 216, 217, 223, 229, 231, 232, 248
method of methods, 32
method of ontology, 10, 155, 160, 161
method of philosophy, *xiii*
methodology, *vii-xii*, 4, 5, 8, 10, 12, 13, 22, 26, 29, 31-4, 49, 58, 60-2,

64, 67, 74, 75, 81, 82, 84, 86, 87, 89-
92, 98, 101-3, 106, 109, 112, 113,
116-18, 120, 123, 128-32, 136, 137,
140, 145, 155, 157, 159, 161, 164,
167, 197, 204, 211, 212, 214, 215,
224, 236, 237, 245, 249, 273, 275
metonymy, 198
Middle Platonic, 86
mimetic, *ix*
mind, the, 23, 35, 57, 58, 61, 72, 88,
89, 100, 101, 108-10, 114, 116, 187,
202, 237
mind's eye, 37, 203, 225
mine, 7, 10, 44, 145, 183, 184, 246
mirroring, *ix, xii*, 16, 29, 51, 60, 87,
102, 107, 149, 155, 159, 163, 182,
199, 211, 223
Misch, G., 46, 58
Möbius strip, 227
Mohanty, J. N., 81, 199, 200, 210
monad, 107, 111, 207, 208, 210, 217,
223, 224
morality, 1, 4, 56, 90, 95, 105, 165,
188
Moran, D., 1, 56, 66, 92, 117, 118
multiform, 134, 142, 160-2, 181, 190,
206, 251
multi-modal, 2, 4, 6,
mundane, *xiv*, 122, 123, 125, 131, 143,
146, 182, 183, 192, 195, 199, 207,
208, 213, 230, 232, 235, 244, 251,
253, 265, 273
Munich Group, the, 118
my being-as-ego, 53, 249
my life, 29, 38, 42, 44, 53, 96, 141, 142,
146, 148, 166-72, 174, 180, 186,
195, 203, 204, 209, 215, 219, 223-5,
231-3, 237, 240, 267, 269, 271, 272
my life as a person, 254-60, 265, 266,
268, 271, 277
my-life-with-their-life, 44, 53, 253,
268
my own, 12, 15, 27, 41, 87, 96, 97, 99,
116, 117, 141, 142, 166, 167, 169,
172, 176, 178, 183, 186, 188, 202,
204, 206, 208, 215, 222, 229, 233,
244, 254, 259, 260, 271, 272, 277

mysticism, *ix*, 30, 60, 76, 135
narrative, 262-4
Natanson, M., *xi*, 51
Natorp, P., 60, 67
natural attitude, *vii, viii, x, xiii*, 4, 6, 7,
12, 19, 21, 24, 29, 30, 37, 42, 43, 49,
52, 54, 66, 68, 70, 71, 77, 78, 81-3,
85, 89, 91, 93-103, 111, 112, 115,
116, 124, 125, 129, 133, 136, 137,
146-9, 153, 157, 164, 171, 180, 182,
183, 191, 192, 195, 197, 199, 200,
206-8, 212, 216, 224, 225, 232, 235,
236, 238, 239, 243, 247, 248, 252,
256-9, 266, 267, 270
natural cause, *x*, 2-4, 78, 109, 110,
129, 193, 204, 236, 249, 253, 270
natural science, 57, 60, 70, 71, 82, 91,
106, 108-10, 113
natural world, 24, 32, 35, 42, 53, 57,
60, 70, 90, 91, 96, 97, 99-101, 103,
108, 122, 125, 128-32, 141, 142,
152, 170-2, 179, 182, 183, 203, 216,
223, 225, 231, 233, 237-9, 243, 246-
9, 251, 254, 257, 264, 266, 269, 270
natural worldview, 71, 91, 111
naturalism, 69, 91, 92, 131
naturalistic, 21, 69, 71, 91, 109, 110,
131, 132
naturalistic abstraction, 131, 132, 216,
224, 254
naturalized, 3, 49, 69, 89, 95, 97, 98,
108-11, 128, 131, 148, 191, 193,
196, 213, 215, 230, 247, 256, 265,
267, 270, 274
Nature, 70, 71, 78, 94-6, 125, 128
148, 153, 179, 189, 202, 203, 231,
237, 247, 249, 257, 270
nature of things, *vii, x*, 1, 20, 30, 31,
49, 50, 54, 70, 83, 91, 92, 94-6, 108,
109, 125, 128, 129, 131, 132, 146,
170, 179, 183, 188, 191, 193, 195,
202, 208, 212, 234, 236, 237, 244,
249, 251-4, 257, 258, 267, 269, 275
Nazis, 119
needs, 94, 141, 257-9, 266
neurological, 16, 27, 135, 194, 233
neutrality modification, 213, 214, 242

Nietzsche, F., 105

noema, 83, 99

noemata, 23

noematic, 87, 116, 158, 172, 173, 181, 212, 225, 226, 230, 234, 275

noeses, 23

noetic, 23, 35, 86, 173, 180, 183, 219, 220, 237

non-action, 39, 40, 86, 134, 139, 151, 184, 219, 222, 227, 230, 240, 241, 248, 250, 253, 263

non-empirical, *viii*, *ix*, 4-7, 13, 16, 17, 20, 33, 34, 37, 73, 74, 232, 274

non-existent, 73, 75

non-intentional, 83, 108, 245, 246

non-intuitive, 88, 106, 239

non-linear, 188, 210, 228, 255, 257

non-phenomenological, 19, 21, 35, 62, 122, 198

non-psychic, 21, 68, 200

non-physiological consciousness, *vi*, *x*, *xi*, *xvi*, 77, 86, 115, 126, 216

nonrandom, 205, 211, 235, 273

non-rational, 7, 107, 121, 124, 134, 139, 144, 186, 237, 244-6, 273

non-reason, 80, 100, 101, 148, 157, 167, 181, 195, 224, 252

non-sense, 202

non-theological, 71

nonthetic, 127, 130, 140, 142, 169, 181, 187, 208, 214, 227, 239, 241, 249, 258, 262,

norm of objective truth, 259-61

norm of practice, 28, 30, 34, 38, 40, 52, 64, 74, 75, 80, 82, 98, 103, 107, 115, 149, 152, 158, 164, 204, 224, 227, 235, 240, 252, 258, 260, 263, 266, 272, 273

normal course of events, *viii*, 2, 14, 18, 35, 38, 40, 42, 65, 71, 80, 82, 83, 85, 124, 125, 130, 137, 142, 144, 148, 150, 156, 167, 168, 189, 191, 194, 202, 203, 233, 249, 253, 257, 260, 261, 263, 266, 269, 274

normalized, 167, 265

normative, 27, 30, 44, 64-6, 69, 75, 86, 96, 101, 103, 107, 109, 121, 126,

130, 134, 165, 176, 177, 181, 187, 190, 196-9, 201, 204, 210, 216, 218, 247, 252, 261-6, 268, 269, 272, 274

norm-consciousness, 165

nothingness, 49, 52, 116, 266

noumena, 1

noumenal, 1, 4, 88, 89

nous, 86-8, 92, 99-101, 145, 207, 209, 212, 234, 236, 237, 275

null-hypothesis, 192

null-point, 100, 255

object constancy, 149, 185, 188

object of the mind, *viii*, *ix*, 7, 18, 22, 23, 27, 34, 35, 39, 54, 64, 70, 76, 83, 116, 121, 130, 138, 147, 151, 153, 172-6, 178, 198, 200, 204, 205, 211, 218-20, 226-8, 230, 231, 245, 248, 250, 256, 258, 268, 270, 273, 276

objectification, 36, 48, 54, 68, 84, 85, 100, 124, 135, 138, 141, 142, 165, 167, 172, 183, 193, 217, 233, 253-5, 257, 263, 267

objectifying-acts, 99, 177, 198

omnitudo realitatis, 19

oneness, *ix*, *xvi*, 83, 120, 136, 188, 227, 256

ontic, *vii*, 10, 49, 52, 78, 95, 97, 125, 127, 144, 145, 147-51, 153, 154, 157, 160, 162, 163, 165, 168-73, 189, 207, 214, 221, 233, 249-51

ontifying-acts, 149, 155

ontology, *vi*, *xiii*, 9-12, 18-21, 24, 31, 35, 39, 40, 42-5, 48-50, 52, 58, 75, 82, 83, 94, 98, 101, 112, 116, 120-2, 124-6, 128, 133, 140, 143-62, 164, 166-9, 172, 174, 187, 211, 215, 218, 240, 245, 249, 259, 264, 275

ordering principle, 94, 250

orientation toward reason, 179

orthogonal, 179, 210, 212, 222, 228

Other, 7, 44, 95, 98, 102-4, 130, 139, 141, 142, 166, 167, 169, 176, 180, 184-6, 190, 206, 209, 214, 217, 218, 223, 234, 241, 249, 251, 253, 258, 259, 267, 271, 275

other minds, 191, 253

otherness, 95, 96, 167, 251, 268

ownness-essence, 186, 188, 226, 253-6, 259, 266, 268
panpsychism, 56
parenthesizing, 8, 68, 78, 79, 89-91, 96, 109, 143, 160, 199
Paris Lectures, The, 67
parapsychology, *viii*
parts and wholes, *ix*, *xiii*, 26, 60, 73, 76, 84, 121, 140, 108, 150, 182, 203, 205, 207, 209, 214
parts-to-parts, 7, 154, 181, 228
parts-to-whole, 7, 147, 154, 161, 178, 181, 228, 241, 263
parts/whole, 6, 40, 64, 123, 127, 150
passivity, 12, 20, 34-6, 40, 50, 57, 63, 64, 71, 86, 101, 102, 106, 134, 142, 148, 152, 154, 157, 162, 163, 174, 179, 181, 183, 197, 198, 200, 205, 208, 213, 222, 226, 227, 235, 240, 241, 243, 244, 250-2, 263-5, 268, 271, 275, 277
pathology, 178, 274
Patočka, J., 48
patterns, *x*, 13, 30, 31, 33, 50, 84, 85, 87, 173, 177, 178, 192, 230, 234, 255, 262, 274
Paulsen, F., 56, 49
Pavlov, I., 21
people, 55, 143, 254, 258, 259
perception, 1-3, 7, 21, 31, 37, 50, 51, 57-9, 63, 67, 69, 79, 81, 83, 86, 93, 95, 104, 123, 125-7, 129, 151, 152, 154-7, 196, 238, 245, 248, 262
performing ego, 37, 42, 121, 132, 137, 145, 149, 152, 158, 180, 183, 194, 209, 240, 245, 255
person, 35, 36, 44, 49, 58, 80, 107, 111, 129, 130, 183, 185, 187, 191, 193, 232, 254-60, 262, 263, 265, 267, 268, 275, 276
personal ego, 12, 141, 186, 187, 249, 254, 255, 260, 277
personal lifeworld, 35-38, 40, 42, 44, 45, 52, 53, 55, 104, 141, 172, 179-83, 186, 188, 200-2, 205, 208, 209, 212, 215-20, 223, 226-8, 230, 231, 233, 240, 244, 247, 249, 253, 255,

257, 260-2, 264-6, 268-73, 276
personality, 253, 258
Pfänder, A., 117, 118
phenomenal, *viii*, 1-4, 7, 16, 76-80, 93, 152, 153, 167, 168, 182
phenomenalism, 79
phenomenognosis, 58, 59, 68, 113, 226
phenomenological anthropology, 258
phenomenological attitude, *x*, *xiii-xvi*, 6, 9, 11, 26, 28, 30, 31, 35, 41, 76, 77, 84, 87, 94, 99, 107, 114, 115, 120, 137, 146, 164, 182, 206, 212, 224, 229, 230, 254, 270, 277
phenomenological *epoché*, 34, 74, 75, 77, 122, 164, 195, 199, 232, 234
phenomenological field, *vii*, 14, 39, 76, 78, 94, 122, 140, 173, 178, 198, 211, 221, 226, 234
phenomenological method proper, *x*, 14, 24, 32, 33, 36, 47, 55, 74, 76, 84, 87, 90, 103, 107, 118, 149, 154, 160, 161, 164, 213, 218, 220, 225, 229, 231, 232, 236, 275
phenomenological philosophy, *vii*, *xi*, *xiv*, 4-6, 8, 11, 14, 16, 23, 24, 29, 30, 32, 38, 41, 45, 51, 56, 59, 65, 90, 91, 113, 114, 117, 170, 232, 273
phenomenological psychology, *vi*, *xi*, *xii*, 5, 6, 8, 9, 11, 13, 14, 19, 22, 25, 28, 29, 35, 39, 42, 43, 51, 53, 55, 68, 70, 76, 111, 113, 116, 120, 128, 132, 145, 146, 150, 154, 159, 166, 173-5, 194, 217, 229, 232-4, 236, 237, 240, 245, 250, 253, 254, 261, 273-6
phenomenological realism, 76, 136
phenomenological reduction, 8, 14, 22, 73-5, 77-81, 88, 158, 180, 205, 211, 214
phenomenological sociology, 258
phenomenologized, 206, 207, 210, 247, 252, 270, 272
phenomenologizing-acts, 218, 223, 230, 235, 277
phenomenologizing ego, 104, 166, 167, 206, 223-5, 235, 253, 275

phenomenology of phenomenology, *ix*, 24, 38, 117

phenomenology of reason, 1, 52, 81, 84, 86, 124, 131, 138 145, 151, 155, 157, 176, 198, 245, 248, 271

phenomenology of the phenomenological reduction, 22, 200, 206

Philosophie der Arithmetik (Philosophy of Arithmetic), 60, 62

philosophy, discipline of, *x*, 11, 29, 46, 56-60, 66, 69, 71, 73, 89, 90, 105, 113, 114, 119, 125, 143, 144, 146, 170, 187, 216, 251, 272

"Philosophy as a Rigorous Science" (the *Logos* article), 60, 69, 71, 91, 96, 109

philosophy of mind, 1, 61

philosophy of psychology, *xii*, 25, 57

philosophy of science, *vi*, *x*, 51, 58

physics, *ix*, 108, 173

physiological, 17, 33, 57, 58, 83, 108, 129, 156, 157, 164, 189, 194, 232, 254

Piaget, J., *xi*, 20, 21, 175

pictorial reasoning, *x*, 34, 37

picturing, *xii*, *xv*, 3, 23, 29 31, 37, 67, 149, 151, 152, 171, 177, 181, 196, 198, 220, 222, 223, 226

place, 7, 9, 32, 45, 47, 51, 79, 94, 95, 111, 120, 132, 137, 140, 141, 148, 149, 155, 159, 162, 166, 169, 179, 185, 188, 204, 217, 222, 233, 237, 240, 247, 254, 257, 270, 275

Plato, *viii*

Platonic *eide*, 7

Platonic realism, 138

Poincaré, H., 105

polar continuum, 70, 188, 257

polythetic, 187, 188, 213, 240, 241, 268, 270

positing, *xiv*, 3, 4, 19, 40-2, 49, 51, 54, 58, 61-3, 66, 69, 70, 73, 74, 76, 79, 89, 91, 101, 132, 136, 143, 144, 160, 161, 185-7, 193, 241-4, 246-9, 251, 255, 268

positive science, 271

possible worlds, 238-40

post-phenomenological phenomena, *x*, 79, 82, 84, 177, 180, 182, 206, 217, 219, 229, 235, 275

praxis, *vi*, *vii*, *ix-xiv*, 9-11, 14-16, 22, 24, 25, 29, 32, 33, 43, 45, 47, 60, 61, 66, 68, 69, 74-7, 79-82, 91, 107, 114, 117, 118, 124, 130, 180, 195, 196, 206, 210, 213, 232, 235, 274

pre-conceptual, 7, 9, 10, 13, 19, 25, 26, 29, 34-8, 40-2, 51, 53, 54, 65, 66, 70, 71, 79, 81-6, 88, 94-6, 99, 100, 102-4, 112, 114-17, 120-8, 130, 131, 134, 136-9, 141, 145, 147, 148, 150-7, 159, 160, 162, 166-9, 173-92, 194-6, 201-3, 205, 207-13, 217, 221-3, 225, 228, 230-2, 235-7, 240-3, 245-7, 249-52, 256, 260, 262-4, 266, 268, 270-2, 276

preconstituted, 44, 96, 125, 130, 178, 185, 250, 251, 253, 261, 263

predelineation, 261

predication, 63, 72, 82, 95, 100, 157, 173, 200, 207, 222, 225, 239, 251

predicating-act, 178

pre-empirical, 83, 247

pre-existence, *viii x*, 2 6, 7, 9, 10, 12, 14, 18, 20, 24 25, 27, 29, 31, 32, 34, 37-41, 44, 45, 48, 52-4, 62, 64, 71, 76-8, 89, 93, 95, 97, 99-103, 107, 108, 110, 114, 116, 122-6, 128, 130, 131, 135, 137, 138, 143-53, 156, 159-64, 171, 173, 174, 176-8, 180-5, 188, 190, 191, 193, 195, 196, 198, 199, 201-5, 207-18, 200, 220-2, 226, 228, 229, 231, 232, 235, 239-43, 246, 247, 250, 251, 254-6, 261, 263-7, 270, 273, 275, 276

pregiven, 21, 30, 38, 41, 43, 48, 50, 52-4, 64, 71, 74, 77, 80, 85, 95, 101, 102, 114, 116, 121, 123-5, 128, 130-43, 145, 147-50, 153, 159, 161-3, 165, 167, 168, 170, 171, 176, 177, 179-87, 189, 190, 193, 196, 198, 199, 201-3, 207, 208, 210, 213, 214, 216, 218, 222, 225-7, 230, 233, 236, 238-41, 246, 247, 249-56, 259, 260 5, 267-9, 271 pregivenness, 38, 44, 52, 53, 102, 116, 123, 124, 138, 140, 142, 147, 164, 168, 177, 190, 195, 240, 242, 255, 256, 258, 264, 268, 270, 275

prejudices, *xi*, 99, 109, 111, 129

pre-linguistic, *xiv*, 7, 88, 104, 235, 247, 249

pre-phenomenological phenomena, *x*, 79, 177, 207

pre-predicative, 61, 99, 100, 174, 175, 251

pre-scientific, 45, 59, 78, 82, 84, 87, 131, 145, 146, 148, 191, 213, 214, 232, 275, 277

presentational object, 90, 92, 98, 120, 121, 125, 137, 151, 159, 162, 168, 170, 198, 205, 207, 209, 212, 213, 217, 234, 236, 242, 244, 245, 256, 275

presentiation, eidos of, 155-9, 162, 190

presumptive, 18, 37, 201, 220, 226, 240, 243

presupposition, *viii, x,* 3, 4, 11, 14, 17, 18, 21, 22, 30, 31, 34, 44, 46-48, 50, 52, 53, 63, 64, 66, 72-5, 78, 82, 89-98, 107, 110-12, 124, 125, 128-32, 141, 144, 148, 157, 179, 187, 188, 191-3, 195, 203, 208, 215, 221, 224, 227, 229, 234, 236, 239, 251, 253, 258-62, 265, 267-9

primitives, *vii, xi,* 7, 8, 12, 22, 33, 35, 84, 92, 157, 175, 241, 273, 276, 277

primordial constitution, 262

principle of all principles, *xi*, 35, 82, 194

privileging attitude, 108, 259

propadeutic, 9, 14, 20, 23, 55, 59, 68, 84, 93, 102, 125, 180, 204, 226

protension, 85, 86, 141, 149, 178, 200, 220, 230, 239, 260, 268

protodoxic, 241

pseudophilosophy, 60

pseudo-science, 42

psyche, *vii, viii,* 13, 33-6, 38, 39, 60, 69, 71, 99, 111, 128, 130-2, 139, 155, 192, 209, 231, 234, 236-41, 247, 248, 251, 255, 266, 271, 275, 276

psychic being, 24, 42, 44, 67, 117, 130, 134, 141, 164, 178, 183, 186, 223, 225, 275, 276

psychic development, 233

psychic life, *vii, xi, xiv,* 14, 19, 24-6, 28, 29, 36, 37, 45, 49, 54, 69, 87, 89, 90, 99, 109, 111, 115, 122, 127, 129, 132, 133, 150, 151, 177-9, 183, 190-6, 208, 212, 216, 225-7, 229, 242, 245, 250, 254, 262, 267, 268, 274-6

psychic nature, 70, 71

psychic order, 71, 73, 82, 84, 99, 103, 125, 126, 130, 133, 137-9, 151, 152, 159, 162, 174, 176, 178, 179, 181, 184, 191, 196, 201, 204, 205, 208-10, 219, 221, 225-8, 230, 234, 240, 247, 255, 261, 262, 267-9, 271, 273

psychoanalysis, *xi*, 21, 43, 193, 234

Psychognosia, viii, ix, xi, xii, xv, 24, 114-16, 173, 195, 206, 211, 234, 245, 274

psychological, the, *vi, vii, ix, xi, xv,* 11, 18, 25, 26, 28, 29, 55, 198, 234, 236

psychological attitude, 25-9, 42, 55, 71, 123, 155, 229, 230, 236

psychological *cogito,* 239, 246, 273

psychological consciousness, 47, 126, 138, 145, 204, 242, 262, 268, 271, 272

psychological ego, 12, 37-40, 42, 47, 52-4, 98, 104, 116, 121, 130, 134, 137, 138, 141, 142, 157, 158, 163, 164, 166, 174, 180, 181, 183, 186-8, 191, 194-206, 208, 212-14, 217-31, 234, 235, 242, 244-53, 255-60, 263-8, 270-3, 275-7

psychological ego-idea, 98, 195

psychological empathy, 259

psychological *epoché,* 34, 37-40, 52, 116, 125, 145, 163, 165, 174, 177, 181, 194-212, 214-19, 221-9, 231, 233, 236, 238-42, 245, 247, 263, 264, 271, 273, 276, 277

psychological reduction, 13, 14, 19-21, 23-5, 37, 39, 42, 68, 117, 125, 168, 180-2, 184, 225-33, 239

psychological subjectivity, 41, 141,

160, 174

psychological theme, 53, 126, 155, 161, 164-6, 180-2, 193, 207, 220, 228, 232, 238, 241, 246, 248, 250-2, 254, 264, 265, 270, 277

psychologism, 11, 15, 16, 19, 20, 23, 58, 60-2, 77, 92, 108, 109, 116, 165

psychology, discipline of, *vi, vii,* ix, *xi,* 5, 6, 9, 13, 17-22, 25, 26, 29, 39, 41-3, 58-61, 68, 69, 72, 82, 89, 108-14, 117, 128, 130, 143, 184, 200, 274

psychophysical, 132, 166, 232, 248

psychosubjectivity, 12, 24, 37, 42, 92, 98, 99, 116, 134, 157, 163, 178, 181, 194, 196-8, 201, 203, 205, 207-9, 227, 228, 231, 234, 244, 248, 255, 262, 272, 273, 276

pure consciousness, 12, 19, 21, 23, 29, 32, 33, 37-40, 42, 43, 47, 48, 58, 68, 71, 74, 75, 78, 79, 81, 83-5, 89, 91, 93-5, 105, 114, 116, 121, 123, 124, 126, 127, 137, 139, 140, 145, 157, 163, 170, 171, 173, 174, 181, 186, 191, 196-8, 200, 203, 208, 216-20, 226, 231, 232, 234, 238, 244, 245, 250, 268, 275-7

pure Ego, 6, 12, 23, 35-8, 40, 42, 52-4, 54, 67, 73, 77, 78, 83, 92, 94-100, 102-4, 112, 116, 120, 124, 126, 127, 130, 133-41, 143, 146-59, 161-6, 168, 169, 172, 174-81, 183-91, 193-215, 217-28, 230-5, 237, 239-51, 253-64, 266-73, 275-7, 262

pure life, 97, 99-101, 191, 232

pure logic, 15, 61, 82, 122, 165, 171, 172

pure phenomenology, 12, 87, 92, 118, 171, 273, 274

pure psychology, *ix-xi, xv,* 12-14, 16, 18-22, 24, 26-9, 32, 35, 37-42, 53, 54, 68, 83, 87, 88, 90, 94, 98, 100, 104, 407, 111, 116, 120-2, 125, 127, 130, 131, 133-5, 139, 140, 142-6, 148, 151, 152, 154, 155, 159-66, 168, 171-4, 177-9, 182, 183, 185, 188-90, 192-202, 205, 206, 211-14, 216-27, 229-38, 240-5, 248-50, 252-5, 264-

6, 269, 273, 274, 276, 277

pure subjectivity, 12, 33, 36, 38, 39, 41, 55, 67, 68, 71, 75, 78, 88, 93-5, 98, 99, 112, 120, 126, 134, 136, 141, 149, 155, 160, 166, 170, 172, 179, 184-6, 199, 209, 210, 218, 222, 223, 231, 233-6, 249, 250, 272

qualitative, *x,* 30, 46

qualities, *ix,* 1, 3, 16, 59, 64, 73, 79, 80, 82, 88, 89, 91, 92, 96, 102, 153, 159, 160, 176, 188

quantifying, 64

quidditive content, 139, 172, 211, 242

radical skepticism, 108, 109, 133, 363

rapport, 190

rational, *viii,* 7, 14, 35, 37, 39-41, 52, 53, 55, 64, 65, 80, 81, 86, 89, 91, 96, 99, 101, 103, 106, 107, 121, 123, 124, 127, 134, 135, 138, 139, 144, 146, 147, 156, 169, 172, 178, 181, 187, 188, 200, 202-6, 210, 217, 222, 226, 228, 231, 233, 237, 240-6, 249, 255, 260, 265, 267, 268, 271-7

rationale, *vi,* 36, 75, 77, 80, 109, 242

rationalism, 30, 106

ray of regard, 33, 34

real world, 14, 59, 194

reason-as-evidence, 86, 99, 100, 102, 135, 149, 153, 156, 175, 179, 191, 198, 214, 222, 228, 230, 239, 253

reasoning, *x, xii- xiv,* 1-5, 7, 9, 17, 32-7, 56, 125, 130, 132, 133, 136-8, 140, 154, 155, 161, 163, 167-9, 171, 173, 174, 179, 184, 185, 189, 198, 201, 209, 211, 213, 214, 216, 217, 225, 230, 232, 233, 235, 239, 241-3, 256, 261, 266, 274, 276

recognition, *x,* 6, 11, 12, 22, 23, 28, 32, 34, 41, 44, 45, 60, 62, 63, 68, 80, 92, 97, 102, 121, 130, 132, 162, 194, 200, 205, 249, 250, 252

*re-*cognition, 102, 123-5, 129, 139, 152, 193, 210, 267

recollection, 34, 62, 69, 85, 195-7

reconstructions, *xv,* 23, 42, 75, 78, 87, 98, 133, 142, 143, 167-70, 180, 181, 186, 195, 201, 205, 218, 219, 233,

235, 275

reconstructive phenomenology, 39, 42, 55, 124, 134, 166-8, 199, 217, 235

reflection on reflection, 115

reflective attitude, 115, 194

reflective thinking, 214, 215

regional ontology, 18-20, 24, 31, 39, 42, 43, 83, 98, 122, 157, 169-71, 192, 245, 276

regression, *xii*, 66, 77, 99, 170, 199

regressive phenomenology, 9, 20, 21, 55, 68, 102, 126, 133, 158, 171, 174, 217, 218, 234, 254

regressive reflections, 7, 14, 23, 75, 124, 125, 127, 134, 137, 139, 143, 145, 149, 157, 166, 168, 199, 263, 275

regulating norm, 70, 130, 261

Reinach, A., 118

reiteration, 53, 183, 188, 189

relational thinking, 89, 207, 208, 210, 216, 244

relational unity, *xiv*

relativism, 61, 65

renewal, 104, 107, 113, 117, 119, 165

repetition, 85

representation, 19, 28, 64, 67, 69, 73, 74, 82, 84, 87, 115, 121, 146, 154-6, 158-63, 166, 169, 174, 182, 185, 190, 192, 194, 195, 199, 201, 206, 231, 236, 245, 251, 261, 269, 271

re-presentation, 77, 115, 155-9, 162, 177, 188, 204, 207, 211, 215

reproductive memory, 86, 159, 162, 196, 217, 255, 262

residuum, 216

retention, 83, 85, 86, 117, 139, 154, 159, 187, 196, 197, 200, 220, 210, 227, 230, 232, 247, 259, 268

retrogression, 37, 52, 53, 251, 253

retro-inquiry, 224, 228, 242, 253

Rickert, H., 67, 69, 89, 104

Ricoeur, P., 70, 148, 262-4

Rorty, R., 199

Sartre, J-P., 45, 48-51, 119, 199

scanning, 220, 226, 230

Scheler, M., 118, 119

Schutz, A., 107, 261

science of essences, *x*, *xii*, 11, 18, 19, 47, 75, 106, 109, 114, 119, 120, 130, 166, 228, 258, 272, 274, 277

science of science, 274

scientific rationalism, 105

sedimentation, *xv*, 46, 200, 203, 206, 215

self, 2, 5, 7, 42, 42, 97, 98, 103, 131, 133, 137, 138, 142, 144, 156, 166, 182, 186, 187, 208, 214-16, 218, 222, 228, 249, 250, 265-7, 272, 277

self-apperception, 184, 196, 229

self-consciousness, 7, 16, 50, 71, 168, 170, 171, 223, 233, 235

self-contained, 106, 107

self-evidence, 6, 8, 12, 15, 16, 26-8, 33, 35, 44, 53, 54, 65, 66, 70, 74, 89, 90, 93, 106, 409, 124, 129, 137, 140, 144, 149, 151-4, 158, 161, 168, 173-5, 177, 189, 198, 200, 201, 222, 226, 227, 230, 231, 235, 236, 251, 253, 266, 269

self-knowledge, *viii*, 1, 2, 10, 16, 17, 21, 22, 26, 28, 30, 34, 38, 42, 48, 52, 54, 55, 61, 67, 70, 75, 80, 83, 85, 96, 103, 111, 122-6, 128, 132, 134-9, 152, 166-8, 170-6, 178-83, 187, 191, 195, 197-200, 202-10, 212-15, 217-20, 222, 224, 225, 229, 235-43, 249, 252, 255, 266, 267, 268, 270, 275

self-objectification, 183, 233, 250

self-preservation, 147, 193

self-reference, 168, 171, 172, 182, 183, 192, 203, 222, 223

self-sameness, 172, 182, 265, 272

self-sufficient, 107, 111, 131, 178, 207

self-validating, 156, 159

semblance, 41-4, 51, 53, 82, 93, 95, 96, 104, 112, 124, 125, 128-30, 132-4, 136, 141, 142, 146-9, 152, 154, 159, 164-72, 174-8, 182, 183, 187-93, 196, 199, 202, 203, 206-10, 212, 217-21, 223, 224, 228-31, 233-5, 239, 240, 244, 246, 249-52, 254-7, 259-61, 263, 266, 269-72, 276, 277

semblance of semblance, 251
sensibility, 3, 75
sensible, 8, 15, 79, 103, 125, 126, 153, 169, 179, 180, 182, 187, 198, 199, 201, 203, 205, 210, 214, 215, 219, 222, 243, 249, 274
sensory data, 39, 123, 126, 127, 130, 150, 156, 157, 164, 241, 262
sensory response, 151, 157, 245
sequence, 1, 32, 47, 82, 100, 160, 162, 174-6, 178, 179, 197, 205, 221, 239-41, 246, 255, 269
"Seventh Cartesian Meditation," 124
shadow, 139, 150, 241-3, 245, 246
shapes, 3, 18, 22, 137, 139, 140, 145, 150, 202, 239, 241, 249-51
sign, 145, 152, 154, 159, 192, 193, 198, 199, 213, 236
signify, 6, 18, 134, 143, 147, 156, 169, 177, 185, 198, 199, 207, 230, 239, 251, 257, 258, 261, 264, 265
similar, vii, x, 2, 21, 35, 41, 42, 47, 53, 58, 59, 63, 68, 86, 90, 98, 101, 106, 115, 116, 125, 132, 135, 146, 148, 152, 153, 155-8, 169, 171, 174-6, 187, 188, 190, 191, 198, 204, 208, 213, 215, 219, 229, 236, 239, 246, 249, 251, 252, 254, 256, 257, 260, 261, 265, 267, 268, 271-5
similarity-and-difference, 44, 53, 249-53, 265, 267, 268, 272
simultaneity, 6, 33, 41, 47, 79, 86, 93, 110, 123, 136, 150, 151, 156, 158, 159, 175, 178, 180, 190, 195, 221, 225, 227, 228, 231, 233, 239, 240, 243, 245, 249-52, 256, 264, 266, 270
social, 4, 33, 48, 50, 52, 91, 110, 239, 258, 259,
social psychology, 261
sociocultural, 21, 69, 101, 108, 110, 111, 124, 147, 176, 180, 188, 199, 201, 209, 212, 214, 216, 227, 239, 251, 256, 260-2, 264, 265, 268, 271, 277
socius, 258, 262
solipsism, 52, 98, 107, 166, 188, 225, 240, 245, 255, 262, 264, 265, 267

solipsistic, 33, 34, 42, 54, 93-6, 101, 146, 158, 159, 166-9, 175, 178, 181, 183-86, 188-91, 197, 202, 209, 210, 217, 218, 220, 222, 229, 232-4, 237, 239, 243, 244, 251, 252, 255, 262, 268, 270, 271, 273, 275-7
solipsistic/intersubjective conflicts, 168
soul, 35, 38, 39, 41, 44, 45, 60, 70-2, 89, 96, 107, 116, 128, 129, 132, 146, 165, 166, 184, 194, 195, 225, 229, 233, 236, 237, 248-50, 252, 254, 266, 271, 272
soulish, 35, 38, 41, 70, 72, 129, 195, 225, 254
space, viii, x, xiii, 4, 22, 61, 62, 78, 82-4, 90-2, 95, 131, 137, 140-2, 145, 154, 176, 189, 204, 208, 214, 227, 233, 237, 239, 247, 249, 256, 257
spatial, 3, 22, 41, 82, 84, 85, 110, 111, 128, 131, 140, 142, 151, 179, 180, 182, 188, 190, 202, 203, 206, 207, 210, 212, 213, 219, 221, 226, 232, 239, 240, 251, 257, 260, 269, 271
spatiotemporality, 19, 33, 52, 85, 91, 94, 100, 103, 111, 128, 130-2, 136-8, 140-2, 145, 147, 150, 159, 163, 164, 169, 171, 179, 183, 187, 191, 200-3, 208-210, 220, 228, 233, 239-41, 246, 247, 256, 258, 269, 270
speech, x, xi, xiii-xv, 4, 6, 9, 23, 26, 33, 34, 37, 39, 41, 63, 64, 73, 78, 80, 85, 86, 88, 96, 99, 101, 102, 104, 121, 122, 130, 131, 136, 141-4, 148, 149, 157-9, 172, 176, 177, 182, 183, 191, 197-9, 203, 208, 213, 216, 218, 225, 228, 230, 231, 235, 237, 250-2, 258, 259, 274
speech-acts, 198, 199
Spiegelberg, H., 113
spirit-life, 35-7, 39, 40, 42, 46, 53, 55, 70-2, 80, 94, 96-101, 104-9, 111, 126, 128, 129, 132, 134, 135, 138, 140, 144, 147, 164-6, 188-95, 203, 211, 218, 225, 231, 231, 234, 236-8, 252-4, 266-9, 273, 277
spiritual formation, 96, 111

spiritual ownness, 35, 100, 106, 132, 165, 138, 189, 254

Stamm-constitution, 265

statistical, *xii*, 5, 11, 35, 173, 211

Stein, E., *vi*, 81, 92, 101, 104, 105, 118, 119, 261

stimulus response, 83, 151

stirrings, 245, 246

strata, *xv*, 6, 31, 123, 128, 140, 141, 161, 163, 169, 203, 205, 214, 225, 234, 269

stream of consciousness, 33, 169, 244, 246

streaming, 46, 169, 177, 181, 200, 210, 225, 227, 240, 246, 250, 268, 269,

stuff, 7, 126, 127, 131, 157, 195, 200, 225, 247, 248, 262, 268, 269

Stumpf, C., 59, 62, 92, 225

sub-consciousness, 86

subject, *ix*, *xii*, 4-7, 10, 12, 15, 20, 22, 26, 29-33, 38, 42, 45, 52-5, 69, 74-6, 78, 80, 82, 84, 86, 87, 92, 94, 95, 98-103, 106, 114, 115, 123-5, 133, 134, 137, 143, 146, 149, 150, 153, 154, 157-9, 163, 165, 167, 168, 177, 178, 180, 182, 184, 188-90, 192, 194, 195, 198, 200-7, 209, 211-15, 217, 218, 222, 224-7, 229-32, 235, 237, 239, 240, 242-6, 254, 257, 260, 270-7

subject-predicate-object, 53, 95, 177, 192

substrates, *xiii*, 12, 19, 38, 97, 128, 141, 143, 148, 154, 161, 169, 194, 232, 237, 250, 271

suprasensible reality, 7

surroundings (*der Außenwelt*), 7, 21, 35, 44, 48, 52, 71, 94, 101, 106, 108, 110, 129, 132, 146, 176, 186, 189, 202, 206, 210, 214, 216, 223, 237-9, 246, 256-8, 260-2, 265, 268, 277

symbolic, *xii*, *xv*, 62-4, 67, 82, 101, 103, 152, 173, 176, 182, 207, 251

symmetrical, 210, 212, 213, 222, 223, 248

synchronic, *x*, 175, 225, 233, 252, 261, 263

synchronic/diachronic simultaneity, 256, 268

syntagmatic, 263, 264

syntax, *xi*, *xiii*, *xv*, 6, 187, 199

synthesis, 33, 35, 47, 49, 50, 52, 83, 87-9, 92, 118, 136, 138, 155, 158-65, 167-72, 175, 183, 187, 197, 203, 205, 207, 216-18, 220, 223, 224, 231, 233, 244, 250, 256, 258, 270, 272, 277

synthesizing-acts, 161, 217, 233

synthetical unity, 99, 141, 207, 220

tachypsychia, 150

techné, 32

teleological, 33, 82, 132, 154, 160, 177, 178, 182, 196, 205, 220, 228, 235, 236, 244, 260

telos, 33, 259, 271, 275

temporality, 31, 56, 77, 83-5, 92, 99, 100, 110-12, 126-8, 131, 137-40, 142, 160, 162, 179, 182, 183, 187, 189, 190, 202, 208-11, 213, 218-22, 228, 23, 254-60, 262, 265, 271

terminology, *vi*, 6, 7, 72, 74, 88, 122, 213, 263

theirs, 7, 44, 246

thematic, 23, 36, 50, 52, 54, 84, 120, 141, 145, 154-64, 166-9, 172, 173, 175, 181, 193, 195, 197, 198, 208, 209, 214-16, 221, 222, 225, 236, 237, 241, 242, 245, 246, 248, 250, 253, 255, 256, 260, 261, 264, 268, 269, 276

theme, 25, 53, 93, 110, 120, 126, 132, 143, 144, 154, 155, 158, 160-5, 180-2, 193, 207, 213, 214, 226, 227, 232, 238, 241, 244-6, 248, 249, 251, 254, 256, 270, 272, 273, 275, 277

theology, 1, 42, 203

theoretical psychology, *xi*, 43

theorizing, 113, 213, 237-9

theory of elements, 8, 9, 23, 29, 37, 40, 58, 86, 87, 89, 120, 155, 160, 161, 163, 169, 172, 179, 180, 197, 198, 219, 220, 234, 245, 256, 269, 272, 273, 276

theory of knowledge, 10, 16, 84, 110,

118, 215

theory of method, 8, 9, 13, 36-8, 40, 42, 44-6, 53, 68, 75, 87, 89, 106, 111, 116, 117, 120, 123, 146, 149, 155, 161, 164, 167, 172, 180, 181, 187, 194, 197, 198, 204, 207, 209, 219, 223, 234, 244, 245, 254, 256, 258, 264, 267, 269, 270, 272, 273, 276, 277

theory of perception, 50, 123

theory of representation, 155, 159

thetic, 127, 130, 140, 169, 181, 187, 188, 214, 217, 227, 239, 241, 249, 259, 262

thing-in-itself (*Ding an sich*), 40, 180

thingness, 201-3, 249, 266

things themselves, *xiv*, 19, 64, 76, 84, 93, 99, 100, 102, 138, 148, 201

thing-world, 165, 240

Thorndike, E., 21

time, *viii*, 4, 14, 45-7, 61, 62, 79, 81, 84, 90-2, 95, 99, 131, 149, 150, 162, 176, 179, 187, 188, 203, 208, 217, 220, 225, 227, 233, 240, 241, 247, 255-7, 262, 270

time-consciousness, 84-7, 100, 103, 137-40, 159, 162, 179, 191, 196, 201, 202, 204, 209, 210, 213, 214, 219, 221, 225, 227, 228, 230, 232, 234, 247, 250, 254, 255, 261, 269, 273

Tito, J.M., 91

topology, *ix*, 57, 112, 204, 277, 275

transcendence, *viii*, 1, 4, 5, 7, 18, 22, 38, 40, 42, 89-91, 93-5, 100, 107, 112, 116, 122, 129, 142, 147, 162, 169, 180, 188, 194, 199, 205, 208, 217, 225, 269

transcendental attitude, 30, 49, 120, 164, 184

transcendental consciousness, 12-14, 18, 20, 21, 23, 24, 28, 29, 34, 37, 38, 40-4, 48-50, 53, 55, 67, 71, 73, 75, 78, 89, 92, 94, 96-8, 100, 101, 103, 111, 112, 116, 118, 121-4, 126, 127, 132, 135, 138, 140, 143-7, 153, 155-7, 159, 161, 163, 166-9, 171, 173,

174, 176, 177, 181, 183-5, 188, 190, 197-203, 206-8, 214, 216-20, 223, 224, 228, 230-4, 246, 247, 254-6, 266, 267, 270, 271, 276

transcendental ego, 12, 23, 37, 42, 47, 49, 52, 54, 68, 95-9, 108, 116, 133, 141, 152, 158, 159, 164, 166, 180-2, 186, 191, 196-8, 205, 206, 209, 212, 216-22, 224, 226, 227, 230, 235, 236, 239, 244, 247, 254-7, 259, 260, 263, 264, 266, 267, 269, 270, 272, 276

transcendental *epoché*, 107-9, 132, 133, 145, 164, 167, 172, 182, 197, 216, 247, 251, 254

transcendental idealism, 41-4, 92, 93, 99, 112, 120, 245, 272, 276

transcendental logic, *xiii*, 23, 49, 63-7, 70, 73, 74, 79, 101-4, 117, 139, 161, 162, 173, 174, 177, 181, 183, 200, 210, 211, 215, 221, 227, 228, 243, 248, 263, 264

transcendental phenomenological psychology, *vi, vii, ix- xii, xiv, xvi*, 1, 5, 6, 8, 9, 13, 14, 25, 29, 36, 39, 42, 43, 52, 55, 68, 107, 117, 120, 145, 146, 173, 174, 184, 194, 131-4, 236, 237, 240, 245, 247, 250, 254, 273

transcendental phenomenology, *vi- ix, xi, xii*, 1, 4, 5, 6, 9, 12, 14, 23, 24, 27, 29, 35, 40, 43, 51, 52, 54, 65, 68, 83, 87, 90, 91, 107, 109, 112, 113, 117-19, 123, 154, 171, 177, 184, 201, 230, 231, 248, 257

transcendental reduction, 19, 22, 74, 75, 109, 112, 123, 132-4, 137, 150, 177, 178, 180, 181, 186, 205, 217-19, 221-5, 227, 263, 270

transcendental reorientation, 55, 164, 165, 167, 178, 180, 183, 184, 189, 190, 194, 224, 231, 266

transcendental subjectivity, 12, 14, 33, 37, 39, 41, 55, 68, 75, 89, 91, 95, 101, 102, 107, 108, 112, 117, 123, 132, 134, 136, 140, 141, 147, 154, 158, 160, 162-4, 167, 169, 176, 178, 181, 183, 190, 191, 197, 201, 209,

213, 215, 216, 218, 220-2, 224, 225,
227, 231, 233-5, 239, 243-5, 248,
255, 256, 259, 266, 271, 273

transcendental turn, 27, 29, 47, 49, 55,
91-3, 98, 118, 134, 150, 161, 191,
193, 194, 220, 275

transcending acts, 24, 28, 38-40, 47,
104, 122, 132, 136, 139, 149, 153,
159, 164, 165, 183, 187, 189, 194,
217, 218, 220, 221, 224-6, 228, 232,
240, 246, 247, 251, 255-7, 260, 264,
266, 268, 270-3, 276, 277

transpersonal, 28, 43

truth, *xiii*, 1, 10, 13, 32, 40, 44, 46, 49-
52, 54, 55, 61, 62, 66, 71, 74, 82,
83, 96, 107, 108, 111, 112, 114,
115, 122, 131, 132, 135, 143, 164-6,
174, 183-5, 187, 188, 191, 193, 195,
201, 206, 207, 213-18, 225, 227,
232, 235, 247, 250, 253, 257, 259-
63, 265, 267, 269-72, 275, 277

truth-seeking, 46, 51, 106, 111, 112,
114, 122, 129, 132, 135, 257, 267

unconscious, 87, 274

unity-form, 142, 151, 161, 162, 190,
204, 205, 233, 251, 252, 267, 273

unity of configuration, *ix*, 8, 26, 37, 77,
79, 82, 104, 430, 134, 141, 150, 151,
153, 154, 158, 159, 161, 162, 169,
178, 181, 200, 203, 211, 213, 220,
226, 227, 250, 264, 270, 271

unity of consciousness, *x*, 20, 40, 67,
76, 84, 141, 162, 163, 177, 217, 227

universals, 78, 122, 177

unreflective, 13, 51, 71, 82, 179, 237

unthematic, 154, 160, 161, 168, 197,
198, 231, 232

validity, 69, 72, 74, 75, 95, 102, 129,
159, 195, 163, 204, 259, 260

value, 31, 48, 50, 65, 91, 210

valuation, *vi, viii, ix*, 2-5, 7, 8, 13, 14,
16, 18, 23, 27-9, 32, 44, 48, 51, 53,
62-4, 67, 76, 77, 79, 83, 86, 94-6,
101, 107, 108, 125, 134, 135, 142,
145, 150, 153, 159, 163, 165, 166,
174, 176, 179-82, 185, 187, 190,
195, 197, 200, 220, 221, 227-9,

240, 241, 248, 250, 251, 258, 263,
265, 267, 270, 271

valuing, 33, 36, 38, 46, 54, 86, 106,
111, 121, 130, 134, 146, 153, 163,
165, 167, 174, 178, 183, 198, 201,
207, 209, 210, 213, 221, 224, 230,
233, 235, 243, 253, 266, 268, 271

van den Berg, J., 47

Verstehen, 46, 49, 52

Vienna lecture, the, 97, 119

volition, 194, 200, 203, 207, 234, 247

Von Helmholtz, H., 21

Watson, J. B., 21

Weierstrass, K., 56, 57, 62

Welch, E.P., 56

Welton, D. *xv*, 24, 113, 118, 196, 197

Weltanschauung, 71, 72, 91, 96, 112

what-ness, 18, 20, 31, 101, 116, 120,
121, 123, 125

will, *vii*, 10, 24, 38, 39, 46, 71, 78, 99,
108, 144, 147, 188, 231-4, 237-9,
251, 255, 266

willing, 33, 80, 87, 100, 106, 121, 163,
234, 237-40, 275

witchcraft, 42

word-meaning, *xii, xiii*, 73

world commonly talked about, *xii*, 27,
29, 31, 33, 37-9, 41, 42, 44, 51, 52,
55, 79, 95, 98, 100, 107, 121, 122,
128, 133, 136, 146, 148, 149, 159,
162, 164, 166, 181, 184, 186, 192,
194, 195, 198, 201-3, 205, 208, 209,
211, 216, 218, 224, 233, 237, 238,
243, 244, 246, 249, 254, 255, 257,
260, 261, 263, 265, 266, 268, 269,
272, 273, 275, 277

world-consciousness, 24, 36, 38, 42,
47, 68, 117, 142, 146, 164, 165, 186,
195, 243, 245, 268, 275

world-constitution, 24, 40, 45, 47,
104, 146, 167, 188, 197, 209, 218,
221-4, 227, 253, 260, 266, 270, 271

world for us all, 44, 95, 104, 166, 187,
197, 219, 227, 235, 253, 260, 269

worldview, 44, 45, 70-2, 96, 97, 111,
249, 266, 275

Wundt, W., 56, 57, 59, 62, 108, 109